New Drama in Russian

Library of Modern Russia

Advisory Board:

Jeffrey Brooks, Professor at Johns Hopkins University, USA
Michael David-Fox, Professor at Georgetown University, USA
Lucien Frary, Associate Professor at Rider University, USA
James Harris, Senior Lecturer at the University of Leeds, UK
Robert Hornsby, Lecturer at the University of Leeds, UK
Ekaterina Pravilova, Professor of History at Princeton University, USA
Geoffrey Swain, Emeritus Professor of Central and East European Studies at the University of Glasgow, UK
Vera Tolz-Zilitinkevic, Sir William Mather Professor of Russian Studies at the University of Manchester, UK
Vladislav Zubok, Professor of International History at the London School of Economics, UK

Building on Bloomsbury Academic's established record of publishing Russian studies titles, the Library of Modern Russia will showcase the work of emerging and established writers who are setting new agendas in the field.

At a time when potentially dangerous misconceptions and misunderstandings about Russia abound, titles in the series will shed fresh light and nuance on Russian history. Volumes will take the idea of 'Russia' in its broadest cultural sense and cover the entirety of the multi-ethnic lands that made up imperial Russia and the Soviet Union. Ranging in chronological scope from the Romanovs to today, the books will:

- Re-consider Russia's history from a variety of inter-disciplinary perspectives.
- Explore Russia in its various international contexts, rather than as exceptional or in isolation.
- Examine the complex, divisive and ever-shifting notions of 'Russia'.
- Contribute to a deeper understanding of Russia's rich social and cultural history.
- Critically re-assess the Soviet period and its legacy today.
- Interrogate the traditional periodizations of the post-Stalin Soviet Union.
- Unearth continuities, or otherwise, among the tsarist, Soviet and post-Soviet periods.
- Re-appraise Russia's complex relationship with Eastern Europe, both historically and today.
- Analyse the politics of history and memory in post-Soviet Russia.
- Promote new archival revelations and innovative research methodologies.
- Foster a community of scholars and readers devoted to a sharper understanding of the Russian experience, past and present.

Books in the series will join our list in being marketed globally, including at conferences – such as the BASEES and ASEEES conventions. Each will be subjected to a rigorous peer-review process and will be published in hardback and, simultaneously, as an e-book. We also anticipate a second release in paperback for the general reader and student markets.

For more information, or to submit a proposal for inclusion in the series, please contact: Rhodri Mogford, Publisher, History (Rhodri.Mogford@bloomsbury.com).

New and forthcoming:

Fascism in Manchuria: The Soviet–China Encounter in the 1930s, Susanne Hohler
The Idea of Russia: The Life and Work of Dmitry Likhachev, Vladislav Zubok
The Tsar's Armenians: A Minority in Late Imperial Russia, Onur Onol
Myth Making in the Soviet Union and Modern Russia: Remembering World War II in Brezhnev's Hero City, Vicky Davis
Building Stalinism: The Moscow Canal and the Creation of Soviet Space, Cynthia Ruder
Russia in the Time of Cholera: Disease and the Environment under Romanovs and Soviets, John Davis
Soviet Americana: A Cultural History of Russian and Ukrainian Americanists, Sergei Zhuk
Stalin's Economic Advisors: The Varga Institute and the Making of Soviet Foreign Policy, Ken Roh
Ideology and the Arts in the Soviet Union: The Establishment of Censorship and Control, Steven Richmond
Nomads and Soviet Rule: Central Asia under Lenin and Stalin, Alun Thomas
The Russian State and the People: Power, Corruption and the Individual in Putin's Russia, Geir Hønneland et al. (eds)
The Communist Party in the Russian Civil War: A Political History, Gayle Lonergan
Criminal Subculture in the Gulag: Prisoner Society in the Stalinist Labour Camps, Mark Vincent
Power and Politics in Modern Chechnya: Ramzan Kadyrov and the New Digital Authoritarianism, Karena Avedissian
Russian Pilgrimage to the Holy Land: Piety and Travel from the Middle Ages to the Revolution, Nikolaos Chrissidis
The Fate of the Bolshevik Revolution, Lara Douds, James Harris, and Peter Whitehead (eds)

Writing History in Late Imperial Russia, Frances Nethercott
Translating England into Russian, Elena Goodwin
Gender and Survival in Soviet Russia, Ludmila Miklashevskaya, Elaine MacKinnon (transl. and ed.)
Publishing in Tsarist Russia, Yukiko Tatsumi and Taro Tsurumi (eds)
New Drama in Russian: Performance, Politics and Protest in Russia, Ukraine and Belarus, J. A. E. Curtis (ed.)

New Drama in Russian

Performance, Politics and Protest in Russia, Ukraine and Belarus

Edited by

J. A. E. Curtis

BLOOMSBURY ACADEMIC
LONDON • NEW YORK • OXFORD • NEW DELHI • SYDNEY

BLOOMSBURY ACADEMIC
Bloomsbury Publishing Plc

50 Bedford Square, London, WC1B 3DP, UK
1385 Broadway, New York, NY 10018, USA
29 Earlsfort Terrace, Dublin 2, Ireland

BLOOMSBURY, BLOOMSBURY ACADEMIC and the Diana logo are trademarks
of Bloomsbury Publishing Plc

First published in Great Britain 2020
This paperback edition published in 2021

Copyright © J. A. E. Curtis, 2020

J. A. E. Curtis has asserted her right under the Copyright, Designs and Patents Act, 1988, to be identified as Editor of this work.

Series design by Tjaša Krivec
Cover Image: *Vitalik–A Show About a Man* by Vitalii Chenskii, produced by Wild Theatre in Kyiv, Ukraine, premiering in 2017 (© Designed by Helena Nikulina
for the performances of *Vitalik*)

All rights reserved. No part of this publication may be reproduced or transmitted in any form or by any means, electronic or mechanical, including photocopying, recording, or any information storage or retrieval system, without prior permission in writing from the publishers.

Bloomsbury Publishing Plc does not have any control over, or responsibility for, any third-party websites referred to or in this book. All internet addresses given in this book were correct at the time of going to press. The author and publisher regret any inconvenience caused if addresses have changed or sites have ceased to exist, but can accept no responsibility for any such changes.

A catalogue record for this book is available from the British Library.

A catalog record for this book is available from the Library of Congress.

ISBN: HB: 978-1-7883-1350-6
PB: 978-1-3502-5318-6
ePDF: 978-1-3501-4247-3
eBook: 978-1-3501-4248-0

Typeset by RefineCatch Limited, Bungay, Suffolk

To find out more about our authors and books visit www.bloomsbury.com
and sign up for our newsletters.

Contents

Notes on contributors	ix
Acknowledgements	xiii
A note on transliteration	xiv

Introduction: Recent developments in Russian, Ukrainian and Belarusian drama   *J. A. E Curtis* — 1

Part I Russia

1. The story of Russian-language drama since 2000: PostDoc, the postdramatic and Teatr Post   *Marie-Christine Autant-Mathieu* — 23

2. Giving testimony in the face of an authoritarian regime: The evolution of documentary forms at Teatr.doc, the KnAM Theatre and the Belarus Free Theatre   *Lucie Kempf* — 41

3. From Stalinist Socialist Realism to Putinist Capitalist Realism: Tracing cultural ideology in contemporary Russia
   Alexander Trustrum Thomas — 53

4. Conversation with Mikhail Durnenkov and Maria Kroupnik (Liubimovka Festival, Moscow, September 2017)   *J. A. E. Curtis* — 69

5. 'Class Act' in Russia and Ukraine: Youth drama projects and social theatre practice   *Maria Kroupnik* — 81

6. Conversation with Sasha Denisova (Moscow, October 2013)
   Susanna Weygandt — 95

7. Conversation with Ivan Vyrypaev (Moscow, May 2013)
   Susanna Weygandt — 99

8. Absence on stage in Ivan Vyrypaev's *July*   *Valeriia Mutc* — 107

Part II Ukraine

9. The watershed year of 2014: The 'birth' of Ukrainian New Drama
   Noah Birksted-Breen — 121

10	The playwright overlooked: Personal reflections on two years in Ukrainian theatre (2017–19) *Jack Clover*	141
11	A new 'dawn' in Ukrainian theatre: A conversation with Maksym Kurochkin (April 2019) *Jack Clover*	151
12	Stages of change: Ukraine's Theatre of Displaced People *Molly Flynn*	163
13	'Ne skvernoslov', otets moy' ['Curse not, my son']: Anna Iablonskaia's *The Pagans* and the search for a language of authenticity *Molly Thomasy Blasing*	175
14	Natal'ia Vorozhbyt's *Viy*: Autoethnography through a Gogolian lens *Jessica Hinds-Bond*	193

Part III Belarus

15	The transformation of the language of 'New Drama' in Belarus, as a reflection of a new model of identity *Tania Arcimovich*	213
16	Conversation with Natalia Koliada, Belarus Free Theatre (London, March 2019) *J. A. E. Curtis*	223
17	Pavel Priazhko: the Text as an Instant Photograph (2012); Conversation with Pavel Priazhko (2011); Essay on Pavel Priazhko's methods *Tania Arcimovich*	237
18	The artistic space shared by Eastern Slavs, and the ways in which that is created: *The Way People Love* by the Belarusian dramatist Dmitry Bogoslavsky *Natalia Osis*	247

Conclusion: Summer of 2019   *J. A. E. Curtis*   259

Recommended reading   267
Index   269

Contributors

Tania Arcimovich is a scholar, curator and art critic. She graduated from the Belarusian State Academy of Arts in Minsk (History of Theatre), then wrote an MA dissertation in Vilnius (Lithuania) on 'Experimental Theatre in the Belarusian Soviet Socialist Republic during the Khrushchev Thaw (1953–1968): Between Modernism and Avant-Garde'. Since 2016 she has been teaching at the European Liberal Arts College in Minsk. She has participated in the international 'Avant-garde Reclaimed' project developed by the Zbigniew Raszewski Theatre Institute in Warsaw, and is currently studying for a PhD at the International Graduate Centre for the Study of Culture in Gießen (Germany).

Marie-Christine Autant-Mathieu is Director of Research at the National Centre for Scientific Research (CNRS) in Paris, and Assistant Director of the Eur'ORBEM institute associated with the CNRS and the Sorbonne University. As a historian of Russian and Soviet theatre, her main fields of research are: theatrical emigration and cultural transfer; the history of the Moscow Art Theatre and the Stanislavsky System; and Russian 'New Drama'. She is one of the coordinators for the Russian section at Maison Antoine Vitez (International Centre for Theatrical Translation). Among her many publications (see www.autant-mathieu.fr), those relevant to this volume include (both as editor) *Théâtre russe contemporain* (Arles: Actes Sud-Papiers, 1997) and *Les Nouvelles Ecritures russes* (Pézenas: Domens, 2010).

Noah Birksted-Breen is a scholar, playwright, translator and theatre-maker. He founded and runs Sputnik Theatre Company (London), the only professional ensemble dedicated to bringing new Russian-language dramas to UK audiences. He is a professional director and translator with productions at the Southwark Playhouse, Battersea Arts Centre and Theatre Royal Plymouth. In 2017 Sputnik was associate producer of Radio 3's Drama of the Week, *Fear and Loathing in Russia Today*, a broadcast of three newly commissioned Russian plays. That same year he also completed a PhD at Queen Mary University of London with the title 'Alternative Voices in an Acquiescent Society: Translating Russian New Drama for British audiences (2000–2014)'. He holds a postdoctoral research position at Oxford University, as part of the AHRC-funded project 'Creative Multilingualism', and has also been a Research Assistant on Manchester's AHRC-funded project 'Cross-Language Dynamics: Reshaping Community'.

Molly Thomasy Blasing is an Assistant Professor of Russian Studies in the Department of Modern and Classical Languages, Literatures and Cultures at the University of Kentucky (USA). She holds degrees in Slavic Languages and Literatures from Harvard

University (BA 2002) and the University of Wisconsin-Madison (MA 2006, PhD 2014). She specializes in twentieth- and twenty-first-century Russian poetry, and is active in the fields of theatre and cinema studies, literary translation and Russian-language pedagogy. Her research has been supported by the National Endowment for the Humanities and the Fulbright Program and has been published in *Slavic Review*, *Slavic and East European Journal*, *Ulbandus Review*, *The Theatre Times* and *Reading in Translation*. She is currently completing a monograph that explores the way the development of photography has shaped Russian poetic writing in the twentieth and twenty-first centuries.

Jack Clover is a freelance writer, theatre director and translator of Russian and Ukrainian. He has created and worked on productions for multiple independent and state theatres across Ukraine from 2017 to 2019. He founded the 'Theatre in Two Weeks' format, encouraging New Writing that quickly reacts to the realities of today's Ukraine. He studied Russian and Czech at University College, Oxford and now lives in East London.

Julie A. E. Curtis is Professor of Russian Literature and Fellow of Wolfson College, University of Oxford. She has published research about writers of the pre-war Stalin era such as Mikhail Bulgakov and Evgeny Zamiatin. She teaches a course in Russian drama, and in recent years has focused her research on contemporary Russian-language playwriting. She has organized a number of workshops on this subject for the AHRC-funded 'Creative Multilingualism' project based at the University of Oxford, and for Manchester's AHRC-funded project 'Cross-Language Dynamics: Reshaping Community'.

Molly Flynn is Lecturer in Theatre and Performance at Birkbeck, University of London and the author of *Witness Onstage: Documentary Theatre in Twenty-First-Century Russia* (Manchester: Manchester University Press, 2019). Her research focuses on social theatre practice in Russia and Ukraine. Her writing has appeared in *New Theatre Quarterly*, *RiDE: The Journal of Applied Theatre and Performance*, *Problems of Post-Communism* and *Open Democracy*. In addition to her work as a teacher and researcher, she is a theatre-maker and a co-founder of the US-based theatre collective the New York Neo-Futurists.

Jessica Hinds-Bond completed an interdisciplinary PhD in theatre and drama at Northwestern University, with a focus on contemporary Russian stage re-makes of the Russian literary canon. She has published book and performance reviews in *Theatre Survey*, *Theatre Research International* and *Theatre Journal*, and she translated the chapter by Pavel Rudnev on Russian theatre for *The Routledge Companion to Dramaturgy* (2015). She is the regional managing editor for Russia for TheTheatreTimes.com, and she works as a freelance editor and indexer for scholarly projects in the humanities.

Lucie Kempf is a Lecturer in Russian Literature and Language at the University of Lorraine (Nancy). She is a member of the research laboratory CERCLE (Centre d'Études et de Recherches sur les Cultures et Littératures Européennes). Her research is focused partly on Russian theatre in the period 1890–1930 (acting techniques, staging and set designs as well as playwriting), and partly on documentary forms in contemporary Russian theatre. With Tania Moguilevskaia she co-edited the volume *Le Théâtre neo-documentaire : résurgence ou réinvention?* (Nancy: PUN, 2013). She is currently working on the first French-language biography of Vera Komissarzhevskaya (1864–1910).

Maria Kroupnik is an art manager, curator, translator, lecturer and researcher at the Cultural Management Faculty of Moscow's School of Social and Economic Sciences. She curates the 'Playwright Plus' educational programme for the Liubimovka Young Russian Playwrights Festival (Moscow), and the Teens' Drama Project/Class Act Russia.

Valeriia Mutc is a PhD candidate in the Department of Slavic Languages and Literatures at Yale University. Her research explores the intersections between Russian fin-de-siècle literature and theatre, with a particular focus on performance studies, theatre studies and cultural histories of theatrical practice in Russia. In her dissertation 'The Dramatic Turn: Chekhov, Gorky, and Tolstoy at the End of the 19th Century', she examines the turn of Russia's famous prose writers towards drama, and applies transmedial narratology to analyse their prose writing alongside their plays, and to discuss its impact on questions of realism and modernism during that time.

Natalia Osis is a PhD candidate at the University of Genoa in Italy. She graduated from Moscow's Gorky Literary Institute with a degree in playwriting. Her many years of experience working in both Russian and Italian theatre have included participation in a number of important festivals such as 'NET' (New European Theatre), the 'Golden Mask' Russian national theatre award and the International Chekhov Festival. In addition to writing scripts, novels and theatrical criticism, she has edited two collections of contemporary drama under the title *Prem'era* (Première) (2002, 2003).

Alexander Trustrum Thomas is a DPhil candidate in medieval and modern languages at the University of Oxford. His research examines contemporary Russian theatre of the past decade through the lens of social, cultural and political changes during the same period. He is primarily interested in radical and transgressive 'new drama', as well as post-dramatic theatre and performance. He co-organized the TORCH-affiliated 'Collaboration in Theatre' conference at the University of Oxford in 2018. He is also a writer and translator, whose work has featured at the Royal Court in London (Teatr. doc's *Torture*, 2019), as well as in *The Theatre Times* and the *Oxonian Review*.

Susanna Weygandt is Visiting Assistant Professor of Russian at Sewanee: The University of the South (USA), where she teaches Russian, performance and post-Soviet culture. She received her PhD from Princeton University's Department of Slavic Languages and Literatures. Her articles on contemporary performance have appeared in *TDR: The Drama Review* (2016), *Stanislavsky Studies* (2019) and *Studies in Russian* *and Soviet Cinema* (2018). Her book manuscript *From Metaphor to Direct Speech: Russian New Drama after 1991* documents a network of playwrights, their aesthetics, and the political implications of their dramas. Together with Maksim Hanukai, she co-edited *New Russian Drama: An Anthology* (New York: Columbia University Press, 2019).

Acknowledgements

This volume arises out of a series of workshops on contemporary Russian-language drama held at Wolfson College, University of Oxford; these were organized under the auspices of the AHRC's Open World Research Initiative project based at the University of Manchester, 'Cross-Language Dynamics: Reshaping Community'. I am very grateful to Professors Stephen Hutchings and Andy Byford for their invitation to take part in the Manchester project, and for their support and guidance throughout. My collaborators Professor Philip Bullock and Dr Noah Birksted-Breen have been a wonderful team to work with. I'm also grateful to Wolfson College and to the University of Oxford for financial and administrative support.

A note on transliteration

In this book the reader will find occasional variant spellings of certain Russian, Ukrainian and Belarusian names and proper nouns. Transliteration practices from Slavonic languages into English vary in any case, and in respect of certain languages can become a reflection of political sensibilities. As an example, the name of the playwright Natal'ia Vorozhbit became widely known in the West from the early 2000s, but in recent years the tendency has been to write her name in Latin characters using the more typical Ukrainian transliteration Vorozhbyt. Rather than attempt to homogenize transliteration across the book, I have left the authors to decide which transliteration seems more appropriate.

Introduction

Recent developments in Russian, Ukrainian and Belarusian drama

J. A. E. Curtis

> In this introduction the 21st-century phenomenon of Russian-language 'New Drama', which flourished as a shared venture in Ukraine and Belarus as well as in Russia, is considered with particular reference to its function as a forum for the exploration of human rights issues in the region. Since 2012 or so domestic and international political developments have had a significant impact on cultural policies in relation to theatre, as they have for other performance arts such as cinema. These have played out in different ways within Russia, Ukraine and Belarus, but have also affected the relationships between theatre-makers from the three countries, and have imperilled the future of Russian-language 'New Drama' as a transnational project.

What difference can theatre and performance make in the post-Soviet world? This could seem like a rhetorical question, but at the time of writing (May 2019) we have just received the startling news that an actor who played the part of the Ukrainian president in a TV comedy show, in the fictional role of a naïve but honest man who finds himself elected to the post despite having no political experience whatsoever, has just been elected in real life as the new president of Ukraine – despite having no political experience whatsoever. He outstripped the previous incumbent Petro Poroshenko by 73 per cent to 25 per cent of the national vote, and after his inauguration appointed a new team of ministers, some drawn from among his colleagues on the TV show, just as his fictional counterpart appoints ministers from among his schoolfriends. We can only imagine what a comparable situation would feel like in an Anglo-American context, with the actor Paul Eddington (who played the hapless James Hacker in the 1980s BBC sitcom *Yes, Prime Minister*) being elected as the next British prime minister; or perhaps Alec Baldwin, who has parodied Donald Trump for the show *Saturday Night Live*, successfully challenging Trump for the US presidency in 2020. Recent years have seen electorates across the Western world making unconventional choices, but rarely has theatrical representation offered such a direct route into political power as it has in Ukraine. Drama there has apparently succeeded in articulating vital social and political issues more effectively than any other artistic, print or social media. How can the actual electoral success in modern-day Ukraine of the actor and comedian Volodymyr Zelensky be understood?

The significance of the roles which theatre can play in the political cultures of the post-Soviet world, and specifically in the East Slavic region constituted by the modern-day states of Russia, Ukraine and Belarus, provides the framework for the investigations and discussions which make up this book. Many of the contributions originated in a workshop called 'Playwriting Without Borders' held at Wolfson College (University of Oxford) in April 2017. Funding for the workshop was provided through the AHRC's Open World Research Initiative project based at the University of Manchester, 'Cross-Language Dynamics: Reshaping Community'. In particular, the workshop was a contribution to its 'Transnational strand', exploring how language shapes identity formation within and across nation states, through transnational linguistic communities and cultural practices. The focus of the 'Playwriting Without Borders' workshop was the phenomenon of 'New Drama', an important recent phase in the evolution of Russian-language drama within Russia, but equally a significant feature of contemporary playwriting in the independent post-Soviet states of Ukraine and Belarus, where Russian was – and still is – widely spoken. However, that situation is now changing, and this book traces some of the ways in which a turn away from the Russian language in the region has become apparent. It also examines the closely related – and largely political – reasons for the fragmentation and dissolution in recent years of the close links which bound the 'New Drama' movement together across those three countries during the first ten to fifteen years of the present century.

The term 'New Drama', as a description of the most influential trend in contemporary Russian-language theatre, came into being almost exactly at the same time as the regime of President Vladimir Putin was inaugurated in the year 2000, and it can be regarded as a twenty-first-century phenomenon. There has been much critical discussion of the term, but essentially it characterizes a move away from the 'well-made' literary play of earlier times, towards a drama which draws upon the speech and the events of real life to represent the world in raw, authentic ways. Much has been made of the impact of seminars conducted in Russia by Elyse Dodgson and other theatre-makers from London's Royal Court Theatre, who visited Russia under the auspices of the British Council in the late 1990s. One British Council staff member whose role was crucial in this process was Sasha Dugdale, who has gone on to become one of the most renowned British translators of contemporary Russian-language drama. As she and others have emphasized, one of the impacts of the Royal Court seminars was almost inadvertent: sessions on documentary and verbatim theatre happened to strike a chord with several of the participants, including Elena Gremina and Mikhail Ugarov, who founded their documentary theatre company Teatr.doc in Moscow in 2002. Since then Teatr.doc, and the annual Liubimovka festival with its competition for contemporary drama which Teatr.doc has hosted, have become identified as the driving force of much of the 'New Drama' movement, although many other theatre-makers and institutions have also been involved.[1] John Freedman, who throughout this period was the very well-informed theatre critic of *The Moscow Times*, comments that:

> 'New Drama' was coined specifically both as the title of a festival and as an ideological slogan. [...] Poetry, literature and metaphors were to be swept aside in favor of reality, simplicity, directness and unblinking honesty. The ideal plot was not something dreamed up by a creative mind, it was drawn from real events and the experiences of real people. That was the theory. What took place was something different and more complex.[2]

Among the main characteristics of 'New Drama' (although as Freedman points out these have actually varied quite widely over time, and with different practitioners) have been the following features:

1. the use of verbatim or documentary texts to give voice to ordinary citizens. This has not only served to demote the significance of the playwright's role in generating a fictional text, although of course s/he retains a powerful editorial role, but has also promoted the visibility of testimonial material, often concerning controversial issues. This in turn has lent some of the writings of 'New Drama' a subversive character, associated with human rights activism, as well as enabling certain therapeutic functions for the theatre;
2. a stripped-down range of staging practices: little or nothing is used in the way of set, costumes, props or stage make-up. One of the slogans of Teatr.doc has been 'A theatre where they don't act' (this could also be translated as 'A theatre where they don't play games'). Moscow's annual Liubimovka Festival in particular has foregrounded the practice of 'rehearsed readings' of plays, which in the majority of cases will never in fact receive a full staging in their authors' home countries;
3. an unabashed frankness in using the vernacular language of everyday speech, including obscenities and many non-standard usages;
4. a remarkable fearlessness in tackling taboo themes such as homosexuality and gender identity issues, youth disaffection, the Orthodox Church and blasphemy, police brutality, prison conditions, political corruption and violence; and it has also resisted attempts to impose monologic narratives about historical issues such as the Stalinist Terror.

One of the striking features about the first ten or more years of 'New Drama' is the extent to which playwrights, directors and theatre critics in the newly independent post-Soviet states of Russia, Ukraine and Belarus actively collaborated with one another, by participating in each other's festivals, freely and unselfconsciously sharing their plays across national frontiers, running workshops together for aspirant theatre-makers in all three countries, sitting on competition juries, and reviewing works or productions, very often without any focus on the specific national origins of the plays' authors. The key enabling factor in these transnational theatrical collaborations has of course primarily been the shared use of the Russian language by the major players in these several different post-Soviet nations.

As far as Russia is concerned, there are some who have argued that this first wave of 'New Drama' had subsided as early as 2009.[3] However, many would now agree that it has continued to thrive and develop, not least in response to political developments since 2012. The election of Vladimir Putin to his third presidential term in that year signalled important shifts in domestic as well as international policies in Russia. Taken together with his period as prime minister from 2008 to 2012 (while his close ally Dmitry Medvedev served as president), this and Putin's further re-election in 2018 has effectively given him uninterrupted power at the head of his country for almost twenty years now. This book picks up the story from approximately 2009, to provide a snapshot of developments in 'New Drama' in Russia, Ukraine and Belarus in the second decade of the twenty-first century, reflecting the rise in political tensions in the region during that period.

Russia

The authoritarian attitude of the Putin regime towards political and other opponents had become apparent even in the early years of the administration. The arrest in 2003 and subsequent ten-year imprisonment of the billionaire businessman Mikhail Khodorkovsky, and the events leading up to the 2009 death in police custody of the anti-corruption lawyer Sergei Magnitsky, which eventually led to the imposition of US sanctions on Russia in 2012, were both signals of aggressive abuses of the legal and penal systems to protect the status quo. Beumers and Lipovetsky have argued that violence was correspondingly intrinsic to the performativity of language in 'New Drama', serving to reflect a degree of turmoil within society and culture and the arbitrary practices of post-Soviet power and financial structures, as well as enacting rituals of transgression.[4]

In its first decade or so Teatr.doc proclaimed its adherence to what its founders Gremina and Ugarov defined as a 'zero position', a commitment to allowing opinions to be heard even if they were unpalatable, and not adopting a one-sided stance. In more recent years many plays performed at Teatr.doc have become more overtly and unequivocally political, and more critical of establishment narratives about events in public life. In 2010 a play for Teatr.doc by Gremina called *An Hour and Eighteen Minutes* (revised in 2012) marked a step away from the relative neutrality of the 'zero position' that the theatre had hitherto adopted. Based largely on documentary sources, the text offered a harrowing account of Sergei Magnitsky's death following upon his unjust arrest and brutal treatment in police custody, in retaliation for his efforts to protect the commercial and legal interests in Moscow of the British-American businessman Bill Browder.

February 2012 saw the notorious Pussy Riot performance in which five members of the feminist punk rock group staged a performance lasting less than one minute in Moscow's Cathedral of Christ the Saviour, in which they called upon the Mother of

God to get rid of Putin and deplored the Russian Orthodox Church's complicity with the Putin regime. The Patriarch Kirill denounced their 'blasphemy', and Maria Alyokhina and Nadezhda Tolokonnikova were charged with hooliganism, accused of inciting religious hatred and sentenced to two years in prison. However, in December 2013 Putin issued an amnesty which slightly abbreviated the Pussy Riot sentences, as well as freeing Khodorkovsky and others.

One reason for these gestures of apparent magnanimity may have been that Russia was about to host the Winter Olympics in Sochi in February 2014, and wished to present a more liberal image to the world. Even so, during the Games the freed members of Pussy Riot attempted to perform a song in front of an Olympics banner, and were physically assaulted by Cossacks wielding whips: nobody was arrested. And as soon as the Games were over, Putin undertook a step which has critically exacerbated international relations ever since, contriving the covert actions which led to the widely condemned seizure of Crimea from Ukraine and its annexation to the Russian Federation, validated by a highly contested referendum in March 2014.

Russia's parliament (Duma) had begun to introduce legislation imposing increasing restrictions on freedom of speech over the previous couple of years: these attempted (not always successfully at first) to restrict public rallies, to block websites run by Putin's opponents, regulate online blogs and promote patriotic values in the arts as well as obedience to the authorities. In May 2014 a new law was introduced (effective from that July) to ban the use of any obscenities in literature, the theatre, cinema and social media. This was essentially the first law enacting censorship of the arts to have been introduced since the Soviet period.[5] In February 2015 Andrei Zviagintsev's film *Leviathan*, which had garnered multiple international awards during 2014, was thus finally released in Russia with all the obscenities duly blanked out. In June 2017, in response to complaints from Zviagintsev that the law on obscenities constituted a restriction on artistic freedom, the Minister of Culture Vladimir Medinsky gave an ominous speech in which he made no concessions on the issue:

> This vocabulary is called 'non-standard' because it does not represent the standard. I don't want my children and your children to go to the cinema, and for obscenities to come from the screen. Or to the theatre. And by the way, certain theatrical institutions in our country are continuing to defy the law. I can promise you that we are not going to tolerate this any further.[6]

Denial of Nazi atrocities and any 'distortion' of the USSR's role in the Second World War (including Stalin's leadership) also became a criminal offence, as the last remaining independent TV channel Rain (Dozhd') discovered to its cost, after it simply invited viewers in January 2014 to debate whether Stalin's strategy with regard to the Siege of Leningrad (1941–4) had been the right one. There was a flood of critical comments by the authorities, the channel was dropped a few days later from cable and satellite TV providers, and it has since had to operate essentially online. Generally speaking, the tendency in the last ten years in Russia has been towards an ever more systematic closing down of independent voices in the broadcast and print media. This has left the state free to shape information in the popular media for propaganda purposes, whether in order to offer an unremittingly negative view of life in Europe and the USA, or brazenly to deny involvement in international scandals such as the downing of the Malaysian airliner over Ukraine in 2014, or the poisoning of the Skripals and others with novichok in Salisbury in 2018. In November 2014 plans were mooted for an alternative Russian version of Wikipedia, to portray the country 'more objectively', and work has since been undertaken on a number of projects designed to control and shape access to the internet for Russian citizens.

In June 2013 Putin had introduced laws specifically to penalize those who offended against religious feeling, such as Pussy Riot. These were taken up vigorously by priests and members of the Church community across the country. Later that year religious activists disrupted a controversial performance directed by Konstantin Bogomolov at the Moscow Art Theatre of Oscar Wilde's *An Ideal Husband*, shouting that it was 'blasphemy'. By 2015 religious activists were disrupting an exhibition of sculptures in Moscow, while protests and picketing of a supposedly offensive production of Wagner's *Tannhäuser* in the Siberian town of Novosibirsk led to the firing of its director and the show being taken off at the behest of the man who had become Minister of Culture in 2012, Vladimir Medinsky. During May 2015 the actor Valery Grishko, who had played the role of the greedy and corrupt priest in Zviagintsev's film *Leviathan*, won compensation in court for defamation by people who had publicly accused him of offending religious feelings simply because he had acted that fictional part; he donated the proceeds to humanitarian causes in eastern Ukraine.[7] This was yet another instance of a truly misguided blurring in the popular imagination of the distinction between fiction and reality. In an article for the BBC in August 2015 a commentator called Vladimir Shevchenko concluded:

> Since Vladimir Putin's return to power in 2012, the Church has become visible in practically all spheres of public life in Russia, from charity drives to science and the army. Pictures of Orthodox priests blessing new weapons and even space rockets have drawn much criticism from online commentators.
>
> Alexander Yakovlev, a top Communist Party ideologue and functionary for many decades, used to say that the KGB 'directly ran' the Orthodox Church and controlled all religious activity in the USSR. Many believe that the KGB's successor, the Federal Security Service (FSB), still has close links to top clerics.[8]

Gremina and Ugarov's Teatr.doc had received notice in the autumn of 2014 that they were being evicted from their premises by the Moscow City authorities, and at the end of December that year police came to interrupt a purportedly 'unlicensed' showing of a film there about the anti-Russian, pro-European protests on Maidan Square in Kyiv. Teatr.doc opened in a new venue in Moscow in February 2015, but in May the dress rehearsal of their play *The Bolotnaya Case* by Polina Borodina, an account from the relatives' point of view of the plight of those arrested for protesting in May 2012 against Putin's re-election, took place in the conspicuous presence of a number of police officers. Soon afterwards their rental agreement was once again abruptly terminated, and they moved into their third venue in six months in June 2015. At the end of that year, the Russian Association of Theatre Critics recognized Gremina as the

'Person of the Year'. In summing up the 2014–15 theatre season John Freedman observed that it had been above all characterized by 'obscurantism' ('*mrakobesie*').⁹

After the Pussy Riot scandal the next cause célèbre, which would attract attention in Russia, Ukraine and Belarus, was the sentencing in August 2015 of the Ukrainian film director Oleg Sentsov to twenty years in jail for supposedly organizing a terrorist conspiracy. He and one other were accused of plotting to set fire to Russian government offices in Crimea after its annexation, and of planning to blow up a monument to Lenin. Both Sentsov and the key prosecution witness claimed at the trial that their testimony was extracted from them under torture, and he is the subject of an ongoing support campaign by Amnesty International as well as by groups such as Teatr.doc and Pussy Riot in Russia, and the Belarus Free Theatre and others abroad. Appeals from leading cultural figures in Russia and abroad for Putin to intervene have been shrugged off. Sentsov undertook a four-month hunger strike during 2018 on behalf of Ukrainian prisoners detained in Russia, which was designed to embarrass Russia during the football World Cup, but he still remains in prison.¹⁰

There was little change in the situation over the next year or so, and the increasing pressures from the state to bring the arts under their control were summed up in October 2016 in this account of a speech to the Union of Russian Theatre-makers by the Artistic Director of the Satirikon Theatre, Konstantin Raykin, whose father Arkady Raykin had been one of the most popular satirical comedians during the Soviet era:

> 'I am very concerned [...] about certain tendencies which have begun to manifest themselves in our lives. These include [...] attacks on art, and on theatre in particular. They are entirely unlawful, extreme, insolent and aggressive, whilst dressing themselves up with phrases about virtue and morals, and all sorts of sacred and elevated notions such as "patriotism", "the Motherland", and "higher morality".' [...]
>
> [However,] Dmitry Peskov [Putin's Press Secretary], commenting on Raykin's speech, declared that the state was perfectly entitled to 'lay down the themes' of those works of art whose creation it was paying for.¹¹

Peskov's views here resonated with those of the Minister of Culture Medinsky, who in June 2015 had published an article in the newspaper *Izvestiia* under the belligerent title 'Those who do not nurture their own culture are nurturing other people's armies'.¹²

The early months of 2017 were dominated by debates in the press about a new film, Aleksei Uchitel''s *Matil'da*, which depicted the love affair (before his marriage) between the future Tsar Nicholas II and a ballerina, Matil'da Kseshinskaya. Even before the film had been completed, and on the basis just of trailers and accounts of the film script, questions were raised in the Duma about the likelihood of the film offending religious feeling in depicting the sexual activity of Nicholas, who was now officially a saint, having been canonized by the Moscow Patriarchate of the Orthodox Church in 2000. When the film was finally passed for distribution that autumn, a number of cinema chains refused to show it, citing security anxieties because of threats received from religious activists. Although the Minister of Culture Medinsky attempted on this occasion to defend the film, many people saw in these events the increasing influence of Bishop Tikhon Shevkunov, known as Putin's 'spiritual adviser', on public affairs in Russia.[13]

In May 2017, the police intensified their investigations into a supposed financial fraud committed at another of Moscow's leading experimental theatres, the Gogol' Centre, where the playwright and film director Kirill Serebrennikov ran a company called Seventh Studio. In a surreal detail, the authorities accused him of embezzling state funds for a production of *A Midsummer Night's Dream*, claiming that it had never even taken place, notwithstanding the fact that the production had been widely reviewed. There was an outcry within Russia and internationally, especially in July 2017 when the Bol'shoi Theatre cancelled the imminent premiere of *Nureyev*, Serebrennikov's biographical ballet about Rudol'f Nureyev. It was said that the ban had been requested by Medinsky himself, because of the ballet's 'propaganda of homosexuality': a legal ban against allowing minors to be exposed to artistic representations of 'non-traditional relationships' was another piece of new legislation, dating back to 2013. Nevertheless, Medinsky later insisted that the fraud case had nothing to do with Serebrennikov's work as an artist.[14] Serebrennikov was then arrested in August 2017 in connection with the charge of embezzlement, and sentenced to house arrest despite vociferous expressions of outrage across the world of theatre and culture. The ballet *Nureyev* eventually premiered in December 2017, and despite only being given a handful of performances (enthusiastically attended by Moscow's cultural elite), it received one of Russia's top prizes for Serebrennikov's scenographic contributions.[15] After constant pressure from his supporters in Russia and around the world, Kirill Serebrennikov was finally released from house arrest – but only on bail – on 8 April 2019, after more than a year and a half of confinement. Irina Prokhorova noted that it was the first time that a cultural leader of the stature of Serebrennikov had been arrested by the authorities since the notorious arrest and murder during Stalin's Terror of the director Vsevolod Meierkhol'd.[16]

Ivan Vyrypaev, aesthetically the most distinguished of Russia's 'New Drama' playwrights, wrote an open letter on 24 August 2017 to other Russian cultural figures, arguing that nothing had changed fundamentally since the Bolshevik era, and that the failure to address and examine publicly the evils perpetrated by Lenin and Stalin had left these issues unresolved in Russian society. Furthermore, he added, this failure has meant that the countries of Eastern Europe and of the former USSR continue to regard the Russian language as the language of their oppressors. Vyrypaev went on to warn his fellow artists against accepting any state funding in Russia, and suggested that their appeals on behalf of Serebrennikov were doomed to fail:

> Who are we appealing to, and what are we asking for? After all, it's just like asking Stalin to forgive Meierkhol'd, but why should Stalin forgive anybody? [...] Do you really not see that the Russian Federation's Ministry of Culture headed by the current Minister [Medinsky], these people are the heirs to that same Communist regime, although they are a little kinder and not quite so cruel: they decide whether to license your films rather than shooting you. So Kirill Serebrennikov has not been shot like Meierkhol'd, just disgraced in public and sentenced to house arrest. So that means times have improved, does it?

Vyrypaev went on to call upon his fellow intellectuals to work for a change of government using non-violent means in the run-up to the 2018 elections, above all by withdrawing from any collaborations or public expressions of support for the Putin regime.[17]

President Putin, who had after all built his career as an international spy working for the Soviet-era KGB, is himself far from denying his nostalgia for the past. Asked in 2005 what he thought about the collapse of the USSR in 1991, he described it as 'the greatest geopolitical catastrophe of the century', and confirmed in 2018 that if he could change anything in history, he would choose to reverse the disintegration of the Soviet empire.[18] In this view he is perhaps not alone: in December 2016 Russia's leading opinion polling organization established that 56 per cent of the population regretted the end of the Soviet regime, not just for economic reasons, but because they had lost the sense of pride they used to feel about living under a great power.[19]

In March 2018, Putin swept to an easy victory again in the presidential elections, inaugurating his fourth term of office in the post: Aleksei Naval'ny, his main opponent, had been disbarred from the race the previous December by the central electoral commission, having been arrested on multiple occasions for his protest activities. A year later, in March 2019, a new law was introduced which banned 'obvious disrespect for society, the state, official state symbols, the constitution or the organs of state power'. This was immediately implemented: news websites, which in early April 2019 had reported some insulting graffiti about Putin in the town of Yaroslavl', started receiving calls from the agency which oversees communications as well as the FSB (security services), demanding that the material be deleted.[20] As the satirist Andrei Bilzho put it, 'Today you're talking about a law which says there can be no criticism of those in power. Tomorrow you'll make praising them obligatory.'[21] In a world shaped by this kind of 'fake news' and blatant media manipulation, the truths that art can tell can only gain further in integrity.

Alexander Trustrum Thomas's essay in this volume investigates the blizzard of new laws and guidelines relating to cultural policy which have been formulated by the Russian Duma since 2012. Since the collapse of the Soviet system in 1991, the world of culture in Russia had been turbulent and heterogeneous, dominated by new forces ranging from raw commercialism to esoteric postmodernism. It is striking that the contributors to Evgeny Dobrenko and Galin Tihanov's important volume of essays *A History of Russian Literary Theory and Criticism*, published as recently as 2011, did not yet really see a clear pattern emerging for the politics of culture in Russia in the second decade of the twenty-first century. Ilya Kukulin and Mark Lipovetsky conclude, for example: 'It is difficult to say whether the contemporary disposition of critical trends is just another guise of the long-standing intellectual struggle between Slavophiles and Westernizers, traditionalists and modernists, and nationalists and liberals, or whether a new inchoate polarity is emerging in twenty-first-century Russian literary criticism.'[22] The cultural policy documents which have emerged in rapid succession since that date have completely transformed that situation. With their emphasis on the state's right and obligation to support artworks which contribute to the nurturing of healthy, patriotic, religious citizens for the future, with 'traditional Russian' values relating to sexuality and gender and a conservative moral outlook, these policy documents tell a story which sounds very familiar to anybody who remembers

Soviet-era ideology and propaganda. In the USSR, the task of using the arts to educate and inspire the populace to support the goals of the Communist Party was to be achieved through the monopolistic set of cultural practices known as 'Socialist Realism'. This had been the 'official method of Soviet literature and literary criticism' which prevailed from 1934 right through until the demise of the USSR in 1991. Katerina Clark's account of the typical 'positive hero' of Socialist Realism, for example, sounds just the same as the models being set up now for contemporary culture:

> The 'positive hero' has been a defining feature of Soviet Socialist Realism. The hero is expected to be an emblem of Bolshevik virtue, someone the reading public should be inspired to emulate, and his life should be patterned to 'show the forward movement of history' in an allegorical representation of one stage in history's dialectical process. [He] should exemplify moral and political (or religious) virtue.[23]

We should not forget that the arbiters of cultural policy – and of course the former KGB officer President Putin himself – still belong to a generation whose formative years were spent under Soviet rule. The notion of a dirigiste state dictating the content and methods of artistic projects is one with which they feel entirely comfortable, and if the politics of communism as such are no longer relevant, then the political goals of an authoritarian ruling class are still well served by these new, tight controls over cultural practices.

And what of those individual artists who do not choose to conform to the state's pressures upon them to identify with the prevailing ideology? The dissident writer Andrei Siniavsky comments on this in a seminal 1959 article, 'What is Socialist Realism?': 'As for anybody who suffers from superfluous differences of thought, the state punishes them severely, by excluding them from both life and literature.'[24] All the indicators suggest that the ideology shaping the KGB-trained Vladimir Putin's cultural policies in the second decade of the twenty-first century is taking us right back to the heyday of Soviet power, and to a revival of Socialist Realism in all its aspects apart from the party political goal of communism itself, which has been neatly replaced by the ideology of the Russian Orthodox Church in its stead.

The spring of 2018 proved to be traumatic for Teatr.doc, when first of all Mikhail Ugarov and then six weeks later his wife Elena Gremina died of stress-related diseases: both were only in their early sixties. Their shocked colleagues in Teatr.doc have since coped with yet another change of premises forced upon them by the authorities, and they are doing their very best to preserve and continue the traditions and the ethos of this institution, which had done so much to shape theatre in Moscow and beyond in the first two decades of the twenty-first century. Whether the deaths of Ugarov and Gremina will prove to mark the true beginning of the end of 'New Drama' as a cultural phenomenon remains to be seen.

Ukraine

The course of events in the theatre world in Ukraine during the last few years is covered extensively in the studies below by Noah Birksted-Breen, Molly Flynn and Jack Clover, based in all three cases on the time they have spent there interviewing and working with Ukrainian theatre-makers. Our ambition for this book has not been to provide a comprehensive account of developments in Ukrainian theatre during this period, a task which would be beyond our competencies, but to explore the ways in which Ukrainian theatre-makers who had hitherto worked fruitfully and more or less unproblematically alongside their Russian counterparts have sought new, independent directions for their work, as the transnational ties which they had shared loosened and frayed under the pressure of political developments.

Individual writers from Ukraine such as Maksym Kurochkin had been involved from the very start in the birth of the 'New Drama' movement at the turn of the twenty-first century. Kurochkin was then based in Moscow, and participated in Elyse Dodgson's 1999 seminar, after which he and others wrote short sketches on the theme of Moscow. Gremina told Sasha Dugdale that it was because of the attention Kurochkin received then that he was commissioned to write one of his early successes, the play *The Kitchen* (2000). Natal'ia Vorozhbit, another Russian-speaking Ukrainian, studied and lived in Moscow for ten years, returning to Ukraine in 2004.[25] She had presented one of her plays, *Gal'ka-Motal'ka*, in 2001, the year when the Liubimovka Festival first established itself in Moscow. She was one of those who participated in a 2005 seminar with the British dramaturg Jeanie O'Hare, which ultimately led to a commission from the Royal Shakespeare Company for her to write a play in Russian about the traumatic events of the '*Holodomor*', the appalling famine of the 1930s in Soviet Ukraine which is widely believed to have been contrived deliberately by Stalin. Her play, written in Russian under the title *The Grainstore*, was developed with the RSC and staged in English at Stratford in 2009 as part of Michael Boyd's 'Revolutions' season. It has only recently been staged for the first time in Ukraine.[26]

These brief glimpses of moments in the theatrical emergence of two of the most important Russian-speaking Ukrainian writers of the transnational 'New Drama' movement, and of the early years of Teatr.doc, are offered simply to underline the extent to which at that time they shared in – and of course also crucially shaped – developments in that movement, irrespective of whether their subject-matter was Ukrainian or Russian. For a significant portion of this time they worked or lived in Russia, entered into collaborations with theatres in Britain and other countries, and apparently shared in the values and adventures of the 'New Drama' movement without tensions based on nationality causing any notable problems. Russian playwrights were similarly travelling to Ukraine and participating in events organized in that country. Again, the necessity of using Russian to communicate did not apparently present a significant problem, since the use of Russian among Ukrainians is very widespread, and facilitates communication and co-operation across the entire post-Soviet sphere.

However, when Vorozhbit returned to Ukraine in 2004, she found that there was little happening on the theatre scene there to compare with the 'New Drama' movement:

There wasn't any interesting contemporary theatre. But together with a few people I knew, I tried to build a community conducive to the creation of a new kind of theatre. For example, we founded the theatre festival 'A Week of Relevant Plays'.[27] That's how we discovered some new names in playwriting and began creating a community for New Ukrainian Drama. Our work is starting to become recognized and some state theatres have begun staging works by contemporary authors. Life here has definitely become more interesting, but we are still at the beginning of this journey.[28]

Vorozhbit recalled that period of easy co-operation with her Russian colleagues as a fond memory, as for example in this reminiscence of Ugarov and Gremina after their 2018 deaths:

I don't remember when we last saw each other. Probably at the 'Week of Contemporary Plays', to which he and Lena [Elena Gremina] often came, to share their priceless lessons. And with no fee. Forgiving us for being disorganised. Because we had a common cause, because of friendship, because they didn't mind sharing and giving. And when he passed away, Ukrainian dramatists and directors were sincere in expressing their grief.[29]

Responding to the emergence of this wave of Ukrainian dramatists who were trying to establish 'New Drama' in Ukraine, including figures such as Oksana Savchenko, Pavel Ar'e and Tat'iana Kitsenko, the critic Oleg Vergelis observed in 2013 that:

Their various texts (which are not always artistically polished) speak about our modern life openly, with anguish and despair, confusingly, haughtily and sometimes naively. This generation of dramatists (whose average age is about 30) seem to me to be 'spiky'. There is much that they are dissatisfied with, they have things to say, but not everybody wants to hear or listen to them. Some of the plays of these several new authors understandably alarm the repertory theatres (obscenities and so on).[30]

Events on Independence Square (the Maidan) in Kyiv late in 2013, with protestors demonstrating against President Yanukovych's decision to abandon a promised rapprochement with the European Union in favour of a renewed closeness with Putin's Russia, ended in bloodshed and well over a hundred deaths. Vorozhbit spent three months on the Maidan with the encamped protestors, gathering witness testimonies on the spot, and together with Andrei Mai created a verbatim play called *Maidan: Voices from the Uprising*.[31] These deeply traumatic events led to the overthrowing of Yanukovych's regime, and were followed by the crisis of the 2014 annexation of Crimea by Russia, and the start of military conflict in eastern Ukraine between Ukrainian government forces and pro-Russian separatists. All these events have revived and sharply exacerbated age-old suspicions and hostility between Moscow and Kyiv, and forced many Ukrainian citizens to confront unwelcome and sometimes uncomfortable questions about their sense of cultural identity and their attitudes towards the Russian state.[32] One feature of the problematization of cultural identity in certain circles has been the choice of whether to use the Russian or the Ukrainian language. Nevertheless, many commentators have emphasized that it would be facile and reductive to assume that Ukrainian speakers are pro-European and loyal to the government, or that

Russian-speakers lean more towards Russia.³³ Ethnic Russians make up a sizeable minority of the population of Ukraine, and many families share mixed backgrounds and are comfortable with both languages, using them fairly interchangeably. President Yanukovych (2010–14) provoked the anger of the most fervent of Ukrainian nationalists when he passed a law in 2012 giving Russian the status of a regional language in public life. One of the very first acts of the new parliament after his flight to Russia in February 2014 was therefore to pass a counter-law, making Ukrainian the sole state language. In May 2017 the Ukrainian parliament introduced quotas for TV, demanding that at least three-quarters of their output should be in Ukrainian: this provoked many complaints from Ukrainians who were Russian-speakers.³⁴ In February 2018 the Yanukovych law elevating Russian to the status of a state language was overturned. In April 2019 Ukraine's parliament passed a law making the use of the Ukrainian language mandatory for public sector workers.³⁵ Nevertheless, in his inaugural speech on 20 May 2019 President Volodymyr Zelensky spoke mostly in Ukrainian, but also used Russian, reflecting his apparent preference for tolerance and flexibility over the issue.³⁶ It is striking that both Vorozhbit and Kurochkin, who used to write entirely in Russian, have turned away from that language, and have learned to write their new drama in Ukrainian instead: and this has been a far from painless or straightforward decision for them.

The worsening of relations between Ukraine and Russia was reflected in the fact that by August 2014 the Ukrainians announced that they would deny entry to their country to up to 500 cultural figures who had declared their support for the Russian annexation of Crimea. Cultural skirmishing of this kind has continued ever since. Along with the further banning of certain individuals (including the French actor Gérard Départdieu, who had recently accepted Russian citizenship), a list of about forty books which it was forbidden to import into Ukraine was published in the summer of 2015, to protect Ukrainians from 'disinformation' and 'xenophobia'.³⁷ Laws were also passed in 2015 ordering the removal or destruction of monuments and other symbols both of the Nazi and of the Soviet past in Ukraine, which naturally contributed to a new, lower visibility for Russian-related artefacts in the public sphere. Most Russian TV channels have also been banned in Ukraine as well. And there was a certain amount of tit-for-tat retaliation, of course, with the Russians closing down a music festival in Moscow in the summer of 2016 when they heard that Ukrainian hardcore punk bands sympathetic to the regime in Kyiv would be involved; and in 2015–16 the director of the Ukrainian library in Moscow was placed under house arrest pending her trial for disseminating 'extremist' material, despite protests from many members of the Russian branch of PEN International.³⁸

In the summer of 2015 Natal'ia Vorozhbit decided, together with the German director Georg Genoux, to set up a new theatre project called Theatre of Displaced People, to provide a space where both active and involuntary participants in the hostilities which had divided Ukraine since the previous year could tell their stories in their own words. Many Ukrainians who had suffered displacement from their homes and disruption of their normal lives have thereby been provided with an opportunity for both healing and empowerment. The story of the Theatre of Displaced People is the specific contribution in this book by Molly Flynn, who has observed and participated in its projects.

Elyse Dodgson of the Royal Court, who like Mikhail Ugarov and Elena Gremina of Teatr.doc sadly and unexpectedly died in 2018, recalled in October 2017 her long association with Natal'ia Vorozhbit: they had met in 2004 at the Liubimovka Festival in Moscow, and she worked with her at the Royal Court on several plays thereafter. Through Vorozhbit, Dodgson also came to know and collaborate with another rising star of Ukrainian drama, Anna Iablonskaia, who was tragically killed in a terrorist bombing at Moscow's Domodedovo Airport in 2011. Iablonskaia's 2010 play *The Pagans* is the particular subject of Molly Thomasy Blasing's contribution to this volume. In 2017 the Royal Court staged Vorozhbit's *Bad Roads*, in which her main protagonist embarks upon a passionate affair with a Ukrainian fighter against the backdrop of the 2014–15 battle for control of Donetsk airport, one of the most deadly episodes of the hostilities in eastern Ukraine.[39] *Bad Roads*, which was initially drafted in Russian, has now been rewritten by Vorozhbit for performance in Ukrainian.

It was striking to hear, however, at a recent event organized by Molly Flynn in London called 'Depicting Donbas', that Vorozhbit and other Ukrainian theatre-makers were beginning to acknowledge their feelings not only of exhaustion, but also possible burn-out, and a sense that Ukrainian documentary theatre may almost have achieved all that it can in reporting first-hand experience. Perhaps contemporary Ukrainian drama is ready to begin on a new and different phase, an emancipation from 'New Drama' itself.[40] The years following upon the painful events of 2014 have been difficult ones for many Ukrainians – the seemingly unstoppable fighting has continued against the backdrop of unchecked corruption in the corridors of power, a faltering economy and weakened currency, while health indicators have taken a turn for the worse.[41] The surprise election of Volodymyr Zelensky suggests that disillusioned voters are willing to seek better prospects even with an untried leader, someone whose only real manifesto has been the optimistic script of his TV comedy show.

Belarus

By contrast with the turbulence of Ukrainian politics over the last decade or two, the political regime in Belarus has remained unchanged. President Alexander Lukashenko has held power there even longer than Putin has in Russia, having been elected to the post in 1994. The only deputy to have voted against the independence of Belarus from the USSR, Lukashenko has displayed his nostalgia for many aspects of Soviet power, to the extent that his security services still bear the old name KGB, a designation which has been replaced in the Russian Federation by the new term FSB. Despite occasional squabbles, the regime in Belarus has remained very closely tied to Putin's Russia. The Bush administration in the US described Lukashenko as 'the last dictator in Europe'.

The arts critic Tania Arcimovich is one of the most authoritative commentators on the cultural scene in Belarus, and her contributions to this volume offer thoughtful insights into the way cultural and language policies have played out in twenty-first-century Belarus, against the backdrop of political events which in many respects reflect trends in modern-day Russian cultural politics. In 2005 a new theatre company was established in Belarus by Natal'ia Koliada and Nicolai Khalezin, who were soon joined by Vladimir Shcherban. This was the Belarus Free Theatre (BFT), whose story is told in this volume in an interview with Natal'ia Koliada. Just like the Ukrainian dramatists who had taken part in the Royal Court seminars and other festivals and competitions characterizing the heyday of 'New Drama', so too there were Belarusians present, including Pavel Priazhko, who has established a very visible reputation in Russia and internationally since that time. Sir Tom Stoppard has described how he met Khalezin and Koliada and became aware of just how important the opportunities offered by the 'New Drama' scene in Russia were to Belarusian playwrights, at a time when they were simply unable to persuade anyone to stage their own work in Belarusian theatres:

> For the two Belarusian playwrights who invited me here, Nikolai Khalezin and Natalia Koliada – husband and wife – a merger with Russia would be the worst thing that could happen; but it's the Russian theatre that has opened its doors to them, and to others like Kureychik, who in 2002 was the first Belarusian to win Russia's major play competition. He came back to Minsk and reported that Moscow was 'like breathing fresh air'. Within two years he had 17 Russian productions of his plays.[42]

Even as recently as 2016, the Belarusian contingent represented at Moscow's Liubimovka festival included Aleksei Makeychik, Lekha Chykanas and Priazhko (he is in fact the single playwright – of any nationality – who has been most frequently performed in the entire history of the Liubimovka). The playwright Konstantin Steshik has given an interview in which he simply claimed: 'Belarusian theatre does not exist.' Arguing that in Belarus the theatres were largely interested in staging the classics, he suggested that although there were occasional attempts to stage contemporary works, 'every significant event relating to Belarusian playwriting actually takes place in Russia. [...] We would never have become established as playwrights in Belarus were it not for the Liubimovka, for "New Drama", and for productions in Russia.'[43] At the same time, however, the Liubimovka's director, the playwright Mikhail Durnenkov, has suggested that since state theatres in Russia have also become increasingly cautious about the content of plays in the current, fraught atmosphere of social conservatism, the majority of the works – whether Russian or Belarusian – which receive readings at the Liubimovka are now more likely to find a staging abroad than they are within Russia.

In February 2010 Noah Birksted-Breen, Artistic Director of Sputnik Theatre, translated and directed a staged reading of Koliada's play *Dreams* in London, in which four women reflect on the disappearances of their husbands, triggered by their oppositional stance to the Lukashenko regime. The BFT's outspokenness about such scandals made their situation more and more precarious and even dangerous, and in 2011 they fled Belarus and sought political asylum in Britain, with influential patrons such as Tom Stoppard and the Czech writer and statesman Václav Havel supporting them. London and the Young Vic Theatre have become their base ever since. As a theatre company in exile, the BFT has used its powerful theatrical productions as well as its 'Ministry of Counter-Culture' internet reporting to highlight human rights abuses in Belarus and to campaign for freedom of speech. Their vision has also become increasingly transnational: they speak out about similar issues affecting Russia and

Ukraine in particular, as well as other countries around the world. Their preoccupations have been similar to some of the characteristic issues addressed by Teatr.doc in Moscow: they have documented police brutality and unjust imprisonment in the aftermath of protest demonstrations against Lukashenko's re-election in December 2010; they have drawn attention to the suppression of political opposition in the run-up to elections; they have highlighted the oppression of dissident figures and minority groups representing, for example, homosexuals or the disabled; and they have campaigned on behalf of prisoners of conscience, such as Oleg Sentsov, the Ukrainian film director accused of terrorist charges in Crimea in 2014.

Another voice articulating opposition to the Lukashenko regime is that of the journalist and writer Svetlana Aleksievich, whose books (written in Russian) have also used documentary techniques to give voice to individuals – often women – who have lived through traumatic events such as the Second World War, the Soviet invasion of Afghanistan, or the nuclear disaster at Chernobyl'. Persecuted by the authorities, and with her books banned in her native country, she spent over a decade abroad from the early 2000s, although she has now returned to live in Minsk, the Belarusian capital. In 2015 she received the Nobel Prize for Literature, to the embarrassment and perhaps the irritation of Lukashenko and Putin, both of whom she has described as dictators. It was striking that two of Russia's leading writers, Dmitry Bykov and Liudmila Ulitskaia, commented that the Nobel Prize was a great achievement and honour for *Russian* literature, with Bykov only adding 'and for Belarusian literature' as a kind of afterthought.[44] Meanwhile the Belarusian playwright and screenwriter Andrey Kureychyk proclaimed of her that: 'A new national leader has appeared in Belarus. She has more authority now than any politician, the President or a minister. And she's someone with normal European values.'[45] Timothy Snyder, writing in *The New York Review of Books*, added:

> It is right, but also not quite right, to celebrate the journalist and contemporary historian, Svetlana Alexievich, this year's laureate of the Nobel Prize in Literature, as a Belarusian writer. The force of her work, the source of its power and plausibility, is the choice of a generation (her own) as a major subject and the close attention to its major inflection point, which was the end of the Soviet Union. She is connected to Russia and Ukraine as well as Belarus and is a writer of all three nations; the passage from Soviet state to national state was experienced by them all, and her life has been divided among them. [...] She clearly identifies with Russians as well as with Belarusians and Ukrainians, as the three new nations move through the uncharted difficulties of sovereignty.[46]

The Belarusian Aleksievich has spoken out against the Russian annexation of Ukrainian Crimea, and continues to occupy something of a transnational position in the culture of the region. This transnational vision which so strongly characterizes some Belarusian writers was similarly reflected in a recent project by the BFT, when Nicolai Khalezin began a collaboration with Mariya Alyokhina (from Pussy Riot) on a production which would be premiered in Britain in 2016 as *Burning Doors*. This hard-hitting, extraordinarily physical piece of theatre traced human rights abuses in Russia and

Ukraine, and had Alyokhina herself reliving her own brutal prison experiences on stage.

In July 2016 Lukashenko approved an elaborate new legal code on cultural policy, containing 257 separate articles. For the first time it gave priority to the use of the Belarusian language rather than Russian in the formation of national identity. And article 81, in terms which anticipate some recent developments in Russia, stated that cultural activities could be banned if they seemed to 'discredit the reputation and honour' of President Lukashenko or the organs of the state. The poet Vladimir Nekliaev, a presidential candidate who was severely beaten up on the day of the 2010 elections, has ridiculed the article requiring that all cultural practitioners would have to hold a certificate to prove their status. The playwright Andrey Kureychyk added that he had no intention of going to the Ministry of Culture to acquire such a certificate.[47] At the end of 2016, after Lukashenko had already spent twenty-two years in power, legislation was proposed to extend the president's term of office from five to seven years.[48] Protests against further repressive measures erupted in Minsk in March 2017, and were again met with a violent response and arrests by the riot police. 'Lukashenko is in a panic, in fear of his own people,' said Natal'ia Koliada hopefully.[49] She and the BFT team have been continuing, as they have done since 2011, to produce illicit underground shows in Minsk and elsewhere in Belarus, rehearsing and directing the shows via Skype from London. Arrests of over two hundred writers, journalists and intellectuals continued during the spring of 2017, with a number of individuals who didn't yet belong to officially registered artistic organizations being charged additional taxes for 'parasitism'. There were further human rights protests in March 2018.

The BFT has also been responsible for another drama project, an annual competition for new plays which ran from 2005 to 2010, started up again in 2014, but has again been suspended now for lack of funds. Known as the International Contest of Contemporary Drama (ICCD), it was notable for accepting plays written in Russian, Ukrainian or Belarusian, and by the time of its seventh contest over 500 plays were being submitted to it on each occasion. The jury was international, including members from Russia and Belarus as well as Britain. Its suspension marks the end, perhaps, of what had been a genuinely transnational phenomenon. As Pavel Rudnev, the Moscow theatre critic, observed:

> A huge problem in Russia, Belarus and Ukraine today is a trend to self-closure, to tightness, to artificial isolation. One of the major themes of the new post-Soviet drama is the catastrophic destruction of communication between people, generations, genders and countries. [...] The mission and meaning of the ICCD contest is not only to encourage and discover Russian-language drama, but also to export this product to other countries. None of the state institutions of these countries are concerned about a similar mission today.[50]

In his 'Foreword' to the 2016 edition of the winning plays from the eighth competition, Nicolai Khalezin commented in similar terms that:

> This edition [...] is a symbol of the power of creative resistance in the face of rising authoritarianism in three Eastern European countries: Belarus, Ukraine and

Russia. [...] ICCD exists to give a voice to writers where there is little or no opportunity for them to be heard in their home countries. Contemporary playwrights are a vital force in these societies; they uncover worlds which are never discussed by journalists or politicians.[51]

The present collection of essays and interviews provides a snapshot of a rapidly changing situation which has transformed the relations between theatre-makers in Russia, Ukraine and Belarus over the past ten years. The Soviet system had created a transnational system of its own, through the imposition across the entire Soviet Empire of the official doctrine of Socialist Realism. The shared use of the Russian language then made possible a fresh, post-Soviet transnational movement in the shape of 'New Drama', freely entered into by theatre-makers in all three countries between about 1999 and 2014. The momentous shifts in Russian culture under President Putin since that year, including a reclaiming of former Soviet territory and a reinstatement of a cultural policy resembling Socialist Realism, have exacerbated political hostilities and personal suspicions. Fruitful collaborations have given way now to more isolationist positions, which almost certainly mark the true demise of 'New Drama' as a genuinely transnational phenomenon.

Notes

1. For a more extensive account of this formative period, see the essays below by Marie-Christine Autant-Mathieu and Lucie Kempf.
2. John Freedman (ed.), 'An Introduction', *Real and Phantom Pains: An Anthology of New Russian Drama* (Washington, DC: New Academia Publishing, 2014), 6.
3. See Birgit Beumers and Mark Lipovetsky, *Performing Violence: Literary and Theatrical Experiments of New Russian Drama* (Bristol: Intellect, 2009), 28: 'If there was a surge of dramatic writing in Russia at the turn of the twentieth and twenty-first centuries, then the peak was reached in the first half of the 2000s; at present, New Drama is already in decline, having influenced, however, contemporary Russian culture in more than one way. By 2008, New Drama had lost its momentum and exhausted itself: society was cushioned in a more stable economy and the commercialised cultural life in the capitals left experiments largely to provincial cities, such as Ekaterinburg and Togliatti in particular.' In the same volume, Sasha Dugdale commented: 'It is mostly accepted that the tidal wave of New Writing has passed. But to my mind the group of new writers who submitted work for the last Royal Court seminar is just as talented as the original group' (19).
4. Beumers and Lipovetsky, *Performing Violence*, 43.
5. See Alexander Trustrum Thomas's essay below, in which he reviews the legislation which has shaped Russian policies in the arts over the last few years.
6. https://moc.media/ru/1743
7. https://tass.ru/kultura/1996328
8. https://www.bbc.co.uk/news/world-europe-33982267
9. http://old.themoscowtimes.com/arts_n_ideas/article/the-year-in-theater-murky-demons-on-the-loose/526033.html
10. Oleg Sentsov was released on 7 September 2019 as part of a prisoner exchange between Russia and Ukraine.

11 http://www.bbc.com/russian/news-37786635
12 https://iz.ru/news/587771
13 http://www.bbc.com/russian/features-42462180
14 https://moc.media/ru/1822; https://www.theguardian.com/world/2017/aug/29/leading-arts-figures-urge-russia-to-drop-flimsy-charges-against-director
15 https://www.calvertjournal.com/news/show/10296/kirill-serebrennikov-wins-top-ballet-prize-for-nureyev
16 https://themoscowtimes.com/articles/russian-culture-at-a-crossroads-the-case-of-serebrennikov-58803
17 https://snob.ru/profile/26058/blog/128291
18 https://www.rferl.org/a/putin-says-would-reverse-collapse-soviet-union-1991-if-could-question-asked-kaliningrad/29076226.html
19 http://www.bbc.com/russian/news-38205589
20 https://www.telegraph.co.uk/news/2019/04/03/russian-sites-delete-putin-graffiti-articles-law-against-disrespecting/
21 https://www.independent.co.uk/news/world/europe/a-gift-for-satire-prominent-russian-humourist-responds-to-new-law-banning-criticism-of-the-state-a8815696.html
22 Ilya Kukulin and Mark Lipovetsky, 'Post-Soviet Literary Criticism', in *A History of Russian Literary Theory and Criticism: The Soviet Age and Beyond* (Pittsburgh, PA: University of Pittsburgh Press, 2011), 304.
23 Katerina Clark, *The Soviet Novel – History as Ritual* (first publ. 1981; Bloomington and Indianapolis, IN: Indiana University Press, 3rd edn, 2000), 46.
24 Andrei Siniavskii, anonymously published in 1960 in *Dissent Magazine*, https://www.dissentmagazine.org/wp-content/files_mf/1410896620On_Socialist_Realism_Winter_1960.pdf
25 See interview with Molly Flynn, 27 May 2014, https://thetheatretimes.com/natalya-vorozhbit/
26 Dugdale in Beumers and Lipovetsky, *Performing Violence*, 14–15, 19.
27 Elsewhere in this volume this festival's name is translated from Ukrainian as 'The Week of Contemporary Plays'.
28 See interview with Molly Flynn, 27 May 2014, https://thetheatretimes.com/natalya-vorozhbit/
29 From a special edition of the Moscow journal *Teatr*, 34 (2018): *Mikhail Ugarov: Teoriya, Praktika, Politika, Pedagogika*, 36.
30 http://gazeta.zn.ua/CULTURE/vzeroshennoe-pokolenie-shest-dramaturgov-v-poiskah-_.html
31 This play is also known as *Maidan Diaries*.
32 Some Ukrainians have been reminded of age-old patronizing attitudes held by Russians towards their culture, as described, for example, by Mark Andryczyk in his account of Soviet-era Ukrainian Socialist Realism: 'a Ukrainian hero in a novel did not merely have to be shown working toward the proletariat's emancipation, and espousing the ideals of communism as Soviet Russian protagonists did, but he also needed to be depicted with his national traits reduced to condescending clichés and quirky peculiarities.' See Mark Andryczyk (ed.), 'Introduction', in *The White Chalk of Days: The Contemporary Ukrainian Literature Series Anthology* (Boston, MA: Academic Studies Press, 2017), 3.
33 Comments by the critic and playwright Nadiia Miroshnychenko and others at the 'Playwriting Without Borders' workshop held at Wolfson College, Oxford in 2015 (JAEC notes).

34 http://www.bbc.co.uk/news/blogs-news-from-elsewhere-40716406
35 https://www.bbc.co.uk/news/world-europe-48085505
36 https://jamestown.org/program/in-inauguration-address-ukrainian-president-zelensky-gives-hints-about-his-policies-at-home-and-abroad/
37 http://www.bbc.com/russian/international/2015/08/150811_ukraine_banned_russian_books_list
38 https://moc.media/ru/642; https://moc.media/ru/1023
39 http://arts-mail.co.uk/1P0Z-57ZJN-GAWW0A-2U3JTO-1/c.aspx
40 'Depicting Donbas' (notes by JAEC), April 2019, Birkbeck College, London. See http://www.bbk.ac.uk/contemporary-theatre/wp-content/uploads/2019/03/Depicting-Donbas-Programme.pdf
41 https://www.theguardian.com/world/2018/apr/14/ukraine-kiev-dakh-theatre-tsesho-music-art-war-russia
42 Tom Stoppard, 'Accidental Tyranny', *Guardian*, 1 October 2005.
43 See website of the Liubimovka festival: http://lubimovka.ru/o-festivale
44 http://www.bbc.com/russian/russia/2015/10/151008_pundits_on_alexievich
45 https://www.bbc.co.uk/news/world-europe-34478536
46 https://www.nybooks.com/daily/2015/10/12/svetlana-alexievich-truth-many-voices/
47 https://www.bbc.com/russian/features-36889399
48 http://www.bbc.com/russian/news-38077033
49 https://www.theguardian.com/world/2017/mar/25/belarus-lukashenko-protesters-riot-police-attack-minsk
50 Pavel Rudnev, in *Belarus Free Theatre: New Plays from Central Europe. The VII International Contest of Contemporary Drama* (London: Oberon Books, 2014), 14.
51 Nicolai Khalezin, 'Foreword' and back cover, *Belarus Free Theatre: Staging a Revolution. New Plays from Eastern Europe (The VIII International Contest of Contemporary Drama)* (London: Oberon Books, 2016), vi.

Part I

Russia

1

The story of Russian-language drama since 2000

PostDoc, the postdramatic and Teatr Post

Marie-Christine Autant-Mathieu

> In her wide-ranging historical survey Marie-Christine Autant-Mathieu considers the transition from Socialist Realist propaganda theatre to glasnost' drama of the late 1980s and beyond, noting the legacy of experimental Soviet theatre from earlier decades as well. She then traces the evolution of new writing in Russia from the late 1990s, and describes the emergence of documentary theatre, especially since the founding of Teatr.doc in 2002, in the broader context of western theories of performance, including the 'postdramatic'. There is a specific focus on the work of the director Konstantin Bogomolov, and on the longstanding collaboration between the director Dmitrii Volkostrelov and the Belarusian playwright Pavel Priazhko. She concludes by considering the threats faced by experimental theatre today.

For two long generations during the Soviet era dramatists had tended to work in close collaboration with theatre directors. But certain authors, even before the liberalizing policy of *perestroika* was inaugurated by President Gorbachev in the mid-1980s, had begun to try resisting this standard practice by regrouping in 'studios' (the playwright Aleksei Arbuzov's studio being the best known of these), or by having their plays staged in alternative venues, on the margins of the official circuit. These semi-clandestine dramatists, who constituted what became known as 'the new wave', had to wait until the 1990s and the collapse of the Soviet Union before fully coming into their own. But with the exception of a few plays by Liudmila Petrushevskaia, Aleksandr Galin and Viktor Slavkin, audiences displayed little enthusiasm at this new historical juncture for texts depicting an often sordid reality, which belonged to an era that was now gone for ever. It was a difficult transitional moment, since post-Soviet theatre directors at first largely preferred to stage classic authors, or else Western plays which had been banned up until this time.

Nevertheless in the mid-1990s, thanks to the pugnaciousness of author-theatre-makers such as Mikhail Roshchin, Aleksei Kazantsev, Mikhail Ugarov and Elena Gremina, thanks to the editorial support afforded to them in journals, and thanks as well to their organizing of seminars, festivals and lectures, a certain groundswell began to make itself felt, which took on more concrete form in 1998 with the creation of the Centre for Playwriting and Directing (TsDR) in Moscow. This would constitute a valuable bridge between Soviet-era playwriting, the 'new wave' of the 1980s and 1990s, and twenty-first-century new writing ('New Drama'). The TsDR, which to begin with had no permanent space or theatre company of its own, staged some sensational productions (Vasily Sigarev's *Plasticine* in 2001 and Vladimir Pankov's *Red Thread* in 2003, based on the text of the same name by Aleksandr Zheleztsov), which attracted much media and audience attention. This independent experimental organization served as a springboard as much for authors as for the theatre directors who became known through it. And so, for example, having introduced Sigarev to audiences, the then unknown director Kirill Serebrennikov astounded spectators at the prestigious Moscow Art Theatre more used to nineteenth-century playwrights such as Chekhov and Aleksandr Ostrovsky by staging *Terrorism* (in 2002) and *Playing the Victim* (in 2004), both works by the Presniakov brothers Oleg and Vladimir.

In a reaction against the dubious discourses of drama which for many years had been sustained during the falsities of Soviet propaganda, and the 'correct' messages offered by conformists, these new authors privileged the language of obscenity ('*mat*'), which they judged to be more alive and more truthful because of its spontaneity;[1] and they dwelt particularly on grotesque, sleazy, absurd or sordid situations in ordinary everyday life. What therefore emerged was a subculture antithetical to the values cultivated hitherto by the intelligentsia, values which henceforth were held up for ridicule in situations or by protagonists who were living in a world where morality was relative and the idea of normality was challenged.[2]

This essay will trace the evolution of new writing in the context of Russian theatre since 2002 (when Teatr.doc was founded and the New Drama Festival was inaugurated), while taking into account not only experimentation within Russia, but also the impact of external influences such as invitations received from avant-garde Western theatre companies and the translation of works of theory, as well as the vagaries of cultural politics, especially since the Pussy Riot affair of 2012.

The origins of 'New Drama'

There are many observers of the Russian theatrical landscape at the turn of the new, twenty-first century, who have doubted that the emergence of 'New Drama' was a 'natural' phenomenon. The media suddenly began to single out for attention a field of experimentation which had been being pursued since the late 1990s:

> The weakness of New Drama consists in the fact that in Russia it took a long time to be born, and it finally came into the world not through its own efforts, but through a Caesarean section, namely through the efforts of the organisers of a seminar given by Britain's Royal Court Theatre in Moscow, together with the energy of M[ikhail] Ugarov and E[lena] Gremina.[3]

The expression 'New Drama', which took over from the term previously used – 'contemporary playwriting' – was copied from the British term 'New Writing'. In 1999 the British Council and the Royal Court gave bursaries for the staging of Sarah Kane and Mark Ravenhill in Russia, they invited to London several Russian authors who got translated thanks to their support and they introduced to them the technique of verbatim writing, based on the recording of live speech.[4]

But although the stories in the media in the years from 2000 to 2002 tended to overstate certain events in their unquenchable thirst for 'scoops', the tendency towards innovation had in fact been under way for ten years already. Above all, the attempts undertaken first of all in isolation, and then around the instigators of Moscow's annual Liubimovka Festival of Contemporary Theatre, already had their roots elsewhere. These antecedents, of which the new playwrights were not always aware, tended to be ignored by the earliest commentators on the new modes of playwriting, even though this should all have been considered in its historical context before being proclaimed as something which had been imported from scratch.

Denying the lies that appeared in print and rejecting the power structures of officialdom had already been the principles adopted by reformers of the immediate post-Stalin 'Thaw' era: the controversial article 'On Sincerity in Literature' by Vladimir Pomerantsev became the trigger from about 1953 for the emergence of a new, youthful drama represented notably by Viktor Rozov and Aleksandr Volodin.[5] During the 1970s and 1980s some postmodern experimentation prioritizing performance (Lev Rubinshteyn), and the practice of collage as a way of challenging assumptions about the value of individual writing (Vladimir Sorokin), undoubtedly provided one context out of which 'New Drama' grew. More specific precursors of documentary theatre were the Soviet authors of the 1920s and 1930s associated with LEF (The Left Front of Art), who had created montages of raw factual material, taken from life; while the 'living newspapers' of the Blue Blouse theatre companies based their work on current affairs, as reported in the newspapers. Other proletarian groups of that period set off in 'brigades' across the country in order to acquire information directly from its sources (in reality these texts, which were attempting to break with the traditions of individual writing, would ultimately serve to create myths about 'the new man').[6] From the 1960s to the 1980s Mikhail Shatrov would become famous for his historical plays about Lenin, Stalin and the Revolution, based on archives, memoirs and interviews.

On the threshold of the twenty-first-century authors seeking once again to reinstate a reality which had not been fixed, manipulated or falsified, based themselves similarly on historical documents, personal diaries and the testimony of the disregarded, the marginal and those who had been excluded from polite society. They privileged the spoken language. Any quest for style and quality in writing seemed to them to mask, deform and dilute the live discourse of the individual prototypes who served as the point of departure for their creative acts.

Teatr.doc and others

The year 2002 was marked by the inauguration of the 'New Drama' festival (2002–9) and by the creation of Teatr.doc. This 'theatre where people don't act', dedicated to documentary techniques, based itself to begin with almost uniquely on verbatim methods.⁷ Based until 2014 in a basement in the centre of Moscow, financially independent and fitted out entirely by its members, this miniature company became an alternative stage. It aroused curiosity and stimulated initiatives by artists keen to establish themselves on an independent circuit. In 2007 a new mini-theatre, Praktika, created by the director and producer Eduard Boiakov and later run by the author, theatre and film director Ivan Vyrypaev, established its own repertory with authors who were close to Teatr.doc.⁸ Teatr.doc in turn extended its range with the creation in 2010 of the DOC centre for documentary cinema, and it opened an experimental platform in December 2016 directed by Vsevolod Lisovsky called Transformator.doc.⁹ As a very dynamic entity which is capable of reacting and adapting to socio-political developments, Teatr.doc has explored topical issues by revealing realities which have been concealed, and since 2012–13 by turning more and more towards Russia's past.¹⁰

The company has made its name by serving as a watchman: it alerts people to things without inciting them to revolt, and it highlights the dysfunctional without tipping over into militancy. Its scope for manoeuvre remains narrow: while it is closely monitored, it is tolerated precisely because of its marginality (each performance is seen by a hundred or so people, mostly young Muscovites who come to reflect upon social issues which are hushed up by the official press and media). In 2005 *September.doc* evoked the Chechen terrorist attack on a school in Beslan; in 2010 *One Hour and Eighteen Minutes* described the death in prison of the tax accountant Sergei Magnitsky; *Two in Our House* in 2011 was about the house arrest of a member of the opposition in Belarus. In 2012 Varvara Faer (also known as Galina Sin'kina) suggested the extent to which folly and the absurd govern the conduct of Russia's leader in her *BerlusPutin*, in which scientists create a monstrous hybrid of Silvio Berlusconi and Vladimir Putin (this was a farcical adaptation of Dario Fo's *Two-headed Anomaly*).

After the demonstrations which took place in 2012 on Moscow's Bolotnaya Square to protest against Putin's re-election as president, Teatr.doc, true to its commitment not to pass judgement and not to make overt protests, but instead to allow the audience to form its own opinion on the basis of testimonies, staged a production called *The Bolotnaya Case* (2014). Participants included individuals who had been found guilty for their part in the demonstrations. This was a step too far, and the forces of law and order put a stop to the undertaking. But in October 2017 the show reappeared under the different title of *The Co-defendants (The Bolotnaya Case 2)*, with a script which allowed two actors and two witnesses of the events to speak.¹¹ The themes of war and patriotism, which are omnipresent in the Russian media, found a different resonance in *War Is Close* (2016), a production devoted to recent and ongoing events in Ukraine, and based on a montage of three texts: the diary of a resident of the eastern Ukrainian town of Luhansk; a plea from the British playwright Mark Ravenhill against the manipulation of information; and the minutes from a trial of anti-Russian 'terrorists'. *When We Came to Power* (2017) depicts a 'utopia, in which a future Russia is governed by civil society'. This show, based on a montage of interviews taken by the theatre directors Gremina, Ugarov, Konstantin Kozhevnikov and Zarema Zaudinova, portrays the coming to power of responsible citizens who get rid of the members of a bellicose government which has been focused on the raising and collecting of taxes, indifferent to corruption and to social injustice.

But documentary theatre constitutes just one aspect of the range of new writings which have begun to flourish in other Russian cities such as St Petersburg, Cheliabinsk, Kemerovo, Perm', Togliatti and Ekaterinburg, and which have manifested themselves in a plurality of styles and genres. There are Maksym Kurochkin's metaphorical and mythological texts; the absurd and grotesque works of the Presniakov brothers; the carnivalesque and hyperreal in the Ural school of playwriting led by Nikolai Koliada; the poetic texts of Ol'ga Mukhina and Kseniia Dragunskaia; the sentimental and resolutely subjective works of Evgenii Grishkovets; and Ivan Vyrypaev's performative and provocative plays.

Even so, people's hopes for a renewal of Russian theatre through the discovery of new authors (as with writers like Chekhov, Ibsen or Strindberg at the dawn of the twentieth century) have been disappointed. Certain promising writers have abandoned the stage, while the very expectation that a play text has to constitute the starting point for a show has been challenged more and more radically.[12] In Russia as elsewhere, although somewhat belatedly, dramatists have redefined themselves through other forms of creative activity: and Teatr.doc's most recent productions show traces of this.

The manifesto of Teatr.doc and its consequences

In 2003, shortly after the founding of Teatr.doc, three of its members – Ruslan Malikov, Aleksandr Vartanov and Tatiana Kopylova – drafted a 'manifesto' defining ten objectives they were seeking to achieve: to take an interest in extreme situations; to propose texts which would provoke discussion; to address provocative themes; to explore subjects which were new to the theatre; to cast a fresh eye on reality; to use innovative writing techniques; to remain clear and simple; to prioritize the social dimension of the work; and to challenge the idea of art for art's sake.[13]

As for their approach to aesthetics, the manifesto identified the constraints under which the theatre director should operate: to use a minimum of sets; to exclude music, dance or any other bodily plastic forms of expression; to avoid metaphorical language; and for the actors: no disguising of their age, and acting without greasepaint unless this was to be a marker of some professional status.

In this way Teatr.doc opened the floodgates by redefining the functions of the author (as interviewer and gatherer of testimonies), of the director (as a modest composer of the montage which would showcase the performers, whose role was to speak rather than to act), as well as that of the spectator, who ceases to be contemplative and is pushed into responding.

In 2011 a book devoted to the 'post-documentary' in the visual arts demonstrated the impossibility of separating off different genres (a para-documentary strain has now infiltrated fictional cinema, while the techniques of framing and staging are becoming more and more apparent in documentary cinema).[14] In the theatre, eight years after the Teatr.doc manifesto, the situation had also evolved. While the autocratic powers of directors in the large theatre companies have not been affected by the foregrounding of facts, of documents and of concrete *realia*, Teatr.doc's experiments advocating an aesthetic of invisibility, an absence of staging, and the abolishing of acting (the actor offers a figuration, not an interpretation of the character) all made possible an opening towards performance arts. Performance, as Joseph Danan defines it, reverts to the theatrical act in the present, in its relationship to the audience. The text in its written form, that is to say in its fixed form, becomes optional and takes on a secondary importance.[15]

These days Teatr.doc does not limit itself to documentary texts based upon verbatim.[16] Storytelling has made its appearance there since 2014 with *Viy*, based on Nikolai Gogol's story of the supernatural (1835), and with *The History of the Russian State* (2015). This in turn has generated workshops on training and practice. In 2017 the spectators were invited to a 'late night session', and listened in a convivial atmosphere to actors telling stories which they had made up (*I Am a Thing!*). Teatr.doc has diversified its approaches in several ways.

These include giving more priority to the artistic and spectacular aspects created by music, dance and plastic expression: after *Doc.tor* (2005) in which the SounDrama group participated to provide rhythm for the text, *Lear the Parasite* or *Uncensored Songs* was presented as a concert production, and *To Forgive Betrayal* was orchestrated by a plastic artist, Dmitry Krivochurov. As a way of keeping up with current trends, sometimes at the expense of its initial credo, the company has become open to new experiences: promenade shows (*Obscure Influences*, 2016); performance shows such as *The Tibetan Book of the Dead* (2016); serial shows (on the poets Pushkin and Tsvetaeva, starting in 2015); exhibition shows (*Monsters*, 2017); and silent shows (*Keeping Silent on a Given Theme*, 2015; *The Silence of the Classics*, 2016, a project by Vsevolod Lisovsky).[17] Outside the small-scale collective of Teatr.doc there has been a similar process of hybridization of different arts and genres, the same turning away from 'the play'; and a similar openness towards new practices has emerged.

Three principles have supported these experiments:

1. In order to protect their independence and freedom of expression, the artists refuse to accept state subsidies and raise the necessary funds for each of their projects themselves. They earn their living in cinema or television, which leaves them free to engage or not with theatre.
2. They refuse political engagement and militancy, justifying this with the argument that objectivity doesn't exist, and that a multiplicity of subjective viewpoints allows one to resist didacticism and the domination of a single opinion.[18]
3. The place and the role of the audience lie at the heart of explorations which prioritize the interactive. Notions of performance and installation inspire directorial projects. In 2014 *Murmansk*, staged at the Meierkhol'd Centre, was one of the first immersive shows, created by Iury Kviatkovsky after the model of the British company Punchdrunk. During the two and a half hours the spectators are free to choose what they want to see as they move around, at their own pace, from one performance space to another, where diverse subjects are presented which involve different procedures derived from narrative, from video or from music hall. The audience member thus makes up his/her own show on the basis of his/her choices. At the conclusion of this 'promenade' all are invited to take part in a collective debate.

Debates around the 'postdramatic'

If new writing as such is no longer at the centre of all that is most topical, it is because it has been confronted by a paradigm shift which became apparent in Russia a decade later than in other European countries. There are multimedia shows where video plays an important part, or performances where the actor-narrator weaves together a text which is sometimes improvised, and which relies upon an effect of presence to grip the spectator here and now, thereby replacing responses which associate immediate pleasure with a gradual process of reflection.[19] All these forms of show put into question the play text as a prerequisite of performance, as well as the work of both director and actors. But in Russia these new ways of making and watching performances have often been rejected, not least due to a lack of tools for analysis.[20]

RoseLee Goldberg's book *Performance Art: From Futurism to the Present* (New York, 1979) was translated into Russian only in 2014,[21] just after Hans-Thies Lehmann's study *Postdramatic Theatre* (Frankfurt, 1999; translated into Russian in 2013), and along with Erika Fischer-Lichte's treatise *The Transformative Power of Performance: A New Aesthetics* (Frankfurt, 2004; translated into Russian in 2015).

Lehmann's book, which became available in Russian only fourteen years after its publication in German, immediately provoked a polemical debate, even though it had long been the bedside book for European and North American theatre scholars.[22] And what taboos does it attack? Analysing dozens of shows in Europe and the USA, Lehmann notes that since the 1980s we have begun to see an end of the play text and the emergence of a 'text which has ceased to be dramatic'.[23] The postdramatic[24] has tolled the bell for narrative, for plot. But that is not all. It marks a stage between traditional theatre and performance, between the 'playwriting state of mind' and 'the performative state of mind'.[25]

Up until the 1970s theatres in Europe staged dialogues and actions, based on a process of imitation rendered through dramatic acting. In this respect theatre was often called upon to reinforce connections in society, aiming to form a community which would unite audience and stage by means of catharsis. By creating illusions dramatic theatre invokes the world in its entirety. But during the 1980s, with the development of new media and technologies, a new practice of theatrical discourse emerged which Lehmann characterizes as follows:

- The emergence of a new way of relating to the spectator. The presence of a performer takes the place of the interpretation of a role by an actor. A shared experience with the audience, thanks to different flows of energy, prevails over what is shown and said on the stage.
- A non-hierarchical, non-relationship between elements. Each detail has the same importance, as in Bruegel's painting 'The Fall of Icarus', where the most essential component is relegated to the periphery. You don't understand the whole thing right away, and signification becomes deferred. There is an appeal not to the audience's immediate intelligence, but to its floating attention.
- The simultaneity of signs goes hand in hand with the fragmentation of perception. The disorientated spectator seeks correlations between exploded particles. Postdramatic theatre creates an unstable sphere of choices.

- On the socio-political level, where dramatic theatre used to have the purpose of emerging into a social praxis, almost all political functions have eluded postdramatic theatre. It no longer resides in the centre of the city as in antiquity. It becomes the concern of a minority, and it no longer reinforces historical or cultural identities. The theatre as an instrument of propaganda, but also the theatre as lectern, educating and purveying public morality, has been left behind. It is not by making politics a theme that the theatre becomes political, but through its modes of representation, through 'a politics of perception which also becomes an ethics of responsibility'.[26]

In 2013, when the translation of Lehmann first appeared, Russian theatre festivals had already been welcoming for over ten years the best 'postdramatic' artists from the West (Marthaler, Ostermayer, Castorf, Lepage, Warlikowski, Wilson, Fabre, Castellucci). Theatre directors such as Butusov, Volkostrelov, Gatsalov, Moguchy, Bogomolov and Iukhananov were inspired by these new ways of approaching theatre and of exploding the text. But instead of drawing upon the German theoretician's analysis in order to appreciate new forms of spectacle, many critics and artists took up positions 'for' or 'against' his propositions, with those who were 'against' limiting themselves to a nostalgia for the past, where 'dramatic' theatre was based on a play structured by a plot and constituted by characters.[27]

This theorization of the inverse of the traditional creative process (going from the text to the performance), the validation of a type of spectacle in which representation is foremost, and where multidisciplinarity and the blurring of boundaries become the norm, was something which shocked people. Aleksei Bartoshevich, who is a professor at the Russian Institute for Theatrical Arts (GITIS), a research director at the Institute for the History of the Arts and a well-known Shakespeare specialist, admitted that he could not understand the enthusiasm of his young students for this 'new bible'. He himself only saw in it a virtuosic juggling with concepts and learned terminology: 'I read Lehmann's book, and I could not rid myself of the feeling that I belonged to a different era, that perhaps I am simply incapable of understanding the complex of ideas out of which the new theatre scholarship is being constructed, and which my younger colleagues pursue so ardently.'[28]

For her part Natal'ia Skorokhod, dramatist and professor at the St Petersburg Theatre Academy, considered that Lehmann's book actually reinforced the scorn of theatres for dramatists, and accentuated the rupture between dramatists and theatre directors.[29] Viktoria Alesenkova, a professor at the Sobinov Conservatory and Academy in the town of Saratov, expressed regret that the Western models cited by Lehmann clashed with the traditions of the Russian theatre: 'The doubts which exist about whether the Russian postdramatic theatre of the last ten years is an independent and original phenomenon of theatre culture, rather than an epigone of the west European model, are just as justified as are the doubts as to whether the west European theatre is a suitable model for imitation at all.'[30]

Among the most violent attacks was that by Iury Barboy, professor at the Institute for Stage Arts in St Petersburg:

> The German theatre specialist Hans-Thies Lehmann is popular to an extraordinary degree. Even theatre directors are prepared to invoke his name, and yet they, better

than anyone, know that it is precisely theatre specialists who are the greatest fools about the theatre. And Lehmann has deserved his popularity: he discovered and pronounced certain seductive words, without which previously the secrets of contemporary theatre had not been known.

Barboy considers that the differences established between the 'postmodern' and the 'postdramatic' were in fact fluid, and he asks whether what followed the postdramatic will in fact be the post-theatrical?[31]

The jeopardizing of traditional dramatic theatre in Russia by forms which have been exported from elsewhere has often been perceived as a trauma: Polina Bogdanova deplored the 'death of drama' and, along with that, the end of 'heroes': 'The postdramatic theatre is the manifestation of a crisis, [...] the manifestation of the end of a certain paradigm, which used to be determined by the birth, the evolution and the death of the dramatic theatre and of drama as its principal component.' But she felt that she could glimpse the beginning of a new way forward, that of 'Theatre-post', in which the functions of the director, the author and the actor would all be freshly redefined.[32]

The approach of the German theoretician Erika Fischer-Lichte, the translation of whose *Transformative Power of Performance: A New Aesthetics* followed upon that of *Postdramatic Theatre*, has proved to be rather more acceptable in Russia, perhaps precisely because she challenged the sharp break Lehmann had identified between the dramatic and the postdramatic. Fischer-Lichte singles out the characteristic which is shared between the show (deriving from theatre) and performance (turned more towards the plastic and visual arts): that is to say, performativity, constituted by the emotions which unite actors and the audience in the here and now.[33] She redefines 'staging' as a procedure which includes the random and the unpredictable, and which is linked to the idea of event:

> I shall define staging as the process of planning (including chance operations and phenomena which emerge in rehearsal), testing, and determining strategies which aim at bringing forth the performance's materiality. On the one hand, these strategies create presence and physicality; on the other, they allow for open, experimental and ludic spaces for unplanned and un-staged behaviour, action and events. The *mise en scène* provides a strong framework for the performance and the feedback loop's autopoiesis, but is nonetheless unable to determine or control the autopoietic process. The concept of staging thus always already includes a moment of reflection on its own limits.

The aesthetics of performativity play with boundaries in order to transgress them, and maintain a link between art and life in an interactive relationship 'not determined by an "either/or" situation but by an "as well as"'.[34]

These frontiers to be crossed and these roles to be blurred are characteristic of the situation of art in general, where competencies have tended to step outside their own realms and to swap their places and their powers. After the dominance of a hypertheatre conceived by directors who imposed their own interpretations and played skilfully with the hybridization of the postmodern, a certain emancipation seems to have become necessary (and even salutary?), on the part of the actors as well as of audiences.[35] The notions of event, of presence, of effects of the real, of live moments, which all lie at the heart of performance, nowadays have spread to theatre stages as well.[36]

Konstantin Bogomolov's writing for the stage

One of the most sensational productions in Moscow of the 2012–13 season, of Oscar Wilde's *An Ideal Husband*, was created and staged by Konstantin Bogomolov. The director's associative method of composition preserved from Wilde's play only the story of a highly placed dignitary whose friend is a singing master.[37] The text, composed of heterogeneous materials selected, rewritten and staged by the director, presents itself as a kaleidoscope of dialogues, dances, stripteases, songs and pantomimes. The farcical comedy links rewritten extracts from Wilde, Chekhov and Shakespeare, and evokes the films of Tarantino, Russian pre-electoral broadcasts, songs from the Olympic Games and TV ads. By dismantling false equivalences, and turning around appearances to the point of nightmarish absurdity, Bogomolov highlights social hypocrisy, the power of money and the omnipresence of the Church in the upper echelons of power. He was outspoken in his provocations. A Russian flag (replaced by the British flag if there were officials present in the auditorium) was placed upon the tomb of a homosexual couple, who die speaking dialogues from *Romeo and Juliet*. Bogomolov mocked the ruling class and 'Putinomics', holding its image up to a distorting mirror. He deployed carnivalesque reversals and established a sort of flirtation, a duel, a game of seduction and repulsion with the audience. Bogomolov was demonstrating the fact that in the twenty-first century the theatre was no longer 'a temple' (his *An Ideal Husband* was put on at the Moscow Art Theatre, the theatre of Chekhov and Stanislavsky), and he attempts to find a new identity for it, one which is misaligned, distanced by a macabre humour and a sinister buffoonery which are always ambivalent and degraded. Art descends from its pedestal and re-joins mass culture, where trash, sideshows (Grand Guignol) and in-house improvisations are at work. Bogomolov carries the rejection of the literary text to its utmost, and he becomes a kind of storyteller himself. He holds between his fingers all the gaudy and incongruous threads of the story he has devised, and which his complicit actors present to us.[38] With his *Musketeers: A Saga* (2015), Bogomolov took a further leap and himself wrote a text largely inspired by the postmodern writers Viktor Pelevin and Vladimir Sorokin, and which was 'a fairly wild mixture of the high and the low, offering a blatant manipulation of rapidly ageing cultural codes'.[39] In this respect he identifies with the position of artists who no longer separate writing from staging. The act of writing a text, its stage design, the movements of the actors, their voices, their costumes, the sounds and the lighting, all acquire significance when combined together, and Bogomolov writes with all these elements. What interests him is the elaboration of 'a new theatrical language, a new mode of existence for the actors, and another way of constructing the subject'.[40]

The outsiders of Teatr Post: Dmitrii Volkostrelov and Pavel Priazhko

Bogomolov carries to its utmost the ambition of an all-powerful artist, who serves in turn as actor, director and storyteller and, following in the wake of Meierkhol'd, proclaims himself the author of the show.⁴¹ In stark contrast to this metaphorical theatre of 'excess', the theatre director Dmitrii Volkostrelov's experiments are based on a *tabula rasa*. The former elevates theatricality and pushes the components of a show to the point of suspending meaning and making way for the sheer pleasure of the acting; the latter has conceived of a non-theatre, or rather a 'pre-theatre', in quest of a primordial form, starting from nothing.⁴² Volkostrelov, who is a pupil of Lev Dodin, founded with his fellow graduates of 2011 in St Petersburg a small independent organization, Teatr Post, whose goal was to bring the plastic and stage arts closer together, using a new theatrical language. In order to achieve this, he worked only with the texts of contemporary authors, and in particular with the Belarusian playwright Pavel Priazhko and the Russian Ivan Vyrypaev.

Volkostrelov borrows his credo from Jean Baudrillard, who observed that nothing is capable of surprising us any more in this world:⁴³

> A reference to some novelty does not assume a transition to a page with that novelty, because a swift glance at the reference is enough to understand everything about the novelty and about everything else. And you see, all of that is what 'post' is. Where can you go further, when you have already arrived? But you have to move, because life, as they say, consists in movement. But is what they say true? Or maybe we should simply stop? This is what we're concerned with: with post-movement, post-stopping, post-life, post-drama, and post-theatre.⁴⁴

Volkostrelov considers representation to be a simulacrum, for the image is neither the reflection of a profound reality, nor the mask or the symbol of that reality: it has no connection with it. Rather than privileging a play which is remarkably written, or the orality of testimonies gathered through verbatim techniques, Volkostrelov comes back to the written texts which dominate our everyday lives – email messages, or social media or Facebook comments – and he gives pride of place to stage directions. These texts, projected on to one or more screens, take precedence over the actors' speeches; they become visual objects for the audience to decipher. The action of the spectator is to make the connection between the actors' words, pronounced in a neutral tone, and the comments and the instructions of the author. This reading produces a certain disjointedness, and it is often difficult to make sense of disconnected exchanges spoken without any attempt at affect.

Volkostrelov's spiritual ancestors are Samuel Beckett, who emptied the stage of objects and words after *Acts without Words* (1956), and the composer John Cage, whose *Lecture on Nothing* the youthful Volkostrelov presented in 2013, and then created his own *Lecture on Something* in 2015.⁴⁵ The praising of boredom as a category of perception (*I Am Free*, 2012), of non-action, the practice of the random and of repetitions (of words, of fragments, or of the ending of the show, which serves to hinder or delay the audience's departure), all lie at the heart of Teatr Post's experiments. Certain productions become similar to lectures (Müller's *Love Story*), or are presented as performances. As a multifaceted artist, Volkostrelov has acted in cinema since 2007 and takes part as a plastic artist in some performances, such as in 2017 in the audio reconstruction of *The Monument to the Third International*, and at the opening of the second MIEFF (Moscow International Experimental Film Festival). In *Shoot/Get Treasure/Repeat*, which was put on at the Meierkhol'd Centre in 2012 with Semen Aleksandrovsky (a Mark Ravenhill project in sixteen short plays presented over eight hours in two distinct spaces), Volkostrelov liberated objects, signs and actions from their concept, their essence, their points of reference and their origins, forcing them to enter into a self-reproduction *ad infinitum*. All that is left is the objectivity of the presence of bodies, of texts and of voices, all disconnected one from another.[46]

The Field (2016), based on a 'performative' text by Pavel Priazhko from 2008, offers an ironic experience of the connections between science and art. 'Dedicated to Modern Physics' states the programme, which only contains authorial stage directions, intercut with scientific definitions taken from Wikipedia (quantum field theory, entropy, chaos theory, attractors, fractals, bifurcation theory, fluctuations, quantum entanglement, Heisenberg's uncertainty principle, Fermi's symmetry, quantum superposition). These definitions, which the worried spectator rushes to read, have nothing to do with the story of the young harvesters which is about to be presented in forty-five numbered episodes, which are distributed in random sequence. A young lad with a board on which a number is posted communicates this to the seven actors involved in the show. One of them gets up, comes to the centre, in front of a blackboard, and chalks up the number of the episode. The interest of the show has shifted. It resides not in what is unfolding on stage (where nothing is happening, and the exchanges remain factual and minimalist), but in the tension among the actors, who don't know in advance which fragment they are going to be performing, and also in the curiosity of the spectators who are trying to find a thread to guide them. But they are lost, because the numbers written in the programme don't correspond to the order of the scenes performed, and the definitions provided in the programme (which remain legible because the auditorium is brightly lit almost until the end) don't provide any help either. 'Things continue to function long after the idea of them has disappeared. They continue to function in complete indifference to their own content', writes Baudrillard, who qualifies the absence of reference to anything as a 'fractal stage': their components radiate in every direction, without reference to anything else at all, by sheer contiguity, and according to a random dispersion.[47]

Teatr Post places the ordinary and the indeterminate at the heart of its experiments, and raises to the level of a principle their absence of 'artistry', of 'empathetic feeling', or of moralizing. Reduced to elementary particles, objects and living beings alike take part in the greater whole, directed not so much by metaphysics as by the laws of physics. 'Humans are ultimately incapable of controlling the "invisible forces" that shape the world. Even if they aspire to govern and define these powers, they will also have to let themselves be governed and defined by them', writes Erika Fischer-Lichte, as the conclusion to her study of performativity.[48]

Volkostrelov and his small company of actors explore new modes of behaviour on stage, in the auditorium, and between the stage and the auditorium: they are distanced, but without the intention of criticizing, they are ludic and participatory. The very concept of an independent, itinerant team, which collaborates with other organizations in Russia (theatres, cinemas, cultural centre and museums) and also abroad, transports this new artistic position beyond the strict art of the stage, and proposes a quest for a new language, the first manifestations of which are very promising.

Experimentation under threat

It is difficult to predict what the future of these experiments will be. Up until now, in Russia, traditional theatre has coexisted with experimentation (even if, in the USSR, rebellious artists were condemned to the underground). But the hardening of contemporary cultural policy, which places upon the artist an obligation to share in the values of society and the state (serving the fatherland, respect for family and community life, in the terms in which these are defined by the Orthodox Church), has jeopardized the independence and the freedom of artists. If these 'indisputable and natural' values, as the Minister for Culture claimed in 2015, are respected, then the state will support creative activity by subsidizing it. This means that traditional art is encouraged, and that experiments can only take place on private stages, at the artists' own expense or thanks to sponsorship.[49] But behind official discourse, which is already very restrictive, the reality is far more complex, for bans can also strike at independent artists, as has been the case with Teatr.doc. The threats which hang over the artists who are hardest to control, such as activists, but also over 'established' creative artists with a reputation, such as Bogomolov or Kirill Serebrennikov,[50] prove that 'the theatre has become one of the most important testing grounds for the war being waged upon culture by the state'.[51]

Russia's increased participation in the globalization of culture, which is inevitable despite the restrictions and the bans imposed by a vigilant state, shatters the whole idea of cultural exceptionalism which official patriotism proclaims so insistently. Many Russians view the appearance from elsewhere of what Patrice Pavis has called 'Unidentified Performative Objects' as an aggression against cultural and theatrical identity, which needs to be defended.[52] As the Minister of Culture has explicitly put it: 'Anyone who does not feed his own culture will be feeding someone else's army.'[53]

This evolution of practices in writing for the theatre provides fascinating material for an analysis of the difficulties and the paradoxes of Russia's opening up towards the international and the intercultural. The decline of the monopoly of the theatre as an aesthetic and fictional object, and the beginnings of a turn towards the performative, all impose new ways of inscribing theatre in the social space, and of linking aesthetics with sociology, with anthropology and with economics, which is something many Russian artists, with the support of the political authorities, resist. For if it is not circumscribed by identifiable spaces and professions, the performative theatrical act may become subversive and serve the purposes of emancipation, something which the authorities who have been in place since 2012 will evidently not tolerate.

Translated from the French by J. A. E. Curtis

Notes

1. This obscene language has been banned in the theatre since July 2014, through an amendment of the law dating from 1 June 2005, 'On the state language of the Russian Federation' (53 F 3).
2. For more on this period of transition and restructuring, see Marie-Christine Autant-Mathieu (ed.), *Les Nouvelles Écritures russes* (Pézenas: Domens, 2010).
3. Alla Shenderova, 'Eta novaia, "novaia", Novaia Drama', in *Pro Scaenium/Voprosy Teatra* 2 (2008): 142.
4. This technique, which emerged in Britain in the mid-1990s, overturned the notion of the dramatic author, the process of dramatic composition and the status of the text. It involved using tape recorders to record data such as testimony or life stories, then staging this material after editing, while retaining linguistic imperfections and the particularity of intonations. Verbatim plays, which imply an absence of predetermined form, can nevertheless allow for aesthetic experimentation.
5. Vladimir Pomerantsev, 'Ob iskrennosti v literature', *Novyi mir* 12 (1953): 218–45.
6. A distinction must be drawn between these 'brigades', whose authors drew upon raw materials for the purposes of propaganda, and the ethnographic expeditions mounted by the theatre director Lev Dodin, particularly when he was preparing with his actors his productions of *Brothers and Sisters* (1985) based on the novel by Fedor Abramov, and Vasily Grossman's *Life and Fate* (2007).
7. This is the motto which Teatr.doc has adopted for its work.
8. Ivan Vyrypaev stepped down from running Praktika in 2016 and has continued to work as a performer and theatre director, and on one-off theatre and film projects.
9. After it was ejected from its location at the Elektrozavod 'art squat' in March 2017, this platform found a home at the M'ars Centre for Contemporary Art in Moscow, on Pushkarev Lane.
10. After the Pussy Riot affair and the re-imposition of censorship, the practice of the indirect has become more and more relevant. The new political culture defined by the Minister for Culture Vladimir Medinsky in 2015 set limits upon freedom of expression. Among the shows which focus on Russian history we could mention *On the Fall of Constantinople and 7 Strategies for Surviving in Times of Change* (2013); *Human Rights Activists*, the starting point for which was an alphabetical list of champions of human rights (2016); and *A Short History of Russian Dissidence*, based on texts dating from the seventeenth to twenty-first centuries (2017).
11. In October 2014 Teatr.doc was ejected from its basement on Trekhprudny Lane on the spurious basis of health and safety infringements. None of the letters of protest, even one from Sir Tom Stoppard, was enough to prevent this happening. Having moved to Spartakovskaia Street in December 2014, the company launched its new season in February 2015, but was obliged to close again in June, after performing *The Bolotnaya Case*: the police came to observe the premiere, and they were subsequently closed down. Since 2017 the theatre has been working on the ground floor of an apartment block on Kazansky Lane, near the Kursk railway station, where it has two small spaces. [Editor's note: by the summer of 2018 Teatr.doc was once again being forced to seek new premises.] The deaths in rapid succession of the two distinguished founders of

Teatr.doc, Mikhail Ugarov and Elena Gremina, in April and May 2018 have been traumatic for the company.

12 Playwrights such as Vasily Sigarev, Evgeny Grishkovets, the Presniakov brothers Oleg and Vladimir, Iury Klavdiev and Iaroslava Pulinovich have rather disappeared from sight; Vadim Levanov died in 2011.

13 This manifesto, composed in 2003 'as a joke', was published by Il'mira Bolotian: '"Dok" i "Dogma": teoriia i praktika', *Teatr* 19 (2015). Available at http://oteatre.info/dok-idogma-teoriya-i-praktika/ (accessed 6 November 2017).

14 Zara Abdullaeva, *Postdok. Igrovoe/neigrovoe* (Moscow: Novoe literaturnoe obozrenie, 2011).

15 Joseph Danan, *Entre théâtre et performance: la question du texte* (Arles: Actes Sud-Papiers, 2013), 7.

16 One could mention their creative work based on documentary materials for shows such as *The Viatsky Labour Camp*; *Dialogues about Art*; *KantCity*; and *My Brother the Policeman*. See www.teatrdoc.ru

17 Teatr.doc has included in its repertory plays by Marius Ivaškevičius, Ol'ga Mikhailova and Maksym Kurochkin, which has led the cultural theorist Mark Lipovetsky to express regret about the weak political engagement of their performers compared to other 'activists', and to wish for an injection of militancy into this 'overliterary' theatre. Mark Lipovetsky, 'Illiuzii dokumental'nosti i drugie illiuzii', *Teatr*. 19 (2015). Available at http://oteatre.info/ (accessed 6 November 2017).

18 In Teatr.doc civic engagement has been expressed through shows reflecting upon homosexuality (*Coming out of the Closet*, 2016); religious extremism (*Fundamentalists*, 2013); and artistic freedom (*Dialogues about Art*, 2015, a reading of the interrogation of the performance artist Petr Pavlensky following his 'Freedom' action).

19 Nick Kaye and Gabriella Giannachi, *Performing Presence: Between the Live and the Simulated* (Manchester: Manchester University Press, 2010).

20 In an editorial for the journal *Teatr*. 13–14 (2013): 3, Marina Davydova expressed regret that in Russia theatre criticism had turned towards the past, focused on exhuming archives, and that a number of her colleagues simply considered contemporary theatre to be impoverished, 'or what was worse, infiltrated by the foreign'. With the opening up of international borders, their tools for analysis have become no longer appropriate. Because of their ignorance of certain terms, it was impossible for them to analyse Robert Wilson, Katie Mitchell or Angélica Liddell. Four years later, the situation did not seem to have moved on much: Ada Shmerling, 'Pionery i geroi', *Teatr*. 19 (2017): 89.

21 Rouzli Goldberg, *Iskusstvo performansa. Ot futurizma do nashikh dney* (Moscow: Ad Marginem, 2014).

22 The book's prologue was translated by Iuly Liderman in the journal *Russky zhurnal* in 2001. The entire book was translated by Natal'ia Isaeva (*Postdramaticheskiy teatr*, Moscow: abc design, 2013).

23 See Gerda Poschmann, *Der nicht mehr dramatische Theatertext* (Tübingen: M. Niemeyer, 1997).

24 According to Lehmann, this term was first used by the godfather of performance art, Richard Schechner, in 1988, who spoke about the 'postdramatic theatre of happenings'. But the origin of the phrase lies with the Polish scholar Andrzej Wirth, who used the term in the 1970s to refer to theatre without texts. The postdramatic does not encompass the concept of the postmodern, which aspires to provide a definition of the age in its globality with reference to the gratuitousness of forms, collages of

heterogeneous elements and the mixing of media. If you abandon the logical unfolding of a story, and if composition is no longer required as an organizing principle, then you position yourself not beyond modernity, but beyond drama.

25 Danan, *Entre théâtre et performance*, 27.
26 Hans-Thies Lehmann, *Le Théâtre postdramatique* (transl. Philippe-Henri Ledru, Paris: L'Arche, 2002), 292.
27 As evidence of this see an interview with the playwright Nina Sadur, who enjoyed success in the 1980s and 1990s: 'In theatre the play is unequivocally the most important thing. But the texts of recent drama do not aspire to anything at all. This is one feature of the destruction of humanity. [...] There used to be respect for the literary language in theatre. And this was not just in relation to the classics. These days that delicacy has not so much been lost, it simply no longer seems relevant.' Nina Sadur and Marina Zabolotnaia, 'Volki i ovtsy', *Voprosy teatra* 3–4 (2012): 187. But in fact Lehmann is at pains to point out that the postdramatic shows no lack of interest in mankind, and that instead of feeling nostalgia for a predefined image of man, one should in fact ask oneself what new ways of thinking and of representation are sketched out for the human subject in the postdramatic. Lehmann, *Le Théâtre postdramatique*, 21.
28 Aleksei Bartoshevich, 'O tekh, kto prikhodit nam na smenu', *Voprosy teatra* 3–4 (2012): 7.
29 Natal'ia Skorokhod, 'Fenomen Zolushki: Analiz postdramy', *Voprosy teatra* 1–2 (2014): 46–9. She observes that in Russia playwriting is taught not in drama schools, but in literature faculties at university.
30 Viktoria Alesenkova, 'Postdramaticheskii teatr: na peresechenii smyslovykh prostranstv', *Sovremennye problemy nauki i obrazovaniia* 5 (2014). Available at https://www.science-education.ru/ru/article/view?id=14772 (accessed 6 November 2017).
31 Iurii Barboy, 'Postdramaticheskii teatr i postteatral'nyi dramatizm', *Peterburgskii teatral'nyi zhurnal* 2/76 (2014). Available at: http://ptj.spb.ru/archive/76/introduction-to-lehman/postdramaticheskij-teatr-ipostteatralnyj-dramatizm-76 (accessed 6 November 2017).
32 Polina Bogdanova, 'Postdramaticheskii teatr', *Sovremennaia dramaturgiia* 2 (2016): 194.
33 See Vladislav Tarnopol'sky, 'Erika Fisher-Lichte: chto budet posle "post"?', *Teatr.* 29 (2017): 22–7.
34 Erika Fischer-Lichte, *The Transformative Power of Performance: A New Aesthetics*, transl. Saskya Iris Jain (Abingdon: Routledge, 2008), 188, 207.
35 See Jacques Rancière, *Le Spectateur émancipé* (Paris: La fabrique, 2008).
36 Joseph Danan, paraphrasing Gilles Deleuze, speaks of a theatre of 'pure purposes', which operates without the backdrop of a plot. Danan, *Entre théâtre et performance*, 39.
37 The 'ideal husband' is a former mafioso who has become Minister for the Rubber Industry. He is married to a very influential and wealthy woman, and lives a life of luxury. But the marriage is a sham, because the man is gay, and is involved with a former assassin who has become a singing star hugely popular in Moscow. Their liaison is threatened by scandal. In a parallel plot there is the story of the Kremlin leader, a sort of Dorian Gray alias Putin, who commissions a portrait in which he will remain eternally young and preserve his power to stay alive. The painter, who has been rewarded with an apartment and other bonuses, becomes a nuisance. The person charged with eliminating him is a mincing priest, who is also gay: like a reincarnation of Harvey Keitel in *Pulp Fiction*, he turns into a monster and swallows the artist. There

are also three sisters (as in Chekhov) who have made it to Moscow and settled down there: these 'new Russians', heavily made-up and with stiletto heels and Prada bags, lounge around in fashionable cafés and talk about the need to work, to work.
38 Anna Banasiukevich, 'Strashnye skazki Konstantina Bogomolova', in Tat'iana Dzhurova, Marina Dmitrevskaia and Oksana Kushliaeva (eds), *Bez tsenzury: molodaia teatral'naia rezhissura. XXI vek. Rossiia*, 82.
39 Ibid., 83. Just like Bogomolov's shows, the works of these two writers, who are often described as 'postmodern', are woven from references to everyday life in the USSR and Russia, and to popular culture (video games, rock groups, TV serials). Saturated with these references, and plunging into the absurd, their texts deliver a powerful satirical view of contemporary society, with totalitarianism being described through allegory, or with recourse to the fantastic.
40 'Rezhisser Konstantin Bogomolov: poshlost' – eto kogda vser'ez', interview by Kseniia Chudinova and Varvara Tunova, 3 March 2013. Available at https://snob.ru/magazine/entry/58126 (accessed 14 January 2015). After the 2012 presidential elections Bogomolov threatened that he would flee to London. He remained in Russia because he needs his own milieu, his language and his culture in order to create. Accustomed as he is to denunciations and to attacks, he insists that his aims are purely aesthetic. 'Current affairs and politics are a trick, which allow me to show something else.'
41 Bogomolov, who defines himself as a theatre director and poet, is also a cinema and theatre actor, including in his own shows (*The Prince*, 2016; *The Magic Mountain*, 2017).
42 Pavel Rudnev, 'Neobkhodimaia antiteza. Dmitrii Volkostrelov', in Dzhurova, Dmitrevskaia and Kushliaeva, *Bez tsenzury*, 331–2.
43 'We have travelled all the paths of the virtual production and overproduction of objects, of signs, of messages, of ideologies, and of pleasures. Nowadays everything has been liberated, the die is cast, and we find ourselves collectively having to confront the crucial question: WHAT ARE WE TO DO AFTER THE ORGY?' Jean Baudrillard, *La Transparence du mal* (Paris, 1990), 11.
44 Dmitrii Volkostrelov on the theatre's site, available at http://teatrpost.ru (accessed 15 September 2017).
45 Volkostrelov is also an heir to the Dada and Fluxus movements, and to Marcel Duchamp's 'readymades', even if he doesn't refer to these explicitly.
46 'The final play, *Birth of a Nation*, unfolds in virtual space. The actors sit at a long table opposite the spectators, some with Notebooks, others with iPads. Projected behind them is the theatre's page on Facebook. Teatr Post posts a message – the play's title and its starting time. And after that the actors, not masked as characters, but in their own names, write comments and replies every few seconds. In real time, so that any Facebook user can join in the conversation, and those who are sitting in the auditorium get out their smartphones, and 'like' the comments. [...] And the fact that in Volkostrelov's theatre this is all happening on Facebook, is of fundamental importance: the thirst for creativity becomes a conscious choice for the new generation, the same one that is bringing about a revolution with the help of the internet. The show ends on a positive note, and everyone who has an account is invited to take part in the celebration of the birth of a new world.' Nikolai Berman, 'Postteatral'nyi sindrom', *Novaia gazeta*, 27 August 2012. Available at: https://www.gazeta.ru/culture/2012/08/27/a_4738873.shtml (accessed 8 November 2017).
47 Baudrillard, *La Transparence du mal*, 13, 14.

48 Fischer-Lichte, *The Transformative Power of Performance*, 206–7.
49 Vladimir Medinsky, 'Kto ne kormit svoiu kul'turu budet kormit' chuzhuiu armiiu', *Izvestiia*, 17 June 2015. Available at https://iz.ru/news/587771 (accessed 28 September 2017).
50 See the banning of Konstantin Bogomolov's show *The Prince*, based on Dostoevsky's *The Idiot*, at the Lenkom Theatre in 2016; and in August 2017 Kirill Serebrennikov, director of the prestigious Gogol' Centre in Moscow, was arrested and placed under house arrest.
51 Konstantin Bogomolov, 24 May 2017, in the first report of *Svobodnoe slovo*, available at https://openrussia.org/notes/709760. During a public discussion at the national 'Golden Mask' theatre festival in April 2014, Bogomolov declared that the theatrical landscape had changed considerably, and compared the collective atmosphere to that found in Ionesco's *Rhinoceros*: artists need to remain constantly vigilant, need to orient themselves in what is going on by trusting their intuition and, above all, they must remain honest. What is hard is not succumbing to self-censorship, and not compromising. (Author's personal notes on this debate.)
52 Patrice Pavis, *Dictionnaire de la performance et du théâtre contemporain*, (Paris: Armand Colin, 2014), 5. See also the Preface by Richard Schechner to *Performance, expérimentation et théorie du théâtre aux USA*, ed. Anne Cuisset, Marie Pecorari and C. Biet (Paris: Editions Théâtrales, 2008), 16.
53 See note 49.

2

Giving testimony in the face of an authoritarian regime

The evolution of documentary forms at Teatr.doc, the KnAM Theatre and the Belarus Free Theatre

Lucie Kempf

> Lucie Kempf explores three variants of documentary theatre as it has been developed since the early 2000s by Teatr.doc (Moscow), the KnAM Theatre based in the Siberian town of Komsomol'sk-on-Amur, and the Belarus Free Theatre, originally from Minsk, but now in exile in London. She considers their different levels of political engagement across the first two decades of this century, and their use of verbatim techniques to create a theatre of testimony. The hardening of political regimes has had an impact on all three theatres, and their various uses of the documentary have shifted during the 2010s.

Since the early 2000s documentary theatre has experienced a phenomenal boom in a certain number of experimental theatres in the nations of the former USSR. This essay will examine recent developments in three of these theatres, who all stage their shows in the Russian language. Two of the theatres are Russian: Teatr.doc is based in Moscow, while the KnAM Theatre operates in Komsomol'sk-on-Amur, nearly 4,000 miles away to the east in Siberia. The Belarus Free Theatre (BFT), as the name suggests, is from the former Soviet Republic of Belarus (now an independent nation), although the artistic directors of this particular theatre have been forced into political exile in London since 2011. The parallels between these three theatres are very numerous. One particularly striking one is that even though their interest in socio-political problems in modern Russia and Belarus have drawn down upon them difficulties with the authorities in their respective countries, who perceive them as members of an opposition, the late Elena Gremina (Teatr.doc), Tat'iana Frolova (KnAM) and Nikolai Khalezin (BFT) have continued forcefully to affirm as one that the theatre they are making is not political.

We will consider the evolution of these three theatres over the last five years, examining in particular whether the hardening of the two political regimes – President

Lukashenko's in Belarus, President Putin's in Russia – has accentuated their convergences or, on the contrary, their divergences.

KnAM is the oldest of the three theatres: it was founded in 1985 (the year that Mikhail Gorbachev became the Soviet leader) by the theatre director Tat'iana Frolova in Komsomol'sk-on-Amur, an industrial city in Russia's Far East. At the time, it was the first independent theatre to be set up in the USSR. Its existence has always been precarious inasmuch as it has never received state subsidies, but on the other hand this has guaranteed its complete creative freedom. Right from the start KnAM focused on contemporary playwriting, but from the year 2000 on it began to create documentary theatre, to which it devoted itself entirely thereafter. Among these works were *A Dry and Waterless Place* (*Sukhobezvodnoe*, 2006), based on a text by Ol'ga Pogodina-Kuzmina, which evokes both everyday life in Russian prisons and the consequences of the collapse of the USSR for the psychological health of ordinary people;[1] and *A Personal War* (*Personal'naia voyna*, 2011), a show about the Russian conflict with Chechnia, based on the memoirs of the journalist Arkady Babchenko.[2] KnAM is relatively unknown within Russia, because of its distance from the European centre of the country, and its lack of finances. By contrast, it commands something of a reputation in Europe, especially in France and in Switzerland, where its shows are regularly performed, and where Tat'iana Frolova runs masterclasses.[3]

Teatr.doc, which was founded more recently, devoted most of its productions to documentary forms from the very outset. The theatre was created in 2002 by the dramatists Elena Gremina and Mikhail Ugarov following three years of collaborations with the Royal Court Theatre. In 1996 this London theatre, which specializes in contemporary drama, had set up an International Department, with the purpose of discovering new writing from abroad. From the late 1990s they ran seminars all over the world.[4] In 1999, they gave a presentation on their working methods to a group of Russian dramatists. The Russian participants came to focus their attention on one particular writing technique proposed by the Royal Court, that of verbatim drama. The collaboration continued over the following two years, and documentary forms developed in different experimental theatres across Russia. Gremina and Ugarov very rapidly adopted verbatim drama for themselves, before going on to create Teatr.doc, whose name clearly proclaimed their focus of interest and their objectives.

During the 2000s, this theatre produced a great many documentary shows, the majority of which were typified by studies of different sub-cultures in Russian society and their linguistic particularities. We could point for example to *Crimes of Passion* (*Prestupleniia strasti*, 2002), a work which was created after a research project undertaken in a women's prison, or else *The Great Guzzle* (*Bol'shaia zhrachka*, 2003), which takes us into the wings of a TV reality show. But the theatre equally responded, sometimes very swiftly, to events in the news: in 2005, just over six months after the hostage tragedy at the school in Beslan, Gremina and Ugarov created a show called *September.doc* (*Sentiabr'.doc*), which they put together on the basis of immediate responses which they collected from a number of Russian, Ossetian and Chechen blogs.

The BFT is the most recent of the three theatres. It was founded in 2005 by Nikolai Khalezin and Natal'ia Koliada. From the outset it was different from the two Russian theatres. Khalezin and Koliada, who came from journalistic backgrounds, right from the start positioned their project as a means of struggling against the cultural homogenization imposed in Belarus by the policies of Lukashenko, who was at that time coming to the end of his second period of office as president of the country.[5] The international connections of Koliada and Khalezin enabled this theatre, which was never officially registered, to secure for itself from the very beginning the support of well-known figures such as Václav Havel and Tom Stoppard. In other words, this small theatre collective (a dozen or so people to start with, including five actors and the director Vladimir Shcherban) inscribed itself at its inception in a posture of resistance to the dictatorship.

Its functioning has always been semi-clandestine. At first the collective performed its shows in a number of alternative venues: spectators were usually informed the day before performances of the place and time where they were to meet. From there, they would be escorted to the place where the performance was to take place, such as a bar, a media agency or a farm in a forest. In 2010 the BFT received permission to work in a fixed location, a dilapidated house, but this was withdrawn from them by the authorities in 2013. Just like KnAM, this Belarusian collective operates partly thanks to support from the West, whether in the form of financial support, collaborations, participation in festivals or going on tour.

Between 2005 and 2010 the BFT created five shows which laid particular emphasis on documentary forms. The most emblematic of these is undoubtedly *Generation Jeans*, a work based on testimony by Khalezin who, alone on the stage, conjures up life in Belarus from an earlier time, before the collapse of the USSR, and then nowadays, under Lukashenko. In this show, constructed around that object which became a symbol of liberty, a pair of jeans, Khalezin narrates both his recollections of his youth in Soviet times, and his arrest under legislation restricting freedom of speech.

The evolution of these three theatres, who have all increased their collaborations abroad, should not be considered only in the context of the former USSR, but also as part of an international shift: since the 1990s, documentary theatre has developed more fully across the world.[6] This burgeoning of the genre took place just after the collapse of the communist bloc, at the moment when one of the great ideologies of the twentieth century lost its credibility. Such a great geopolitical upheaval would go on to have an impact on the forms of documentary theatre: by contrast with the historic models offered by Erwin Piscator and Peter Weiss, modern documentary theatre is often characterized by the absence of an overarching point of view.[7] If Piscator and Weiss proposed a Marxist framework for the interpretation of the documents out of which they created their shows, we can observe today a wish by theatre-makers to abstain from any judgement, and to leave the spectator free to choose his/her own reading of the facts. The approach of Anna Deavere Smith in the 1990s, or that of Gremina and Ugarov in the 2000s, illustrate very well this great wariness with regard to all forms of political engagement.[8]

The second characteristic of neo-documentary theatre is the importance which it accords to personal testimony. Among the many types of document which it uses, this indeed occupies a privileged place and it often constitutes the very subject-matter of the shows, particularly, but not exclusively, in verbatim plays.[9] Through its emotional charge and the empathy which it provokes among audiences, personal testimony seems better equipped to account for reality than any other kind of document, as though the prism of individual experience has these days become the best means for apprehending reality.

Each in their own fashion, all three theatres adopted during the 2000s this dual tendency of neo-documentary theatre. Personal testimony played an essential part in their shows. Thanks to verbatim techniques Teatr.doc gave a voice to people who, in Russian society of the 2000s, had been deprived of one – such as the homeless in *The Battle of the Moldavians for a Cardboard Box* (*Bor'ba moldovan za kartonnuiu korobku*, 2003). Khalezin and Frolova proceeded somewhat differently. Their companies also undertook projects involving research on the ground and the collection of documents in advance of shows, but they equally often had recourse to the personal recollections of the actors themselves. The BFT's *Generation Jeans* (2006) was entirely made up of Khalezin's recollections, while *Discovering Love* (*Postigaia liubov'*, 2009) relates the tragic story of a couple who were friends of the theatre, Irina and Anatoly Krasovsky.[10] As for Frolova, she evoked the death of her own mother in one of her first documentary shows, *My Mum* (*Moia mama*, 2005).

This way of using personal testimony has an impact on the aesthetics of the performances. Teatr.doc had above all been seeking to discover an authentic language, and therefore made verbatim into something of a trademark. They were aiming to create a space for the emergence of a new discourse, pronounced originally by the 'contributors', and then reconstituted by the actors in a fully authentic way.[11] For this reason, the acting as well as the staging of their shows were both characterized by great restraint. The documentary approaches at the BFT and KnAM, by contrast, did not fall within the realm of verbatim. At the BFT the actors gave testimony themselves, above all bringing their own lives on to the stage rather than the words of others. The shows at KnAM also included an undeniable autobiographical component, but combined personal testimony with literary texts. The aesthetics of this theatre are characterized by a significant attention to form, notably the use of video material: 'Documents need absolutely to reach the heart, to address the emotions and not just the rational mind of the spectator', declares Frolova.[12]

Furthermore, all three companies have maintained a considerable wariness as far as political engagement is concerned. In the West they have generally been perceived and presented as representatives of the opposition to the regimes of Putin and Lukashenko: Khalezin was openly criticizing Lukashenko's authority, while Gremina and Frolova both tackled a particularly controversial subject, the Russian conflicts with Chechnia, in *September.doc* (Teatr.doc, 2005) and *A Personal War* (KnAM Theatre, 2011) respectively. And nevertheless, as soon as you ask them about their political engagement, they all deny this vehemently. Gremina and Ugarov affirmed that they were simply making theatre, nothing else, and that even when they addressed highly disputed topics such as the terrorist attack on the school in Beslan, they were not taking sides. For her part, Frolova states: 'It is quite obvious that we are not interested in politics and in political theatre. What interests us is to seek for things within ourselves, and then to share our discoveries with other people.'[13] And Khalezin considers that, since Bertolt Brecht, there is nobody who has made political theatre.[14]

We should therefore note that the artistic directors of these three theatres associate political theatre with the assuming of a point of view which overarches the concept of these shows. And of course the very notion of political theatre recalls disagreeable memories for people in the countries of the former USSR, specifically the theatre of agit-prop, which was instrumentalized by the Soviet authorities. We should not forget that political theatre there served not, as it does in the West, to contest the existing regime, but instead to buttress that authority. At this point it becomes possible to understand these artists' visceral suspicion of political theatre, even when their artistic practice positions them de facto in an attitude of protest, whether direct or indirect, in relation to the state ideologies of Belarus and of Russia. They prefer to speak of their theatre as civic theatre.[15]

Nevertheless, the BFT is distinct from the two Russian theatres. From the very start it was created with the purpose of constituting an 'aesthetic opposition' to the Lukashenko regime, and it has developed in the manner of an underground organization, against the backdrop of intimidation and even arrests. Ever since *Generation Jeans*, their discourse has been extremely polemical. In Russia, where political pressures were far less acute than in Belarus during the early 2000s, Teatr.doc and the KnAM were above all preoccupied with social questions, and the positions they adopted were more restrained. After *September.doc* Gremina and Ugarov formulated their 'zero position', that is to say the artistic *credo* of their theatre: whatever the question that was being tackled, each opinion has the right to be expressed and heard. Teatr.doc categorically refuses to impose a single point of view concerning reality on the spectator, even at the risk of ambiguity. At the time of the premiere of *September.doc* at the 'Passages' Festival in France in 2005, the show was taken to be anti-Chechen.[16] But in Moscow, on the contrary, it was perceived as being pro-Chechen.

Nevertheless, in both these theatres the subject-matter of their shows began to change towards the end of this period, especially after the swapping of roles in 2008 and 2012 between Vladimir Putin and Dmitry Medvedev as president and prime minister of the Russian Federation, which then saw Putin controversially restored to the presidency in 2012. If the aesthetic principles remained the same, the subjects they treated became quite clearly more politicized. In 2010 Teatr.doc staged *An Hour and Eighteen Minutes*, a show dedicated to the story of the death of the accountant Sergei Magnitsky in prison.[17] Gremina tied her colours to the mast quite clearly, from the very beginning of the play: 'They put people on trial, and as for us, we're going to put them on trial. [...] The trial which didn't take place, but which must take place.' As for Frolova, she created the 2010 show *A Personal War*, a piece about the conflict with Chechnia, whose concluding words can scarcely be challenged: 'If you think that Chechnia belongs to the past, then you are mistaken, [...] because nothing has changed. This war was far from being the last one. [...] Prepare yourselves.'

What has been the evolution of these three theatres as they faced up to the hardening of political positions during the 2010s, in Belarus as well as in Russia? What strategies have they adopted? Has their initial wariness as regards political engagement been affected?

2011 represented a decisive turning-point for the BFT. After the widespread electoral fraud associated with the re-election of Alexander Lukashenko for his fourth term as president on 19 December 2010, a large protest demonstration took place on the streets of Minsk. It was suppressed violently by the forces of law and order and led to over 700 arrests. Khalezin and Koliada, threatened with imprisonment, were forced to flee the country and take refuge in the United Kingdom. This forced exile obviously had consequences for the way the BFT was to function in the future. Part of the company had stayed behind, and continued to work with the 'Londoners' through the medium of Skype. Khalezin and Koliada have continued their activities in the UK, with plays in Russian or in English, staging shows such as *Trash Cuisine* (2012), *The Time of Women* (2013) and *Burning Doors* (2016).

In Russia things became more tense in 2012, after Putin was elected to the presidency for the third time. The decisive factor here proved to be the 'white ribbon' protest movement in late 2011 to early 2012. As in Belarus, the protests emerged as a consequence of electoral fraud. There were large demonstrations in the major cities, especially in Moscow. They too were suppressed with violence, and followed by arrests.

It is certainly the case that Teatr.doc and the KnAM were not as directly affected by the hardening of the regime as the BFT had been. Even so, the working environment at Teatr.doc became more complicated. On 3 December 2014 the forces of law and order, accompanied by two representatives of the Ministry of Culture, obliged them to close the theatre on the grounds of 'extremism'. The theatre rented a new venue and re-opened its doors on 14 February 2015. But on 6 May, after the premiere of *The Bolotnaia Case* (*Bolotnoe delo*), a show which involved the friends and families of the victims of the suppression of the 'white ribbon' movement, the private firm which had rented the premises to the theatre withdrew the arrangement under political pressure. The theatre was compelled to rent another venue, which it currently occupies.[18] Since then, they have regularly had to have dealings with the security services, who attend the more controversial shows, take photographs and make the weight of their presence felt. The theatre has gained the support of lawyers financed by Open Russia ('Otkrytaia Rossiia'), a non-governmental organization created by the exiled Russian businessman Mikhail Khodorkovsky.

The KnAM theatre has not experienced the same kind of direct pressures, despite its active participation in the local version of the 'white ribbon' movement. The attitude of the authorities in Komsomol'sk-on-Amur is a passive one, and consists in ignoring their existence and denying them any financial support. For this reason, the theatre has, on several occasions in recent years, had to appeal to the generosity of its audiences to cover the costs of its heating bills. Frolova believes that her company is safeguarded by two rather different factors: firstly, their small size and their distance from Moscow allow them to go more or less unnoticed; and secondly, their success abroad affords them a kind of protection. Nevertheless, for their most recent show *I Haven't Yet Started to Live* (*Ya esche ne nachinala zhit'*), they preferred to follow the example of the BFT in order to avoid the risk of being closed down by the authorities: the performances of their show were not advertised anywhere, and the audience members, all regulars at the theatre, were simply informed of the details by telephone.[19]

Khalezin and Koliada have remained faithful from London to the policies adopted by the BFT since its creation: they produce documentary shows which revolve around outspoken denunciations of every kind of attack on liberty of expression. Their favoured target remains Belarus under Lukashenko, although they also address human rights issues in Russia and Ukraine. Their show *The Time of Women* (2013) draws upon their autobiographical tradition, and intimately stages the recollections of three female journalists and activists imprisoned in Belarus after the demonstrations on 19 December 2010, Irina Khalip, Natal'ia Radina and Nasta Palazhanka.[20] In a London apartment full of Christmas decorations they recall their detention, and the moral pressures to which they were subjected.

By contrast, in *Trash Cuisine* (2012) and *Burning Doors* (2016) we can see a broadening of their themes. If Belarus remains strongly present in the former play, which deals with capital punishment, this is considered alongside other countries: Thailand, the UK, Argentina and the USA. The most challenging episode in the show is indeed the testimony given by a lawyer about his client's final moments, after he has been condemned to the electric chair in the USA. *Burning Doors* focuses on repressive Russian prisons and the stories of three artists imprisoned for having expressed their beliefs in public: Maria Alyokhina from Pussy Riot; Oleg Sentsov, a Ukrainian filmmaker from the Crimea who was arrested after the Russian annexation of the peninsula in 2014 and condemned to twenty years of confinement; and finally Piotr Pavlensky, who was incarcerated after a performance supporting the Maidan movement in Ukraine.[21]

In parallel with the broadening of its focus, the BFT has considerably intensified its work on the human body since 2011. It is true that violence has always been physically present in their shows, such as for example in *Being Harold Pinter* (2007). But it became more accentuated in *Trash Cuisine*, and then again in *Burning Doors*, where the acting pushed the actors to the limits of their physical capabilities. At times they performed suspended from a rope, dealt one other physical blows, stripped off entirely, or else had their heads plunged into a bathtub in a simulation of a drowning. Nevertheless this violence remained metaphorical: it was choreographed and stylized, and when certain stage images became simply unendurable, the actors reminded us of the fact that the action was taking place in a theatre. In comparison with their shows of the 2000s, the BFT's cries of protest against oppression have become more physically incarnated: these days the dialogues are intersected by long episodes where oppression and rebellion find purely physical expression.

Teatr.doc has an extremely intensive rhythm of creative activity. If we are to draw overall conclusions about the way they have evolved since 2012, we could note two tendencies: at first, their faithfulness to their original interests and aesthetic positions, and later a more marked politicization of the subjects they treat, with two different strategies, depending on the show. They continue to take an interest in social questions, as for example in the plight of Russian homosexuals in *Coming Out of the Closet* (*Vyyti iz shkafa*, 2016). This show perfectly matches their criterion of the 'zero position', since speeches are distributed among characters without any stigmatization of people's discourse, and with a profound respect for the individuality of people's testimony, as well as a sober staging.

Nevertheless, the hardening of the regime has induced a de facto intensification of politics in their themes: giving an opportunity to speak out to the friends and relations of those who fell victim to the repressions in 2011–12 after the Moscow demonstrations (*The Bolotnaya Case*, 2015), or evoking the conflict in Ukraine (*War Is Close*, 2017), is quite enough to situate Teatr.doc in explicit opposition to the regime.²² We should nevertheless note that, in comparison with the KnAM theatre, Teatr.doc has adopted a dual strategy: in certain shows, the most political questions are approached indirectly. In 2012, for example, the theatre staged *Two People in Your Home* (*Dvoe v tvoem dome*), a show about Belarus and the house arrest of one of Lukashenko's rivals for the presidency, Vladimir Nekliaev. If Gremina had explained in 2012 that the political methods of the Belarusians interested her because she suspected that the Russian authorities were taking inspiration from them, she equally claimed that addressing the question head-on would surely have prevented Teatr.doc from performing their shows in Belarus, and maybe even from crossing that country in order to visit Europe.²³ And so she adopted a dislocated perspective: *Two People in Your Home* depicts the forced cohabitation of Nekliaev and his wife with two security service agents. The show makes us laugh, because Nekliaev's wife makes the two policemen's lives intolerable, and she even manages to get them to do some domestic chores before they leave.

One can see a similar kind of displacement, in a less humorous form, in the 2013 show *150 Reasons for Not Defending the Motherland* (*150 prichin ne zashchishchat' rodinu*), which is presented as 'fifteenth-century verbatim', and evokes the capturing of Constantinople by the Ottomans in 1453. It depicts the fall of the city as being the result of an accumulation of individual choices, and obviously it makes one think of present-day Russia. Gremina considers this to be a crucial new stage in her work, because she conceived of it as an experience where history would be 'actualized'. She wanted to show how difficult it is to survive in an era of global transformations, when those in positions of power take decisions, rather than individuals.²⁴ People who are regulars at Teatr.doc have stated that the resonance of this show, which remains in their repertory, has been especially powerful, particularly since the Maidan events and the beginning of the conflict in Ukraine.²⁵

Other shows address political questions in a much more direct manner: this is the case, for example, with *The Bolotnaya Case* (2015), which reuses a technique they have drawn upon since 2012. At that point Teatr.doc invented the form of 'a theatre of real witnesses', by inviting for single performances people who were involved in current events to testify from the stage, such as the lawyers defending Pussy Riot and the journalists who covered their trial in August 2012. *The Bolotnaya Case* stages the experiences lived through by those who were close to those imprisoned in the aftermath of the 'white ribbon' movement. In *War Is Close*, Teatr.doc tackled the Ukrainian conflict, with three different perspectives on it. The show opens with the diary of an inhabitant of Luhansk, in eastern Ukraine, who is first of all incredulous at the threat of an armed conflict, and then finds himself plunged into war. In a second phase, the theme is universalized thanks to a text by the British playwright Mark Ravenhill on the conflict in Syria. And finally the last part of the show tackles the trial and sentence of Oleg Sentsov, just as in *Burning Doors*. Just like Khalezin, Gremina attacks the issue of cowardice, inasmuch as Sentsov's guilty sentence was clinched thanks to the testimony of another of the accused, who heavily incriminated him before declaring during the trial that his confessions had been extracted from him under torture. If Khalezin bases himself on a quotation from Mikhail Bulgakov's 1940 novel *The Master and Margarita*, about cowardice being the worst of sins, in order to insist upon the need for individual responsibility, Teatr.doc by contrast underlines the courage of the young man who denied his previous testimony. Both shows highlight the issue of physical torture in Russian prisons.

The KnAM theatre's evolution has been somewhat different. Since 2012 they have devoted themselves to working on the collective memories of the inhabitants of Komsomol'sk-on-Amur. This anchoring of the theatre in the local community is indeed very powerful: the history of the city interests Frolova because it reflects the titanic efforts of the Soviet regime to create by force a new life for a New Man. And indeed the official mythology still proclaims nowadays that the city was founded in the early 1930s by a group of heroic young communists (members of the Komsomol organization), whereas in fact it was constructed by labour camp prisoners from the Gulag, and in appalling conditions. Having very rapidly become an industrial centre, Komsomol'sk-on-Amur was abandoned to its fate after the collapse of the USSR: in the absence of any investment many factories closed down, while others reconfigured themselves with great difficulty. The 1990s were marked by grave social problems: the impoverishment of the population, a dramatic increase in crime, pollution and a sense of hopelessness about the future. The situation has not significantly improved since then, and the city is currently suffering from a massive exodus of its population.

Since 2012 Frolova has devoted a cycle of six shows to the study of the city's collective memories, by undertaking the collecting of testimonies on a large scale. Her efforts have focused in particular on two generations: on the one hand, those who were born in the 1930s, and who were marked by the collective traumas of the persecutions in the Stalin era and the Second World War, and then the young, those born after the collapse of the USSR. The theatre was undertaking a dual project: it was a question not only of repairing the collective memory, to restore a less falsified past to the city's inhabitants, but also of trying to understand the apathy of modern-day young people in Russia. Four of these shows have only been performed in Komsomol'sk-on-Amur. The two others, which we are about to discuss, were aimed at wider audiences: they have been performed several times in France as well as in Switzerland. These are *I Exist* (*Ia est'*, 2012) and *I Haven't Yet Started to Live* (2017).

These two shows tackle Soviet history rather as in the works of the Nobel Prize-winning Belarusian author Svetlana Aleksievich; that is to say, by being based on individual testimonies. *I Exist* is focused around the inhabitants of Komsomol'sk-on-Amur, whereas *I Haven't Yet Started to Live* broadens the themes by envisaging the history of the nation from 1917 until 2017. The first show was conceived just after the 'white ribbon' demonstrations. Frolova had indeed gone out on to the street with a sign on which she had simply written 'I exist'. 'Why were the militia so violent in the way they treated us? Because we exist?'[26] The show, which concludes with a quotation from Pussy Riot's Nadia Tolokonnikova, asks questions about the violence of the state towards individuals. It is constructed principally around two elements: on the one hand the testimonies of the actors themselves, who reconstructed the tragic history of their own families across two generations, and on the other hand a reflection on the connections between memory and forgetting, based on a text by Bernard Noël and also on the testimony of one of the female actors whose mother was suffering from Alzheimer's.[27] *I Exist* functions rather like memory, through the association of ideas:

each successive stage image summons up a new one. Their work on form, and particularly on the use of video, is very well developed. The show is not only performed on screen and with screens, when the actors film themselves on stage, but also behind transparent screens of plastic, on to which they project images or make drawings, as though their own memory was itself a screen on to which their memories could be projected.

I Haven't Yet Started to Live is structured around a number of episodes, more or less in chronological order, which retrace the history of the nation while at the same time being interleaved with reflections upon the distress and apathy of the young, to whom preceding generations have proved incapable of transmitting anything but fearfulness and lies. 'We are all the same', states one of the actors, 'the children of executioners, or of their victims. If there were no victims in a family, that's because there were executioners. And *vice versa*.'[28] The show stresses two turning points in recent Russian history, two irremediable errors: firstly, the regime did nothing in the post-Stalin era after 1956 to undertake anything like the Nuremberg trials; and in 1993 the executive powers brought an end to democratization by sending tanks out against the Duma in Moscow. It is interesting to note that when Frolova tackles the subject of modern-day Russia, she too emphasizes police oppression and detention conditions in Russia: she specifically evokes the case of Il'dar Dadin, who was imprisoned and tortured after the 'white ribbon' movement.

In conclusion, we can see that these three theatres, despite their strongly felt diffidence about political theatre, have created shows which have turned them willy-nilly into opponents to the regimes in their countries. This tipping over into opposition is more marked for the two Russian theatres, whose original purposes had been less confrontational than that of the BFT. The two European theatres, the BFT and Teatr.doc, gaze in each other's directions: the BFT is interested in developments in Russia, Teatr.doc is interested in Belarus, and both are concerned about the Ukrainian conflict. Even if Khalezin's exile has increased the distance of their connections, they have maintained interests in common.[29] The concerns of the more distant KnAM are a little different, since Frolova has focused her artistic endeavours around the leitmotif of collective memory, in an undertaking which one could almost describe as therapeutic. But she shares with Gremina and Khalezin a number of points of reference which structure her projects: the suppression of protest movements against electoral fraud; the courage of the political opposition, specifically of the members of Pussy Riot; and denouncing the use of torture in Russian prisons.

Translated from the French by J. A. E. Curtis

Notes

1 Ol'ga Pogodina-Kuzmina is a novelist, dramatist and scriptwriter born in 1969, who lives in St Petersburg.
2 Arkady Babchenko (born 1977) is a freelance journalist and war correspondent for various Russian media outlets, and in particular the newspaper *Novaia Gazeta*. He was

called up in 1995 and served in the North Caucasus during the first Chechen war. Demobilized in 1997, he joined up again at the time of the second Chechen war. He published a short novel, *Alkhan-Iurt* (Moscow: Yauza, 2006), in which he described the massacre of civilians perpetrated in December 1999 by Russian troops under General Vladimir Shamanov. He became notorious in May 2018 for faking his own murder in Kyiv (Ukraine), apparently in order to escape a real attempt on his life.
3   These take place approximately every two years. Their most recent visit was in November–December 2017, when they toured the show *I Haven't Yet Started to Live* (*Ia eshche ne nachinala zhit'*).
4   In Germany, Uganda, Palestine and Brazil, to cite just a few examples.
5   Khalezin was a member of the Executive Committee of the Belarusian organization Charter 97, which was set up along the lines of the Czechoslovak Charter 77, to defend human rights and democracy in Belarus. See Virginie Symaniec, 'Le théâtre en Biélorussie. L'officiel et le dissident', in *La documentation française/Le courrier des pays de l'Est* 6, no. 1058 (2006): 47–55.
6   See Alison Forsyth and Chris Megson (eds), *Get Real: Documentary Theatre Past and Present*, (Chippenham and Eastbourne: Palgrave Macmillan UK, 2002); Will Hammond and Dan Steward (eds), *Verbatim, Verbatim* (London: Oberon Books, 2008); Lucie Kempf and Tania Moguilevskaia (eds), *Le théâtre neo-documentaire, résurgence ou réinvention?* (Nancy: Presses Universitaires de Nancy, 2013).
7   Tania Moguilevskaia, 'Notes sur l'invention du théâtre documentaire marxiste', in ibid.., 25–42.
8   Marie Pecorari, 'La vérité nue: retrait de la technologie, retour du corps dans le théâtre d'Anna Deavere Smith', in ibid., 197–210; Tania Moguilevskaia, 'Position zéro: contre la manipulation: Entretien avec Mikhail Ougarov et Elena Gremina, fondateurs et directeurs artistiques du Teatr.doc', in ibid., 143–57.
9   The most striking passage in *Rwanda 94* (1999), a show by the Belgian company Groupov under the direction of Jacques Delcuvellerie, is testimony which lasts for nearly 40 minutes taken from a survivor of the genocide, Yolande Mukagasana.
10 Anatoly Krasovsky was a businessman in Belarus, who was opposed to the regime. He disappeared on 16 September 1999, together with the vice-president of the Belarusian parliament, Viktor Gonchar. The criminal investigation was soon abandoned.
11 By 'contributors' we mean the people originally interviewed.
12 Interview with Tat'iana Frolova, March 2017.
13 Ibid.
14 Interview with Nikolai Khalezin, January 2018: 'In my opinion political theatre is a theatre which proclaims some sort of political idea. But if that is the case, then the most recent person to have proclaimed any sort of concrete idea was Bertolt Brecht. We don't proclaim political ideas, and for that reason I reject that label.'
15 'grazhdanskii teatr'.
16 This festival, which has always been focused on the theatres of Eastern Europe, was established in Nancy in 1996. At first it took place annually, then from 2003 on, every second year. The KnAM theatre took part in 1999, 2001 and 2011, Teatr.doc in 2005, and the BFT in 2007 and 2009.
17 Sergei Magnitsky, a tax accountant, had uncovered a very extensive corruption scandal implicating highly placed figures. He was promptly accused of corruption himself, and placed on remand. He died in custody of pancreatitis, the authorities having failed to provide him with appropriate medical attention.
18 During the summer of 2018 Teatr.doc was forced yet again to seek new premises.

19 After the premiere one local campaigner for human rights warned Frolova that she risked being imprisoned for this show under three different articles of the Russian Penal Code. However, the show was performed in France in the autumn of 2017.
20 Irina Khalip is a Belarusian journalist, the Minsk correspondent for Russia's *Novaia Gazeta*, and is married to one of the other candidates in the presidential elections of 2010, Andrei Sannikov. She was kept in prison for a month after the demonstration of 19 December 2010, before being placed under house arrest. Natal'ia Radina is a journalist, and the editor of the independent website Charter 97. Having been incarcerated after the demonstration, she was released a month later and forced into exile in 2011. Since then she has lived in Lithuania, where she has continued her activities on behalf of Charter 97. Nasta Palazhanka is a militant human rights campaigner, and has been the Vice-President since 2011 of the Youth Front; she too was put in prison after the demonstration.
21 The title of Khalezin's show is a reference to one of Pavlensky's performances, which involved setting fire to the door of the Lubianka, the secret police's headquarters in Moscow.
22 *Bolotnoe delo*; *Voyna blizko*.
23 Elena Gremina, 'Position zéro: contre la manipulation' in Kempf and Moguilevskaia, *Le théâtre neo-documentaire*, 143.
24 Interview with Elena Gremina, January 2018.
25 Ibid. Gremina noted that in 2014 a female spectator from eastern Ukraine fell ill during the performance, but nevertheless declined to leave the auditorium.
26 Opening lines from the show *I Am*.
27 Bernard Noël, *Le livre de l'oubli* (Paris: P.O.L., 2012).
28 Concluding words of *I Haven't Yet Started to Live*.
29 Gremina and Khalezin kept in touch by Facebook. Frolova has lost touch with Khalezin since his forced move to London.

From Stalinist Socialist Realism to Putinist Capitalist Realism

Tracing cultural ideology in contemporary Russia

Alexander Trustrum Thomas

> Alexander Trustrum Thomas investigates the numerous laws affecting the freedom of cultural production which have been passed since Vladimir Putin was re-elected to the Presidency in Russia in 2012. It is impossible to understand what has been happening in the world of theatre over the last five-ten years without reference to this wider cultural policy. These laws impose bans or restrictions on the representation of controversial issues (homosexuality, 'blasphemy', political corruption etc.) and limit the language in which these might be depicted (banning the use of obscenities). When these are considered alongside new guidelines for cultural policy in the future, it becomes apparent that a fundamental shift is taking place in Russian cultural life in the second decade of the twenty-first century, reflecting a rigid social conservatism and reinstating many precepts reminiscent of Soviet-era Socialist Realism. An all-encompassing ideological monopoly over culture would seem to be what the Russian state is aspiring to achieve, with the body of the individual becoming the site for policy making. The example of the house arrest of the theatre and film director Kirill Serebrennikov on spurious fraud charges is used in this essay to illustrate the application of these politically-motivated restrictions in the theatre world.

Cultural policy in Russia during the 2010s

Since the inauguration of Vladimir Putin for his third presidential term in 2012, a minimum of ten different laws have been passed that can be said directly or indirectly to affect the freedom of cultural production in the Russian Federation.[1] The three best known of these are collectively dubbed the 'censorship laws', and all appeared within a year of each other over the course of 2013 and 2014. They relate to language usage (the so-called law on *mat*, or obscene lexicon), to sexual orientation (the 'homosexual propaganda' law) and finally to religious feelings, or more specifically the prohibition of anything that causes offence to such feelings. These laws coincided with a significant change in cultural policy around that time, in line with the broader domestic and foreign policy shifts of Putin's return to the presidency in 2012. This period was characterized by the annexation of Crimea, military intervention in Ukraine, the consolidation of power in the hands of the federal security services, an information war both internally and with the West, as well as a renewed hard-line stance against protests and political opposition in general. Before addressing the implications of this conservative authoritarian turn, it is worth considering what preceded it, namely an unprecedented period of financial and political investment in the cultural sphere, the genuine materialization of promises made by Dmitrii Medvedev (president 2008–12) to invest in the contemporary arts as the foundation of future social cohesion, for the benefit of the next generation of citizens.

This 'golden age' in the history of post-Soviet Russian theatre (which was true not only in financial terms, but also in terms of the number of premieres, the number of spectators, and other indicators) ran from 2011 to 2014.[2] After this the three-year funding cycles ran out and, rather than being renewed or built upon, were replaced by a radical cultural conservatism, epitomized by policy statements from the new Minister of Culture, Vladimir Medinsky, as well as the passing of the aforementioned censorship laws.[3] This culminated three years later in the scandal surrounding the theatre director Kirill Serebrennikov and his company Seventh Studio (*Sed'maia Studiia*), which was both born out of and was a major beneficiary of the Medvedev cultural investment programme. In many ways, the history of Seventh Studio and the ongoing legal case around it (known colloquially and in the media as Theatre-gate, or *Teatral'noe Delo*) epitomizes the extent of the shift in cultural policy from Medvedev to Putin, and illustrates the major challenges faced by the cultural sphere in the post-2012 era.

There are other factors that put external pressure on theatrical production besides overbearing state legislation, municipal-level harassment, and the use of financial threats and deprivation, one of these being the ever-growing and increasingly assertive power of the Russian Orthodox Church. This has been cited as the greatest problem facing the cultural sphere in the current era by Boris Mezdrich, the theatre manager who was fired from the Novosibirsk Opera House after Orthodox activists picketed a production of *Tannhäuser* there in 2015.[4] The problem, which is widely acknowledged by theatre professionals, is that there are no effective mechanisms of defence or protection for cultural production from conservative-nationalist and religious activists. Moreover, the laws that have been passed over the last few years have had the opposite effect, emboldening those elements of society that see so-called 'non-traditional' culture in purely negative terms (most unfortunately this includes the Minister of Culture himself). The two crucial documents here, called the 'Fundamentals of State Cultural Policy' (2014), and the 'Strategy of State Cultural Policy up until 2030' (2016), are both legislative 'white papers' or projects that have been signed into law by the president, but do not constitute legally binding criteria or statutes (henceforth referred to as the 'Fundamentals' and the 'Strategy'). As such, they function more as instruction manuals for the new state ideology, indicating how cultural production should manifest itself, the direction it should take, and the kind of language that should be used in approaching the formulation and implementation of cultural policy at the institutional and regional level.

Focusing on these two pieces of legislation that specifically address cultural policy, we can observe a clear somatic turn, which is to say a turn to the body of the individual as the site of policymaking. This was one of the trademark features of Soviet-era Socialist Realism as a doctrine, shaping cultural ideology in similar ways through treating the body as the raw material in its processes. It is perhaps unsurprising to see this focus re-emerge now, given that it has already occurred in other areas such as education and national security, as the emphasis on political loyalty and the corresponding patronage network continues inexorably to extend into all areas of civic life. The absence of real targets or policy commitments in these policy documents should not belie their significance – they transparently reveal the desire of the government to bring the cultural sphere into line behind the state apparatus, as it has already done so successfully with the media, business, and the Church, thereby reinforcing its own power structures and the 'managed democracy' of the political system.[5] The 'Fundamentals' sets out as its aims 'regulating the processes of cultural development' [...], in order 'to secure a higher quality of society' [...] and 'the formation of moral, responsible, independent-minded creative personalities'; and in the final instance it sees culture as an 'integral part of the strategy of national security of the Russian Federation', in order to achieve the 'harmonisation of social relations' and the 'preservation of a unitary cultural space and the territorial integrity of Russia'.[6] 'Culture', as narrowly defined by this state legislative document, is to be utilized to further political ideology on multiple fronts (domestic, foreign, social, economic).[7] There are strong currents of Russian exceptionalism running through the decree, with reference to its position as 'uniting two worlds – East and West', and its 'historic path' that has defined its 'cultural uniqueness' and the 'specificity of the national mentality'.[8] These notions, while often repeated and held up as truisms, are never defined in any concrete way, existing more as signifiers for how the document should be read and understood. They are indicators of intended meaning, establishing a feedback loop between the state-author and the reader, whose responsibility it is to interpret and implement the policy. Indeed, although the 'Fundamentals' is not legally binding, the document already functions as the determiner of artistic policy in theatres that do not have a strong, independent-minded leadership. Tellingly, the editor of the journal *Theatre* (*Teatr*), Marina Davydova, stated that the experience of reading the 'Fundamentals' reminded her of reading a resolution by the Central Committee of the Soviet-era Communist Party.[9] This is the new language of Putinism, and it must be learnt, much as one had to learn to 'speak Bolshevik' (partly through the interpretation of decrees) in the Soviet Union.[10]

Starting from the premise that legislation is performative, the passing of a new policy into law, which is to say the moment at which it becomes a part of the legal code that defines the officially sanctioned zone of cultural permissibility, is an act of redrawing, a redefining of the Norm. This performative dimension of lawmaking extends down to the level of language usage in the text itself. A good example of this is the introduction and subsequent proliferation, through citation and reiteration, of a constructed linguistic binary such as 'traditional/non-traditional', which first appeared in 2013 as a single-sentence addendum to the 2010 law on 'the protection of children from information causing harm to their health and development', but has its origins in earlier Duma debates from 2003 and 2009, as a result of which it entered the political and public discourse.[11] This new clause wrote into law the notion that information alleged to cause harm to children's health and development also includes 'denying family values, propagandizing non-traditional sexual relations, and fostering disrespect to parents and/or to another member of the family'.[12] There are clearly lots of questions here, not least the highly problematic conflation of notions of sexuality, family hierarchy and values broadly conceived, but my attention here is on the appearance of the term 'non-traditional'. The immediate consequence of this legislative intervention is that this term becomes a real, legitimate language usage in political and cultural discourse, drawing an officially sanctioned ontological distinction between 'types' of sexuality – traditional and non-traditional – a status that the term did not previously have.[13] What we see following from this is that the notion of the 'non-traditional', which is here applied specifically to sexual relations (i.e. homosexuality), then gets taken up and applied more generally to other spheres, and ultimately to cultural production itself. This gets played out in the 'Fundamentals', where in fairly open terms an opposition gets drawn between traditional culture as good and healthy, and non-traditional culture as 'pseudo-culture' and therefore bad, not real culture, and undesirable.[14] This sentiment was publicly echoed by the Minister of Culture himself, who negatively assessed contemporary art as being akin to the Emperor's New Clothes, and as such, not something that the state should be financing.[15] The notion of 'tradition' subsequently becomes a guiding principle in cultural policy, and proliferates in both the 'Fundamentals' and the later 'Strategy'. This is significant because it becomes the premise for an actively interventionist cultural policy, especially relating to youth culture and educational development, and also serves as a more general justification for imposing through legislation upon the body of the individual as a subject. Given the highly traditional, conservative nature of Soviet Socialist Realism, which propounded a neo-classical and realist aesthetic, the parallels between then and now in terms of state artistic policy are only getting stronger.

Another example of this legal language working performatively also appears in the 'Fundamentals', which states early on that one of the main aims of the new state cultural policy is 'the formation of the harmoniously developed personality'. This phrase has a history that traces back to the 1920s at least, when it appeared in Proletkul't theory.[16] It was also a central tenet of Socialist Realism. Furthermore, when this cultural policy aim is placed alongside the new politicized antagonism of the traditional and the non-traditional, it becomes clear that artists are essentially once again expected to become 'engineers of the human soul' (to quote Stalin's notorious phrase), proactively taking a correct, moral and patriotic approach to their art in accordance with ruling state ideology. There is talk of the 'qualitative renewal of the personality' in order to fulfil this plan.[17] The deployment of this language reintroduces the notion of the 'positive hero' so central to Socialist Realist culture.[18] This idealized so-called 'personality' would have a textbook knowledge of correct and pure 'literary Russian' (which they use at all times, acknowledging no other registers of language), as well as a commanding grasp of the moral, ethical and aesthetic principles of art and culture (of the traditional kind), grounded as these should be in the traditional family unit as the the foundation of all social values.[19] The 'literary Russian' language question has its own history, which traces back to 1920s debates that informed the later development of Socialist Realist literary dogma.[20] In recent legislation, this resurfaces most strongly in the 2014 law on 'uncensored lexicon', which bans all so-called 'obscene language' from the public realm, printed or spoken (including books, cinemas, theatres, music and public performances of any kind).[21] Like Socialist Realism, this is a deeply infantilizing approach to cultural policy, as pointed out by the late Elena Gremina in her commentary on the document, and it becomes a way of depriving non-conformist art and work deemed to be immoral or even amoral from receiving state subsidies, therefore functioning as another mechanism of censorship on cultural production (known informally as 'financial censorship').[22] There are other notions in the 'Fundamentals' that feed into this, such as the assertion that the cultural sphere forms a part of national security and that it therefore must be regulated and serve a military-patriotic agenda. Gremina best captured the sense of the 'Fundamentals' with the following assessment: 'They [the authorities] see culture as a servant of ideology, and with the help of this document they are trying to squeeze culture into a "Procrustean bed" of ideology.'[23] The metaphor of the Procrustean bed is ideal for conceptualizing the effect of these legislation restrictions – with the inscription of each new law, the parameters of the Norm are pulled in towards the normalizing centre of power (the state apparatus), making legally Other that which was previously comfortably the Norm.

The sheer impossibility of conformity to the model of the 'harmoniously developed personality' is akin to the 'New Soviet Person' trope in Socialist Realism –both can only be the products of fiction rather than of any reality. This generic unrealizability necessitates and generates transgression of its own norms. As such, a legislative policy based on such an impossible model of homogeneity is itself entirely cynical. It demands a pathological multi-polarity from the subject, in order to perform acts of conformity while simultaneously not ever truly conforming. This is how the technical power to overdetermine cultural ideology achieves its aims – the 'othering' of the subject, caught in a state of permanent instability. On the one hand, Hannah Arendt asserts a 'state of permanent instability' as an inherent characteristic of totalitarianism.[24] This can be extended to Socialist Realism, as a totalitarian artistic genre. On the other hand, Mark Fisher, in his diagnosis of 'Capitalist Realism', talks of 'capitalism's perpetual instability'.[25] Given that post-Soviet Russia is a *capitalist* state, not a socialist one, any comparison between Putinist cultural policy and Socialist Realism has firm limits. However, when considering the current system as a Capitalist Realist phenomenon, the Socialist Realist past can offer a productive context. The comparison of cultural policy in Russia under Stalin and Putin respectively reveals the many traits that Socialist Realism and Capitalist Realism have in common *as genres*. The fact that products of genre such as the 'harmoniously developed personality', which first appeared then, can and should reappear now, is evidence of this. Fisher states in regard to Capitalist Realism of the twenty-first century what could just as easily have been written about twentieth-century Socialist Realism, that 'the effect of permanent structural instability', the 'cancellation of the long term', is invariably stagnation and conservatism, not innovation'.[26] The conservative turn to 'tradition' in cultural policy under both Stalin and Putin would seem to bear this out.

Alongside the introduction of these highly ideological and contingent concepts of 'traditional' attitudes to sex and gender, and of 'literary language', the notion of 'history' has also become no less subject to the machinations of state legislative power. We see in the post-2012 legislation a concerted effort to take 'history' as such in hand, which is to say, to control historical narratives through the performative act of legislating. In the opening pages of the 'Foundations', it is stated that the purpose of the document is to create a new cultural policy in order to avert the 'threat of a crisis in the humanities' in Russia.[27] Two characteristic features of such a crisis would apparently be the 'negative evaluation of significant periods of national history', and the 'dissemination of a false impression about the historic backwardness of Russia'.[28] Here are the first signals of what is later developed in the 'Strategy' into a juridico-legislative outlawing of the possibility of evidence-based historiography, especially if it negatively evaluates the dominant trope of neo-Soviet great-power triumphalism, in which positive memories of the Soviet era become an integral part. History, therefore, is 'remembered' by those in power and reinscribed as a singular narrative, leaving all alternative, competing narratives outside the normative parameters of the politico-judicial space. This attempt to set historical narratives in stone, and the total denial of their inherently contingent nature, does not of course necessarily erase the collective 'social' memory, although it does come to dominate it, especially given state control of education and the media. The act of collective forgetting, then, becomes an important feature of this phenomenon as well.[29] In the context of the Capitalist Realist reality of Putin's Russia, however, this is perhaps unsurprising. Fisher states that, 'In these conditions of ontological precarity, forgetting becomes an adaptive strategy'.[30] In other words, selective memory and forgetting is a survival strategy under the ontological instability of Putinism, just as it was under Stalinism.

It is important to view this 'petrification' of history and the introduction of the notion of the 'traditional' into political discourse as part of one and the same trend. 'History' and 'tradition' are actively employed as the conceptual weapons in the fight against a culture of 'all-permissibility and violence'.[31] Daphne Skillen states that 'all-permissibility' [*vsedozvolennost'*], with its Dostoevskian undertones of 'egoism, narcissism and random acts of violence', is a pejorative word in Russian.[32] In cultural Putinism, closely allied as it is with the resurgent Russian Orthodox Church, history and tradition are the forces of enclosure and social cohesion that protect society from a harmful culture of permissiveness associated with the 'godless gay West'.[33]

Further manifestations of a preoccupation with history appear in the 'Strategy' in relation to the fostering of the so-called 'harmoniously developed personality', two key elements of which, we are told, will include the 'immortalising of the memory of the casualties of the Great Patriotic [i.e. Second World] War', and 'the study and popularization, including through media projects, of the history of national culture and of national history'.[34] Both of these policies involve the petrification of history in the image of the dominant political narrative, which, with the continual invocation of the 'memory' of the Great Patriotic War and the rehabilitation of the figure of Stalin, increasingly resembles a neo-Soviet chauvinism. The questions that continually reoccur to a critical reader of this legislative document are: Which memories? What history? Whose culture? These are questions that are naturally left unanswered in the documents, but it should nonetheless be apparent by now who and what decides the answers.

Bound up with the notion of the 'harmoniously developed personality' is a focus on youth, and on the human body in the process of development. This is one of the main developments in the 2016 'Strategy' when compared with the earlier 'Fundamentals' – a shift towards the body of the child as the performative site of policy inscription in the shaping of the next generation of citizens. Early in the 'Strategy', it is stated that new programmes 'for the provision of all types of cultural activity' will include 'the expansion of children's and youth movements', as well as 'the patriotic upbringing of youth'.[35] This also has its own, separate policy document, to cover the years 2016–20.[36] Passed into law only two months before the 'Strategy', its language feeds into the elaboration of the latter legislation. The emphasis in these policies, which is on the 'patriotic education' of young people, relies heavily on the military – military history, military culture, and the effective militarization of youth culture. This process of militarization through education is nothing new in Russia, and in fact, as Michel Foucault convincingly demonstrated, military discipline is the genealogical origin of discipline in many other European social(izing) institutions, including the school, the hospital and the prison, meaning that these seemingly disparate and unrelated social spheres share much in common.[37] Nonetheless, the evidence from these cultural policy documents shows that in recent years the militarization of youth culture and education in Russia has accelerated and become an active government priority. The 'Strategy' states that this will be achieved through a 'system of monitors' and 'quality indicators' to assess the 'relative proportion of young people between the ages of 14 and 30 who participate in events relating to patriotic education'.[38] There are clear parallels here with the Soviet Komsomol (Communist Youth League) system, which had a similar military-patriotic function and also extended its definition of 'youth' to the ripe age of twenty-eight. This imposition of the state's political ideology on to young people as they are still developing is clearly part of one and the same trend as the aforementioned laws on 'homosexual propaganda' and 'uncensored lexicon', which are both specifically directed at the control and censorship of material available to minors. Indeed, the debates around the introduction of these laws and other similarly restrictive measures are always framed in narratives of child and youth 'health'.

Fisher describes Capitalist Realism as 'more like a pervasive *atmosphere*, conditioning not only the production of culture but also the regulation of work and education, and acting as a kind of invisible barrier constraining thought and action'.[39] It is this *atmosphere* that pervades theatrical production in late Putinism. To borrow an idea from Simone de Beauvoir, we can say that one is not born, but rather *becomes* Other.[40] This is to say that the phenomenon of Russian 'New Drama' is 'other' not intrinsically, as the authorities would have us believe. It is not some alien, foreign seed fallen on Russian soil.[41] It is 'other' only extrinsically, which is to say, circumstantially, due to the ever narrowing paradigm of the Norm in the political, and by extension, social and cultural realms. As the late Mikhail Ugarov wrote, 'In our country, with its deviant government and its perversions at every level, an appeal to adhere to the norm can draw accusations of extremism'.[42]

Policy in practice: the case of Kirill Serebrennikov and the theatre

The case of the theatre and film director Kirill Serebrennikov is demonstrative of how censorship of the arts functions in contemporary Russia under Putinism (and of how it deviates from Stalinism). Concerning the hardening of cultural ideology through the paradigm of the traditional/non-traditional binary, the scandal over the director's ballet at Moscow's Bolshoi Theatre in 2017 is revealing. The ballet's subject matter was Rudolf Nureyev, the world-renowned Soviet ballet dancer who came out as gay after he defected to the West in 1961. The explicit depiction of his homosexuality in Serebrennikov's ballet caused the production to be repeatedly delayed, before the director was arrested in August 2017 on unrelated and evidently spurious charges of embezzlement and placed under house arrest, where he remained until April 2019.[43] Serebrennikov's arrest was the culmination of a number of years of rising tensions between the director and the authorities, as the question of whether state funding for theatres should entail political loyalty to the regime reached a head – a battle that Serebrennikov fought hard but inevitably lost. The production of the ballet was completed without him, then eventually performed twice in 2017 before an audience of the political and cultural elite, and now languishes on the theatre repertoire list with no further dates scheduled.[44] Although the production does not break any laws as such, the depiction of Nureyev's homosexuality on stage falls beyond the boundaries of the narrowing norms as set out in the 'Fundamentals' and 'Strategy', and embodied in the three 'censorship' laws against gay propaganda, religious offence and obscene language. The question of 'history' is significant here too, in that an attempt has been made to control the collective 'memory' of an historical figure, rewritten according to the ideological norms of the dominant political power – Nureyev as a public figure has been chopped down and made to fit the 'Procrustean bed' of ideology. The authorities brought the meanings of this production under control through the crude yet typical devices of power – by removing the embodiment of the idea (Serebrennikov himself) from the public sphere, by regulating the 'abnormalities' in the production, and finally by restricting its performance and thus those who were able to see it, despite the considerable demand for tickets (both of the performances were sell-outs).

Serebrennikov was no stranger to the machinations of state cultural policy prior to *Nureyev*. In 2013, two of his productions for the theatre – *Punks*, based on a novel by Zakhar Prilepin, and Martin McDonagh's *The Pillowman* – were the subject of police investigations on suspicion of breaking new so-called 'anti-terrorist' laws.[45] The pressure on theatres to conform to the new laws and to the social norms set out within them in turn fosters a culture of self-censorship, where the instability generated by apprehension and uncertainty before the law performs the work of the censor. A number of prominent theatre-makers have cited self-censorship as a real and significant problem, a part of the new reality of cultural production in Russia.[46] The case of actors in the provincial town of Pskov, who simply refused to act in Varvara Faer's verbatim drama *The Bath-house Attendant* in the wake of the aforementioned scandal surrounding a production of Wagner's *Tannhäuser* at the Novosibirsk Opera House in 2015 is an example of this – the latter production had provoked demonstrations and threats of violence from patriotic Orthodox Christian fundamentalists, and the Pskov actors were not prepared to take the risk of being caught up in similar scandal.[47] This incident set a highly problematic precedent, and the fact that the Ministry of Culture did nothing to support or protect the actors in either case further confirms that cultural figures are not safe to practise their profession in the current climate. Unfortunately, with state funding making up on average 73.1 per cent of theatre budgets, and covering as much as 90 per cent of the cost of a ticket in some theatres, there is little chance for the performing arts to resist such pressures on their work to conform, a problem that is only compounded by hardening state cultural policy.[48] Owing to the stranglehold of financial censorship, which presents a major obstacle to nonconformist theatre, the new political diktats relating to the arts and society will continue to dominate and determine cultural production for the foreseeable future.

Conclusion

The very pervasiveness of censorship mechanisms – legislative, financial and self-censorship – present exceptionally challenging conditions for nonconformist theatre-making under developed Putinism. The laws concerning sexuality and gender, language and history have had the cumulative effect of weaponizing culture in the service of the broader political aims of the state. This brings it into line with previous politically weaponized social institutions, such as the media and the church, as well as the education and welfare systems.[49] This is expressed as such in the 'Strategy', which states that current planning policies 'do not fully account for the strategic significance of cultural potential'.[50] One of the bases for this 'new model of cultural politics', as it becomes known in the 'Strategy', is 'the harmonious combining of the interests of national security, [and] of unity within the cultural sphere'.[51] The perception of the cultural sphere as a latent branch of national security, combined with the belief in the necessity of 'unity' as a prerequisite for its realization, goes some way towards explaining the coercive means that the regime has adopted towards cultural policy since 2012.

Individuals find themselves subjected, as it were, to the impossibility of conformity. A politically motivated process of collective forgetting and 'correct' remembering, reinscribing and petrifying historical narratives in the official version of events, is taking place according to the reigning ideology. Ambitions to militarize youth culture have seen the body moved back to the centre of policymaking. Culture is once more treated as a weapon of political ideology, as it was in Soviet times.

As Skillen points out, the notion of a so-called 'managed democracy' in Russia under Putin is 'a nonsense, an oxymoron that fitted in the postmodernist arsenal of wordplay'.[52] Similarly, recent cultural policy represents a new paradoxical paradigm, in which the impossibility of conforming to this 'new model' generates a state of instability for those that are necessarily subject, and subjected, to its ideological norms. Although the periods are so distant from one another and the realities so different, it is clear that the mechanisms of power underlying Putinist Capitalist Realism are qualitatively similar to those of Stalinist Socialist Realism, and in fact demonstrate a great deal in common as performative systems of operation.

Russia under Putin is showing the symptoms of an exacerbated Capitalist Realism, brought on by nearly three decades of exposure to the untrammelled excesses of the brand of deregulated neoliberal capitalism sold to the country after the collapse of the Soviet Union. As such, the striking similarities between now and the period of high Stalinism do not represent a return to the past, but show the present system reaching a kind of entropic stage of development akin to the stagnation and conservatism of developed socialism. Capitalist Realism relies on hopelessness to sustain its own illusion – that there is no alternative to the status quo. As Fisher states, 'it is now impossible even to *imagine* a coherent alternative'.[53] This reality is experienced even more acutely in Russia than elsewhere, due to the hyper-extended nature of Putinist capitalism. There is no better summary explanation for the two-decade success of Putinism than this inconceivability of an alternative. If, for Fredric Jameson, postmodernism is the 'cultural logic of late capitalism', Putinism can be thought of as the cultural logic of Russian hyper-Capitalist Realism. On the one hand this presents formidable challenges to cultural production in contemporary Russia, as has been witnessed especially acutely since 2012. On the other hand, the outcomes are still far from decided while voices of resistance and alternative discourses refuse to be silenced, and continue to take the stage in the boldest of small theatres.

Notes

1   In chronological order, these are:
    1. 'O zashchite detei ot informatsii, prichiniaiushchei vred ikh zdorov'iu i razvitiiu', N 436-F3, 29 December 2010;
    2. 'O vnesenii izmenenii ... v chasti regulirovaniia deiatel'nosti nekommercheskikh organizatsii, vypolniaiushchikh funktsii inostrannogo agenta', N 121-F3, 20 July 2012;
    3. 'O vnesenii izmenenii ... v tseliakh zashchity detei ot informatsii, propagandiruiushchei otritsanie traditsionnykh semeinykh tsennostei', N 135-F3, 29 June 2013;
    4. 'O vnesenii izmenenii ... v tseliakh protivodeistviia oskorbleniiu religioznykh ubezhdenii i chuvstv grazhdan', N 136-F3, 29 June 2013;
    5. 'O vnesenii izmenenii ... v sviazi s sovershenstvovaniem pravovogo regulirovaniia v sfere ispol'zovaniia russkogo iazyka', N 190238-6, 5 May 2014;
    6. 'Ob utverzhdenii Osnov gosudarstvennoi kul'turnoi politiki', N 808, 24 December 2014;
    7. 'O deiatel'nosti na territorii Rossiiskoi Federatsii inostrannoi ili mezhdunarodnoi nepravitel'stvennoi organizatsii, v otnoshenii kotoroi priniato reshenie o priznanii nezhelatel'noi na territorii Rossiiskoi Federatsii ee deiatel'nosti', N 129-F3, 23 May 2015;
    8. 'O gosudarstvennoi programme "Patrioticheskoe vospitanie grazhdan Rossiiskoi Federatsii na 2016–2020 gody"', N 1493, 30 December 2015;
    9. 'Strategiia gosudarstvennoi kul'turnoi politiki na period do 2030 goda', N 326-r, 29 February 2016;
    10. 'O vnesenii izmenenii ... dopolnitel'nykh mer protivodeistviia terrorizma i obespecheniia obshchestvennoi bezopasnosti', N 374-F3 & N 375-F3, 6 July 2016.

Additionally, new laws have criminalised the spreading of fake news and "disrespect to authority". The three laws are: 'Ob informatsii, ob informatsionnykh tekhnologiiakh i zashchite informatsii' (N 149-F3), 'O SMI' (N 2124–1) and 'Oskorblenie predstavitelia vlasti' (N 319). Restrictive changes to these laws all received preliminary government approval in January 2019 and were implemented shortly afterwards. See: 'Komitet gosdumy podderzhal zakonproekty Klishasa o zaprete feikovykh novostei i oskorblenii vlasti v internete', *Novaia Gazeta*, 21 January 2019. www.novayagazeta.ru/news/2019/01/21/148524-komitet-gosdumy-podderzhal-zakonoproekty-klishasa-o-zaprete-feykovyh-novostey-i-oskorblenii-vlasti-v-internete (accessed 24 February 2019).

2 See John Freedman, 'Contemporary Russian Drama: The Journey from Stagnation to a Golden Age', *Theatre Journal* 62,3 (2010), 389–420; and Nika Parkhomovskaia, '2008–2012: Teatral'nye innovatsii v deystvii', *Teatr* 32 (2017), 16–20.

3 Vladimir Medinsky became Minister of Culture on 21 May 2012. He is well known for his criticism of contemporary art and support of military-patriotic culture and themes in the arts. He has complained of a culture of 'unhealthy liberalism' in the theatre. See 'Medinskii "zhaleet" khudrukov, dopuskaiushchikh netsenzurnuiu leksiku v teatral'nykh postanovkakh', *TASS*, 15 November 2018. tass.ru/kultura/5797454 (accessed 24 February 2019).

4 Mezdrich was subsequently *persona non grata* in state theatres and it was three years before he was able to find a new position, at Praktika in Moscow. For the scandal, see: 'Novosibirsk: Direktor uvolen iz-za "Tangeizera"', BBC Russian, 29 March 2015. www.bbc.com/russian/russia/2015/03/150329_russia_novosibirsk_theatre_director (accessed 24 February 2019).

5 For research on the so-called 'managed democracy' of the Putin-era political system, see Andrew Wilson, *Virtual Politics: Faking Democracy in the Post-Soviet World* (New Haven, CT: Yale University Press, 2005).

6 'Reguliruiushchikh protsessy kul'turnogo razvitiia v Rossiiskoi Federatsii' [...] 'obespechit' bolee vysokoe kachestvo obshchestva', [...] 'formirovanie nravstvennoi, otvetstvennoi, samostoiatel'no mysliashchei, tvorcheskoi lichnosti' [...] 'neot"emlemoi chast'iu strategii natsionalnoi bezopasnosti Rossiiskoi Federatsii' [...] 'garmonizatsii obshchestvennykh otnoshenii [...] sokhraneniia edinogo kul'turnogo prostranstva i territorial'noi tselostnosti Rossii'. 'Fundamentals', 1–3.

7 Culture is defined as 'the sum total of formal and informal institutions, phenomena and factors which influence the preservation, production, translation and dissemination of spiritual values (ethical, aesthetic, intellectual, and civic, etc.)'. 'Fundamentals', 4.

8 'Fundamentals', 2.

9 'Obsuzhdenie "Osnov gosudarstvennoi kul'turnoi politiki RF"', Meierkhol'd Centre, Moscow, June 2014 (unpublished transcript). A video recording of the meeting is available at: https://www.youtube.com/watch?v=kCXLBeSksaA

10 See Steven Kotkin, *Magnetic Mountain: Stalinism as a Civilization* (Berkeley, CA: University of California Press, 1995), 191–221.

11 Dan Healey claims that the 'traditional/non-traditional' opposition had been circulating 'in media and popular sexological discourse for some twenty years' before the introduction of the new law in 2013. See Dan Healey, *Russian Homophobia from Stalin to Sochi* (London: Bloomsbury Academic, 2018), 10. For an overview of the genealogy of this new term, see ibid., 6–13.

12 '[…] *otritsaiushchaia semeinye tsennosti, propagandiruiushchaia netraditsionnye seksual'nye otnosheniia i formiruiushchaia neuvazhenie k roditeliam i/ili drugim chlenam sem'i'. O zashchite detei* (2013 edn), 4.
13 However, this distinction can be traced back at least to Stalin's reintroduction of the pre-revolutionary law against sodomy in 1933–4, which was re-repealed in the 1990s.
14 The term 'pseudo-culture' does not appear in the official text of the 'Fundamentals'. However, it was clearly present in an earlier draft, because it was criticized by the director Kirill Serebrennikov at an official consultation on the draft document with cultural figures at the Meierkhol'd Centre in Moscow in June 2014.
15 See Aleksei Iablokov, 'V 2014 gody gosudarstvo vser'ez voz'metsia za kul'turu', *Vedomosti*, 11 October 2013. www.vedomosti.ru/lifestyle/articles/2013/10/11/v-2014-godu-gosudarstvo-vserez-vozmetsya-za-kulturu#cut (accessed 24 February 2019).
16 See Konstantin Rudnitskii, *Russian and Soviet Theater, 1905–1932*, trans. by Roxane Permar (New York: Harry N. Abrams, Inc., 1988), 45.
17 '*Kachestvennoe obnovlenie lichnosti*'. 'Fundamentals', 3.
18 See, for example, Regine Robin, *Socialist Realism: An Impossible Aesthetic*, trans. by Catherine Porter (Stanford, CA: Stanford University Press, 1992), 299. For a more general history of Socialist Realism as a genre, see Katerina Clark, *The Soviet Novel: History as Ritual*, 2nd edn (Chicago: University of Chicago Press, 1985).
19 'Standard Russian literary language' [*etalonnyi russkii literaturnyi iazyk*] is the term used in the 'Fundamentals' for that which should be promoted and used. See 'Fundamentals', 8.
20 In 1928 Viktor Shklovsky criticized Maksim Gor'ky, who played a key role in the defining of what became Soviet Socialist Realist literary language norms in the 1930s, stating that 'he takes the prose of the eighteen-nineties as his linguistic norm. He takes purely temporary rules, and practises [them] as literary dogma'. For this and more, see Robin, 176–7.
21 Work that does contain 'obscene' language is strictly prohibited to minors, and must visibly show a warning sign on the front cover or venue entrance (the exception to this is film/cinema, where there is zero tolerance). Lexicon defined as 'obscene' by state communications department Roskomnadzor includes all Russian words derived from four generally known root words – prudishly listed as those beginning with '*b*', '*p*', '*kh*' and '*e*' in Russian. See: 'Roskomnadzor poiasnil zhurnalistam, chto takoe mat', BBC Russian, 25 December 2013. https://www.bbc.com/russian/russia/2013/12/131225_roskomnadzor_obscene_words_list (accessed 24 August 2018).
22 'Obsuzhdenie', Meierkhol'd Centre, 2014.
23 '[…] *kul'turu vidiat sluzhankoi ideologii, s pomoshch'iu etogo dokumenta kul'turu pytaiutsia vtisnut' v «prokrustovo lozhe» ideologii*'. 'Obsuzhdenie', Meierkhol'd Centre, 2014.
24 Hannah Arendt, *The Origins of Totalitarianism* (New York: Harcourt Brace, 1951; repr. Schocken Books, 2004), 509.
25 Mark Fisher, *Capitalist Realism: Is There No Alternative?* (Alresford: Zero Books, 2009), 54.
26 Ibid., 76.
27 '*ugroza gumanitarnogo krizisa*'. 'Fundamentals', 3. This phrase is exactly repeated in the 'Strategy'. See 'Strategy', 6. The idea of creating a new cultural policy will be later developed in the 'Strategy' into the officially titled 'new model of cultural politics'. It is defined as, among other things, 'the spreading of Russian traditional social values' and 'the harmonious combining of the interests of national security, unity in the cultural sphere, and the ethnocultural diversity of the country'. See 'Strategy', 35.

28 'negativnaia otsenka znachitel'nykh periodov otechestvennoi istorii, rasprostranenie lozhnogo predstavleniia ob istoricheskoi otstalosti Rossii'. 'Fundamentals', 3. Likewise, 'Strategy', 6.
29 Yuri Lotman considers 'forgetting' as one of three forms of collective memory in any given culture, which is to say that forgetting is no less active a process than remembering, and is just as important. See Yu. A. Lotman and B. A. Uspensky, 'On the Semiotic Mechanism of Culture', *New Literary History* 9, no. 2 (1978): 211–32 (215–16).
30 Fisher, *Capitalist Realism*, 56.
31 'vsedozvolennost' i nasilie'. 'Strategy', 7.
32 Daphne Skillen, *Freedom of Speech in Russia: Politics and Media from Gorbachev to Putin* (Abingdon: Routledge, 2017), 18. In several of Fedor Dostoevsky's novels, from *Crime and Punishment* (1866) and *The Demons* (1871–2) through to *The Brothers Karamazov* (1879–80), the young male protagonists arrogantly and deludedly claim 'all-permissibility' for themselves, i.e. the right to exercise free will in an untrammelled way – with tragic consequences.
33 Peter Pomerantsev, 'Non-Linear War', LRB Blog, 28 March 2014. www.lrb.co.uk/blog/2014/march/non-linear-war (accessed 25 February 2019).
34 'Strategy', 31–2.
35 'Strategy', 4–5.
36 It is entitled '*O gosudarstvennoi programme "Patrioticheskoe vospitanie grazhdan Rossiiskoi Federatsii na 2016–2020 gody"'* (N 1493, 30 December 2015).
37 Michel Foucault, *Discipline and Punish: The Birth of the Prison*, trans. by Alan Sheridan (London: Allen Lane, 1977; repr. Harmondsworth: Penguin, 1991), 140.
38 'Strategy', 36–7.
39 Fisher, *Capitalist Realism*, 16.
40 The original is: 'One is not born, but rather *becomes*, a woman.' See Simone de Beauvoir, *The Second Sex* (New York: Vintage Books, 2003), 301.
41 The theatre critic Grigorii Zaslavsky wrote in 2004 of 'a foreign bottle with poisoned ink' that has 'sailed from England'. See Birgit Beumers and Mark Lipovetsky, *Performing Violence: Literary and Theatrical Experiments of New Russian Drama* (Bristol: Intellect, 2009), 36.
42 Maksym Kurochkin, Ivan Ugarov and Zarema Zaudinova, *Lena and Misha*, trans. by Sasha Dugdale (unpublished, 2018), 25.
43 For a brief history of the troubled production, see: 'Otmena "Nureeva": tri versii sluchivshegosia', BBC Russian, 10 July 2017. bbc.com/russian/features-40372730 (accessed 9 February 2018).
44 See Bolshoi Theatre website: https://www.bolshoi.ru/performances/1025/roles/#20171210190000 (accessed 9 February 2018). Paradoxically, the audiences for the two sold-out performances were largely drawn from the political as well as the cultural elite.
45 'Spektakl' Serebrennikova "Chelovek-Podushka" proveriaiut sledovateli', *RIA Novosti*, 3 July 2013. https://ria.ru/culture/20130703/947409699.html (accessed 9 February 2018).
46 This has been stated, for example, by Marat Gatsalov of the Aleksandrinsky theatre, Mark Zakharov of the Lenkom theatre, and Konstantin Bogomolov. See, respectively: 'Khudruk Novoi stseny Aleksandrinki: "Samotsenzura ub'et teatra kak vid iskusstva"', *Rosbalt*, 13 April 2015: www.rosbalt.ru/piter/2015/04/13/1388293.html; Artur Solomonov, 'Mark Zakharov: samotsenzura igraet vse bol'shuiu rol'', *Artursolmonov.ru*, 24 December 2014: artursolomonov.ru/mark-zaharov-samotsenzura-igraet-vse-bolshuyu-rol/; Shestakova, Anna, 'Chto takoe politicheskii teatr: Opros izvestnykh moskovskikh rezhisserov i

khudrukov', *Teatr*, No. 8 (2012): oteatre.info/chto-takoe-politicheskij-teatr-opros-izvestnyh-moskovskih-rezhisserov-i-hudrukov/ (all accessed 26 February 2019).
47 'Pskov: teatr ne otmenit spektakl'' iz-za zhalob akterov', BBC Russian, 14 April 2015. http://www.bbc.com/russian/society/2015/04/150414_pskov_theatre_play_scandal> (accessed 9 February 2018).
48 See 'Strategy', 8. See also Transparency International's report on the state funding of theatres, by Igor Sergeev et al., 'Kak rukovoditeli gosudarstvennykh teatrov platiat gonorary sami sebe', *Transparency International Russia*, 23 October 2017. https://transparency.org.ru/special/teatr/ (accessed 8 February 2018).
49 For evidence of the latter, see: Eleanor Bindman, *Social Rights in Russia: From Imperfect Past to Uncertain Future* (Abingdon: Routledge, 2018).
50 '*Deistvuiushchie dokumenty strategicheskogo planirovaniia Rossiiskoi Federatsii ne v polnoi mere uchityvaiut strategicheskuiu znachimost' potentsiala kul'tury*'. 'Strategy', 10.
51 'Ibid., 35.
52 Skillen, *Freedom of Speech in Russia*, 265.
53 Fisher, *Capitalist Realism*, 2.

Bibliography

Primary Sources (Chronological)

'O zashchite detei ot informatsii,... propagandiruiushchei otritsanie traditsionnykh semeinykh tsennostei', N 436-F3, 29 December 2010. http://www.consultant.ru/document/cons_doc_LAW_108808/ (accessed 24 August 2018).

'O vnesenii izmenenii... v chasti regulirovaniia deiatel'nosti nekommercheskikh organizatsii, vypolniaiushchikh funktsii inostrannogo agenta', N 121-F3, 20 July 2012. http://www.consultant.ru/document/cons_doc_LAW_132900/ (accessed 24 August 2018).

'O vnesenii izmenenii... v tseliakh zashchity detei ot informatsii, propagandiruiushchei otritsanie traditsionnykh semeinykh tsennostei', N 135-F3, 29 June 2013. http://www.consultant.ru/document/cons_doc_LAW_148269/ (accessed 26 February 2019).

'O vnesenii izmenenii... v tseliakh protivodeistviia oskorbleniiu religioznykh ubezhdenii i chuvstv grazhdan', N 136-F3, 29 June 2013. http://www.consultant.ru/document/cons_doc_LAW_148270/ (accessed 24 August 2018).

'O vnesenii izmenenii... v sviazi s sovershenstvovaniem pravovogo regulirovaniia v sfere ispol'zovaniia russkogo iazyka', N 190238-6, 5 May 2014. http://asozd2.duma.gov.ru/main.nsf/%28SpravkaNew%29?OpenAgent&RN=190238-6&02 (accessed 24 August 2018).

'Obsuzhdenie "Osnov gosudarstvennoi kul'turnoi politiki RF"', Meierkhol'd Centre, Moscow, June 2014 (unpublished transcript).

'Kontseptsiia gosudarstvennoi semeinoi politiki Rossiiskoi Federatsii na period do 2025 goda', N 1618-r, 25 August 2014. http://www.consultant.ru/document/cons_doc_LAW_167897/ (accessed 24 August 2018).

'Ob utverzhdenii Osnov gosudarstvennoi kul'turnoi politiki', N 808, 24 December 2014. http://www.consultant.ru/document/cons_doc_LAW_172706/ (accessed 24 August 2018).

'O deiatel'nosti na territorii Rossiiskoi Federatsii inostrannoi ili mezhdunarodnoi nepravitel'stvennoi organizatsii, v otnoshenii kotoroi priniato reshenie o priznanii

nezhelatel'noi na territorii Rossiiskoi Federatsii ee deiatel'nosti', N 129-F3, 23 May 2015. http://www.consultant.ru/document/cons_doc_LAW_179979/ (accessed 24 August 2018).
'O gosudarstvennoi programme "Patrioticheskoe vospitanie grazhdan Rossiiskoi Federatsii na 2016–2020 gody"', N 1493, 30 December 2015. https://mvd.consultant.ru/documents/1055819 (accessed 24 August 2018).
'Strategiia gosudarstvennoi kul'turnoi politiki na period do 2030 goda', N 326-r, 29 February 2016. http://www.consultant.ru/document/cons_doc_LAW_194820/ (accessed 24 August 2018).
'O vnesenii izmenenii . . . dopolnitel'nykh mer protivodeistviia terrorizma i obespecheniia obshchestvennoi bezopasnosti', N 374-F3 & N 375-F3, 6 July 2016. <http://www.consultant.ru/document/cons_doc_LAW_201078/> http://www.consultant.ru/document/cons_doc_LAW_201087/ (accessed 24 August 2018).
Kurochkin Maksym, Ugarov Ivan and Zaudinova Zarema. *Lena and Misha*, trans. by Sasha Dugdale (unpublished, 2018).

Secondary sources

Arendt, Hannah. *The Origins of Totalitarianism*. New York: Harcourt Brace, 1951; repr. Schoken Books, 2004.
Beumers, Birgit, and Mark Lipovetsky. *Performing Violence: Literary and Theatrical Experiments of New Russian Drama*. Bristol: Intellect, 2009.
Bindman, Eleanor. *Social Rights in Russia: From Imperfect Past to Uncertain Future*. Abingdon: Routledge, 2018.
Clark, Katerina. *The Soviet Novel: History as Ritual*, 2nd edn. Chicago: University of Chicago Press, 1985.
Fisher, Mark. *Capitalist Realism: Is There No Alternative?* Alresford: Zero Books, 2009.
Foucault, Michel. *Discipline and Punish: The Birth of the Prison*, trans. by Alan Sheridan. London: Allen Lane, 1977; repr. Harmondsworth: Penguin, 1991.
Healey, Dan. *Russian Homophobia from Stalin to Sochi*. New York: Bloomsbury Academic, 2017.
Iablokov, Aleksei. 'V 2014 gody gosudarstvo vser'ez voz'metsia za kul'turu'. *Vedomosti*, 11 October 2013. www.vedomosti.ru/lifestyle/articles/2013/10/11/v-2014-godu-gosudarstvo-vserez-vozmetsya-za-kulturu#cut (accessed 24 February 2019).
'Khudruk Novoi stseny Aleksandrinki: "Samotsenzura ub'et teatra kak vid iskusstva". *Rosbalt*, 13 April 2015. www.rosbalt.ru/piter/2015/04/13/1388293.html (accessed 26 February 2019).
'Komitet gosdumy podderzhal zakonproekty Klishasa o zaprete feikovykh novostei i oskorblenii vlasti v internete'. *Novaia Gazeta*, 21 January 2019. www.novayagazeta.ru/news/2019/01/21/148524-komitet-gosdumy-podderzhal-zakonoproekty-klishasa-o-zaprete-feykovyh-novostey-i-oskorblenii-vlasti-v-internete [accessed 24 February 2019].
Kotkin, Stephen. *Magnetic Mountain: Stalinism as a Civilization*. Berkeley, CA: University of California Press, 1995.
Lotman, Yu. A., and B. A. Uspensky. 'On the Semiotic Mechanism of Culture'. *New Literary History* 9, no. 2 (1978): 211–32.
'Medinskii "zhaleet" khudrukov, dopuskaiushchikh netsenzurnuiu leksiku v teatral'nykh postanovkakh'. *TASS*, 15 November 2018. tass.ru/kultura/5797454 (accessed 24 February 2019).

'Novosibirsk: Direktor uvolen iz-za "Tangeizera"'. BBC Russian, 29 March 2015. www.bbc.com/russian/russia/2015/03/150329_russia_novosibirsk_theatre_director (accessed 24 February 2019).

'Otmena "Nureeva": tri versii sluchivshegosia'. BBC Russian, 10 July 2017. bbc.com/russian/features-40372730 (accessed 8 February 2018).

Pomerantsev, Peter. 'Non-Linear War', LRB Blog, 28 March 2014. www.lrb.co.uk/blog/2014/march/non-linear-war (accessed 25 February 2019).

'Pskov: teatr ne otmenit spektakl' iz-za zhalob akterov'. BBC Russian, 14 April 2015. http://www.bbc.com/russian/society/2015/04/150414_pskov_theatre_play_scandal (accessed 9 February 2018).

Robin, Regine. *Socialist Realism: An Impossible Aesthetic*, trans. by Catherine Porter. Stanford, CA: Stanford University Press, 1992.

'Roskomnadzor poiasnil zhurnalistam, chto takoe mat'. BBC Russian, 25 December 2013. https://www.bbc.com/russian/russia/2013/12/131225_roskomnadzor_obscene_words_list (accessed 24 August 2018).

Rudnitskii, Konstantin. *Russian and Soviet Theater, 1905–1932*, trans. by Roxane Permar. New York: Harry N. Abrams, Inc., 1988.

Sergeev, Igor, et al. 'Kak rukovoditeli gosudarstvennykh teatrov platiat gonorary sami sebe'. *Transparency International Russia*, 23 October 2017. https://transparency.org.ru/special/teatr/ (accessed 8 February 2018).

Shestakova, Anna. 'Chto takoe politicheskii teatr: Opros izvestnykh moskovskikh rezhisserov i khudrukov'. *Teatr.* 8 (2012). oteatre.info/chto-takoe-politicheskij-teatr-opros-izvestnyh-moskovskih-rezhisserov-i-hudrukov/ (accessed 26 February 2019).

Skillen, Daphne. *Freedom of Speech in Russia: Politics and Media from Gorbachev to Putin*. Abingdon: Routledge, 2017.

Solomonov, Artur. 'Mark Zakharov: samotsenzura igraet vse bol'shuiu rol''. *Artursolmonov.ru*, 24 December 2014. artursolmonov.ru/mark-zaharov-samotsenzura-igraet-vse-bolshuyu-rol/ (accessed 26 February 2019).

'Spektakl' Serebrennikova "Chelovek-Podushka" proveriaiut sledovateli'. *RIA Novosti*, 3 July 2013. https://ria.ru/culture/20130703/947409699.html (accessed 9 February 2018).

Wilson, Andrew. *Virtual Politics: Faking Democracy in the Post-Soviet World*. New Haven, CT: Yale University Press, 2005.

4

Conversation with Mikhail Durnenkov and Maria Kroupnik (Liubimovka Festival, Moscow, September 2017)

J. A. E. Curtis

> Mikhail Durnenkov has been one of the key figures of the 'New Drama' movement, writing plays together with his brother Viacheslav, and also on his own. In recent years he has served as one of the Artistic Directors of the annual Liubimovka theatre festival in Moscow. He is a fine writer, but also a born pedagogue: he runs the festival's rehearsed readings and discussions with firm efficiency and wit, and always offers respectful and constructive suggestions to young writers. Maria Kroupnik has been closely associated with Teatr.doc and the Liubimovka festival, and as well as her lecturing work has become a key figure in delivering Edinburgh's 'Class Act' workshops to young people across Russia, as described by her later in this volume. Our conversation touched upon the prospects for contemporary drama in Russian theatres, the functions of the Liubimovka festival, the level of participation by Ukrainian and Belarusian authors before and after the 2014 annexation of Crimea by the Russians, and the prospects for future collaborations with them.

JAEC Why is there not much contemporary drama being staged in mainstream Russian theatres at the moment?

MD Because there hasn't been a hand-over at management level. All the major state theatres are still run by very old men in Moscow, with perhaps the exception of the Theatre of the Nations [Teatr Natsiy], or by middle-aged people, and then there's the Gogol' Centre – well, we'll see what their fate will be [the Gogol' Centre's Artistic Director, Kirill Serebrennikov, was placed under house arrest for nearly two years in 2017–19]. And so it all ends up going into decline [...] and there's no new generation taking over. Young people are the ones who should stage contemporary drama. [...]

There are certain things which help to maintain the present system. Despite the severity of the laws, there's the fact that people don't feel obliged to observe them –

they're compensated for by not necessarily being implemented. [...] Nobody feels confident in the future in this country, not a single person. And so each person seizes what they can at every opportunity, every moment, because tomorrow... there's a very characteristic proverb for Russia, which is 'Never say never!'... You could end up in poverty or in prison at any moment, so for as long as you're on top, you need to lead a full life, take everything from life... [...]

Another reason why contemporary plays aren't put on in those mainstream theatres is financial. Theatres these days are required to do quite a lot in the sense of earning money, [...] so theatres are regarded as businesses, and therefore they want guaranteed takings, and if the auditorium is large, and if it's a well-known institution, then they'll go for a classic with a big reputation, whereas with a young dramatist there's always a risk, the question will be – is it going to sell? And on the other hand, then there are ideologically motivated critics: a mass audience comes along, and the theatre has to consider its moral convictions – what is good, and what is bad? And audience perceptions are hard to work with – I know people who are very innocent and who leave a show utterly offended by the words 'sperm' and 'bum'. And when it's the most shocking words, then each time there'll be letters and complaints. And we've been obliged to remove things from shocking scenes – not in Moscow, of course, but when we go elsewhere in Russia.

JAEC You have a small auditorium at the Liubimovka Festival, but there seems to be a flood of young people here, a new audience has emerged. Does that change anything?

MK The spectator who comes to the Liubimovka is different from the typical theatregoer who comes to Teatr.doc, but there is some overlap.

MD For a start, half of the people who come to the Liubimovka are theatre-makers themselves. And unlike those who come to Teatr.doc, we get young theatre critics and specialists coming, and young directors and young actors, half the auditorium, people who have some sort of connection... and also foreigners. 'Ordinary' spectators make up about a quarter probably. [...] Some people might feel indignant about it, but we hold this festival for the benefit of the young dramatists we've invited, for the readings and discussions, it's to help them. Sometimes people tell us we're too kind, but we're not being kind, we're working for that person who's sitting up at the front, so that s/he should reflect and start to write better. It's for the authors. There's an element of 'show': people have got used to coming to these readings, and they like them, but we don't care whether the play pleases them, what we're seeking is constructive opinions for the authors.

MK In that respect it was very valuable to us to hear what, for example, Andrei Ivanov [a Moscow-based playwright] had to say this year: that his play had come into being because of the energy he had gained previously at the Liubimovka: that meant that it had all worked.

MD Yes, it worked. And you may have noticed that we mention it if a certain author was commended previously, and now he's made it into the main programme: we particularly keep track of this, of how an author develops and grows, to give him three chances as a minimum to show himself in the main programme, and to see whether he changes and rises to a higher level – and if not, we take someone else. We're not like an agency for actors, we can't concern ourselves with a single individual for his entire life – but for as long as he has a certain creative immaturity, with his first play, we enable him to develop, to develop very rapidly, and to become a professional author, and make his own way.

JAEC   And even those who are on the 'non-competition programme' [a showcase for plays by more established authors], they're playwrights who have come through the Liubimovka previously...

MD/MK   Yes!

MD   We try to make sure that there are new authors there, that there are Liubimovka authors. [...]

MK   And it's incredibly important for our authors if their plays get taken up somewhere abroad: their rankings immediately improve.

MD   It's also important that they should get to look around, that they shouldn't remain provincial authors, shouldn't reinvent the wheel...

MK   That's why international projects are very important to us: it enables us to take authors out there, let them get to know a different system, and we can unpack it for the authors. Our educational programme is also devised in order to push back some of these frontiers. [...]

JAEC   And how are Russian-speaking authors from other countries perceived, since they've always participated? How do people regard this – is it unimportant, or all part of the whole picture?

MD   Our authors have very often come from other countries. My inner conviction is that any differences have largely been stylistic, rather than in people's psychological make-up. The Belarusians are distinctive as far as form is concerned. So until recent times the differences were mostly formal: in style, form, relationship to time, chronotopes. Any difference in regime has an influence on the chronotope.

JAEC   So the political and the social do have an impact?

MD   Yes, they're impossible to separate, so the Belarusian plays are always concerned, so to speak, with the future. But now the differences in themes have increased. Russian plays have started to move towards the marginal, in the sense of depicting marginal types in society, people at the bottom of society, society's outsiders, because nobody else is treating this subject – official culture pays no attention to it, and there's no outlet for that social energy, whereas dramatists are continuing to describe all this just as before. And this difference between realities is growing more and more, in what's being shown on TV and what non-commercial, individual dramatists are writing. And I am concerned about this, because if previously I had some notion of where these plays might get staged, then nowadays I am less and less sure who needs them in this country, in the sense of productions.

JAEC That's very apparent: your audiences at the Liubimovka are extremely young, and the authors are too, and they're mostly writing about their own lives.

MD To take another example, we have an author here, the Ukrainian Natal'ia Blok, and her play [*All This Fucking Mess Upsets Me*, 2017] is sharply differentiated and free, and you can feel that the author allows herself to say anything she wants. Why? Because nothing is going to hinder this author, and she even allows herself irony when she writes about what things are like in Ukraine at present. [...]

JAEC We've been talking about whether you can feel the differences in the plays and the language of playwrights from different countries. I think I'm right that it's become quite a rarity for plays to be staged in Moscow by authors, say, from Ukraine?

MK [...] In drama there's the example of the Meierkhol'd Centre which staged a play by Natasha Vorozhbit, and then there's the Liubimovka, which every year brings authors here and allows plays to be heard from Ukraine.

JAEC Are you taking any particular measures to encourage authors from there? Or do they just submit their work?

MD They don't 'just submit' ... We make use of our one key tool, which is our reputation. Our reputation is that we don't work with the state, and we don't take money: because if we were to accept grants from the Ministry of Culture, say, we would deprive ourselves of our Ukrainian playwrights. We speak out on political themes, and articulate positions which show that we are always ready to hear people, and we try to make sure that our selection panel includes people from these countries. This year it was Den Gumennyi – every year we have Ukrainian selectors, but this year he couldn't come to the festival itself because he has a project in the Donetsk region, a humanitarian mission, and so he's there, and he couldn't come. [...] So this is again a question of reputation: he is the guarantee of our integrity. Den Gumennyi is running Post Play, which is an independent theatre in Kyiv: there's a very powerful movement now of independent theatres there, perhaps about seventy, and this is one of them. Earlier we had Natasha Vorozhbit, but she has begun to work a lot with young people, and so she doesn't have the time to do it.

JAEC If I remember rightly she has said that she didn't want to come any more, for ideological reasons? [...]

MD She won't ever come here now. There will be a possibility for us to meet when we're with Nicola McCartney[1] in Edinburgh in November [2017]; and maybe we'll be able to get to the premiere of her new play in London. We'll be there in Edinburgh to celebrate twenty-five years of the 'Class Act' scheme. [...] The main thing for us is to preserve our position as an independent competition, which doesn't depend on all these political difficulties, and to keep the competition going. But all we can do is keep the door open, we can't entice people here.

JAEC So you say that the most important thing is your reputation. Is it possible to say that the present situation has been shaped by the fact that in the past you had so many projects in common, because you all used to travel back and forth between Russia, Ukraine and Belarus: what were relations like in the past, say, with Belarus?

MD There were a lot of contacts! I can remember, for example, from my own experience, I used to go to the Week of Contemporary Drama festival in Kyiv – it's a sort of large cooperative forum. I gave a masterclass and talked there with dramatists, and gave a talk. Or else I used to travel to Belarus, and opened (it's been going for about five years now) a Centre for Playwriting and Directing. Directors in Belarus don't often put on Belarusian playwrights, and at the invitation of the Belarusian Centre for Playwriting and Directing, I was invited to, if you like, run a seminar. We went to a place near Minsk – ten dramatists and ten directors – and we worked together, divided into pairs and wrote new plays. And now that has been happening every year since then.

JAEC So all these joint undertakings came about quite naturally – you had shared purposes and interests?

MD Yes, yes... For example, Nicola McCartney invited me to work with 'Class Act' in Ukraine, but I couldn't go to Kyiv at that point.

JAEC And so the 'New Drama' movement, and verbatim drama, that was all a shared endeavour?

MD Up until 2014 we might have described Natasha Vorozhbit as a Russian dramatist, or a Kyiv dramatist, or a Ukrainian dramatist, but now nobody can say anything imprecise like that anymore.

MK There was a situation where Ukrainian dramatists were more often staged in Russia than in Ukraine.

JAEC Russian-language dramatists?

MD Yes, Russian-language ones – there was very little writing in Ukrainian previously, and now they are almost all going over to writing in Ukrainian. [...]

JAEC So the Russian language remains crucial?

MD That is so for the time being ... But it's already changing. So, for example, the shift of one sector of Ukrainian theatre-makers to using Facebook in Ukrainian is a marker of that: the fact that they're describing their everyday life on Facebook in Ukrainian, that's a symbol. And in Belarus too, but the fact that they have two languages there makes things more complicated ...

JAEC [...] This year at the Liubimovka there's not a huge number of Ukrainians: it's not particularly noticeable, but maybe there are slightly fewer than previously? Or is it as ever?

MK As regards the submitted plays, it's pretty much as ever. But maybe there are fewer people who've actually come from there, that's my impression.

MD Ukrainians, you mean? I think there are fewer, but I'm hoping it's some sort of hiccup. If you looked at the statistics, it would be a bit up and down. But people submitted their plays, some people who had submitted previously submitted again, but they didn't all get through to the final stages.

JAEC My impression is that when there were quite a lot of Ukrainians here, they wrote largely about youth problems and social problems,

MD Ukrainians? And always about the war ...

JAEC ...yes, about the ongoing conflict within Ukraine, but not particularly about the international context of that, about Ukraine's relations with Russia. Maybe that's for a lot of different reasons? They want to send their plays here, to Moscow ...

MD Drama concerns itself with people in a war, and not with war in the political sense. They don't want to say that it's right or wrong, [...] what they're saying is: 'we are concerned about the soldiers in the war, not what side they're on' – and so the humanist tradition is being carried forward. The theme of the war is one which it is quite impossible to stage in Russia at the moment, but it's an obligatory element of Ukrainian playwriting.

JAEC But, for example, the occupation of Crimea – that's not a theme for the Ukrainian writers?

MD No, it's the internal fighting. The war. But see how terrifically they're developing, they've come a long way. Take for example that play [*All This Fucking Mess Upsets Me*] by Blok, which I like very much, very much indeed. She has already allowed herself self-irony about it all. [...] These are people who have already got used to the idea that war is happening, that they are surviving it, and they allow themselves to take a couple of steps back, and to take a look at things from the side. And of course I observe all this with huge delight. There's a great freedom to it; and it reminds me, when Natal'ia Blok talks about what's happening, [...] about lesbians gathering together, and someone is involved who is of an indeterminate gender, someone else who's described as '*ono*', using a neuter pronoun, this is all our 1990s all over again ... it's that kind of freedom!

JAEC   So as far as the question of collaborating with Ukrainian dramatists is concerned, how do you see that developing in the future?

MD   The Belarus Free Theatre used to organize their drama competition with texts submitted in several languages. And at that point you start to ask yourself, is it possible to compare plays written in different languages? It's probably possible, but the people who are going to select the plays and be on the jury, they're going to need to be able to read all those languages fluently. [...] So, for example, Natasha Vorozhbit is equally fluent in Russian and in Ukrainian, and she needs to choose now. I'm afraid that we are not going to be able to do that, and as soon as the Ukrainians switch over to using the Ukrainian language, then we're going to lose them. We're already losing our links in fact, because of the unwillingness of Ukrainian dramatists to come to us here, and the difficulties our people have in trying to travel to see them: all this weakens our connections with them.

JAEC   Because previously there were lots of links, for example festivals, and these were largely friendly relations?

MD   And creative ones as well. You'd get grants for joint projects, for example.

MK   And these were professional links, because we would travel to Ukraine to festivals, to hear plays, and to run masterclasses – Elena Gremina and Mikhail Ugarov and Mikhail Durnenkov. There was a time when the Week of Contemporary Drama festival was developing very actively, and they gathered together people from different regions of Ukraine, and in certain regions other centres sprang up which began to make themselves known. But now the focus of attention of our Ukrainian colleagues is in a different direction, towards Europe, towards Great Britain, (**MD**: towards Germany!), towards Germany and towards international projects.

MD   They're working really well with the Germans, whereas Russia, for example, has traditionally been linked to Great Britain, to the Royal Court and all that. We're seeing Ukrainian dramatists winning German theatre competitions.

JAEC   And for the Belarusians it's Poland?

MD   Poland ... but in Belarus there's also a very strong Goethe Institute with lots of activities, and they often get staged in Germany and in Austria, German-speaking countries.

JAEC   And what about Belarus? I've looked through your programmes over a period of ten years, and I've noticed that Pavel Priazhko is the author who has been more frequently staged than any other, not only from Belarus, but altogether.

MK Dmitry Bogoslavsky too.

MD You mean at the Liubimovka?

MK He's a writer who has been sending his plays to the Liubimovka for many years already, he's very productive, and he's very good.

MD Priazhko is a really modern artist, and that means that every new work of his is some sort of new experiment. He doesn't repeat himself, and it's not work that is targeted at a particular theatre. There's an attempt to discover his own limits, and to go beyond those. And by way there's also Konstantin Steshik, who's also featured here: he's also a researcher, although he has his own lyrical intonations, which are more or less similar in all of his plays. But Priazhko: with some of his plays, it's as though a completely different person had written each one, and that's what makes him so interesting, he's always opening up new facets.

JAEC Yes, I was just intrigued that at a Moscow festival the most popular writer should be someone who's appeared from elsewhere – but perhaps this isn't in fact an important issue? This year you have quite a lot of Belarusian authors.

MD Yes, and quite a few of them are here as part of the 'off-competition' programme, which includes Konstantin Steshik, Dmitry Bogoslavsky and Oleg Mikhailov.

MK And also Andrei Ivanov, who has now moved to Moscow.

JAEC Yes, I couldn't quite understand . . . He lives where?

MD He lives here.

JAEC So does he consider himself a Belarusian author, or . . .

MD Minsk-Moscow! For the moment it's Moscow. In Belarus that's also in fact a question: if they were to start staging Belarusian authors in Belarus, then I don't think there would be such a steady flow of them at the Liubimovka as before.

JAEC I was talking to Tania Arcimovich [a Belarusian commentator on the arts], who told me that in recent times dual-language plays have started to appear in Belarus, and she was saying that there was a bit of a problem with that, because who was going to listen to them?

MD And there are no directors. They don't have independent theatres. There is an interesting situation there: I was in Minsk not long ago and spoke to people who lived in Belarus, and there are two cultural coalitions there. One is pro-Moscow, and they say that they should develop further, and go on to 'conquer Moscow', to put it bluntly – so that's a sort of Soviet legacy. And then there are others who say very interesting things, for example: 'We're going to create our own theatres here, some independent ones, right here –

underground ones of course, because under President Lukashenko's regime it's quite impossible to speak out about any contemporary topics, that's forbidden …' […] So you stick to your own home soil – it's a kind of patriotism, but a genuine one, not state patriotism.

JAEC The state there has had a rather complicated attitude towards the Belarusian language.

MD The language … yes, of course, that's a political issue: they're linked to Russia as though we were a unified state, and the state supports this dichotomy, this dual-language system, because there's a reason to do so – and the ban on contemporary topics in the theatre of course drives their authors towards us.

JAEC Or to London, in the case of the Belarus Free Theatre!

MD Or to London … but towards us is easier, because we can speak the same language. So that Dmitry Bogoslavsky has become a successful author in Russia, and Konstantin Steshik too, he has no fewer productions than I do, and that's completely normal in a theatre sense in Russia. The Belarusians also hold amazing festivals with shows from all over the world, on all topics, I've looked at their programmes. But at the same time there's a complete ban on staging anything of the sort themselves in Belarus.

MK So you can watch other people's theatre, but not your own …

JAEC In London of course we can watch shows by the Belarus Free Theatre, and I'm struck by the fact that they stage shows which touch upon themes which are Russian, Ukrainian, Belarusian and so on. That's an interesting position, and probably a correct position to assume, that they don't only talk about Belarus.

MD But in a sense you don't get to choose your position. Teatr.doc is a theatre of documentary plays, but as a result it's become a persecuted theatre staging political plays, not because they especially like political plays, but because they suffer harassment, and they respond – and anyway, what else can you talk about in such circumstances, can you sing about flowers when you're being beaten over the head with a stick? Enough! You can sing about the stick, about the war, about your pain, and in that sense Teatr.doc doesn't choose its own repertory. It is a very painful matter for artists today – I as a dramatist can't not write a play which cannot be staged in Russia, do you understand? I'm a hostage of artistic truth.

JAEC So you too have forbidden themes?

MD Yes, and we cannot ignore them. If you want to remain an artist you must speak about these themes, and if you don't you will die as a creative personality. It's a kind of dependency. And in that respect I was talking about the marginalization of Russian playwriting, yes? And at the same time another process is taking place, with a different vector, and that is the provincialization of art. Because the circle of themes which excludes all that is most controversial leaves you only with the most general things – and it was the same thing in Soviet-era art. When that became cut off from the outside world, it became extremely naïve, and in some senses toothless. It was about the battle between the good and the kind. And this provincialization means that there is a real dearth of well-made plays in Russian drama. And so this same Dmitry Bogoslavsky brought us his anti-war play [*Points Along the Axis of Time/Tochki na vremennoy osi*]: but it's very provincial, because it's oriented towards ... all that's good, in a country where all you are allowed to say is that war is a bad thing. Nothing about which war, war with whom, the causes of the war, it's forbidden to say who profits from the war – you can't say anything about that, but you can say that war is a bad thing. And this sort of naivety is precisely the kind of provincialization which affects us. And so we can talk about say, transgender rights, but we will sound provincial about it, because this issue has already been resolved in the rest of the world. They already have rights, and we're discovering that, we're here shouting that transgender people need rights! Who needs such plays here, and who needs them in the rest of the world, where this question has already long ago been resolved, do you understand? If I had to make a choice I would take the marginal over the provincial, because provincialism is the death of a contemporary artist. You can't be a contemporary artist if they have closed your mouth.

JAEC So what does this say for the future of the Liubimovka Festival?

MD Again: we started from all that at the beginning of the 2000s, all the plays – I'm generalizing here – had prostitutes, the homeless, drug addicts; and now once again we're going to be seeing plays about prostitutes and the homeless. Russian drama is distinct from British drama not only in its themes, but also in its forms. Form is as much a matter for consideration as themes. And from the Liubimovka programmes in this sense you can single out Ivan Vyrypaev, who is someone who works with form, never with themes.

JAEC What do you feel about the Minister of Culture Medinsky's recent comments, when he was threatening to clamp down harder on those theatres which use obscenities?

MD I hadn't heard that. Well, to hell with him!

JAEC But you don't expect any problems or hassle?

MK No, we don't expect any problems in that respect: we're not a state theatre, we state an age limit on our posters, so formally we observe the laws on age restrictions. We don't observe the law on obscenities, but that's a risk we take consciously, because it's important for us that what is heard are the words written by the author, as they were written.

MD Take *From the College* by Andrei Ivanov – how could you take the obscenities out? You have to understand this situation ... It's the most likely play this year to be proposed for a production grant. But no state theatre will take it. And then the dramatist will be obliged to sit down and rewrite the play, without the obscenities – and how much worse will it become then?

JAEC   So it's like with Andrei Zviagintsev's film *Leviathan* . . .

MD   They simply muted the bad language . . . And in fact that recent law on obscenities is unconstitutional, it infringes a fundamental right enshrined in the constitution, which is freedom of speech. And for us the most important document is still the constitution. And as for Kirill Serebrennikov, well one of my shows went on at his theatre, with plenty of obscenities, it was called *The Brothers*, and I asked him, 'But what about the law?' And he said: 'I'll simply pay the fine, I'm prepared to do that.'

JAEC   Let me ask you: why is Serebrennikov being persecuted at the moment?

MD   We don't know the true reasons, but the very fact of it having happened is more important than the real reasons.

JAEC   Does it reflect some other kind of struggle?

MD   Well, possibly some kind of broader struggle, but the fact that it's precisely him and precisely now, that's a signal for all the rest of us, because he's one of the most outspoken of artists. And even if it is what they call a battle 'between the Kremlin towers', as they say, the most important thing is not that battle but the fact that we will all now have to engage in self-censorship so as not to end up in his kind of situation.

MK   Or we have to be prepared to pay fines, and answer to these people . . . In fact it's not easy to understand why they decided to resurrect this legal case, which had been lying around since 2015, at this particular moment, and maybe we will never know the real reasons why. But this story has several different layers, which are important for us, for people who are working in the fields of culture and the arts. The fact is that we have no protection at all from arbitrary actions, that no normal human logic is at work here. It also reveals the situation that has been thrust upon us, that we are in the position of being hostages, because the laws and the regulations of financial affairs are set up in such a way that it is impossible to do work of high quality without infringing those regulations.

JAEC   And does all this affect your own plans and projects?

MD   Well, you have to think. Either you stay here and carry on, or try to obtain a different citizenship and leave the country. There aren't any other possibilities for the moment.

JAEC   But that's difficult at the moment!

MD Well, Serebrennikov had foreign citizenship, and an apartment in Germany, [...] but none of that helped. On the contrary, it made it even worse, because they keep people like him under guard since they do have the opportunity to emigrate.

MK And this is yet another demonstration of the fact that this is an act of hostage-taking!

MD Yes, and Putin simply said: 'Are we supposed to free him because he works in the field of culture? What makes him any better than the rest?' And that's also a signal, that 'I know all about it. Do you think I didn't know? I know.' I've been reading some Soviet history, and every time then when it was a question of arrests at this sort of level, it was on the personal order of Stalin. So what has changed?

JAEC But unlike Stalin, I don't think Putin goes regularly to the theatre!

Translated from the Russian by J. A. E. Curtis

Note

1 Nicola McCartney is a charismatic Scottish playwright, director and dramaturge, who has played a crucial role in collaborations with many Russian and Ukrainian theatres and writers. As stated on the University of Edinburgh's website, 'She is ambassador of the Traverse Theatre's flagship public engagement project, "Class Act", pioneering it in India, Russia and Ukraine since 2004'.

5

'Class Act' in Russia and Ukraine

Youth drama projects and social theatre practice

Maria Kroupnik

> Maria Kroupnik has made a study of the 'Class Act' drama project for young people which originated at the Traverse Theatre in Edinburgh in the 1990s. She reflects upon the original methodology, aims and achievements of the project in Scotland. She also describes and analyses the numerous variants of the original scheme which have since been developed in towns right across Russia, many of them with her own involvement, as well as in Ukraine, where the project has been developed on the initiative of the playwright Natal'ia Vorozhbit. The phenomenon of 'Class Act' being extended to both Russia and Ukraine is an example of a flourishing transnational collaboration in the arts.

'Class Act' is a Scottish theatre project originating in Edinburgh, which has been running for nearly thirty years. It has now gained an international dimension, and thanks to its creative power to foster intercultural communication and exchanges it has developed a number of variants as far afield as Russia and Ukraine. This study of 'Class Act' adopts the methods of participatory observation, and of qualitative data collection through interviews and through collecting oral and written feedback from the organizers of and participants in 'Class Act' projects across Russia and Ukraine.[1] In my own role as the producer of many of the projects in Russia, and at the same time as a researcher, I will also use a self-reflective approach. We will consider the differences and similarities between the UK's 'Class Act' and its counterparts in Russia and Ukraine, in terms of the projects' design and delivery, and the issues of reciprocal enrichment arising from this transnational process of communication, dissemination and partnership. This study also considers the values and the ethical and aesthetic discourses of the social/applied theatre sphere. Without offering detailed conclusions, this is simply an opportunity to summarize the information collected so far, in order to introduce the project to an international academic readership, and to note some findings that will be developed further in my own research into the sphere of social theatre in Russia and the UK.

'Class Act': historical overview

In 1990 Jane Ellis, the Traverse Theatre's Education Officer, and Jenny Wilson, a Leith Academy drama teacher, came up with an idea called 'Writers About', a drama project for high school students in Edinburgh.[2] For the first time, professional playwrights connected to the Traverse Theatre began to work with teenagers, facilitating the creation of their first short plays. These adolescents then worked with directors and actors to see their finished pieces performed on the main stage at the Traverse, for an audience of the young writers' peers, friends and families. In 1993, the project was renamed 'Class Act'. Jane Ellis remembers:

> We used to have lots of school parties who would come in and have tours around the theatre. Some of them would ask how you went about writing a play, so that was the start of what was originally a little experiment, and we just ran with it after that. The first year was really successful, or we wouldn't have done it again. I suppose we were trying to get more young people into the theatre as well. It was always quite easy to get teachers interested in Shakespeare because that was on the curriculum, but not so much in new work. So by getting both English and drama departments involved, we could tap into the curriculum as well. After that, the teachers were mad for it, and we ended up with something like twenty-eight schools in the Lothian being involved. We developed it and took it out to the Borders, but at the start, we weren't aware of anything else like 'Class Act', so initially at least we had no idea what we were doing – and I think it's incredible that it's still going.[3]

What Ellis does not describe here are all the challenges involved in preparing, negotiating and organizing the project, to say nothing of its creative, aesthetic, ethical, social and cultural complexities and impacts. Over the past twenty-six years, 'Class Act' has worked with over eighty schools in Scotland (in Edinburgh, Glasgow and Lothian) and over 1600 pupils, including Gaelic language speakers.[4] 'Class Act' has become an annual programme at the Traverse Theatre, involving several leading Scottish playwrights. A number of charitable foundations and organizations, including the Andrew Lloyd Webber Foundation and the Cross Trust, support it financially. In 2001, the project was adopted more widely across the UK, and from 2004 it became international, reaching Russia with the help of the British Council office in Moscow, and extending all the way to Mumbai in India by January 2018.[5] My own involvement in 'Class Act' arose from work I was doing for the marketing and communications department of the British Council's Moscow office during 2005–7. Following an initiative of the translator and theatrical expert Tat'iana Oskolkova, and of Anna Genina, head of the Arts Department of the British Council in Russia, 'Class Act' was inaugurated by being tested out in several cities, first of all in the east of European Russia, on the river Volga: in 2004 in Togliatti, in 2005 in Samara and Moscow, and then again in Moscow in 2006.[6]

In 2004 the Scottish theatre-makers Nicola McCartney, Douglas Maxwell and Jemima Levick first introduced 'Class Act' in Togliatti, and a group of local playwrights

(Vadim Levanov, Viacheslav Durnenkov, his brother Mikhail Durnenkov and Yuriy Klavdiev) worked alongside them to learn the methodology, the guidelines and the values of the techniques involved. That project brought together a group of pupils from the local secondary school and from an orphanage. In 2006, there was a presentation of a 'Class Act' gala during the Festival of Contemporary British Drama at the Meierkhol'd Centre in Moscow. Once the British Council had stepped back from its initial role in promoting 'Class Act' in Russia, the project was taken up and delivered by a number of Russian enthusiasts in many different locations and circumstances around the country. These are some of the major projects that have been successful, some of which have continued to this day:

1. 'Teatr v klasse' ('Theatre in a Classroom', in Togliatti): this ran from 2004 to 2011 under the leadership of the playwright Vadim Levanov and his students Olya and Dasha Savin, who have maintained and continued to reinvent the project since the death of Levanov in December 2011.[7]
2. 'Klass Mira' ('Class of Peace', in Moscow and in Sochi): this ran from 2007 to 2014. The creative company 'Game 3000', which was managed by Maria and Andrei Popov, organized it. They were the first among these independent initiatives to involve a nationally renowned theatre – Moscow's Sovremennik ['Contemporary'] Theatre, but that was only for a one-off project. The distinctive features of this project included the competitive selection of the participants (through an all-Russian children's competition), its work with disabled children, and its exploration of different genres and types of art, including theatre, cinema, and the musical and visual arts. The project formed part of the cultural programme organized around the Winter Olympic Games held in Sochi in 2014.[8]
3. The 2008–9 'Climate Act Theatre Project' (in Moscow and St Petersburg), or as it was called in Russian the 'Teatr klimaticheskogo deistviya' ('Climate Action Theatre'), was not strictly speaking a typical 'Class Act' project, since it prescribed the topic for the participants' creative work – the issues of climate change and of the environment. This topic formed part of the UK's public diplomacy agenda at that time. The British Embassy in Russia fully sponsored the project, and provided the venues for the drama workshops.[9]
4. 'Klassnaya Drama' (a Teens' Drama Project) is a classic project for teenagers using 'Class Act' techniques. Between 2011 and 2017 it ran in the cities of Moscow, Perm', Mozhaisk, Voronezh and Kazan' in European Russia, and in Tiumen' in Siberia, and was produced in a variety of partnerships.[10] Between 2011 and 2013 it existed under the umbrella of the 'Bol'shaya Peremena' (Big Break) International Festival of Theatre for Children. In 2015, in partnership with the 'Zhivoi Gorod' (Living City) Foundation for the Support of the Contemporary Arts and the 'Ugol' (Corner) Creative Laboratory, it took place in Kazan', on the Volga. This was the first bilingual project, where the young writers created plays written both in Russian and in the Tatar language. The Kamal Tatar State Academic Theatre presented the three Tatar-language plays and Kazan's Theatre for Young Spectators presented the fifteen Russian-language ones.[11] In 2017, in

partnership with the 'Solntse Sibiri' (Siberian Sun) Theatre and with the 'Cosmos' Youth Theatre Centre the project ran in Tiumen', and brought together schoolchildren and disadvantaged adolescents who had committed minor crimes or were having other socialization problems.[12] One of the most recent projects ran in 2018 in Voronezh, within the framework of the 'Shakespearia' International Educational and Theatrical Festival at the Kol'tsov Drama Theatre.[13]

This project usually works with diverse groups of teenagers, including pupils from more and less successful schools and from varied backgrounds (Moscow, Voronezh); children with disabilities (in Kazan' and Moscow); and children from orphanages and foster care (in Perm'). Separately from this, there was a 2012 project which was a partnership between Moscow's documentary theatre Teatr. doc and the Centre for Criminal Justice Reform. It was held in the Mozhaisk Juvenile Correctional Colony, as part of a nation-wide programme called 'Theatre plus Society'. This resulted in a two-day showcase of a theatre miscellany called 'My Way', made up of eight short plays.[14]

5. Another very important institution for the promotion and production of 'Class Act' projects in Russia was the 'Kul'tproekt' (CultProject) cultural agency, which unfortunately no longer exists. It initiated and produced several festivals and projects using the 'Class Act' methodology:
   - In 2013 the Afanas'ev Puppet Theatre in Kirov (five hundred miles north-east of Moscow) created the 'Pervyi Akt' ('First Act') project with the participation of the playwrights Viacheslav Durnenkov and Maria Zelinskaia.[15]
   - In 2013/2014 there was a 'Class Act Social Laboratory' project in the Krasnoiarsk Youth Theatre in Siberia.[16]
   - In 2014 there was a project run by the director Oleg Lipovetsky in the National Theatre of Karelia, near the Finnish border.[17]

6. In addition, I should mention a number of projects initiated by other theatres and cultural centres which have also used the 'Class Act' methodology of youth work through playwriting. For example:
   - In 2013 the ZIL Cultural Centre, based in a Moscow district where there used to be a famous car factory, invited a Teens' Drama Project to become part of some summer camp workshops for children.[18] The ZIL Cultural Centre made that opportunity available to children from nine up to sixteen. A creative team of four playwrights (Maria Zelinskaia, Nina Belenitskaia, Liubov' Strizhak and Gulnar Sapargalieva), together with five directors (Anastasiia Patlay, Zhenia Berkovich, Yuriy Alesin and Lyubov' Strizhak (Moscow) and Aleksei Zabegin (St Petersburg)) worked on thirteen plays written by the participants. On 29 August 2013 a theatrical miscellany of these new works was presented in the Constructor Hall of the ZIL Cultural Centre.[19]
   - In 2014, the Baltic Fleet Theatre initiated projects at Kronshtadt (the naval base close to St Petersburg) and at the On.Teatr Laboratory in St Petersburg respectively, with the playwright and director Yuriy Klavdiev, who had started out in Togliatti.[20]
   - In 2015 the ZIL Cultural Centre (Moscow) initiated a Theatre Laboratory for teenagers called 'Grani' (Borderlines).[21] This laboratory diversified the 'Class

Act' techniques, and consisted of acting, art and design, and playwriting workshops. More than forty Moscow teenagers took part in the project. Twenty-two of them contributed to the final production, 'The Borderlines', directed by Aleksandr Sozonov and presented in the Constructor Hall of the ZIL Cultural Centre. Maria Zelinskaya, an experienced playwright, led the drama workshop and helped the young authors to write five plays. Dmitry Gorbas worked with children in the art and design workshop and created the set for the show, and a small exhibition of their preparatory sketches. Il'ia Romashko and Natal'ia Gorbas delivered actor training. Daria Razumnikova made a video installation and worked with her live camera during the show. Professional actors reinforced the team of teenagers. Both of the acting tutors (Il'ia Romashko and Natal'ia Gorbas) performed, and other adults acted as extras in the final production. The Moscow 24 TV channel filmed and broadcast the show and it is still available online.[22]

- In 2015 the Bol'shoi Drama Theatre (St Petersburg) initiated a documentary theatre project 'Novye Liudi' (New People) for teenagers, where playwrights used some of the elements of 'Class Act' in order to impart to them the basics of drama and playwriting, combining these with documentary theatre techniques. This was the second time a mainstream national theatre had become involved.[23]

- In 2016 the Russian Drama Theatre in Ulan-Ude (in Buriatiia, near the border with Mongolia) initiated playwriting laboratories for teenagers called 'Territoriia ROSTa (*Rastem, Obshchaias' S Teatrom*) ('Territory for Growth' – the acronym means 'We grow by getting to know theatre'), and has already produced these for three years in a row. They are trying to develop not only new audiences for the theatre, but also to revive playwriting in the national Buriat language.[24]

- In 2017 in the small Siberian town of Niagan' the Young Spectators' Theatre initiated playwriting laboratories for teenagers under the title 'Ia est'' ('I exist') and, as in Ulan-Ude, these are ongoing.[25]

At this stage of my research it is impossible to give detailed descriptions of each and every project that has been undertaken in Russia. Records have not been kept systematically. Even the playwrights who have been involved in several projects have difficulty in remembering the exact dates and places of all the individual projects and activities. For example, Viacheslav Durnenkov, when answering my questions about the exact dates and organizers of the 'Class Act' projects in Russia in which he had participated, told me that at first he was mostly assisting the Scottish playwrights, and then worked independently and with a variety of playwrights involving more than thirty different projects across Russia since 2004. What we can say is that many of the Russian projects are working not only with the design and approaches appropriate for socio-cultural projects, which suggest creative ways of tackling social issues through cultural and artistic activities, but also within the specific guidelines, values and methodology suggested by the Scottish playwrights who first developed it, and who then taught it to playwrights in Ukraine as well as Russia.

Structure and Organization: 'Class Act' in Scotland

The Traverse Theatre collaborates with Edinburgh City Council and other bodies, and selects five or six schools to participate in the project every year. To begin with, the playwrights visit the schools to deliver one-to-two-hour masterclasses for the schoolchildren once a week, for a period of eight to ten weeks. During this period, there is a session with the actors, who come to the schools to read the drafts of the plays. At the end of these eight to ten weeks, the plays are ready for rehearsal and are distributed to the directors. The young authors participate in the rehearsal process, communicate with the directors and actors, become acquainted with the technical aspects of creating theatrical performances, give interviews to journalists and, of course, watch their shows together with parents, friends and the general theatre audience. The project tracks the promotional and advertising campaigns, as well as the ticket sales process. By the day of the performance, the Traverse team organizes the publication of a volume of their plays, ready for distribution. The teenagers thus experience the complete cycle of creating a performance, from an initial idea right up to the final applause in the auditorium and an award ceremony. The playwright Douglas Maxwell has commented upon the effects of the project:

> It is amazing how little the formula has changed. And one of the reasons we are still doing it is because it works. [...] The outcome works, and the process works. We know that it hits its goals. How it works and what are the outcomes – is a mystery. Because it is like an art. You can't work out why we need it, and what it does. [...] We can see in their faces how it works... Magic happens. The child's voice is leading the whole thing, even if it says something duff and silly. And all the adults do follow the voice. The professional actors, directors, technicians follow the voice. It's got something to do with confidence... It's quite something to be an individual, but also working as a team. It's got something that comes from the feeling that it may be a disaster. Then, it works. It is a great laugh, fun to be in a classroom and to make up stories with children. And as for the professionals, watching 'Class Act' is like coming back to the basics of drama, which we forget in our professional lives, intellectualizing it.[26]

However, changes do take place in the educational system, and more recently Scottish playwrights have been complaining that the schools have perceptibly cut the time available for the project work with their pupils. Now they have only five sessions of about an hour each to deliver the playwriting workshop, and then one day of rehearsals. It is certainly quite difficult in such circumstances to push the participants to achieve a more or less complete result. However, the Traverse's administrative and creative teams succeed in doing the best that is possible, even with such limited means.

Structure and organization: 'Class Act' in Russia and in Ukraine

The Russian and Ukrainian organizational models differ from the Scottish one. Only the 'Theatre in the Classroom' project has used the exact Scottish model, when playwrights in Togliatti went into schools to deliver a workshop for their pupils. Other Russian projects have been using a more intensive out-of-school model, which means six to seven days for the drama workshops with four to five hours of work a day, plus four to five more days of rehearsals. That means something like twenty-eight to thirty-two hours for the drama workshop and the writing in total. The Scottish playwright Nicola McCartney observed this model in 2011 in Moscow, and commented that it gives a deeper experience to the participants, as well as giving the playwrights more time for work with individuals and for facilitating the creation of the new texts. This model is also more effective in terms of creating a 'safe space' for trust to be built, for fun, and for real equality to develop in the creative process of theatre-making. Another reason for placing these drama workshops outside of the school system is that school life has its own rules and routines, levels of power distribution and subordination. These might interfere with the creative process of writing and have an impact on the work of the participants, not allowing them to open their minds and start to think outside the box.

The specific features of this model took shape party due to the lack of resources in Russia – money, venues and time. The issue of time is important for the schedules of the playwrights, who have to do various other jobs in order to make their living. This is equally true of the schedules of the theatres or theatre venues, which are able to allocate only a limited number of days in the rehearsal rooms and on the stage in order to produce the final showcases. Theatres in Russia do not face the same expectations that British cultural institutions do as far as outreach and access work is concerned. Some of them have engaged with 'Class Act' projects on a one-off, experimental basis, but have not developed or sustained their commitment in subsequent years. Much depends on the energy of the producer, who often initiates the projects, offers his or her expertise to the theatre, takes on much of the fundraising and organizational work, helps to draft participant application forms and audience questionnaires, establishes the guidelines and framework for the project, invites school participation and supervises the delivery of the project at all stages. In other words, personal involvement is a key factor in the dissemination and the success of 'Class Act' projects in Russia.

In Ukraine the 'Class Act: Skhid-Zakhid' ('Class Act: East–West') project was launched in 2016 by a creative team organized by the playwright Natal'ia Vorozhbit.[27] The idea of the project was to use theatre practices in order to build better trust and understanding between teenagers from the opposite border regions of the country, which have been suffering from the internal military conflict in Ukraine arising from Russia's annexation of Crimea in 2014. The Ukrainian 'Class Act' is organized rather differently from the Russian projects. It begins with a process of selection, choosing cities in the Eastern and Western regions of the country, and certain schools situated there. As the curator and leader of the project, Natal'ia Vorozhbit explains:

> We had the idea of finding children in the East and West border regions and bringing them to Kyiv, in order to show them the cultural capital and the diversity of interesting things happening there. Children from both border regions, even in their choice of further education destinations, were tending to consider either

staying in their native towns, or going to Russia if they lived in the East; or going to Poland and other European countries if they lived in the West. They had little understanding of their own country as a whole. They do not understand fully where it is that they are living. Most of the children did not travel, and had never been to Kyiv. Often this is due to economic reasons. We also wanted to distract the attention of the children from the Donbas region away from the war and terror they have faced. We wanted to help them to befriend one another.

Our team got together and we started looking at the map, researching towns and regions and googling them. We looked into local myths and stereotypes which we wanted to understand. For example, the city of Novovolynsk in the West is suffering from just the same industrial decline, and from the closure of the coalmines, as in the Donbas in the East. When we found one town called Schast'e ('Happiness'), how could we not go there?

We selected troubled schools, or – in the East – schools damaged by war.[28]

Once the geographical selection process is completed, the project team arranges visits to the schools and selects the classes which they will be working with. Usually it is three classes in each school. A team of several people comes to the school and works for an hour and a half a day with each selected class, for five days in the East and three days in the West. This can involve creative masterclasses, communicative meetings and talks, as well as after-school shared time spent walking in the town. We hand out five topics and ask them to write some texts, truthfully telling us what they think. We promise that only our team will read all those texts. Through this personal communication, we get to find out the individual stories of those children. Then we come together in Kyiv as a team, and read the texts in order to select the talented ones, or those written by young people who are facing trauma or misfortune which he or she needs to overcome.[29]

With the selection process complete, the organizational process begins, and then the children, with their parent or accompanying teacher, come to Kyiv for the main part of the project. Another difference about the Ukrainian 'Class Act' is that the curators and playwrights designate the pairs in which children will be working within the project (one participant from the East and one from the West). Then each pair has five days to write a text. Each day playwriting masterclasses take up four to five hours, and then additional events, excursions and classes take place. The authors themselves choose the language of the play: it can be written in Ukrainian, in Russian, or in both at once. After two to three days of work, the actors and directors visit the project in order to meet the children and try out some of the texts that are already taking shape in the workshops. The children have the opportunity to meet the actors and decide if they want to write a role for someone in particular. The project has attracted TV and film stars to be the actors in the final show. When the texts are ready, rehearsals start, and last for four to five more days. Overall the Ukrainian 'Class Act' process aims to be completed within ten days. While the plays are in rehearsal, the children continue to be supported and have the choice of either attending the rehearsals or joining in the cultural programme devised by the organizers (excursions, museum and theatre visits, and so on).

In both the Russian and the Ukrainian schemes there is a first reading by the authors of the finished plays, to which the actors and director are invited; one obligatory attendance at a rehearsal for each author; and finally they must be present at the final showcase performance of the project. Each project finishes with an award ceremony, where all the authors are invited on to the stage and are presented with diplomas, a collected volume of their plays, and other souvenirs, in the presence of their tutor-playwrights and the directors.

The aims, values and creative practices of 'Class Act' in Scotland and abroad

Douglas Maxwell, a playwright and one of the founders of the 'Class Act' methodology, has this to say about the scheme:

> 'Class Act'. It is all about process. It is about taking young people through the entire theatre-making process, all the risks, highs, all the excitement, but without any of the seemingly mandatory pitfalls. Obviously, there are important educational benefits involved in this; literacy, creativity, performance and communication skills etc. But I think it's the ownership they love the most. Throughout every step of the process, this thing is theirs: their idea, their words, their vision, all followed through by professional adults who take their cue from them. In other words, we are hired guns working for them, using our skill to get them from a blank page to a place where they're sky high from applause.[30]

This is an accurate and quite precise description of the playwrights' role in the project, but the methodology is also shaped by the basic principles that drive both the participants and the whole project forward. One of the key 'Class Act' principles is *respect*:

> 'The personality of the child is very important', says the playwright and director Kira Malinina, 'as well as a respectful attitude towards him or her. In everyday schools we usually meet something entirely opposite ... "Hey, you, go, hurry up, and come here". Children appreciate the respect, and this interest in their inner processes. When the interest is genuine, it helps a child to open up, to become more attentive to him/herself and more sensitive to what is happening all around. I can say that it helps a child to believe that the world of adults is interested in him or her, that each is seen and accepted as he/she is, with nobody trying to tailor him/her to "fit in".'[31]

'We treat the teenagers as professional playwrights', commented the playwright and director Nicola McCartney.[32]

Another major principle and value of the 'Class Act' scheme is the *conscious, serious joy* of communication and creativity. It often happens that participation in a project becomes for a teenager the first experience of a serious and equal conversation with adults, when he/she is carefully listened to and ideas and visions are analysed at various levels, but it can also be the first experience of shared joy, laughter and playing games on an equal footing. It is important that the project should provoke in every participant vivid emotions.

Finally, and equally crucially, a core value and principle of 'Class Act' is *freedom of expression*. Participants are free to select their topic, choose any idea they want to work with, select their protagonists and the language they need to speak, according to the story and its internal rules. The playwrights are not there to recommend better versions of the plot or dialogue; they only ask questions, helping to give form to the ideas and find ways out of any difficult creative issues that the young authors face during the writing. "'Class Act' teaches humility. You must not do anything for the children. Your professional solutions can often spoil a child's original idea. You can learn through the children how to perceive the world directly, and then watch the audience responses to stories told in a very simple way," says Natal'ia Vorozhbit.[33]

Among the multiple aims of 'Class Act' various practitioners have listed the following: finding potential playwrights for the future; attracting and diversifying new, well-informed theatre audiences; the personal development of the teenage participants; the development of their literacy, and of their interest in further education. Nicola McCartney says:

> We teach them to communicate with each other in a civilised way. To discuss their work without offending one another. Their self-esteem increases, and the teenager becomes more mature. The schoolchildren start to learn better. They gain the ability to express their own thoughts – and of course, there is the correcting of their spelling ... But the main goal remains the same – to write a great play.[34]

The project is aimed both at disadvantaged teenagers, with low self-esteem and reduced motivation, and at ordinary schoolchildren. 'Class Act' gives a teenager a chance to learn how to analyse his/her own life through the examples of his/her protagonists, their intentions and their actions. And as well, this is a chance to see theatre as an accessible and interesting professional field, where each can discover and realize him/herself.

At the 2017 'Class Act' Symposium in the Traverse Theatre, we were told that over the more than twenty-five years of the project's existence, their work in disadvantaged areas with adolescents has shown that after participating in the project, the children's performance and indicators of educational and social success in their schools have improved. In addition, the number of students who decided to continue their studies at college level has increased, and some have later become playwrights and theatre professionals. Moreover, most of the children also became spectators, who repeatedly returned to the theatre which had once given them such an unforgettable experience.

It is virtually impossible to track any comparable effects of the projects in Russia and in Ukraine. However, some information is available about the 'graduates' of the 'Class Act' projects that I myself organized in Moscow and in the city of Voronezh. Some of the children have decided to study acting and entered professional theatre schools. Some have joined theatre studios in the universities where they have chosen to study. One theatre producer – Anastasia Iushkova – is now working in one of the most vibrant contemporary theatres in Moscow, the Gogol' Centre. She was a participant in the project called 'Borderlines' in Moscow's ZIL Cultural Centre in 2015, mentioned above.

The most valuable evidence of the significance of the 'Class Act' projects can be found in the testimonials from the participants, from the teenagers themselves. I want to conclude with the words of a schoolboy, Stas Pantya, who was a participant in the Moscow 'Climate Act' project in 2009: 'Participation in the project created an opportunity for me to discover new interests, gave me freedom of imagination, and taught me how to frame this fantasy on a sheet of paper ... this project provided me with many interesting acquaintances, emotions and memories.'[35]

Translated from the Russian by J. A. E. Curtis

Notes

1. I have collected email questionnaires from the playwrights who participated in the diverse versions of 'Class Act' projects across Russia and Ukraine.
2. Neil Cooper, Coffee-Table Notes. An Archive of Arts Writing by Neil Cooper. Effete No Obstacle. Available at http://coffeetablenotes.blogspot.ru/2011/03/class-act-21.html (accessed 15 August 2018).
3. Ibid.
4. This statistic was given at the first panel discussion of the 'Class Act' Symposium in the Traverse Theatre by Sunniva Ramsey, 24 November 2017 (audio recording. author's archive). Mentioned at https://www.traverse.co.uk/whats-on/event-detail/1309/class-act-international-symposium-2017.aspx (accessed 15 August 2018).
5. 'Nicola McCartney, Sunniva Ramsay and the Traverse Theatre – Class Act Mumbai', 12 January 2018. Available at: http://coffeetablenotes.blogspot.com/2018/01/nicola-mccartney-sunniva-ramsay-and.html
6. Traverse's Class Act project: 'It's about children finding their voice', *The Scotsman*, 26 January 2011. Available at: https://www.scotsman.com/lifestyle/traverse-s-class-act-project-it-s-about-children-finding-their-voice-1-1498488 (accessed 15 August 2018).
7. Some materials and video fragments of their latest showcases can be found at the project's webpages on the Russian social network VKontakte: https://vk.com/teatr_v_klasse (accessed 15 August 2018).
8. Some materials can be found at the project's web page at: http://www.igra3000.ru/chelovek/events/class-mira.htm (accessed 15 August 2018).
9. You can find some media coverage of the project at: https://ria.ru/eco/20090126/160153494.html, https://www.kino-teatr.ru/teatr/history/1/1188/, https://ilmira-b.livejournal.com/67310.html, https://www.prolab.ru/fotovystavka-teplo-eshhe-teplee-vzglyad-na-novyj-klimat.html, http://www.vodokanal.spb.ru/presscentr/news/svezhij_vzglyad_na_novyj_klimat/, https://www.kommersant.ru/doc/1104628, http://www.pomoyka.org/part_news/2863/, https://wwf.ru/resources/news/arkhiv/sokhranenie-klimata-kak-iskusstvo/
10. Some materials can be found at the project's Facebook page: www.facebook.com/TeensDramaProject/; on the VKontakte page: https://vk.com/teensdramaproject; and in my article in the Russian/German online magazine on cultural and educational

practices, KUBI: http://www.goethe.de/ins/ru/lp/prj/kub/dos/ru15252130.htm (accessed 15 August 2018).

11 Some materials can be found on the project's VKontakte webpages: https://vk.com/teens_drama_kazan; and in media coverage: http://ptj.spb.ru/blog/vkazhdoj-muzyke-bax-vkazhdom-rebenke-bog/, https://ramis-nazmiev.livejournal.com/tag/%D0%9A%D0%BB%D0%B0%D1%81%D1%81%D0%BD%D0%B0%D1%8F%20%D0%B4%D1%80%D0%B0%D0%BC%D0%B0, http://mincult.tatarstan.ru/rus/index.htm/news/462110.htm, https://www.kzn.ru/meriya/press-tsentr/novosti/49737_s_16_po_29_avgusta_vpervye_v_kazani_proydet_klassnaya_drama/, http://www.sobaka.ru/kzn/city/theatre/39049, http://www.kazan.aif.ru/culture/person/klassnaya_drama, https://kazanfirst.ru/articles/59950, http://history-kazan.ru/16046-klassnaya-drama-v-kazani (accessed 15 August 2018).

12 Some materials can be found on the project's VKontakte pages: https://vk.com/cooldrama: and in media coverage: http://tumentoday.ru/2017/07/31/unikalnyj-teatralnyj-proekt-dlya-trudnyh-podrostkov-startoval-v-tyumeni/, http://www.vsluh.ru/news/culture/321454, https://t-l.ru/230383.html, https://moi-portal.ru/foto/334265-proekt-klassnaya-drama-/ (accessed 15 August 2018).

13 Some materials can be found on the Festival's page: https://www.facebook.com/shakespearialand/, and in media coverage: http://vestivrn.ru/novosti/ves-mir-teatr-yunyie-voronezhtsyi-smogli-pobyit-rezhissrami-i-stsenaristami_2018-5-29_14-55, https://moe-online.ru/news/society/1012558, https://riavrn.ru/news/voronezhskie-artisty-sygrali-spektakl-po-pesam-mestnykh-shkolnikov/ (accessed 15 August 2018).

14 Some media clips can be found at the Teatr.Doc page – http://www.teatrdoc.ru/news.php?nid=371; and in diverse media; the TV Culture channel – https://tvkultura.ru/article/show/article_id/71064/, Gazeta.ru- https://www.gazeta.ru/culture/2012/11/30/a_4874005.shtml?updated, and *The New Times* – https://newtimes.ru/articles/detail/57432/ (accessed 15 August 2018).

15 Information about the project can be found at http://afisha.newsler.ru/teatr/2013/12/05/kirovskix-detej-besplatno-obuchat-teatralnomu-iskusstvu, http://kirovkukla-ru.1gb.ru/news/text98, http://kirovkukla-ru.1gb.ru/show116 (accessed 15 August 2018).

16 Details and media coverage can be found at http://www.ktyz.ru/project/view/7#about (accessed 15 August 2018).

17 Details and media coverage can be found at http://mincultrk.ru/kultura/kulturnaya_zhizn/dramaturgicheskaya_laboratoriya_dlya_podrostkov_v_ramkah_proekta_granicnet (accessed 15 August 2018).

18 See http://cao.mos.ru/presscenter/news/detail/840800.html?pdf_file=y (accessed 15 August 2018).

19 Photo-reportage of the ZIL Cultural Center's showcase can be found at URL: https://www.facebook.com/pg/ClassActRussia/photos/?tab=album&album_id=557617097620564 (accessed 15 August 2018).

20 See http://ptj.spb.ru/blog/kogda-drama-stanovitsya-klassnoj (accessed 15 August 2018).

21 See https://www.m24.ru/videos/teatr/15032015/78535, http://zilcc.ru/news/1735.html (accessed 15 August 2018).

22 Showcase of the 'Borderlines' production, 15 March 2015, ZIL Cultural Centre. URL: https://www.m24.ru/videos/%D1%82%D0%B5%D0%B0%D1%82%D1%80/15032015/78535 (accessed 15 August 2018).

23 See https://art1.ru/2015/01/28/bdt-zapuskaet-dokumentalnyj-proekt-novye-lyudi-45726 (accessed 15 August 2018).

24 Details and media coverage can be found at http://grdt.ru/teatr/laboratoriya-territoriya-rosta/, https://www.baikal-media.ru/news/culture/319245/?sphrase_id=75838302, https://www.baikal-media.ru/news/culture/339957/, https://www.infpol.ru/99283-v-ulan-ude-postavili-pesy-kotorye-napisali-podrostki-video-/, https://gazeta-n1.ru/news/69034/, http://burdram.ru/media/news/dramaturgi-vyacheslav-durnenkov-i-anastasiya-bukreeva-est-mnogoe,-chto-otlichaet-rebyat-iz-buryatii.html (accessed 15 August 2018).

25 Details and media coverage can be found at http://www.ntyz.ru/novosti/ja-est-premera-spektaklja-po-pesam-podrostkov-goroda-njagani/, http://www.ntyz.ru/novosti/vtoraja-dramaturgicheskaja-laboratorija-ja-est-ischet-svoih-geroev/, http://www.ntyz.ru/novosti/2-dramaturgicheskaja-laboratorija-ja-est-proshla-v-njaganskom-tjuze/, http://www.ntyz.ru/novosti/heshteg-ja-est-v-dekabre-premera-spektaklja-po-pesam-podrostkov-goroda-njagani/, https://ugra-news.ru/article/11042017/46749 (accessed 15 August 2018).

26 Douglas Maxwell 'Class Act' Symposium in the Traverse Theatre, 24 November 2017 (audio recording. author's archive).

27 See https://www.facebook.com/ClasActUkraine/, https://dt.ua/ART/nataliya-vorozhbit-pislya-class-act-odna-z-uchasnic-vigrala-grant-na-navchannya-u-shveycariyi-282960_.html (accessed 15 August 2018).

28 Natal'ia Vorozhbit interview, 25 January 2018 (audio recording, author's archive).

29 Ibid.

30 Douglas Maxwell 'Class Act Handbook', 15 April 2008, Traverse Theatre (author's archive).

31 Maria Kroupnik, 'Class Act: Sekrety tekhnologii', http://www.goethe.de/ins/ru/lp/prj/kub/dos/ru15280558.htm (accessed 15 August 2018).

32 Nicola McCartney, 'Class Act: teoriia i praktika', *Peterburgskii teatral'nyi zhurnal*, 3, no. 73 (2013): 10. http://ptj.spb.ru/archive/73/theatre-leader-school-73/class-act-teoriya-ipraktika/ (accessed 15 August 2018).

33 Natal'ia Vorozhbit interview, 25 January 2018 (audio recording, author's archive).

34 McCartney, 'Class Act', 11. http://ptj.spb.ru/archive/73/theatre-leader-school-73/class-act-teoriya-ipraktika/ (accessed 15 August 2018).

35 Climate Act project feedback forms, 2009, Moscow (author's archive).

6

Conversation with Sasha Denisova (Moscow, October 2013)

Susanna Weygandt

> This is an interview with the theatre director Sasha Denisova, who has directed several verbatim performances across Russia. In Moscow she is known mostly for her staged productions of *Light My Fire* (*Zazhgi moy ogon'*, 2012) and *Alice in Wonderland* (*Alisa v strane chudes*, 2013) (see descriptions below). Denisova speaks here in detail about the ways she works with verbatim techniques.

SW   I have read about different versions of verbatim. At the Maiakovskii Theatre [in Moscow], for instance, there is a new version of an Ibsen play made entirely of recorded, modern-day speech from the street. That's verbatim. Then there are the verbatim performances that are performed only once, in Teatr.doc's Eye Witness Theatre. Actors read the text only once. One of Teatr.doc's Eye Witness Theatre performances was about the Pussy Riot trial, during which lawyers from the actual trial discussed how the news media were covering the trial. This performance took place on one night only. Could you please tell me a bit about how the stories for your performances come together?

SD   We don't start with ready-made text. The actors record text during the interviews they conduct with people from certain social groups, and bring those recordings with them to rehearsal.

SW   Could you tell me about what type of recorded text your actors bring back to the theatre? What are the qualities in the recorded speech that they are looking for?

SD   We're looking for how the recorded speech tells a story of a fate and a destiny. We are looking for how the personalities of the speakers (interviewed on the street) are reflected in the speech that they are uttering. We feel that these qualities of the speaker and his/her life are reflected through speech in a way that they never could be by a writer, for instance, a writer of realism. Human speech communicates those qualities that writing can't convey. For instance, here's a situation: a man sits down to talk about sending someone flowers, and then all of a sudden he jumps to talking about his brother who has just tragically died. Speech captures the pulse of someone's life, and it's from that pulse that we deduce how the person lives.

SW The recorded speech brings to life the person who is speaking.

SD Yes, but it's also the actor's craft that brings this person to life. The actor doesn't stand on stage, repeating in cold blood the lines of a verbatim play. The actor has spent a considerable amount of time with the person whose speech has been recorded, and the craft of the actor conveys the life of this person in a true way. From the position of an observer – one of non-identity with the role – the actor peers over the recorded speech's phonetic patterns and content – abbreviated words, slang and swear words – and emphasizes those speech mannerisms characteristic of a particular social culture. The verbatim actor gives 'evaluations' (*otsenki*) of the facts in the everyday life of the interviewee. The actor places vocal emphasis on the moments when the interviewee laughed. For instance, when the interviewee laughs at a major tragedy in his life, this grotesquery is immediately underscored by the actor's pauses or vocal emphasis. The actor is like the light on the stage, highlighting strange but important phrases that the speaker mentioned, in order to convey meaning to the audience.

SW The actor is the amplifier. He underscores important moments and strange moments in the recording. The actor looks at the text from a distanced position and looks to see what interesting and strange moments should be emphasized in the performance.

SD Yes, the actor has observed and studied this personality and knows the moments when the person was trying to cover something up in his life or trying to boast about something important in his life. So it's different from 'playing the role' in the traditional sense of creating physical verisimilitude with the character. Yet at the same time, during the moments when the actor gives 'evaluations' of the character's speech, the actor might play up or place vocal emphasis on an important moment in the speaker's life because this is, after all, theatre. [...] I give my actors exercises in observation to do. I station them at different areas in town – at a café or hospital – where they follow a method of observation and record text that then becomes the basis of several scenes that we perform on stage.

SW Might you be able to compare the verbatim method to other acting methods?

SD The actor doesn't approach the text like one would using traditional methods, for instance psychological realism, because then the actor only focuses on his or her role to the exclusion of other things. I want the actor to be open – open to life. Rehearsal starts when the actor presses 'play' on his or her voice recorder. From that time on, the actor should focus very closely on the speech that is being recorded in the live interview. Focus on how the interviewee is sitting, what secrets the interviewee is conveying. Try to understand, like a psychologist, the psychology of the speaker. The first couple of times it's very difficult for actors to do this because it's a whole different way of relating to people. But then actors start to enjoy it because they are getting to know deeply a whole new person. When we are walking down the same streets every day we ignore so many people and don't think about who they are or how they live. Automatically, we block out curiosity about strangers.

Translated from the Russian by Susanna Weygandt

Light My Fire (Zazhgi moi ogon', 2012)

The innovator behind *Light My Fire* is Sasha Denisova, a journalist, columnist for *Russian Reporter* (*Russkii reporter*) and playwright who has created and directed several verbatim performances, including *Country Villages.net* (*Derevni.net*) (in Barnaul, Siberia) and *Plus-minus Twenty* (*Plius-minus dvadtsat'*) (in Tashkent). Denisova is also a playwright at the Meierkhol'd Centre in Moscow, where she wrote and directed the award-winning drama *Mayakovsky Fetches Sugar* (*Mayakovsky idet za sakharom*, 2012). Her verbatim plays are about museum workers in Kirov, farmers in the Altai Republic and Muscovites who survive terrorist attacks. *Light My Fire* opened the 2012 New Play Project, a programme within the Golden Mask Festival that showcases innovative Russian plays. *Light My Fire* received a Golden Mask award that year. The play also opened a new chapter in the creative endeavours of Teatr.doc. At Teatr.doc Denisova and her colleagues have always been interested in the challenges and rewards of telling stories about the lives of people from various parts of the social spectrum. For this project Denisova decided to focus on one group of 'different people' – the iconic American music legends of Jim Morrison, Janice Joplin and Jimi Hendrix. These roles were played by actors at Teatr.doc who have, over the years, become iconic within their own artistic circles – Arina Marakylina (who acted in several of Vyrypaev's productions), Aleksei Iudnikov and Talgat Batalov. The actors re-enact and improvise moments of the high points and everyday lives of the legendary subjects.

Alice and the Government (Alisa i gosudarstvo, 2013)

The playwright and director Sasha Denisova and the choreographer Aleksei Zherebtsov of the contemporary dance troupe Liquid Theatre joined forces to produce not only a satire about contemporary Russian society, but also full instructions as to how to survive in this type of government. The performance centres around Lewis Carroll's *Alice in Wonderland*. In the contemporary adaptation written by Sasha Denisova, Alisa, a high school student, loses consciousness after worrying about and studying for a test. When she regains consciousness, she meets characters from Lewis Carroll's story and also a group of pensioners (represented by dancers from Liquid Dance Theatre), to whom Alisa addresses a question: 'But why is there a government if retired women don't receive a decent amount to live on in retirement?' This play received the 2013 Golden Mask Award.

Conversation with Ivan Vyrypaev (Moscow, May 2013)

Susanna Weygandt

> Ivan Vyrypaev made his name as one of the most inventive and experimental playwrights of the 'New Drama' age with his play *Oxygen* (*Kislorod*, 2002), a meditation on love and violence shaped by musically poetic variations on the Ten Commandments. Here he considers with Susanna Weygandt the nature of his drama and the challenges of directing and performing his plays. This is followed by a description of two of the plays he discusses, *Illusions* (*Illiuzii*' 2011) and *July* (*Iiul*', 2006). 'July' is examined in more detail in the following essay, by Valeriia Mutc.

SW As a writer and a director, when you write plays, do you picture your plays being performed in any specific type of theatre with any specific style of acting technique?

IV I have my own theatre method. It differs from most performance techniques. It's a little difficult for me to explain because it's an entire method, created from a director's point of view. It is always with me. I might sit down as a writer to compose my dramas, but the method is always with me and the approach to acting is always with me. I don't keep track of the productions of my plays that others direct, but I have noticed that they are staged more often in Europe than in Russia. I don't travel to see all these performances, but what I have seen of them was not very successful. They were staged using an older approach to acting, and it's just not possible to stage my plays with that approach. When directors read my plays, they like the content and find the story interesting but they don't understand that the content of my plays is also very tightly connected to the performance approach. They don't know this approach. They start staging and, accordingly, things start falling apart. If the director is one of my acquaintances, then he or she starts calling me and says, 'Ivan, we don't understand what's going on and why nothing's working out. All the actors love the text and they want to go forward with it, but nothing's working out.' And this is because there's a particular approach to performance rooted in all my plays.

As it turns out, I'm doing a lot of commissioned playwriting at the moment. When theatres commission my plays – most often German theatres – they don't tell me what to write. They just say, please write a play, and that's it. It's quite a comfortable situation. I want to write plays anyway, and to be doing it with a commission is ideal. But when I finish a play, I always think, oh, what a nightmare. Someone's going to stage it poorly. But nevertheless, my plays are staged at different theatres because, most likely, the directors like the ideas in them. I've seen about five or six of my plays staged by other directors and of all of those, there were two that were very interesting. About three didn't quite come together. But that's my opinion. The audience judges the work in a different way. In Paris I saw *Delhi Dance*. I wasn't so keen about it, but the audience liked it a lot. And it seemed, at least to me, that in the French theatre, which has *its own* [emphasis I.V.] particular acting method, that the actors weren't playing 'sincerely', but in the audience's eyes, that lack of sincerity is an acceptable, normal style of acting.

SW Your approach to acting is new and unique. You mention that it differs from older approaches to acting. Do you mean, for instance, that it differs from, say, Stanislavsky's?

IV Today there is no separation between the audience and the actor. There's no 'fourth wall'. The actor should be himself. He should have a very strong connection with the audience. And at this moment he performs to the audience. For instance, if you were to play Hamlet, don't try to feel the emotions you intuit Hamlet has but, more naturally, try to reveal your honest reactions to what happened to Hamlet. Experience not the emotions of Hamlet, but rather your own emotions about Hamlet. The actor should understand his character's life story and tell the audience about it in a direct, frank manner. Rarely does the actor even appear in costume. The actor enters the stage as if he were meeting with his best friend in a café, and revealing all the details of something special that has just happened to someone whom he knows. The actor sincerely reflects on what happened to his character. Of course, Stanislavsky's actors were raised according to the same principle, but they hit the fourth wall in their delivery. That which comes into the actor's mind about Hamlet, his impression about what Hamlet went through, is what the actor gives to the audience. It's when the actor conveys this impression to the audience that he builds a connection between himself and the audience. The actor doesn't hide anything behind the curtain. And in this way, the audience has contact with a real person, the actor. If the actor emphasizes playing the role, then the audience can only identify with Hamlet, and Hamlet doesn't exist. The audience would just be getting a sense of how well/not well the actor plays Hamlet, and that's not strong enough to maintain a close bond between the actor and the audience for the duration of the performance. But I'm a real person and I'm going to tell you about Hamlet. Wait for me at the theatre at 7 p.m.

SW This is what it's like in your performance of *Illusions*.

IV Yes, but it's not necessary for the actor to speak facing in the direction of where the audience is seated. The actor may speak to his partner on stage, but the actor's centre of attention is always on the audience. And once the audience understands that, the audience empathizes not with Hamlet, but with the actor. When the physical material of the role – costume, make-up and mimicry – when the barrier of conventions that stands between actor and spectator disappears, the dramatic text and its deeper ideas are brought closer to the audience. Characters remain in my plays because of the stories attached to them. The character is the means through which we communicate. But the role itself is largely an obstacle to the actor–audience bonding.

SW   I've seen how stunningly this works in your performances.

IV   As the actor reveals to the audience his true emotions, and his reactions as to what happened to his character, the audience identifies with the actor, as a friend does when listening closely to a story. A very close contact with the audience occurs. A direct dialogue between the actor and spectators takes place. This highly intimate style of performance happens in *July* (*Iiul'*), *Illusions* (*Illiuzii*), *Dream Works* and *The Drunks* (*P'ianye*). As for your question about Stanislavsky's system, I'd like to say that I'm a great admirer of his system. What I admire about Stanislavsky's system is the emphasis on performing the objective. It's just that Stanislavsky didn't show this to the audience, but to the fourth wall. But the playwright and performer Evgenii Grishkovets, for instance, he cultivates an amazingly close connection with the audience.

SW   Yes, it's as if as soon as he walks on stage the connection is made, and it lasts.

IV   Grishkovets directs his words to the audience throughout his performances, grasping their reactions and modifying his speech based on the degree of their engagement. I was thrilled to see Robert Wilson acting in a similar style when he toured Moscow last October, performing his self-directed *Krapp's Last Tape* (Beckett). Wilson was in full make-up and gestured, but the entire time he delivered every word to the audience as if speaking only for them.

SW   Speaking of Grishkovets and Beckett, your plays, too, all have very long monologues. For instance, *July*. The play is one long monologue. When Polina Agureeva entered the stage, she entered as a narrator. The most important component of her performance was her voice, her style of speech.

IV   Yes, this is because the hero of my plays is the text. It's the same thing in Shakespeare's plays. All of the action is contained in the text itself. Plus, back then there weren't resources for a travelling troupe to have an elaborate mise en scène. The stage directions, which were read, provided the description of the play's settings. In Shakespeare's theatre the voices of the actors were the most important part of the performances. And for me, a play is pure text; or rather, it's text brought to life.

SW   I've also noticed that in 'New Drama' plays, the main tendency includes experiments with speech and contemporary slang. There are stage directions, but they don't indicate vibrant, physical actions. At the same time, there's radical speech. Language is a substitute for physical action. For instance, in *Delhi Dance*, the dance could have been better represented in the stage directions, but instead you place an accent on the literariness of the dialogue. An impression of the dance is rendered through the dialogue. Characters of the play describe in detail the elongated limbs of the dancer.

IV   Yes, this is because if you see the dance, then the dance is nothing more to you than the one you just saw. But if you hear it, then you will have your own dance. As soon as you hear it, an image of the dance manifests itself. The word comes to life – that is, within you the image is born. This is the whole point of theatre. Theatre is based on text and the text is brought to life. It comes to life in front of the audience.

SW   If the emphasis in 'New Drama' is on radical speech, then doesn't that mean that the characters' dialogue is key to building their roles? It seems to me that we understand characters in contemporary plays not through scenic movements, but through their speech mannerisms.

IV   Absolutely.

SW   This comes to the forefront in *July*. The stage directions indicate that a female actress plays the role of a man. It's not at all important how convincing she is at physically resembling a man. The actress, Polina Agureeva, is trained in speech, voice and diction, and it's important how she brings attention to the sounds of her character's speech.

IV   Yes. In *July* there is no 'male role'. There is no role, period. There is the text of the male character's monologue. If a man played this part, then it would be just like any monologue performed for the goal of a convincing portrayal of a character. The audience would identify only with the character, which isn't a real thing. But they wouldn't identify with the actor, whose passion and emotions about what is going on in the story are real. And the actor is real. What is more, the disconnect between the female voice and the male's story opens up space for looking at the text from a distance. The text is 'elevated', if you will; it's put up on a platform.

SW   Is the distancing device you use a different kind of estrangement from the kind in Brecht's theatre?

IV   Yes, absolutely. This is a different type of distance from Brecht's. In Brecht's theatre the actor is not his or her real self, but is a persona who just came out of character, who is not necessarily his or her natural self. It's playing theatre inside of theatre. But my actors play real life in the theatre. Of course, it's not as intense as vomiting or getting naked on the stage. But it's amazing how far theatre has come, for instance, from the theatre of masks in ancient Greece. Then, the audience saw nothing, the audience only listened. It was all about the voice. There was nothing on stage but the voice. By the time of Shakespeare, there was the voice together with the character. The actor wore a costume, and the audience began to see the character. Then came Ibsen, then psychological realism. Then life appeared on stage in Stanislavsky's theatre. The actor, his voice, gesture and demeanour created a 'real' character. Then came the corporeal stuff of the sixties and vomiting on stage and eating on stage. Then came Grotowski and Peter Brook. Now, today, we are returning to the sacred on the stage. We've come all this way to return to the very beginning, to ritual. Before theatre, before art, there was ritual. Chanting and worshipping pagan gods came first and then came Greek tragedy, then the Renaissance, Shakespeare, Molière, then realism and Ostrovsky, then Grotowski and post-modernism. Where are we going? We are returning to sacred acts and to theatre as a ritual. Theatre is becoming sacred again. And now we're returning to the beginning, when it all started with the voice. Moreover, theatre, since the beginning, has functioned to help the audience analyse something fundamental in their lives: their spirituality, their society, their sexuality. This is something that a modest, poor theatre can achieve. And in fact, it happens more often in the small, poor theatres than in the large opera halls that sell very expensive tickets. Theatre should be art, and art should be creation. Art should bring people together to focus on an aspect and see it from a different perspective. The audience, when seeing the things that bother them, rises above those things. That's what theatre does.

SW I'd like to ask if you plan on staging *July* again in the future.

IV Do you think there would be an interest in it in America?

SW Yes, without a doubt.

IV I'd like to return to the text of this play. I feel like I'm ready.

SW But Elena Koval'skaia told me that you've decided not to stage this performance again.

IV I want to return to it. I could, in two hours, sit down and rewrite parts of it, but I'd never do that. It's already created, it's already a historical document, and it shouldn't be altered.

SW I'd like to ask you about another play, *Illusions*. One drama critic's review shed light on the play's own unique theory about love. But how can the audience feel a deep emotion when the plot of the play is constantly being interrupted? The text is full of jokes and ironic phrases, and it seems to me that these components prevent the audience from fully empathizing with the characters and their experiences. What do you think?

IV Well, the idea is simple. It's about illusions. As soon as you get used to a certain reality, it suddenly changes.

SW Yes, and this is exactly how we live in real life.

IV Yes, and so the question arises: what is consistency? What is permanency? The answer to this question is within each audience member. You watch a play about unrequited love, which leaves you going out of the theatre, nevertheless, with a bright feeling, and that feeling is the thing that stays with you constantly. All things change, even love. But all things always remain in the environment. The environment is eternal and is part of us, and we are a part of it. If we hold on to just one component of this environment, of this life, then, absolutely, it will disappear. But if we can grasp the whole picture and try to see more and more, and wider and wider, then we'll have more of a sense of consistency and permanency. What I'm saying is that little details are never permanent. But they are embedded in a larger process, and this larger process is permanent, unending. It never ends and it never began. It's always been. There's no future and no past. Everything is one. But within its details are the future, past, tragedy. And within these details we search for a new life and try to make sense of tragedy.

SW Your work is very conceptual. When I read, for instance, *Oxygen* and *July*, I would follow the plot, and then I'd start to follow not the plot but rather the words in your plays that repeat. The phrase-repeat, like the refrain of a song. I started to await the repeated phrases because they are familiar to me.

IV It's like looking at an object from a different perspective, at different intervals of time. Do you remember the house in which you lived when you were a child?

SW Yes, I do.

IV OK, in your house there were things that you looked at and played with when you were eleven years old. Then, in the same house, but when you were at the age of twenty, you looked at these things, and they were the same, but you looked at them from a different perspective. This proves that you have changed. And so has your perspective on things. It's a very interesting process. We always think that the world around us is changing, but it's actually our perception that is changing. The world changes according to our perception. The same thing happens in the theatre. You hear one phrase in the beginning of the play, and then hear the same phrase at the end of the play, but by the end of the play your perspective has changed, and so that same phrase seems new and different to you. These repeated phrases give the audience the ability to experience a moment of change. There's a new development within ourselves at the same time as the universe is developing.

SW Within the timeframe of the theatrical performance.

IV Yes, the universe is changing every second, we simply don't notice it.

SW May I ask what kind of literature you're reading at the moment?

IV Right now [May, 2013], since I'm the artistic director of Praktika Theatre, people are sending me plays to read all the time. I've been reading many Belarusian plays. By Pavel Priazhko, for instance.

SW Can you identify any similarities in style between your plays and his?

IV To me, Priazhko's plays are experiments with text. His *Life Has Gone Well* (*Zhizn' Udalas'*), as staged by Mikhail Ugarov, is written directly for the audience and performed directly for them. People go to the theatre and buy tickets because theatre is something that they absolutely need. Here, at Praktika, all the seats are full. Yes, our theatre is small, but all the seats are full. This is because people need these performances.

Translated from the Russian by Susanna Weygandt

Illusions (*Illiuzii*, 2011), written by Ivan Vyrypaev

The play's protagonists are two elderly couples. On his deathbed, Danny tells his wife Sandra for the last time how much he loves her. He speaks tender words to her and thanks her. After his death Sandra admits to Danny's best friend, Albert, that she has loved Albert her whole life. Albert takes his turn to discuss with his wife Margaret how his whole life he has loved Sandra. And at that moment Margaret tells him that she cheated on him with Danny. Within this melodrama is a performance in which there is neither make-up, nor costumes, nor any actor's devised playing.

July (*Iiul'*, 2006), written by Ivan Vyrypaev

July is a seventy-page monologue told from the perspective of Petr, a maniac serial-killer. One traumatic event happens in the beginning of the play: Petr's house burns to the ground. The rest of the monodrama is dedicated to his recovery from the fire as the sixty-four-year-old Petr flees his house of ashes to take refuge in an insane asylum in Smolensk. Petr derives a transgressive pleasure from killing and eating. *July* was written during Vyrypaev's 'dark period' when he was interested in the aesthetics of cruelty and when he was watching films by Quentin Tarantino. Along the way to Smolensk, Petr's different emotional states – power, salvation and love – are expressed through his murder of a fox, a dog, a priest and a woman whom he loves.[1] Every life he takes offers the possibility of him becoming a new Self. In *July* the physical acts of violence committed by Petr are omitted from stage directions. However, there is one, noteworthy stage direction: there should be one performer of the play, who should be female. The ostensible opposite typecasting marks Vyrypaev's fascination with the aesthetics of sound and speech in his monodrama, first, and lack of interest in physical identification between actor and character.

Note

1 There is a reference here to Evgenii Grishkovets's play *How I Ate a Dog* (*Kak ia s"el sobaku*, 1999).

Beumers and Lipovetsky frame Petr's cannibalism in Julia Kristeva's theory of the Abject, which posits that the subject projects the object of pleasure on to himself out of an impulse to overcome fear of himself and his own identity: 'Peter kills not only those whom he considers his enemies or rivals, but also those he esteems and loves, and on whom he projects himself' (2009, 259).

8

Absence on Stage in Ivan Vyrypaev's *July*

Valeriia Mutc

> In this essay Valeriia Mutc offers a close reading of Ivan Vyrypaev's play *July* (*Iiul'*, 2006), a chilling monologue by a psychopath murderer in which the part of the male character Petr is performed by a female actor. Mutc is particularly fascinated by the ways that audience engagement is enhanced through the absence of the character from the stage, raising questions about who is actually responsible for making meaning.

At the very end of Ivan Vyrypaev's play *July* (2006), the reader is faced with a difficult decision. After the monologue of the maniac and murderer Petr, readers are reminded of their own participation in the narratological development of the play. In a short stage direction, they are made acutely aware of their complicity in the action. The stage direction states:

> The movement stops, nature freezes, we are waiting. Autumn, winter, spring, and then summer. The very middle of summer is July. Everything has become different, and yet it has not started anew, but is moving forward. Everything is moving forward. And we are following it.[1]

The voice of the playwright enters the text, inviting the reader first to wait with him and then to follow the narrative further. The use of the first person plural form *my* ('we') engages the reader and explicitly calls for us to become absorbed in the narrative progression, making this stage direction a central meta-fictional moment of the play. One is reminded that *July* is, in fact, a theatrical narrative, meant to be staged. Even though the main character dies at the end of the play, once the story is staged, it will be performed again and again, suggesting that ultimately no one can escape the power of a theatrical narrative but must travel through its curved enclosure of repetition. Additionally, the last sentence of this stage direction is purposefully ambiguous in Russian and can be translated both as 'we are following it', and as 'we are following him'. The former refers to 'everything', to time, and stands in for the narrative itself. The latter alludes to the main character of the play, Petr.

Petr, however, is hardly the right person to follow. In fact, he is a maniac, who kills everyone he meets, often devouring them afterwards. He traverses the spaces of Russia, performing his highly ritualistic killings, and finally perishes in a mental health institution, only to realize there is no escape for him even after death. *July* presents the monologue of Petr, which ends with the character dying and succumbing to the overpowering timeline of the play: 'Eternal, forever and ever, never-ending July.'[2] It is after this ambiguous resolution that the meta-fictional stage direction appears in the play script. By blurring the line between following the narrative progression and following the maniac, the narrator implicitly invites the reader to make a decision about Petr's life and death, and to evaluate ethically whether to participate in the narrative further. The stage direction thus presents the reader with the most important ethical dilemma of the play.

However, in the 2006 production of the play at Moscow's Praktika theatre, directed by Viktor Ryzhakov, this stage direction is not verbalized or performed in any way. During this moment in the play, the solo performer, the actress Polina Agureeva, leaves, and the spectator sits alone in the darkness for a couple of minutes, looking at an empty stage. In the play-text, readers are explicitly encouraged to follow the playwright and to consider their place in the narrative progression. In the theatre, the spectators are instead confronted by emptiness, with no apparent indication of the authorial desire for their engagement. In the entire performance the moments of emptiness and darkness amount to approximately seven minutes and constitute one tenth of the whole production. They often correspond with the meta-fictional instances in the play script, when the reader is addressed by the playwright, as in the stage direction discussed above. Emptiness in the performance thus assumes the function of meta-fictionality in the text, engaging the spectator and making one aware of the act of watching.

This essay will examine the process of audience engagement by means of emptiness on stage in Ivan Vyrypaev's *July*. It will ask what happens during this time when the stage is empty. Why did Vyrypaev and Ryzhakov choose to leave it empty during the most crucial moments of the play, when a direct interaction with the reader is initiated in the text?[3] This technique is a reflection on the conditions of performative presence in modern theatre, a spectral intervention into the space of the stage, not dissimilar to the ghost entering the scene in Shakespeare's *Hamlet*. It also grants the director an opportunity to escape the dominating power of the plot, to represent something else on stage. Finally, rather like the stage direction from the play, emptiness is an invitation for the spectator to participate in the narrative, and to take an active part in its unfolding. In the moments of absence on stage, the audience is faced with an ethical dilemma about the story of Petr. The spectators have to question their participation in the narrative as a whole and take an ethical stance on the subject.

In my argumentation, I work with Jacques Derrida's and Shoshana Felman's reflections on the performative in speech and theatre, and consider Samuel Weber's discussion of spectrality and disembodied voice in theatre. Derrida's and Felman's consideration of the performative is especially fruitful for examining how the text is foregrounded in *July*, defying the primacy of the actor and the narrator. When the disembodied narrative is the only thing left on stage, the place of the spectator in theatre is reconsidered. Following

Weber's interpretation of spectrality, I argue that in the moments of absence on stage, the audience becomes cognisant of the different temporalities involved in a theatrical narrative, and has to consider its own role in the narrative unfolding. Erasing the actor and, sometimes, the narrative, Vyrypaev points out the underlying structures of theatre, which constitute a struggle for power not only in the framework of theatre, but in our everyday reality. By doing so, Vyrypaev participates in a discourse on performance, which is evident in contemporary Russian theatre and exposes ethical dilemmas that underlie our entire social existence. These ethical questions are treated as universal by the playwright, not confined to any particular space or time. The broad geography of his texts and his life only further highlights this fact.

Vyrypaev's artistic life was shaped by new perceptions of space and mobility that came with the turn of the century in Russia. He started his career as a theatrical director in the eastern Siberian town of Irkutsk and then moved to Moscow, where in 2005 he co-founded the Praktika theatre. He now alternates between Moscow and Poland, continuing his work on cinema and drama. However, whether his works are set in the Russian provinces (*Oxygen*, 2003), Tibet (*Salvation*, 2015) or Copenhagen (*The Iran Conference*, 2017), the questions they raise are markedly universal and blur spatial borders between provincial and central, native and foreign. *July* was written after Vyrypaev's move to Poland and, while being in many ways different stylistically from his earlier works, it deals with similar themes, such as identity, representation and the idea of self, as well as the ethical choices required of people in a continuously expanding modern world. *July*, which was successfully produced in Russia, Ukraine and Poland, presents questions of universal human existence in the face of the new challenges of the twenty-first century. Unlike Vyrypaev's later works, however, the play script of *July* and its subsequent performances raise these questions on a meta-textual level, calling for distrust of the narrative itself. This is achieved primarily by highlighting the primacy of the text in the absence of the actor and the narrator, prompting questions about who is responsible for meaning-making in theatre.

The importance of the text in *July* is emphasized by its very structure, which mimics the techniques of documentary theatre, initiated in Russia with the active participation of Vyrypaev. The playwright was among the first members of Teatr.doc, a documentary theatre located in Moscow. When in 2005 he started his own theatre, Praktika, *July* became one of the first plays written after his move.[4] The play has many of the usual attributes of documentary theatre: it is intended as a one-person play, it is narrated in the first person and past tense, and it follows the progression of the narrating subject's life. However, it immediately becomes evident that *July* is scarcely the artistic retelling of a personal experience – not only is it terrifying in its cruelty, but also the narrator dies and the play continues without him. Furthermore, the stage directions at the beginning of the play clearly establish that it has to be performed not by the text's male protagonist/narrator, but by a woman, who enters the stage 'with the sole purpose of performing the text'.[5] This stage direction indicates that the actress is supposed to perform a text, and not a role. Vyrypaev carefully erases all implications of 'acting' from the play; for example, the actress is never actually defined as such and instead is called a 'woman-performer'.[6] She is a puppet in the hands of the director, the playwright and the narrative, cognitively absent from the story that she tells.

While presenting this story, the solo performer, Polina Agureeva, approaches it only as a text, which she has to mindlessly *transmit*. This performance highlights her mediating function both on a verbal and visual level. At the beginning of the play, she walks out of the darkness that surrounds the stage, clad in an elegant dark dress falling to the floor, holding sheets of paper with the text in her hands. The bright white sheets become the first thing the audience notices. The audience's attention is drawn to the predominance of text, as well as its overpowering materiality in comparison to the ephemeral Agureeva. The performance prioritizes the text on a visual level, making the actress cognitively absent, even when she is physically present. In one critic's assessment, Agureeva creates the illusion of being merely a tool for the transmission of the text: distant and unattainable, she floats with the waves of the narrative, but does not allow their substance to enter her body.[7] For Birgit Beumers and Mark Lipovetsky, Agureeva's performance makes her a female 'Other' to the male narrator, with the latter's consciousness being secondary in relation to her own voice.[8] It is precisely because of her 'mediatory' function that she can resist Petr's narrative and not be consumed by it. This function is most visible in the instances before and after the moments when she is not on stage. The first time the stage is left empty in *July*, Agureeva's performance is purposefully distant, with her metallic voice and perfect diction, which she uses to retell the inner monologue of Petr's insanity, and which is accentuated by the introduction of an echo. Most likely talking over a pre-recorded track of her own voice, Agureeva spits out words in a completely absent manner. While being physically on stage, her psychic and emotional connections are elsewhere. It is at this moment she most resembles a machine, transmitting the story in someone else's voice.

Text is usually in the background of a theatrical performance. We assume that there is one, but it has to be 'forgotten' to preserve the theatrical illusion. The audience has to pretend that the words they hear are being produced for the very first time. By bringing the play script on stage and ensuring that Agureeva's performance is mechanical and emotionless, Vyrypaev subverts theatrical conventions, making his spectators aware of the fact that a performance is always determined by an already existing script, or a narrative more generally. Vyrypaev thus takes away the pretence that the actor is living through the situation in real time and that the action is unfolding in front of the audience. Agureeva's mental and physical absence on stage highlights the fact that she is not an active creator of the narrative, and makes the spectator wonder who is the author of these words. As Agureeva physically leaves the stage, she abandons the spectator to ruminate on the conditions of authorship in theatre. The spectator is encouraged to ask who is the original 'sender' of the message. If Agureeva is nothing more than a medium, then who stands behind meaning-making in theatre, and who can be considered an author?

An obvious candidate for meaning-making in the text is Petr himself. After all, he is the narrator of the events in *July*, as all of the play is given in the first person. However, the possibility of his control over the narrative is quickly undermined. Petr is himself stuck inside the repeatable narrative produced by his own insanity, and cannot escape its power. He exists in a narratological nightmare, in which he cannot even distinguish between his own thoughts and someone else's. This mental state is represented by the recurring symbol of July, which Petr both praises and hates simultaneously, and from which he cannot escape, no matter how much time passes. Petr is as much a hostage of the narrative as its creator.

Birgit Beumers and Mark Lipovetsky have remarked that the text becomes an object of the performance in Vyrypaev's drama.[9] In another one of his plays, *Genesis-2* (2004), Vyrypaev claims as much himself: 'The main hero of this play is the text.'[10] Vyrypaev's characters often struggle against the power of the narrative. This is most aptly captured by the female character in *Oxygen* (2003) who rebels against the narrator by accusing him of being partial: 'I won't be able to say so, because you did not write this text for me, on purpose.'[11] In *July*, this struggle is speechless and is embodied by Agureeva's physical and mental absence on stage. It is in the moments when she is not there that the spectator feels the sheer power of the narrative, which can continue without her or Petr. For example, at the end of the play, Petr dies and Agureeva leaves the stage, freeing the space for the disembodied voice of Petr's sons, who come to collect his body. These ruptures in the fabric of the narrative suggest that Petr does not preside over it, but is captured by it. However, this capacity of the narrative to continue after the symbolic death of the narrator opens up new terrifying possibilities for Petr. It serves as a symbolic guarantee that his violence will continue even after he is gone. Vyrypaev paints a disheartening image in which this 'durability' of violence might be a universal phenomenon preconditioned by language itself.

This notion of authorship and meaning corresponds to Derrida's argument in 'Signature Event Context', where he argues that language must be capable of functioning in the absence of its original presence. Both the sender and the addressee ought to allow for the possibility of their absence in order for language to exist. Even the sign itself is preconditioned by the absence of the object from present perception. The iterability of any text is most important for its meaning:

> Could we maintain that, following the death of the receiver, or even of both partners, the mark left by one of them is still writing? Yes, to the extent that, organized by a code, even an unknown and nonlinguistic one, it is constituted in its identity as mark by its iterability, in the absence of such and such a person, and hence ultimately of every empirically determined 'subject'.[12]

According to Derrida, all writing must be able to function in the 'radical absence' of its sender and receiver, which originates from the impossibility of ever having an absolutely determinable context. A speech act on stage is mediated, while its original meaning resides elsewhere, and Vyrypaev only highlights this by his choice of the performer. However, for Vyrypaev, this mediation is also a promise. Petr presents a story of his life, filled with violence and murder. By making it into a repeatable theatrical narrative, he makes certain that his story will not perish, even in the absence, or death, of the sender, i.e. himself. If the absence of Agureeva signifies her resistance and foregrounding of the text, the absence of Petr signifies his presence somewhere else, be it in some undetermined space off stage, or in language itself.

Most of Petr's crimes are language-based, highlighting the fact that the violence of his story, however terrifying, is not one of a kind, but is a recurring event in history. In a way, Petr attributes most of the guilt for his crimes to language, often misinterpreting what he hears. A speech act for Petr is performative, meaning that he is incapable of seeing the difference between saying something and doing it. Shoshana Felman in *The Scandal of the Speaking Body*, writes about this precise question in connection to Molière's Don Juan. She claims Don Juan thinks about language in terms of its performative function. For him the speech act does not correspond directly to the truth lying behind it.[13] Don Juan's antagonists, on the other hand, approach language as a cognitive instrument and assess it only in relation to its constative function.[14] Like Don Juan in Felman's interpretation, Petr understands the speech act as performative: anything that is pronounced is acted out, and there is virtually no difference between saying something and acting it.

The man can only tell his story by enacting it, which accounts for the lack of difference between verbal and physical acts of violence. However, he is constantly running up against the limits of the narrative. After the murder of a priest, Petr envisions an angel addressing him, claiming that the killing is 'not news any more'.[15] The denial of the novelty of Petr's crime originates neither in him having committed similar crimes before, nor in the existing precedence for murders committed by someone else, but rather in the ultimate inescapability of a theatrical narrative, which leads Petr along a predictable path. As Felman demonstrates, there is nothing in the framework of the theatrical narrative that can be classified as 'first' or 'original'.[16] The impossibility of conceptualizing the event's novelty becomes a guarantee that Petr's terrible violence will continue in the future, even in the absence of the narrator himself.

Petr's story becomes an example of how a narrative preconditions an action, and how his actions will be repeated, as long as the text lasts. The maniac's story does not correspond to the truth outside of itself, but rather aims to produce an event in the timeline of the performance, in the here and now of stage time. The play explores the conditions of a theatrical event by narrating Petr's crimes, instead of showing them. His actions are determined by the primacy of the text and the absence of conventional theatrical representation. To commit a murder, Petr needs a verbal affirmation or an imperative to do so, which his victims unknowingly give him. The maniac approaches the world as an instruction manual for murder. For example, reading the Bible and liturgical texts, Petr decides that, in order to ensure his friend's future life in Heaven, he has to kill him while he still remains innocent. In other instances of the same misappropriation of language, Petr summarizes the significance of marriage through reference to a Russian idiomatic expression 'to ask for one's hand and heart', which the maniac interprets literally: he tears out his beloved's heart and amputates her hand.[17] Before that, Petr asks his lover if she is ready to disappear, which the woman responds to affirmatively, although what she means is the disappearance and dissolution of herself in love: 'All of me became love, I am all love. I am love and I am lying on the table. Love is food. Love is a dish on a festive table.'[18] Petr interprets this metaphor as a command to eat the woman. Any speech act for him is equivalent to an action, and even his own story pursues the same goal of making the narrative produce an event over and over. What is terrifying about Petr's violence is not just its utmost cruelty, but the fact that it exists in language even in the absence of the maniac. From telling the unique story of a mentally ill person, *July* becomes a narrative on how certain violent acts will repeat themselves in history, simply because they are inherent to humanity and its ways of communication. Thus, when Agureeva leaves the stage and when the narrator dies in the play, Vyrypaev draws attention to the primacy of the narrative and to its potency for invoking terrifying meanings in theatre and in everyday life. However, the playwright also offers a possible solution to his audience, which resides in the audience's capacity for distancing itself from the events of the play, and for making an active choice about its participation in the violent narrative.

In order to explore this possibility, the play simultaneously introduces two temporal frameworks. The first one is the repeated cyclical temporality of Petr's insanity, summarized in the symbol of 'never-ending July'. The narrative of the story highlights both teleological movement towards a greater good – the death of the maniac – and simultaneously, the enclosure of Petr in cyclical time, which is symbolized by perpetual July, deprived of temporal coordinates: 'It was July, winter was approaching spring.'[19] This cyclical time is shared with the spectator, who is similarly stuck in a theatrical repeatability, faced with a distrust towards the language on stage. However, Vyrypaev offers an alternative, in which the spectator can choose to stand behind the narrative meaning in theatre. This alternative comes in introducing a different temporality in the moments of absence on stage.

Early in the play, Petr confesses that he once hit his wife, causing her to lose her mind. Petr's outrage and violence were prompted by a seemingly inconspicuous remark by his wife: like the angel's exclamation mentioned above, the wife objects to Petr's violence, saying, 'this is nothing new'.[20] After Petr attacks her, the woman seemingly goes insane and leaves their house without saying a word, never to return. Paradoxically, she turns out to be the only person who survives Petr's violence. In order to survive violence, one has to write oneself out of the narrative by leaving the stage, both literally and metaphorically. The story of Petr's wife is told abruptly and does not constitute a major part of the play. However, the woman's disappearance – that is repeated in the absence of Agureeva – interrupts the cyclical structure of the theatrical narrative in *July*. The wife is the *first* to survive Petr's violence, defying the narrative repeatability of the plot and introducing a different temporality to the play, not that of the meaningless inescapability of July, but that of real time, of the spectator. By being absent on stage, she is present somewhere else, becoming a spectral intervention into the space of the stage.

This endurance of meaning beyond the theatrical stage is connected to the discussion of spectrality in theatre. Samuel Weber in *Theatricality as Medium*, building on Derrida's discussion of *Hamlet* in *Specters of Marx*, suggests that spectrality and theatricality are complicit: like the spectral, the theatrical stage encompasses a multiplicity of different temporalities and spatial dimensions, with its figures always being somewhere else as well. A ghost is always present and absent at the same time, 'being tied to a particular locale, and yet not to any single one'.[21] The stage, according to Weber, 'remains a temporal stage, which comes only in going, and which, in departing, leaves room for what is to come'.[22] However, this time it is not Petr who continues to exist even after his narratological demise, but the wife, and with her, the spectator. The audience is out of reach of Petr's violence, once it makes a decision about its own exclusion from the narrative of the story. In a way, the audience is encouraged to build a fourth wall, not so much between the stage and the auditorium, but between themselves and the narrative. The spectator can intervene with a different temporality in Petr's narrative, discrediting its power. The introduction of this evasive spectral temporality accentuates the fact that what is peeking through the cracks of a theatrical performance is a reality of other places and other temporality, which is ultimately brought to the theatre by the spectator. It is the spectator who 'survives' the play every time:

> As generic work, theatrical presentation is thus elevated above the restrictive limitations of its *localizability*, which for living beings is inseparable from *mortality*. Every self-contained 'story' tends *as such* to be a story of salvation, every *Geschichte*, a *Heilsgeschichte*; every ending is a happy one for the viewer, listener, or reader who 'survives' it.[23]

The possibility of a spectator surviving Petr's violence, and an alternative to the suffocating inescapability of Petr's narrative, appear in the places of rupture – the places of emptiness on stage. When Agureeva abandons the stage, the spectator is left alone, in an attempt to process what just happened, while looking at an empty stage. The audience is invited to self-observe, immersed in a state of powerful sense-deprivation: the loud music prevents people from talking to each other and the relative darkness does not allow for looking around. It is here that the spectator brings another temporality on stage, putting himself or herself in a position outlined by Weber: the audience knows that the performance will continue and that they will be the ones to 'survive' Petr's violence and escape the narrative 'doom' that looms over the characters of the play. In allocating to his audience the spaces of emptiness, Vyrypaev encourages it to question their implication in Petr's violent story and to react to it emotionally, counteracting Petr's narrative.

Empty stage as a technique was historically linked to the exploration of the emotional response of the audience. It was introduced in Russia in the Moscow Art Theatre's performance of Anton Chekhov's *The Seagull* (1898). At the beginning of the play, actors would casually enter and leave the stage for prolonged periods of time, continuing their conversations as if no interruption happened. The audience would be looking at an empty stage for minutes, listening to the characters talk in the background. Konstantin Stanislavsky, the director of the production, believed that such instances would make the performance more realistic and would cause the audience to be more emotionally attuned. However, at the time some critics argued that, while intending to create a more authentic image of the 'flow of life,' the production also immersed its audience in a state of emotional and physical inactivity. This notion was developed at the beginning of the twentieth century by the theatre critic Ilya Ignatov, who in his book *Theatre and Spectators* (1916), argued that theatre teaches its audience emotional restraint.[24] The spectator learns not to react to what he or she witnesses on stage, and subconsciously transfers this principle into real life. Ignatov was not alone in this belief. It is precisely for this reason that the long tradition of anti-theatricality was hostile to the depiction of social evils on stage. The audience can either become numb to others' suffering or start to replicate in their lives the bad patterns they have witnessed on stage. The emotional response of the audience always has been tied to an ethical choice about the characters' fate.

In *July* the moments of absence on stage trigger this ethical dilemma. These moments have the power to remove the spectator from a theatrical illusion for a second, and remind the audience that it is participating in a theatrical event as opposed to real life. Yet in theatre the spectator does not have the power of expressing his or her disdain, and is incapable of breaking through the fourth wall and creating a rupture in a theatrical performance. Even when no one is on stage, the mechanisms of self-regulation, actualized in the theatrical audience, prevent it from interrupting the performance. The ethics of this inactivity in *July* are considered in the moments of absence on stage, when the shared responsibility of the audience for the narrative progression is revealed.

At the end of *July*, the empty auditorium is filled with mechanical and muffled sounds, transmitted by a bad radio signal and reminiscent of a train station. The spectator hears voices, announcements, various noises, but it is impossible to tell who is speaking – a woman or a man – or whether anyone is speaking at all. This abundance of disjointed sounds, reminiscent of the noise produced during public gatherings, introduces a new subject to the stage – the collective voice. It is imagined as the voice of the audience – a voice of reason which belongs to a different temporality, that of a collective reality outside of theatre. This temporality then manifests itself in the appearance of a different perspective – this time in the voice of a man, which is supposed to stand for Petr's sons, who have come to collect his body and take it to their home in the northern city of Arkhangel'sk. The sons introduce the voice of the rational, which corresponds to the voice of the audience. Petr is not rejected by it. On the contrary, he is being 'made sense of', he is no longer a divine double who can murder God, but a mentally ill person who has had a hard life: 'We know about all your misfortunes and your suffering, your life turned out to be hard, as they say, I wouldn't wish it on my enemy.'[25]

While Petr remains stuck in a repetitive narrative that continually leads to death, his sons introduce another temporality, in which Petr's life has ended. The spectators are supposed to associate themselves with the sons and become the performance's sole survivors, left looking at an empty stage, which shows the absence that stands behind the performer's words. This ultimate absence exposes the representational tools at the theatre's disposal: a table, a stool and a microphone. The objects which remain on stage are mundane and unremarkable, unable to tell a story by themselves, leaving it for the spectator to decide whether an empty stage contains any narrative, and whether that can be told without an actor or a narrator. The audience feels its agency in the aftermath of this confrontation with Petr, as well as with the narrative. In those moments, they are given the opportunity to make an ethical decision about Petr's fate. Is this documentary story about a maniac, an unfortunate tale of a mentally ill person, a theatrical rendition of events which never took place, or a universal story of humanity which will repeat itself over and over? The spectator may even reject any decision and choose to abandon the story altogether. Regardless of what he or she chooses, however, this injection of outside temporality into the theatrical timeline puts things in perspective and forces one to be decisive about the ethical implications of the play. Ultimately, emptiness forces the spectator to take a more active role than would typically be expected of an audience member.

Derrida's model of language as the absence of an original presence invites us to consider the theatrical performance in its *iterability*. As one can never determine the absolute context of each performance or mark any of them as original, each play can only be analysed in the multiplicity of its manifestations. However, the empty stage provides an opportunity to expose the theatrical conditions that underlie any performance and allows the spectator to be active about the ethical implications of the play. *July* highlights latent points about a theatrical narrative that usually remain untold and unseen, and forces the spectator actively to question the conventional conditions of theatrical presence. By making the text material and present on stage, Vyrypaev points out how the more conventional absence of textual material enables the illusion of an original event, of something that has happened for the *first* time. In *July*, on the contrary, narrative is foregrounded and prioritized, making Petr's story terrifying in its repeatability. However, instances of emptiness on stage allow for audience members to place themselves inside the play and to consider the possibility of surviving inside the narrative, at the same time tearing it apart by introducing the different temporality of the 'outside' world.

Vyrypaev's exposition of theatrical conditions through the use of absence leads us towards the underlying structures of power not just in theatre, but in our everyday existence. Coming from the 'New Drama' movement, which increasingly became politically engaged, Vyrypaev considers the idea of theatre as a contained version of reality in its fullness, a *theatrum mundi* of contemporary society. The many absences in *July* – that of the actress, of the narrator, and of standard theatrical temporality – force the spectator to take a more active stance and to evaluate the possibility of following the narrative further. Ultimately, the possibility of this choice is as universal as the violence exhibited by Petr, and can always lead to a symbolic 'survival'. After all, any play for Vyrypaev is 'a form of eternity', and it is the theatre that connects the spectator to this eternity, which is both internal and external to ourselves.[26]

Notes

1 Ivan Vyrypaev, *P'esy* (Moscow: Tri kvadrata, 2016), 79. 'Dvizhenie ostanavlivaetsia, priroda zamiraet, zhdem. Osen', zima, vesna, a potom i leto. Samaia seredina leta – iiul'. Vse stalo drugim, no ne zanovo nachalos', a poshlo dal'she. Vse poshlo dal'she. I my poshli za nim.' All translations are my own, unless stated otherwise.
2 Ibid., 79. 'Vechnyi i vo veki vekov neskonchaemyi iiul'.'
3 This essay considers the production by Viktor Ryzhakov as reflecting Vyrypaev's own beliefs about how his plays should be directed, and thus, for the sake of clarity, I will refer to the production in question as Vyrypaev's own.
4 'Ivan Vyrypaev', Teatr.doc, http://www.teatrdoc.ru/person.php?id=1 (accessed 19 December 2017).
5 Vyrypaev, *P'esy*, 54. '... Vyshla tol'ko dlia togo, chtoby ispolnit' etot tekst.'
6 Ibid., 80. 'Zhenshchina-ispolnitel'nitsa.' Note here the similarity with Teatr.doc's motto: 'A theatre where no one acts' ('Teatr, gde ne igraiut').
7 Pavel Rudnev, 'Lektsiia kannibala', Vzgliad, https://vz.ru/columns/2006/12/15/60800.html (accessed 19 December 2017).
8 Birgit Beumers and Mark Lipovetsky, *Performing Violence: Literary and Theatrical Experiments of New Russian Drama* (Chicago: Intellect, 2009), 262–3.

9   Ibid., 241.
10 Ivan Vyrypaev, *13 tekstov, napisannykh osen'iu* (Moscow: Vremia, 2005), 156. 'Glavnyi geroi p'esy - tekst.'
11 Vyrypaev, *P'esy*, 30. 'Ia ne mogu tak skazat', potomu chto ty spetsial'no ne napisal mne etogo teksta.'
12 Jacques Derrida, 'Signature Event Context', in *Limited Inc* (Evanston, IL: Northwestern University Press, 1988), 7–8.
13 Shoshana Felman, *The Scandal of The Speaking Body* (Stanford, CA: Stanford University Press, 2003), 14.
14 Ibid.
15 Vyrypaev, *P'esy*, 60. 'Eto ne novost'.'
16 Felman, *The Scandal of The Speaking Body*, 21–3.
17 'To ask for one's hand and heart' in Russian means 'to propose', to put a ring on a woman's hand and to win her heart over.
18 Vyrypaev, *P'esy*, 75. 'Ia vsia stala liubov'iu, ia vsia i est' liubov'. Vot ia – liubov', lezhu na stole. A liubov' – eto pishcha. Liubov' – eto bliudo na prazdnichnom stole.'
19 Ibid., 60. 'Shel mesiats iul', zima uzhe priblizhalas' k vesne.'
20 Ibid., 58. 'Eto ne novost'.'
21 Samuel Weber, *Theatricality as Medium* (New York: Fordham University Press, 2004), 188–9.
22 Ibid., 199.
23 Ibid., 188–9.
24 I. Ignatov, *Teatr i zriteli* (Moscow: Tipografiia tovarishchestva Riabushinskikh, 1916). For more information on Ignatov and theatrical audiences of the nineteenth century, see: Olga Kuptsova, '"Ekzazheratsiia chuvstv": osobennosti emotsional'nykh reaktsii teatral'noi publiki 1830–1840-kh godov', in *Rossiiskaia imperiia chuvstv: Podkhody k kul'turnoi istorii emotsii*, ed. Jan Plamper, Shamma Shakhadat and Marc Elie, 131–43 (Moscow: Novoe literaturnoe obozrenie, 2010).
25 Vyrypaev, *P'esy*, 77. 'Znaem my o vsekh tvoikh bedakh i stradaniiakh, nelegkaia u tebia okazalas' zhizn', takogo, kak govoritsia, i vragu ne pozhelaesh'.'
26 Ibid., 12.

Bibliography

Beumers, Birgit, and Mark Lipovetsky. *Performing Violence: Literary and Theatrical Experiments of New Russian Drama*. Chicago: Intellect, 2009.
Derrida, Jacques. 'Signature Event Context'. Translated by Samuel Weber and Jeffrey Mehlman. In *Limited Inc*, 1–21. Evanston, IL: Northwestern University Press, 1988.
Derrida, Jacques. *Specters of Marx: The State of the Debt, the Work of Mourning, and the New International*. Translated by Peggy Kamuf. London: Routledge, 1994.
Felman, Shoshana. *The Scandal of the Speaking Body*. Stanford: Stanford University Press, 2003.
Lehmann, Hans-Thies. *Postdramatic Theatre*. Translated by Karen Jurs-Munby. London: Routledge, 2006.
Ignatov, I. *Teatr i zriteli*. Moscow: Tipografiia tovarishchestva Riabushinskikh, 1916.
Kuptsova, Olga. '"Ekzazheratsiia chuvstv": osobennosti emotsional'nykh reaktsii teatral'noi publiki 1830–1840-kh godov'. In *Rossiiskaia imperiia chuvstv: Podkhody k kul'turnoi*

istorii emotsii, edited by Jan Plamper, Shamma Shakhadat and Marc Elie, 131–43. Moscow: Novoe literaturnoe obozrenie, 2010.

Rudnev, Pavel. 'Lektsiia kannibala'. Vzgliad. https://vz.ru/columns/2006/12/15/60800.html (accessed 19 December 2017).

Vyrypaev, Ivan. *P'esy*. Moscow: Tri kvadrata, 2016.

Vyrypaev, Ivan. *13 tekstov, napisannykh osen'iu*. Moscow: Vremia, 2005.

Weber, Samuel. *Theatricality as Medium*. New York: Fordham University Press, 2004.

Part II

Ukraine

The watershed year of 2014

The 'birth' of Ukrainian New Drama

Noah Birksted-Breen

> Noah Birksted-Breen made two research trips to Ukraine during 2017, to observe the contemporary drama scene there and interview theatre-makers. Against the background of late-twentieth and twenty-first-century Russian drama, on which he is an expert, Noah identifies the political events of 2014 as marking a decisive break in the close relations which up until then had characterised the worlds of modern Ukrainian and Russian theatre. In this comprehensive survey, he considers how aesthetic considerations as well as institutional structures have shaped the development of Ukrainian theatre since the collapse of the USSR in 1991, and argues that 2014 marks the beginning of a fully independent 'Ukrainian New Drama'.

A watershed year in Ukrainian cultural life occurred in 2014. Every aspect of the civic sphere – including theatre-making – was affected by the popular uprising (known as 'the Maidan') in Kyiv's Independence Square in 2013–14. This essay documents how this pivotal episode in contemporary Ukrainian history, as well as the occupation of Crimea by pro-Russian troops and Russian military intervention in eastern Ukraine in 2014, translated into the realm of theatrical production. I will propose that this dramatic year may be conceptualized as the birth date of 'Ukrainian New Drama'. I suggest that, between the mid-1990s and 2014, most post-Soviet Ukrainian playwrights actively participated in the 'New Drama' movement in Russia, writing as part of a transnational cultural sphere, primarily for Russian audiences – and in Russian. The sudden shift in civic and geopolitical contexts in 2014 led to an abrupt re-forging of identity: a re-focusing on national audiences – which found immediate expression in the choice of dramatic narratives as well as, to a lesser extent, by privileging the Ukrainian language. With the Maidan as a prototype for collective civic action, many post-Soviet playwrights re-conceptualized their own position as influencers, or even activists, within a national public discourse. Their revitalized sense of purpose also served as a de facto 'postcolonial' rejection of Russian state interference in Ukrainian affairs, at a time when Russia was reasserting its territorial claims in Crimea and in eastern Ukraine. From 'New Drama' into 'Ukrainian New Drama', there was a significant continuity of a postmodern aesthetic in much contemporary dramatic writing. What changed abruptly in terms of theatrical production was the perceived need for new institutions which would support experimentation by contemporary playwrights, to develop their own distinctive theatrical forms in order to forge a legitimate national playwriting movement. From 2014, small collectives of playwrights and directors created an emergent 'fringe' sector outside of the state-run repertory system, as a vehicle for 'Ukrainian New Drama' – a term which some theatre-makers and critics began to use. After the Maidan and still at the time of writing (April 2019), playwriting by the post-Soviet generation exhibits a relatively diverse range of postmodern theatrical forms as well as underlying nonconformist ideologies – suggesting that its aesthetic trajectory is still in contention.

I have structured this essay as a chronological overview of the development of post-Soviet contemporary playwriting from 1991 to 2017. I reflect upon a small number of significant productions during this period, particularly those which disrupted dominant theatrical conventions in Ukrainian theatre, such as the documentary texts *Maidan Diaries* by Natal'ia Vorozhbyt (2014) and *The Militiaman* by Dan Gumennyi and Yana Gumennaia (2015), as well as the semi-autobiographical drama *Vitalik* by Vitalii Chenskii (2017). This essay draws significantly on primary research conducted in the field, through two week-long research trips to Kyiv in July and October 2017. I attended productions and rehearsed readings, as well as interviewing over a dozen theatre-makers from a range of theatres from Kyiv and other cities in Ukraine, in particular Lviv (in the west) and Zaporizhzhia (in the east).

Ukrainian theatre in the 1990s

The collapse of the Soviet Union in 1991 led to sovereign independence for Ukraine. The overthrow of communism removed Soviet-era censorship in the arts. Yet this positive development for freedom of artistic expression was offset by economic collapse, widespread among all post-Soviet states. The move to a market economy witnessed the removal of significant state subsidies for culture. Besides radical reductions in material support, the authorities demonstrated risk-averseness and a lack of creative imagination. The Ukrainian theatre director Vladislav Troitskii has characterized cultural politics after 1991 as being institutionally conservative: 'In the years of independence, the theatre sector basically didn't develop. [...] Many Ukrainian theatre directors returned after training at the drama schools in Moscow, but they came back here and it turned out there was no demand for their work.'[1]

This cultural conservatism in Ukraine shaped the landscape in contemporary playwriting, although this phenomenon was not limited to theatre. The novelist Oksana Zabuzhko has described her aim along with fellow fiction writers 'to create for national literature a national Ukrainian market, literally out of nothing',[2] while a similar endeavour was undertaken by the Lviv-based performance poetry collective Bu-Ba-

Bu, to create a vibrant poetry scene in Ukraine.³ The success of these initiatives was dependent upon an ability to circumvent rigid institutional structures, by founding or collaborating with small private publishing houses in the case of Zabuzhko,⁴ and by performing poetry live as a means of accessing the public without the encumbrance of poetry journals, for Bu-Ba-Bu.

There was at least one significant attempt to create 'alternative' theatrical infrastructures, by Troitskii, who founded a studio theatre – Teatr Dakh (meaning 'roof' in Ukrainian) – which ran as a producing company between 1994 and 2012. Dakh offered opportunities to the post-Soviet generation of actors to gain professional experience beyond the traditional repertory theatres. However, this studio privileged directorial theatrical innovation over dramatic writing, so it did not significantly further the cause of contemporary playwriting in Ukraine.⁵ Through the 1990s, playwrights were entirely dependent upon existing state-run institutions to support them. One of the best-known playwrights from the post-Soviet generation, Natal'ia Vorozhbyt, had her first play *Lives of the Common People* staged at the Youth Theatre in Kyiv in 1995 – but it would be more than a decade until a Ukrainian theatre produced one of her works again.⁶ Furthermore, not a single university or drama school offered a professional playwriting course in Ukraine.⁷ Simultaneously, from the mid-1990s, a vibrant 'underground' theatre sector began to emerge in Russia. Re-enacting a centuries-old tradition of the Ukrainian intelligentsia, numerous young playwrights (who later gained international critical acclaim) moved to Russia in the mid-1990s. Furthermore, as a consequence of many centuries of colonial oppression first by Tsarist Russia and later the Soviet Union, the majority of Ukrainians were bilingual in Russian and Ukrainian. In other words, there was no language barrier to hinder this emigration. Without any state support from the domestic theatre sector, as Troitskii summarizes the situation, Ukraine 'drove away all of its theatrical innovators'.⁸

Two of the writers who came to exemplify Ukrainian playwriting, Vorozhbyt (mentioned earlier) and Maksym Kurochkin, went to study playwriting at the Gor'ky Literary Institute in Moscow, and they participated in the creation of 'New Drama' – the Russian-language experimental 'fringe' playwriting movement emerging in Russia from the mid-1990s.⁹ Both dramatists took part in the Royal Court's seminars in 1999,¹⁰ on documentary forms of playwriting, including verbatim,¹¹ although they were influenced by its ethos rather than rigidly adopting its testimony-based writing practice. Kurochkin's *The Kitchen* played at the Mossoviet Theatre in Moscow in 2000 to huge audience acclaim and largely negative reviews:¹² it was a founding production of 'New Drama'. *The Kitchen* mixed historical allusions with jokes referencing the American animated series *Beavis and Butthead*,¹³ creating a rupture of existing theatrical conventions through a 'mash-up' of the traditional categories of high art and mass entertainment. It took Vorozhbyt longer to emerge as an established dramatist. A production of her play *Galka-Motalko* by the CDR¹⁴ in Moscow in 2005, which brought her to the attention of Russian theatre critics, narrated a vivid tale of a disillusioned teenage athlete at a boarding school for sports champions. The eponymous hero faces abuse by her trainers and sniffs glue with her friends.¹⁵

These critical successes abroad for Ukrainian playwrights were – at least, initially – detrimental to theatrical culture in Ukraine. The Ukrainian theatre critic Sergei Vasil'ev has described the post-1991 era in this way: 'It is revealing that there was no dissemination whatsoever of 'New Drama' on Ukrainian stages (regardless of the fact that Ukraine had delegated its most famous creative artists to Russia, starting with Maksym Kurochkin and Natal'ia Vorozhbyt and ending with Marina Lado and Anna Iablonskaia).'[16] This creative 'brain drain' to Moscow was not reversed until around the mid-2000s.

Ukrainian drama between the Orange Revolution and the Maidan

Another phase of development of a playwriting culture in Ukraine evolved incrementally, particularly in Kyiv, from the mid-2000s until the Maidan. The cultural shift in this period is emblematized by Vorozhbyt's ten-minute text *I Join Them* (2005), commissioned and produced by the New Play Company in London, about the Orange Revolution of 2004–5.[17] This documentary play depicts the playwright's own involvement in the country's first major post-Soviet uprising, which resulted in the annulling and re-running of a presidential election, ultimately favouring the pro-European candidate Viktor Iushchenko. The work marked Vorozhbyt's return to Kyiv as her main city of residence. The title reflects the author's literal as well as metaphorical engagement with citizen-activists in her native city. In retrospect, she has described this period as a problematic homecoming:

> I returned from Moscow in 2005. [...] I lived a fairly isolated life in Kyiv for a few years. I kept travelling back and forth to Moscow to work. There was more or less no contemporary drama being staged here at all. Nobody was programming it and there were no festivals of contemporary playwriting. [...] Then something like three or four years went by and I met Andriy Mai, the director, who had also studied in Moscow.[18] We decided that we were bored and we wanted a movement similar to the Liubimovka [a festival of new plays in Moscow]. [...] We thought up a festival, which is called Week of the Contemporary Play. [...] A professional setting emerged where playwrights meet once a year to read plays to each other. [...] These are plays about 'today', about oneself: many are personal and many are reflections on social issues.[19]

Inspired directly by the 'New Drama' movement in Russia, as Vorozhbyt acknowledges,[20] this new festival was one key element in creating a contemporary playwriting culture in Ukraine, by offering a platform for first-time and non-professional dramatists writing in either Ukrainian or Russian. Week of the Contemporary Play in Kyiv disrupted Soviet-era dramatic conventions of 'timeless' plays on universal themes. Instead, the festival produced readings of plays which created socio-political interventions in contemporary society, both thematically and by depicting graphic content as well as using obscene lexicons. Equally, it privileged a range of postmodern malleable and unconventional dramaturgies. Week of the Contemporary Play enabled post-Soviet dramatists to begin to perceive themselves as part of a likeminded artistic community. In other words, this period from the mid-2000s witnessed the emergence of a significant institution supporting a playwriting culture, or rather subculture. Run largely on voluntary labour, the festival offered the freedom to experiment aesthetically, and the opportunity to write ideologically nonconformist play texts, outside of the state-funded systems of theatrical production.

Although Week of the Contemporary Play was the first play festival in the capital city, another Ukrainian festival gained the distinction of being the first national 'new play' festival. In 2009, the International Festival of Contemporary Playwriting, Drama.UA, was created in Lviv. This festival was also dedicated to promoting contemporary Ukrainian playwrights writing in Ukrainian,[21] unlike Week of the Contemporary Play which accepts submissions in both Ukrainian and Russian (in response to the fact that most Ukrainians are bilingual). Drama.UA's policy was 'a political decision, because prior to 2014 we didn't have a lot of Ukrainian-language contemporary texts, whereas we had lots of Russian-language ones'.[22] Drama.UA, like Week of the Contemporary Play, was a collective project, although it emerged out of five years of work by the Art Workshop 'Drabyna' (meaning 'ladder' in Ukrainian), an NGO founded in 2004 to support amateur playwriting.[23] The legacy of Drama.UA, in developing a new generation of professional playwrights through public rehearsed readings, was limited by its closure after four years, although below I consider a new phase in the company's work after the Maidan. Overall, by 2013, two national playwriting festivals had been launched and one endured as a longer-term venture. But the question remained: would the dominant state-run theatrical sector respond to the new generation of playwrights being 'discovered' at these festivals? Between 2005 and 2013, repertory theatres continued to overlook most dramatists for their programmes, in spite of the incremental creation of a playwriting subculture. By 2009, Vorozhbyt was consolidating an international reputation beyond the post-Soviet sphere, when the Royal Shakespeare Company commissioned and produced her play *The Grain Store* in Stratford-upon-Avon. Written in Russian for the benefit of her long-time translator Sasha Dugdale, Vorozhbyt's play depicts the attempt of one community to survive the Holodomor (the name given to the mass starvation of the Ukrainian people in the 1930s, apparently caused by Stalin's policies). In spite of a successful run at a globally renowned UK theatre, no Ukrainian state-run theatre produced her epic drama subsequently. Since the Holodomor entered political discourse under President Iushchenko (2005–10), this neglect of 'homegrown' playwriting talent appears to be a legacy of *theatrical* risk-aversion, as much as a resistance to 'political' themes. Were it not for the civic and geopolitical political events of 2013–14, the de-politicized and risk-averse mechanisms of state-led theatrical production would probably have remained intact. The Maidan and Russian military actions ushered in change in at least four related guises: a liberalizing-but-patriotic shift in the dominant national and local cultural politics; a greater willingness by some repertory theatres to engage with 'political' and experimental forms of playwriting; a greater appetite by young playwrights to depict overtly politicized subject matters; and a commitment by the post-Soviet generation to creating new 'types' of independent theatre institutions to sidestep the repertory theatres – a Ukrainian 'fringe'. Taken together, these four areas – even where the changes were relatively modest in scale – nevertheless amounted to the emergence of a significantly altered theatrical landscape.

The impact of the Maidan and Russian military expansionism on theatrical production

The Maidan in 2013–14, as well as Russia's proxy occupation of Crimea and its military intervention in eastern Ukraine in 2014, altered the contexts in which theatrical production functioned in Ukraine. Many theatre-makers supported, or participated in, the Maidan because of the liberalizing, pro-European vision of these public protests which occurred on the 'Maidan Nezalezhnosti' (Independence Square) in central Kyiv and to a lesser extent in many cities across Ukraine. These protests, which began after President Viktor Ianukovich suspended Ukraine's Association Agreement with Europe, led to the ousting of the sitting president. Political victory came at great personal cost, with over a hundred people killed by the security forces during the demonstrations. However, the Maidan (or 'Euromaidan' as it was also called) triggered a strong sense of civic purpose among the protestors including the post-Soviet generation, who witnessed a tangible result to their civic activism. The Maidan was swiftly followed by two divisive Russian military interventions affecting Ukraine. In March 2014, the occupation of Crimea – a peninsula falling within Ukrainian jurisdiction since 1954 – by pro-Russian troops was consolidated by a highly contested referendum, not recognized by international law to date, due to allegations of fraudulence. Crimea became a de facto Russian territory – raising the spectre of Russian military aggression against Ukraine's territorial integrity. When a pro-Russian, anti-Maidan protest movement emerged in eastern Ukraine in the spring of 2014, it was partly led and partly aggravated by Russian-backed militia.[24] The anti-Maidan groupings formalized into a breakaway region – the Donbas – aiming to achieve independence from Ukraine; this military conflict continues even at the time of writing.

The election of President Poroshenko, a pro-European businessman, in 2014 appeared to consolidate Ukraine's de facto political independence from Russia. The incoming president used culture as one means of forging a national consensus around a patriotic public discourse. Specifically, at the federal level, the authorities stated an intention to create a 'blacklist' to prevent five hundred Russian cultural luminaries who supported Putin's aggressive expansionism from entering Ukraine, through visa bans.[25] This state-led policy was partly symbolic, serving to accentuate an 'us versus them' attitude towards Russia, but it had real-world consequences: it reduced the number of Russian-created cultural outputs reaching Ukraine. Prior to 2014, a mainstay of Ukrainian theatre were commercial companies which toured from Russia. Since Russian-created television programmes continued to be broadcast in Ukraine after 1991, these touring productions attracted Ukrainian audiences by featuring Russian 'star' actors. However, this touring to Ukraine decreased significantly as a result of the 'blacklist'. Rather than turning away from theatre-going, many Ukrainian audiences began to demonstrate an interest in 'homegrown' talent, with even small-scale state-run studio theatres benefiting from a surge in audience interest.[26]

Responding presumably to the increased visibility of the post-Soviet generation, Kyiv's city authorities experimented with a liberalization of local cultural policies in an attempt to accommodate younger theatre directors. In 2014, the Kyiv Ministry of Culture appointed almost half a dozen artistic directors from the post-Soviet generation to small or medium-sized venues – including the director Stas Jirkov at the Golden Gates. This step embodied a pro-Maidan, pro-European ethos, since these new directors tended to be European-facing in their tastes. Jirkov's priority in his opening seasons included tackling the themes of war, but also 'Ukraine in a European context'.[27] While ostensibly a positive step for theatre in Kyiv, this cultural policy favoured directors who were – according to some detractors among their peers – 'artistically daring but more loyal to government politics, they would not stage critical theatre and radical theatre'.[28] The progressive character of this policy was further curtailed because it was implemented cautiously in terms of its scale.[29] Even so, those theatres selected for a 'changing of the guard' directly advocated for younger generations of playwrights writing postmodern texts. By July 2017, Jirkov had staged four productions written by his contemporary, Pavlo Ar'e (born in 1977), thereby offering a regular platform for this young Lviv-born dramatist in the capital. In other words, these state and city-led cultural policies played a role – albeit modest in scale – in reversing the marginalization of nonconformist contemporary Ukrainian playwriting.

These cultural policies coincided with a greater willingness to take artistic risks by some repertory theatres. A production which set a new precedent in the theatre landscape was the documentary play *Maidan Diaries* by Vorozhbyt, directed by Mai. In 2014, the *Maidan Diaries* ran at the Franko National Theatre, one of Kyiv's two national theatres (the Ukrainian-language one). The playwright distilled around eighty hours of video recordings – taken from protests occurring in the streets of Kyiv between November 2013 and February 2014 – into a fragmented narrative which examined the real-life stories and actions of the people involved; the play was bilingual, in order authentically to record the testimony of each interviewee. This level of engagement with a contemporary socio-political event was unprecedented at the mostly apolitical repertory theatres. It also evidenced a new level of 'political engagement' with Ukrainian national politics by a contemporary playwright. This real-life drama includes graphic descriptions of violence on the Maidan, including the brutality meted out by state's security forces:

Old woman When I lie down in bed to go to sleep I see that boy they brought back to the protestors' encampment. Skinned. Only his face was white, all the rest was red. I don't know what they did to him. Burned him maybe, God only knows ... Only half an hour before I'd given him some soup. And now they were bringing in his body.[30]

Mai has characterized *Maidan Diaries* as 'theatre with a message',[31] and described how, with this production, 'I realised my first attempt to make political theatre'.[32] In Mai's production, audience members were invited to speak into microphones during the performance, to recount their own personal experiences and perspectives on the Maidan,[33] which augmented the act of socio-political intervention implicit in the play text. It is highly significant that such an overtly 'political' play, eschewing conventional artistic forms in favour of documentary testimonies from real-life people whose voices would rarely (or never) be represented in theatres, was included in a national theatre's repertoire. This production served as a new 'high watermark' for what was permissible on a state-run stage.

While *Maidan Diaries* was artistically nonconformist and politically 'engaged', it nevertheless advocates for an ideology which is not inherently critical of the post-Maidan Ukrainian state. The playwright includes a small number of brief dialogues about problematic aspects of the Maidan, which challenge the overly simplistic representation of a 'people's uprising', such as the involvement of the far-right political group Pravy Sektor,[34] as well as the alleged political 'behind-the-scenes' orchestration by American and Russian political actors.[35] Yet, the overarching construction of the narrative serves a clear purpose: Vorozhbyt's text mythologizes the Maidan as a place of solidarity among peaceful protestors. While 'New Drama' in Russia was largely characterized by its political oppositionality towards the state, *Maidan Diaries*' most significant intervention was in relation to dominant theatrical conventions. The 'politics' which Mai refers to is, at most, a statement of postcolonial independence, but not one which invites any further reflection upon the difficult relationship of governance to grassroots democracy post-Maidan, or one which offers any legitimacy to the anti-Maidan movement in eastern Ukraine as an alternative people's movement, intent on rejecting post-1991 oligarchic control of Ukraine.

In spite of its relatively narrow ideological parameters, the affective power of *Maidan Diaries*, and its explicit engagement with recent political events, represented a striking boldness of programming in Ukraine, and signified a shift in the cultural landscape. As Mai put it:

> Since the Maidan, the political vector points towards Europe, so if a production relates to Europe, the repertory theatres have to do it, on the one hand. On the other hand, there's a war going on in the country. If the war is going on, and you don't do a play about the war ... and you're a state theatre, people will ask 'why are you saying "no"? Why are you putting on Ray Cooney and earning box office income? You're receiving state subsidies!'[36]

However, in spite of this 'moral' pressure to accommodate topical contemporary playwriting, many repertory theatres continued to programme their repertoires cautiously as before, continuing to favour canonical classics and commercial comedies as the mainstay of their repertoires. In spite of his renown in Russia as well as his growing recognition in the Anglophone world, Kurochkin has not been commissioned to write original dramas by any Ukrainian repertory theatres at the time of writing, only to adapt Ukrainian classics.[37] Presumably his unconventional, postmodern artistic style did not suit programmers' tastes. By hiring him to adapt classical works, directors could benefit from (in the playwright's own words) the 'image of a person who supports contemporary playwriting',[38] without having to take any significant artistic risk. Kurochkin observed that a younger wave of Ukrainian dramatists, from a 'second' generation of post-Soviet dramatists born around or after 1991, are succeeding at play festivals but rarely being produced in the large-scale theatres:

> Week of the Contemporary Play taught us to draw young people into the profession but didn't teach them how to take the next step. To some extent, we led them into

a dead end. What can we offer them when there's no direct career ladder? I'm optimistic that Ukrainian theatre and film will blossom, but producers and theatre practitioners don't yet have the habit of thinking of Week of the Contemporary Play as a direct resource to find new playwrights to commission.[39]

Maidan Diaries raised the glass ceiling for topical, experimental playwriting. It also contributed to Vorozhbyt's recognition across the country: alongside her subsequent film and theatre commissions, she became a highly visible public commentator on contemporary issues. Around the same time, apparently also in relation to a shift in the cultural landscape, Ar'e's dramas were also programmed in an increasing number of regional repertory theatres.[40] The canonization of two young living playwrights was a positive development, but without immediate benefit for their contemporaries. However, it sent a powerful symbolic message to younger generations. The journalist-turned-playwright Anastasia Kosodiy (who has gained acclaim at playwriting festivals subsequently) has cited the 2014 production of *Maidan Diaries* as her reason for turning to dramatic writing. That production afforded her a renewed belief in theatre's socio-political relevance.[41] There was also another phenomenon after 2014, which would influence Kosodiy, who is a 'second generation' post-Soviet playwright (born in 1991). Young playwrights, particularly those of the first post-Soviet generation, began to create independent theatre companies, as a potential trajectory out of the 'dead end' facing them, and in order to circumvent the institutional rigidity of the state-run sector.

The birth of a post-Maidan fringe

The civic activism of the Maidan emboldened younger generations, who channelled their energy into new social or creative outlets after 2014: creating impromptu night clubs in abandoned spaces, setting up European-style 'hipster' cafés[42] and – relevant to this essay – founding independent studio theatres in empty and sometimes run-down buildings. Within a couple of years of the Maidan, more than half a dozen theatrical ensembles were founded by directors and playwrights of the post-Soviet generation, mostly in the capital city, as part of an emergent Ukrainian 'fringe'.[43] Among the first independent producing companies were PostPlay, Wild Theatre, the Theatre of Displaced People[44] in Kyiv and Drama.UA in Lviv (the latter was transformed into a producing company in 2014).[45] These ensembles extended the existing theatrical ecology, providing an outlet dedicated almost exclusively to productions of contemporary playwriting (as opposed to the rehearsed readings at the festivals). Vorozhbyt's *The Grain Store* received its Ukrainian premiere in a translation from Russian into Ukrainian, at Drama.UA,[46] suggesting that this 'fringe' might supplant the repertory theatres as a site of new play production, at least for the most 'political' or aesthetically unconventional works. To some extent, Teatr Dakh was a forebear of the post-Maidan fringe in the 1990s – yet there are significant differences. While Dakh was run as a top-down private venture,[47] these fringe venues were, for the most part, collectively run on a voluntary basis, emphasizing ideologically oppositional new work, usually contemporary playwriting – but also new theatrical forms and genres, such as devised work, socially engaged theatre and performance art.

While the fringe became a recognizable phenomenon in Kyiv and Lviv after 2014, it was not limited to these major cities. In 2015, PostPlay toured a production across several regional cities, including the eastern city of Zaporizhzhia – home town of the playwright Kosodiy. Kosodiy saw PostPlay's performances and subsequently, inspired by this troupe, co-founded a theatre company in her hometown, called 'Zaporizhzhia New Drama', with the actor-manager Viktoria Petrova. By her own account, their company is the only theatre in Zaporizhzhia producing contemporary plays.[48] This direct and material lineage between the fringe in larger cities and further afield was not accidental. Several of the new fringe companies made conscious efforts to establish professional collaborations and networks beyond their own cities, apparently in order to enrich their work and guarantee their sustainability through the creation of a nationwide independent theatre sector. Viktoria Shvydko, the Artistic Director of Drama.UA from 2013, emphasized how her company's festival served as a forum for dialogue and cultural exchange between a post-Soviet generation across Ukraine, as well as with theatre-makers from other European countries. She suggested that many playwrights and directors from diverse Ukrainian cities met at Drama.UA, which led directly to the creation of new ensembles. She offered three examples: Theatre of Contemporary Dialogue[49] in Poltava in 2011 (formalized in 2015), Totem Centre Theatre Lab[50] in Kherson in 2012 and PostPlay[51] in Kyiv in 2015. All three emphasize artistic experimentation and exhibit a nonconformist socio-political orientation in their work. The founding dates of these companies serve as a reminder that the Ukrainian fringe was already nascent in the early 2010s in various cities; however, the initiatives founded prior to 2014 were focused on discrete projects (primarily rehearsed readings and outreach workshops), rather than full productions. The significance of this post-2014 fringe is that this new institutional 'type' was, for the most part, intended to function as alternative sites of theatrical production beyond the state-run theatre sector.

Naturally, the fringe manifested a spectrum of artistic forms and ideologies since its very purpose was to promote theatrical 'risk-taking'. The phenomenon of independent ensembles emerged so recently that it is difficult fully to evaluate its scope and future legacy. Nevertheless, it is already possible to observe that most of these companies exist along a spectrum which places an equal emphasis on marrying postmodern artistic experimentation with socio-political intervention. What diverges between companies is the extent to which they perceive their mission as ideologically oppositional to the state. An illustration of the 'least oppositional' end of the spectrum, privileging liberal ideals and artistic innovation over criticism of official ideology, would be Wild Theatre's production, *Vitalik – A Show about a Man* by Vitalii Chenskii, which premiered in 2017. Its episodic narrative centres on explicit descriptions of the eponymous hero's attempt to find love, often finding male fantasies and masturbation instead. The play weaves confessional first-person narration with apparently authentic Facebook posts. Chenskii depicts the semi-autobiographical protagonist as torn between different 'versions' of himself, alternating between indecisive and 'macho'.[52] The narrative offers a metaphorical resonance with the country's growing east–west schism, since the first-person narrator describes his conflicted attachment to his hometown of Mariupol' in eastern Ukraine, even after moving to Kyiv.[53] Wild Theatre's production augments this sense of personal and metaphorical schism, by using two actors to play Vitalik – a younger one who performs him as a sensitive and neurotic man, while an older one offers a 'macho' characterization.[54]

The pre-publicity text warns audiences that the performance is appropriate for viewers who are '18+. We use obscenities, and some scenes may offend [lit. traumatize] with their frankness'.[55] This ideological vision of theatre-making – as an existential postmodern exploration of the self – is in stark contrast to the state-funded repertory system, where theatrical production tends to be aligned with moral purpose as a means to confirm dominant ideologies. One complimentary review of *Vitalik* for a major Ukrainian newspaper specifically offers this advice to audiences attending the production, with reference to the national theatre in Kyiv (the Russian-language one): 'Don't bring friends who love the Russian Drama Theatre and joyful productions, [who attend theatre saying] "I want to relax and have a breather".'[56] In other words, some fringe companies – including Wild Theatre – embody progressive liberal values in their productions, as a rebuff to mainstream and conservative ideals. Yet, even though *Vitalik* offers a portrait of masculinity in crisis, it offers a male, heterosexual perspective. While the play questions the narrator's misogyny with a certain ironic knowingness, it never offers alternative ideologies – such as feminist or queer, and therefore allies itself to the most progressive elements of the Ukrainian state. For that reason, Dan Gumennyi – another post-Soviet playwright – has described Wild Theatre as 'bourgeois theatre, but from time to time, bourgeois theatre leads to productions which are important for this country'.[57] By his own account, Gumennyi himself continues to work as a playwright in 'bourgeois' 1000-seater repertory theatres in Ukraine[58] – and so does his wife and regular collaborator, Yana Gumennaia. The fringe company PostPlay, which the husband-and-wife team co-founded as artistic director and producer respectively, positions itself at the other ideological end of the spectrum within the independent sector. As a company, it attempts to extend the experimentation of the fringe yet further in challenging both existing aesthetic forms and also normative ideologies, including productions in their repertoire which are overtly critical of the Ukrainian state. Their founding production, *The Militiaman* by Dan Gumennyi and Yana Gumennaia (2015), was a verbatim script, based on an interview with a civilian-turned-militiaman who took part in the war in the Donbas on the side of the Russian forces. The play text humanizes this fighter, the kind of individual whom the state would perceive to be a 'terrorist': 'I just needed to buy my child a bike at Christmas... I went to war because of the money... I'm not *for* Russia or *for* Ukraine.'[59] Through this nuanced and humane exploration of one man's lived experience of the ongoing conflict, the playwrights challenge the patriotic narratives about the war; subverting the 'us versus them' governmental rhetoric. They further criticize the state by documenting the real-life protagonist's presence in Kyiv (where they interviewed the subject of their play) – implicitly questioning how a 'terrorist' travelled freely to the capital. State incompetence, and possible complicity by security forces with 'warring' factions, is woven into the texture of their play. The creative team politicized their production beyond the play text itself, in two ways. Firstly, this monologue play was performed by Galina Dzhikaeva, in other words, a female actor was delivering a male insurgent's testimony. This device offered a Brechtian distancing effect, encouraging the audience to engage critically with the testimony, rather than assuming any singular didactic message. Secondly, Dzhikaeva delivered improvised sections of text in Ukrainian, interspersed throughout the main text in Russian, the primary language of the real-life militiaman. The actor improvised these Ukrainian sections, revising them for each performance, based on the latest developments of fighting in the Donbas. In this way, the production remained topical – thereby offering a greater potential for socio-political intervention.

PostPlay has extended its experimentation further since the company's inception. In 2017, members of the company introduced a new programme which divided into four strands of work, which received pithy and in some cases playful titles: 'Not Theatre', 'Not Dance', 'Political Theatre' and 'Performance Art'. They appear to place an equal emphasis on what is called 'participatory theatre' in the West, such as productions in which members of the LGBT community or refugees perform their own testimonies on stage. Detractors of this radical approach to theatrical production – with no precedent in modern Ukraine, as far as I am aware – would suggest that PostPlay's performances are of less artistic merit, precisely because they eschew existing notions of 'good art' in favour of activist theatre. By the company's own account, most critics do not attend PostPlay's productions and, if they do, they rarely write reviews.[60] This critical dismissal of the most nonconformist fringe companies is a useful reminder of the disincentive for the independent ensembles to position themselves in overt opposition to official state ideology. PostPlay has attracted critical attention from European countries, particularly Poland and Germany.[61] Even so, the company's material position is insecure, compared to less overtly 'political' venues (such as Wild Theatre) which gain greater critical acclaim and have the potential to earn more box-office revenue from a larger audience base. PostPlay overcomes some of this instability by self-organizing as a collective, while also subsidizing their own work through other paid work as playwrights in the state sector – an irony which suggests that even the most radical companies in the fringe may never gain total material independence. In summary, the overall picture is of an independent sector which has become firmly established, even within a few years of the Maidan. The diversity of their ideological positions and artistic forms suggests that the fringe is indeed a site of 'alternative' theatrical production, created by and for the post-Soviet generations. In terms of this essay, its significance is that it serves as a vehicle to support and develop 'Ukrainian New Drama'.

'Ukrainian New Drama'

My central proposition is that there is a post-Soviet form of dramatic writing, which may be labelled 'Ukrainian New Drama', with 2014 serving as an effective 'start date'. While this term is used by some younger directors and playwrights themselves, there is no consensus among them on exactly how to define it, or about its 'start date'. The critic Anastasia Golovnenko has suggested that Kurochkin's *The Kitchen* in 2000, written in

Russian, is the first work of 'Ukrainian New Drama'.⁶² Mai has stated that 'Ukrainian New Drama' exists, but that many representatives of this movement – including himself – choose not to use the term, stating instead that they write 'new texts' (as opposed to 'new plays');⁶³ in other words, he emphasizes postmodern dramaturgy over any specific cultural landscape. Speaking in 2017, Kurochkin felt that it was still 'too early to call this a movement, but there is a clear phenomenon emerging'.⁶⁴ These positions can be resolved, in my view, by bringing historical context back into the frame. As discussed earlier, Ukrainian playwrights were actively engaged in forging the transnational and Russian-language 'New Drama' movement in Moscow, from the mid-1990s. Their practice took on a decidedly *national* character after the Maidan, with a literal and metaphorical re-focusing of their dramaturgy on national audiences and the creation of a fringe subculture, which was intended – to paraphrase Zabuzhko (cited earlier) – 'to create for national playwriting a national Ukrainian market, literally out of nothing'. Like the 'New Drama' movement which preceded it and helped to shaped it, 'Ukrainian New Drama' emerged as a socio-cultural phenomenon without a singular or unified aesthetic manifesto. It may be distinguished from contemporary playwriting more broadly by its postmodern character, which challenges conventional dramatic forms, and its underlying ethos of subverting dominant ideologies in favour of anti-capitalist, queer, feminist or other 'alternative' ideologies.

This term 'Ukrainian New Drama' encapsulates the acute sense among most post-Soviet playwrights that they had no choice but to re-forge their identity after 2014. As Kurochkin explains, it is a 'huge trauma that the question of my nationality now arises', since he was never reductively labelled as 'foreign' during his years in Moscow.⁶⁵ The feeling of no longer belonging to a *transnational* subcultural sphere, but instead only to a national theatrical landscape, has translated into an incremental shift towards the use of the Ukrainian language by many post-Soviet dramatists. While the 'language question' has been 'political' for centuries, a process of intensification occurred after the outbreak of military conflict in eastern Ukraine. Prior to 2014, due to centuries of suppression by successive Russian imperial forces,⁶⁶ the majority of Ukrainians were bilingual in Russian and Ukrainian⁶⁷ as well as sometimes speaking the rural dialect of *surhik*.⁶⁸ The exception was in western Ukraine, where the Ukrainian language was dominant in the towns: it is no coincidence that Ar'e (from the western city of Lviv) chose to write his plays in Ukrainian. Kosodiy has characterized the Ukrainian language prior to 2014 as having the feel of a non-spoken 'literary language'.⁶⁹ Referring to the period after pro-Russian troops became entrenched in eastern Ukraine, Kosodiy has described how 'you just have to talk for a year in Ukrainian and then it becomes natural. It happened to lots of my friends – they made this political decision to switch to Ukrainian.'⁷⁰ Kurochkin decided to surmount the same language barrier after 2014, and he also moved back with his family from Moscow to live in Kyiv, in 2017. As he notes, he had to persevere in order to learn Ukrainian well enough for it to serve him in his everyday and professional life: 'It bothered me before that my Ukrainian wasn't perfect. Before, it was a serious obstacle. Now, I don't think about it. I already write TV scripts in Ukrainian. I haven't yet written a play in Ukrainian, but I could.'⁷¹

Similarly, whereas Vorozhbyt only wrote plays in Russian prior to 2014, she expressed an ideological preference for writing in Ukrainian in 2017. She acknowledges that Russian is her 'native language',[72] and she continues to write in Russian where it is a requirement – such as for film or international commissions. It should be noted that the inverse process occurred in the Donbas, where there was a significant increase in the use of Russian.[73] 'Ukrainian New Drama' continues to be written in both Ukrainian and Russian – with an incremental evolution towards the former. The privileging of the Ukrainian language by many younger playwrights in their professional and daily lives after 2014 reinforces the notion of a postcolonial identity among post-Soviet dramatists – with 'Ukrainian New Drama' as the most significant emergent theatrical form.

Conclusion

The political turmoil of 2013–14 led to a shift in the theatrical landscape in Ukraine. The post-Soviet generation was able to assert itself in the sphere of theatre more fully than at any time since 1991. Earlier experiments bore fruit. The festivals created in Lviv in 2009 (Drama.UA) and in Kyiv in 2011 (Week of the Contemporary Play) capitalized on an appetite among younger theatre-makers finally to smash the monopoly held over theatrical production by the older generations, which had left the theatre sector stagnant since the collapse of the Soviet Union. A renewed belief in civic action – as embodied in the Maidan popular uprising in 2013–14 – translated directly into the creation of a theatrical 'fringe'. The larger cities witnessed the first wave of independent companies, such as Wild Theatre and Postplay in Kyiv as well as Drama.UA (reinvented as a production company) in Lviv, among others – but with a little delay other ensembles were created further afield from the capital, including 'Zaporizhzhia New Drama' in the east of Ukraine. This fringe offered theatre-makers artistic freedom, which they have used to explore new aesthetic forms and 'alternative' ideological perspectives. These independent companies staged theatrically innovative work which was either implicitly or explicitly critical of dominant state ideologies. The agenda of the Ukrainian state, which has often incorporated nationalistic and militaristic rhetoric as well as regressive policies with regard to social justice and anti-corruption policies, has found at least a partial counterweight in the buoyant subcultural sphere created by a post-Soviet generation of theatre-makers – the post-Maidan independent fringe. The significance of the fringe was that it has served as a site for developing 'Ukrainian New Drama', which may be defined broadly as a stylistically diverse set of postmodern theatrical texts, which rupture many of the conventions of traditional realist theatre practice. After the Maidan and the outbreak of Russian-backed militarism in eastern Ukraine, there was an increased impetus among playwrights to forge nonconformist dramatic writing for national audiences, designed to contribute to a national theatrical tradition. Some dramatists who had previously written in Russian to contribute to the Moscow-based 'New Drama' movement such as Kurochkin and Vorozhbyt, opted to start writing play texts in Ukrainian, except where it was unavoidable to write in Russian for particular commissions. Doubtless, like its forebear 'New Drama', this emergent dramaturgy will elicit endless scholarly and popular debates about its merit and character, yet it seems to me indisputable that, since 2014, it is possible to observe 'Ukrainian New Drama' as a distinctive phenomenon, both aesthetically and as occupying a particular niche within the socio-cultural sphere in Ukraine and at times receiving productions overseas. While in many ways this new theatrical form is a positive contribution, offering a vehicle to the post-Soviet generation to articulate its political perspectives, what scholars and critics will need to follow is the extent to which 'Ukrainian New Drama' serves to accrue cultural capital to a younger generation of middle-class Ukrainians without significantly challenging dominant ideologies, or whether it offers a genuine site of questioning and contestation of society-wide prejudices, taboos and state oppression.

Acknowledgements

I would like to express my gratitude to Dr Ivan Kozachenko, Postdoctoral Research Associate in Ukrainian Studies at Cambridge University, for his extensive notes on the first draft of this chapter.

Notes

1. Interview with Vladislav Troitskii (2017).
2. Oksana Zabuzhko, 'Being a Writer in Contemporary Ukraine: Drawing the Landscape while Standing on a Powerboat', University of Cambridge, 29 March 2013. Available at: https://sms.cam.ac.uk/media/1449548 (accessed 16 May 2017).
3. Michael Naydan, 'Ukrainian Avant-Garde Poetry Today: Bu-Ba-Bu and Others', *The Slavic and East European Journal* 50, no. 3, Special Forum Issue: Contemporary Ukrainian Literature and National Identity (Fall, 2006): 452–68.
4. Zabuzhko, 'Being a Writer in Contemporary Ukraine'.
5. Dakh produced only one Ukrainian playwright: Vladimir Klimenko (born in 1952), known popularly as Klim (*The Dakh Theatre*, 2012), who is more widely known as an innovative director, and therefore not relevant to this essay, although it is a subject which merits further scholarly study.
6. Marysia Nikitiuk, 'Natalia Vorozhbyt', *Teatre teatral'nyi zhurnal*, 23 February 2009. Available at: http://teatre.com.ua/modern/natalja_vorozhbyt (accessed 9 February 2017).
7. That situation remains unchanged at the time of writing (January 2019), with only a professional screenwriting course offered at university level, according to the director Andriy Mai (2017).
8. Interview with Vladislav Troitskii (2017).
9. I have written about the foundation and characteristics of 'New Drama' in my unpublished doctoral thesis, held in repository at Queen Mary University of London's library (Birksted-Breen, 2017).
10. The most comprehensive account of the Royal Court International Department's involvement in Russia is in the monograph by Elaine Aston and Mark O'Thomas, *Royal Court: International* (Basingstoke: Palgrave Macmillan, 2015), with a section specifically on its engagement in Russia, 136–40.
11. Verbatim is a form of documentary theatre-making which uses voice recorders to record the exact speech patterns of the real-life prototypes who are represented on stage.

12 John Freedman, 'Maksym Kurochkin Cooks Up Great Drama', personal website, 4 November 2009. Available at: https://johnfreedmanarchive.wordpress.com/2017/07/12/maksym-kurochkin-cooks-up-great-drama (accessed 13 February 2018).
13 Ibid.
14 The Centre for Playwriting and Dramaturgy (often abbreviated as CDR – *Tsentr dramaturgii i rezhissury*).
15 Marina Zaionts, 'O, sport, ty zhut!", *Itogi*, 7 June 2005. Available at: http://www.smotr.ru/2004/2004_centr_galka.htm (accessed 13 February 2018).
16 Sergei Vasil'ev, 'Ukrainskii teatr ot Soiuza do Maidana', *Teatr*, no. 17, 2014. Available at: http://oteatre.info/ukrainskij-teatr-ot-soyuza-do-majdana/ (accessed 4 December 2017).
17 This play ran at the Actors' Theatre in central London in 2005, in my translation.
18 Mai trained as a director in Kyiv; he subsequently moved to St Petersburg for professional training at the Malyi Theatre with Lev Dodin, as well as completing a Master's at the Meierkhol'd Centre in Moscow. See Dar'ia Slobodianik, '"Dnevniki Maidana": neotlozhnaia refleksiia', *Levyi Bereg*, 1 December 2014. Available at: https://lb.ua/culture/2014/12/01/287804_dnevniki_maydana_neotlozhnaya.html (accessed 13 February 2018).
19 Interview with Natal'ia Vorozhbyt (2017).
20 Ibid.
21 Interview with Viktoria Shvydko (2018).
22 Ibid.
23 Ibid.
24 Ivan Kozachenko, 'Retelling Old Stories with New Media: National Identity and Transnationalism in the "Russian Spring" Popular Uprisings', *East/West Journal of Ukrainian Studies* 4, no. 1 (2017): 140–2.
25 The first visa bans were introduced in 2015 – with fourteen Russian actors and singers named on it. By early 2018, the blacklist had increased to include 118 Russian cultural figures. Kateryna Botanova, 'Ukraine's Blacklists in Defence of Democracy and National Security Are Doing It No Favours', *Open Democracy Russia*, 9 February 2018. Available at: https://www.opendemocracy.net/od-russia/kateryna-botanova/ukraines-blacklists-in-defence-of-democracy (accessed 10 February 2018).
26 Interview with Stas Jirkov (2017).
27 Ibid.
28 Interview with Galina Dzhikaeva, Dan Gumennyi and Yana Gumennaia (2017), citation by Dzhikaeva.
29 Jirkov suggested that four theatres – among the city's twenty – had been included in this policy of changing the management. Interview with Stas Jirkov (2017).
30 Natal'ia Vorozhbyt, *Maidan Dairies*, trans. by Sasha Dugdale (unpublished text, 2014).
31 His phrase in Russian was 'teatr vyskazivaniia'; interview with Andriy Mai (2017).
32 Ibid.
33 Slobodianik, '"Dnevniki Maidana"'.
34 Vorozhbyt, *Maidan Dairies*.
35 Ibid.
36 Ibid.
37 Interview with Maksym Kurochkin (2017).
38 Ibid.
39 Ibid.

40 Interview with Anastasia Golovnenko (2017).
41 Interview with Anastasia Kosodiy and Jack Clover (2017).
42 Starr (2016).
43 I am using the term 'fringe', since it resembles the Western 'alternative' models of theatrical production, originating with the Edinburgh Fringe Festival in 1947. In my experience, the term 'fringe' is not used by the theatre-makers themselves, although it has gained currency in Russia since the 2000s to describe the 'New Drama' phenomenon.
44 See Chapter 12 by Molly Flynn.
45 Interview with Viktoria Shvydko (2018).
46 Ibid.
47 Theatre Dakh was funded primarily through private sponsorship by its founder, Troitskii, and he assumed responsibility for programming.
48 Interview with Anastasia Kosodiy and Jack Clover (2017).
49 Theatre of Contemporary Dialogue began as a youth theatre group, run by the playwright Irina Garets, in 2011. In 2015 the group formalized their company as the Theatre of Contemporary Dialogue. Its primary aim is to 'create topical and socially important plays, videos, workshops, training, and to form the cultural space of Poltava region'. The head of the company since 2015 is Ganna Kiyashchenko. See http://theater-ua.com.ua/theater/5953a057ebe4b769461320f3 (accessed 22 January 2018).
50 Totem was founded in 2012 as 'an artistic group working at the combination of performing arts, journalism and social sciences in such spheres as documentary theatre, oral history and public activities'. See http://cmitotem.wixsite.com/totemlab/fan-gallery (accessed 22 January 2018).
51 PostPlay Theatre is a collective company, founded in 2015. The artistic director is Dan Gumennyi and the producer is Yana Gumennaia. Postplay perceives itself to be a 'true theatrical underground'. See https://www.facebook.com/postplaytheater (accessed 22 January 2018).
52 Ol'ga Bud'ko, 'Sovremennyi Odissei: V Kieve proshli prem'ernye pokazy spektakli *Vitalik*', *Novoe vremia*, 8 July 2017. Available at: https://nv.ua/style/art/theater_art/v-kieve-proshli-premernye-pokazy-spektaklja-vitalik-1449000.html (accessed 13 February 2018).
53 *Vitalik* by Vitalii Chenskii (unpublished play text), 8.
54 Ibid.
55 Citation from Wild (Dikii) Theatre's website available at http://wild-t.com.ua/vitalik (accessed 22 January 2018).
56 Angela Velichko, 'Vitalik-Uliss: chem interesen novyi spektakl' "Dikogo teatra"', *Ukrains'ka Pravda*, 4 July 2017. Available at: http://life.pravda.com.ua/columns/2017/07/4/225086 (accessed 22 January 2018).
57 Interview with Galina Dzhikaeva, Dan Gumennyi and Yana Gumennaia (2017).
58 Ibid.
59 Dan Gumennyi and Yana Gumennaia, *The Militiaman* (unpublished text, 2015).
60 Ibid.
61 Ibid.
62 Interview with Anastasia Golovnenko (2017).
63 Interview with Andriy Mai (2017).
64 Interview with Maksym Kurochkin (2017).
65 Ibid.
66 In the Russian Empire, Catherine the Great abolished Ukrainian autonomy in the late eighteenth century, leading to 'administrative russification [. . .] whereby Ukrainian

noblemen, merchants, and artisans were for the most part absorbed into their respective imperial estates, which were linguistically and culturally Russian'. Natan Mair, 'Jews, Ukrainians, and Russians in Kiev: Intergroup Relations in Late Imperial Associational Life', *Slavic Review* 3 (Autumn, 2006): 479. The Soviet Union continued to enforce Russian as the official language in Ukraine. The level of suppression becomes clear in movements to resist this cultural censorship, such as the Ukrainian Renaissance of the 1920s, which was a movement spearheaded by politicians and artists, aiming to give greater prominence to Ukrainian cultural identity and language, with only limited success prior to further suppression. Myroslav Shkandrij, trans. and ed. *Mykola Khvylovy: The Cultural Renaissance in Ukraine*. University of Alberta, 1986: 1–26.
67 Ukrainian is a distinctive, Slavic language – as old as Russian. Russian speakers struggle to understand Ukrainian.
68 It should be noted that, in addition to Ukrainian, there is a Ukrainian dialect called *surhik* [pronounced *surzhik*] – which is a spoken dialect, mixing elements of Ukrainian and Russian, into a distinctive register associated largely with rural speakers.
69 Interview with Anastasia Kosodiy and Jack Clover (2017).
70 Ibid.
71 Interview with Maksym Kurochkin (2017).
72 Interview with Natal'ia Vorozhbyt (2017).
73 Ivan Kozachenko, 'Retelling Old Stories with New Media': 150.

Bibliography

Articles and news features (online)

Billington, Michael. 'Broken Voices'. *Guardian*, 31 March 2005. Available at: https://www.theguardian.com/stage/2005/mar/31/theatre1 (accessed 4 December 2017).

Botanova, Kateryna. 'Ukraine's Blacklists in Defence of Democracy and National Security Are Doing It No Favours'. *Open Democracy Russia*, 9 February 2018. Available at: https://www.opendemocracy.net/od-russia/kateryna-botanova/ukraines-blacklists-in-defence-of-democracy (accessed 10 February 2018).

Bud'ko, Ol'ga. 'Sovremennyi Odissei: V Kieve proshli prem'ernye pokazy spektakli *Vitalik*'. *Novoe vremia*, 8 July 2017. Available at: https://nv.ua/style/art/theater_art/v-kieve-proshli-premernye-pokazy-spektaklja-vitalik-1449000.html (accessed 13 February 2018).

Freedman, John. 'Maksym Kurochkin Cooks Up Great Drama', personal website, 4 November 2009. Available at: https://johnfreedmanarchive.wordpress.com/2017/07/12/maksym-kurochkin-cooks-up-great-drama (accessed 13 February 2018).

Kozachenko, Ivan. 'Retelling Old Stories with New Media: National Identity and Transnationalism in the "Russian Spring" Popular Uprisings'. *East/West Journal of Ukrainian Studies* 4, no. 1 (2017): 137–58.

Mair, Natan. 'Jews, Ukrainians, and Russians in Kiev: Intergroup Relations in Late Imperial Associational Life'. *Slavic Review* 3 (Autumn, 2006): 475–501.

Naydan, Michael. 'Ukrainian Avant-Garde Poetry Today: Bu-Ba-Bu and Others'. *The Slavic and East European Journal* 50, no. 3, Special Forum Issue: Contemporary Ukrainian Literature and National Identity (Fall, 2006): 452–68.

Nikitiuk, Marysia. 'Natalia Vorozhbyt'. *Teatre teatral'nyi zhurnal*, 23 February 2009. Available at http://teatre.com.ua/modern/natalja_vorozhbyt (accessed 9 February 2017).

Shkandrij, Myroslav, trans. and ed. *Mykola Khvylovy: The Cultural Renaissance in Ukraine*. Edmonton: University of Alberta, 1986.

Slobodianik, Dar'ia. '"Dnevniki Maidana": neotlozhnaia refleksiia'. *Levyi Bereg*, 1 December 2014. Available at: https://lb.ua/culture/2014/12/01/287804_dnevniki_maydana_neotlozhnaya.html (accessed 13 February 2018).

Starr, Megan. 'The Best Coffee in Kiev, Ukraine', personal blog, 16 October 2016. Available at: https://www.meganstarr.com/kiev-coffee (accessed 10 July 2017).

Vasil'ev, Sergei. 'Valerii Bil'chenko: "Vmeste s esteticheskim slukhom my teriaem chuvstvo sovesti"'. *Den'*, 2 September 1998. Available at: https://day.kyiv.ua/ru/article/kultura/valeriy-bilchenko-vmeste-s-esteticheskim-sluhom-my-teryaem-chuvstvo-sovesti (accessed 1 December 2017).

Vasil'ev, Sergei. 'Ukrainskii teatr ot Soiuza do Maidana'. *Teatr*, no. 17, 2014. Available at: http://oteatre.info/ukrainskij-teatr-ot-soyuza-do-majdana/ (accessed 4 December 2017).

Velichko, Angela. 'Vitalik-Uliss: chem interesen novyi spektakl' "Dikogo teatra"'. *Ukrains'ka Pravda*, 4 July 2017. Available at: http://life.pravda.com.ua/columns/2017/07/4/225086 (accessed 22 January 2018).

Zaionts, Marina. 'O, sport, ty zhut!'', *Itogi*, 7 June 2005. Available at: http://www.smotr.ru/2004/2004_centr_galka.htm (accessed 13 February 2018).

Books

Aston, Elaine, and Mark O'Thomas. *Royal Court: International*. Basingstoke: Palgrave Macmillan, 2015.

Knowles, Richard. *Reading the Material Theatre*. Cambridge: Cambridge University Press, 2004.

The Dakh Theatre: Kyiv, 1994–2012. Kyiv: Dukh-Litera, 2012.

Lecture

Zabuzhko, Oksana. 'Being a Writer in Contemporary Ukraine: Drawing the Landscape while Standing on a Powerboat', University of Cambridge, 29 March 2013. Available at: https://sms.cam.ac.uk/media/1449548 (accessed 16 May 2017).

Interviews (in Russian and English, translated where necessary into English by this author)

Dzhikaeva, Galina, Dan Gumennyi and Yana Gumennaia, 19 October 2017, Kyiv.
Golovnenko, Anastasia, 18 October 2017, Kyiv.
Kosodiy, Anastasia and Jack Clover, 6 December 2017, London.
Kurochkin, Maksym, 21 October 2017, Kyiv.
Mai, Andriy, 20 October 2017, Kyiv.
Nezhdana, Nadiia, 6 July 2017, Kyiv.
Rybakova, Alla, 9 July 2017, Kyiv.
Shvydko, Viktoria, 4 January 2018, Lviv (by Skype).
Troitskii, Vladislav, 11 July 2017, Kyiv.
Vorozhbyt, Natal'ia, 11 July 2017, Kyiv.
Jirkov, Stas, 5 July 2017, Kyiv.

Play texts

Gumennyi, Dan, and Gumennaia, Yana. *The Militiaman*. Unpublished text, 2015.
Vorozhbyt, Natal'ia. *The Grain Store*, trans. by Sasha Dugdale. London: Nick Hern Books, 2009.
Vorozhbyt, Natal'ia. *Maidan Dairies*, trans. by Sasha Dugdale. Unpublished text, 2014.
Vorozhbyt, Natal'ia. *Bad Roads*, trans. by Sasha Dugdale. London: Nick Hern Books, 2017.

Useful reference

Birksted-Breen, Noah. 'Alternative Voices in an Acquiescent Society: Translating the New Wave of Russian Playwrights (2000–2014)'. Unpublished doctoral thesis, 2017.

10

The playwright overlooked

Personal reflections on two years in Ukrainian theatre (2017–19)

Jack Clover

> Jack Clover draws upon his direct experience of working together with a number of Ukrainian playwrights and theatres to offer a picture of the current situation in the country. Being a playwright himself, he pays particular attention to the question of how respectful theatre directors are to the texts of plays. As he surveys the writers, directors and institutions which make up the 'Ukrainian fringe', he makes a case for the year 2018 marking the true birth of a new theatre in Ukraine. In this respect he sees things slightly differently from Noah Birksted-Breen, who suggested in the previous essay that 2014 was the real watershed year.

Since February 2017 I have been working on and off as a freelance director and playwright in Ukraine. I have witnessed first-hand various aspects of what Noah Birksted-Breen aptly labels the 'Ukrainian Fringe'. His article offers an excellent account of the manner in which the events of 2014 gave birth to a new theatre in Ukraine. I will approach a similar question, not from an academic position but instead from a more subjective standpoint. There are three overarching observations that I hope these sketches will affirm. Firstly, the events of 2014 (the Euromaidan Revolution, the Annexation of Crimea and the ongoing War in Donbas) transformed lives and challenged all the existing forms, language, methods and aesthetics of Ukrainian contemporary theatre, to an extent that cannot easily be understated. The only comparable period in the history of theatre in the country would perhaps be the 'Ukrainization' which took place in the 1920s. Secondly, the fragile group of independent theatres, playwrights and documentary theatre practitioners that have become active after 2014 represents an exciting and unprecedented 'new dawn' in Ukrainian Theatre that is unique within Europe, to quote Maksym Kurochkin (April 2019). Thirdly, this phenomenon (with an emphasis on 'Ukrainian New Drama') is materially and aesthetically under threat. Not only do exciting new platforms and writers disappear as quickly as they emerge but existing institutions (theatres and universities) are often woefully under-equipped and unwilling to work respectfully with a contemporary text. I believe that now, five years after the revolution and war began, a battle for the soul of Ukrainian theatre is under way: a battle between writer and director, content and form, empathy and manipulation.

My sketches will be backed up by interviews with four Ukrainian theatre-makers whose lives and work have been transformed since 2014: Galina Dzhikaeva (actor, director and co-founder of PostPlay Theatre, Kyiv), Maksym Kurochkin (playwright active before 2014 in Russia and Ukraine), Olena Apchel (head director at the Lesia Ukrainka Academic Theatre, Lviv) and Anastasia Kosodiy (a leading Ukrainian playwright of the post-Euromaidan generation). With the exception of Apchel their work has already been discussed by Birksted-Breen.

Olena Apchel and 'decolonizing the actor'

Olena and I meet late in the evening in her office in Lviv's Lesia Ukrainka Theatre. The premiere of my production of Kosodiy's play *Timetraveller's Guide to Donbas* occurred a few days before, so now Olena has only a few days to prepare for the revival of her magnum opus *Horizon 200,* a 'post-documentary' play about miners from different parts of Ukraine. The play is almost four hours long and aims to deconstruct and analyse mainstream Ukrainian theatre's existing tools of manipulation. This evening's rehearsals were long and heated.

Olena remarks dryly that her story with regards to the war is a little more 'Hollywood' than that of most Ukrainian theatre directors. She has a personal connection to both Donbas and Crimea. The village where she was brought up is now in the 'Grey Zone' between Ukrainian and Russian-controlled territory in Donbas. Her family home itself was shelled from the Ukrainian side. Some of her family are still there, and while shelling is now rare civilian casualties from mines still occur. She has a dream to set up an art residency in the village when the war ends, though she admits that such a programme may not be interesting or helpful for those who live there. In 2014 Olena was part of the first wave of Ukrainian volunteers to travel to Donbas when the unrest began. She served for a period in 2014 as a military medic.

Olena's father has lived in Crimea since the 1990s. Olena tried to travel to Crimea to visit him in the summer of 2017. She was arrested on the border. She was apparently on a blacklist because of interviews she had given. She was interrogated and threatened, then unexpectedly a Russian guard opened her cell in the middle of the night and told her to walk. Olena speaks of her first reaction to the 'New Drama' that addressed the war:

> There was a micro conflict/scandal – I don't know what to call it. There was a festival organized by Tania [Tat'iana] Kitsenko called 'Writing in the Cross-hairs'. It was 2015, and they collected all these texts that were written quickly after the Maidan. When I read these texts [...] I remember feeling, 'This is complete nonsense, I am coming back from the front and I'm washing blood out of my fingernails and [I know] the reality is thousands of times stronger than this, albeit honest, dramatic writing'. I said, 'Stop! I can't do theatre at the moment, because I

truly do not know how to talk about the war, everything I know is not like that.'
[...] I thought I couldn't return to the profession.

It was not only 'New Drama' that seemed inadequate to Apchel at that time, but even the work of PostPlay Theatre or the Theatre of Displaced People that worked with documentary testimony also seemed to her to strike false notes. Her opinion has changed since then. However, to this day she has not addressed the war directly in her own work. It seems it is a topic too close to home for her to gain an artistic distance.

Instead, her focus seems to be more on shifting the conventional forms of an actor's existence on the stage, in order to prepare actors for working on a contemporary text or document, even if those texts haven't emerged yet. This in my opinion seems to be the aim of *Horizon 200* (text compiled by Apchel and Oksana Danchuk). The piece is broken down into various *études*, where the actors often step out of character to explain to the audience which well-tried methods of manipulation they will use in the next scene.

In most cities in Ukraine an actor's education is dominated by teachers who were themselves taught during the Soviet period, when the theatre was an instrument of political and cultural control. Even among young actors like those at Lviv's Lesia Ukrainka Theatre (or Teatr Lesi for short) echoes of agitprop can linger in the position of an actor's hand, the timbre of a vowel or a forced smile. This realization became most clear to me in my recent work in a government theatre in Sumy (in north-eastern Ukraine), where the young and talented actors were treated like factory workers and spoke of their own work as 'service', as if they were part of a Red Army Choir.

I see Apchel's approach in *Horizon 200*, and in her work in Teatr Lesi as a whole, as a kind of decolonization of the actor, and in turn of the audience's expectations. The shock of the events of 2014 awoke young theatre-makers to the enemy within, to the Soviet relics surviving in their own aesthetics. Despite almost thirty years having passed since the break-up of the Soviet Union, the conscious process of stamping out these relics has only just begun.

Olena tells me she is most interested in the 'near-frontline state' both physically and psychologically. That feeling when you travel '20–25 kilometres away from the front and people are sitting and working on their laptops in cafes'. This empathy gap between those who were at the front or have lost loved ones and those who haven't is an unavoidable reality of life in modern Ukraine. Olena adds: 'Between people [theatre-makers] who have experienced the trauma and those who haven't there is a big difference, but it's hard to say what it is.' This difference is hard to define on the stage but it often boils down to micro details such as one actor's intonation on one line. For example in the opening monologue of Kosodiy's *Timetraveller's Guide to Donbas*: 'What? You say/a basement in Luhansk/What? You say/basements that's where you get tinned foods/and where they torture/people/often for tinned foods.'

Apchel tells me how the performance of those lines containing the sudden reference to torture in my production in her theatre prompted a strong negative reaction from her: 'It didn't happen in the rehearsal, but in the performance Nastia [Anastasia Lisovska, actress] changes the timbre of her voice as if to manipulate me emotionally, and that really irritates me because anyone who actually has that kind of experience would never talk about the war [with that affected intonation], they would just talk calmly.' Apchel noticed the false note, while I missed it. When working with a new Ukrainian text the success of a production can hang upon such details. There is a scarily fine line between empathy and dehumanization.

Apchel's astute ear for, and intolerance of, old tools of decoration and emotional manipulation (whether or not the work is related to the war) is shared by an entire generation of socially engaged theatre-makers (Kosodiy, Dzhikaeva, Apchel, Den and Yana Gumennyi, Olga Maciupa, Piotr Armianovskii, Natasha Blok, Iryna Harets, Rosa Sarkisian and others). However, the very fabric of the state theatre system in Ukraine is a Soviet relic and was conceived as an instrument of manipulation, a system that instead of provoking critical thought nips it in the bud. This is the system against which representatives of the Ukrainian Fringe are fighting.

Teatr Lesi

A relatively major victory in this battle occurred in Lviv in 2017. The Lesia Ukrainka Academic Dramatic Theatre in Lviv is unique in Ukraine. In 2014 the actors went on strike in protest against a tyrannical and belligerent artistic director who was also supposedly embezzling the theatre's funds. The director eventually was forced out but the theatre was left virtually without a repertoire. The playwright and director Pavlo Ar'ye ran the theatre for over a year, during which time he added some of his own plays to the repertoire and invited young directors (Artem Vusyk, Igor Bilyts) from Kyiv and Kharkiv to stage them along with other work. However, the greatest modernizing shift began in 2017 when the team behind Drama.UA (Viktoria Shvydko, Olha Puzhakovska (nee Mukhina) and Oksana Danchuk) took over the theatre, with Puzhakovska taking the managerial role. Apchel came at this time too to take the head director position. This was the first occasion when a team from an independent non-governmental organization that focused on contemporary Ukrainian playwriting took over a government theatre. As a result, when Kosodiy's play *Timetraveller's Guide to Donbas* won the Drama.UA playwriting award in 2018 it was awarded a full production on the main stage, not just a rehearsed reading in a studio space. However, to call Lesi a theatre of the contemporary playwright is a stretch. A short visit to Apchel's rehearsal shows that a director-led hierarchy is still very much in place, but it certainly is an experimental theatre of contemporary drama, a place where the methods of the 'Ukrainian Fringe' meet the mainstream with mixed but exciting results. While there are hundreds of factors behind this shift I do believe that the positive attempt at reform in a government theatre that is happening in Lesi could not have happened before 2014.

Bad Roads

A relatively major defeat in this battle occurred during the Ukrainian premiere of Natal'ia Vorozhbyt's *Bad Roads*. On paper the signs were looking good: a powerful piece of 'Ukrainian New Drama' (perhaps the most powerful dramatic text addressing the war to emerge so far), a young rising star female director Tamara Trunova, a new independent stage (Stsena 6, Kyiv). In fact, according to the documentary theatre practitioner and dramaturg Dima (Dmitry) Levitsky these facts alone made this production a positive and important step, and I agree with him on those grounds. However, in relation to a director's treatment of 'New Drama' it was worrying. Galina Dzhikaeva explains her reaction as a member of the audience:

> I left in the first act. I went into hysterics. Went home and drank a bottle of flavoured vodka that was lying in the kitchen. [...] The problem isn't in the text but in the director's vision. There was an absolute feeling of a director from an ivory tower with a horrible position of superiority painting a picture of what they think is happening in this country. I had a great desire to grab the director by the scruff of the neck and push her nose into the dirt, into those conditions where our forces live, make her spend one night under bombardment. Then she would have created a completely different production. [...] Watching this aesthetic [decorative] vision was traumatic for me. [...] I took it as an insult to those people [who live with the war].

While Trunova is a young director, she is still a product of the Ukrainian director-led aesthetic school that believes their role is to twist and decorate a text. I am in a difficult position in criticizing this piece because I have my own vast 'ivory tower', being a British director approaching Ukrainian issues and the war in particular. My production of *Timetraveller's Guide to Donbas* in Lviv which Dzhikaeva saw on the first night was also disappointing to her but for slightly different reasons.

My point here is not to give a poor review of a colleague's work, but to highlight the challenge that Ukrainian writers face when the majority of establishment directors (with the notable exception of Andriy Mai and Georg Genoux, though both seem to work more in Germany now) do not seem to respect text. Or more importantly, do not know how to approach a contemporary text. Apchel worries that due to the absence of good new directors 'New Drama' will 'go off' (literally 'spoil'). This is a very big concern. Whenever a dramatic text breaks out of the fringe scene of rehearsed readings (be it Drama.UA, or The Week of Contemporary Plays) it is often staged in a manner that discourages young, socially engaged Ukrainians from writing plays, and forces exciting artists that are dealing with the trauma related to the recent events such as Dzhikaeva (an internally displaced person from Crimea) to remain in the realm of documentary theatre and performance art, whereas their sensitivity would be thoroughly appreciated in approaching a piece of 'New Drama'.

Moscow's Teatr.doc tour to PostPlay Theatre, November 2018

Now for an aside. The tour of Teatr.doc to Kyiv last year in my opinion marked a full stop: the end of an era that has lasted since the fall of the Soviet Union, in which the most exciting Ukrainian theatre practitioners looked to Moscow for answers and new forms.

Dzhikaeva noted her great respect for those in Teatr.doc who fought against injustice in their political and judicial system, but admitted that she learned nothing new from the tour – in fact, it left her with the feeling that the work of PostPlay was more interesting. I recall a humorous moment when Den Gumennyi left a post-performance discussion cursing and shouting, coming into the bar where we were standing. A member of the audience had just praised Teatr.doc saying how wonderful it was that they came because 'we don't have documentary theatre here'. Galina said that she and Den responded, saying: 'Look, here we are, come and watch our plays – but of course they don't come.' This indicates a deeply ingrained inferiority complex that is common in post-colonial Ukraine: the presumption that in Moscow, or in Europe, the art is better. I admit that I am often a beneficiary of such an assumption. But such an inferiority complex, while Moscow is literally waging a hybrid war against Ukraine, was rather depressing to encounter.

There were many high points. The actors' aptitude in delivering a documentary text without decoration and their way of existing on the stage was very refreshing, and it is rare to find this approach among professional actors in Ukraine. *Two in Your Home* (E. Gremina), and *New Antigone* (E. Kostiuchenko) moved me greatly and reminded me that despite the great personal cost that Ukrainians have paid, especially over the past five years, it is a great and fragile privilege no longer to live in the kind of police state that their Slavic post-Soviet neighbours still have to endure. For me the unexpected highlight of the tour was the one-man performance *Carrier*, in which the actor and author of the piece Aleksei Iudnikov in an epic two-hour stint re-told frame by frame the recent scandalous blockbuster about Tsar Nicholas II's love life, *Matil'da*. In some ways, I felt I gleaned more about today's Russia from those two hours than from the rest of the tour put together.

Another impression I gained was that the general format of protest performance followed by a long unmediated discussion seemed rather self-righteous and unchallenging. This sounds harsh considering the oppression that these artists face each day. I did not see every performance that week and they varied greatly, but often the slightly complacent nature of the after-show discussions dissolved the complex feelings of empathy that the performances evoked. The war and the change in relations between Russia and Ukraine bizarrely seemed to be an elephant in the room throughout the tour. Not that the topic was not discussed, but rather it was treated as a domestic Ukrainian problem with the exception of *War Is Close* (D. Bel, M. Ravenhill, E. Gremina) which included material from the arrest of Oleh Sentsov and from a diary of a man living in Luhansk in 2014. This gave me a small hint of the sense that Kosodiy told me she felt in Liubimovka in 2014–16, or that Kurochkin felt living in Moscow from 2014 to 2017, or Apchel felt when speaking with former colleagues from Russia, whereby even the greatest friends, allies, brave artists, activists and intellectuals in Russia who condemned their government in clear terms still lived on the other side of an information war, and still did not fully engage with the depth of the 'betrayal of classical proportions', as Kurochkin describes it, that the events of 2014 amounted to.

There was a great sadness behind the trip, as the tour was dedicated to Teatr.Doc's founders Elena Gremina and Mikhail Ugarov who both died suddenly last year. The guests returned to Russia with a sense of uncertainty for their future. In Kyiv, there was a huge feeling of gratitude to Gremina and Ugarov, mixed with a greater certainty than ever that it's now time to turn away. In Apchel's words, 'everything we could have taken [learnt] from Russia we have taken'.

Ukrainian independent theatre

Now for a quick word about independent theatres in Ukraine. The vast majority of theatres in Ukraine are funded by the state, either through a local council or directly through the Ministry of Culture. The system is a relic of a Soviet command economy. In Lviv, for example, tickets for a theatre production average between 80 and 150 hryvnia (£2–5). While the administrations of government theatres love to sell tickets, and are incentivised to do so by local councils, the money they receive from ticket sales is a fraction of what they need to survive and pay monthly salaries for their extensive list of employees. However, ticket prices stay very low because theatre is viewed as public service and a right for all.

Making contemporary theatre into business in Ukraine is very difficult, as prices will always be undercut by government theatres. However, companies such as 'Wild Theatre' (Kyiv) and 'Beautiful Flowers' (Kharkiv) have managed to succeed at doing so. 'Beautiful Flowers' are a hit physical-theatre troupe in Kharkiv that have been creating their own socially conscious work since 2011. 'Wild Theatre' is a post-2014 phenomenon and has somehow managed to make theatre cool again in Kyiv: an astounding feat. Their productions often include work by living writers – Maksym Kurochkin, Natasha Blok, Martin McDonagh, Ihor Bilyts, Vitalii Chenskii – though the productions remain very director-led and rely on in-yer-face aesthetics to draw a crowd.

Natal'ia Blok's play *Woman! Sit Down!* (a very personal text addressing domestic violence and abuse in marriage) was staged by Wild Theatre in December 2018. The performance toured the country and offered some free showings in various regional centres. According to their poster, the show was supported by UK Aid, the British Embassy and the United Nations Population Fund among other domestic and foreign NGOs, presumably on account of its brave and uncompromising approach to the topic of domestic abuse and women's rights. All of this made me even more astounded to find out that Blok only received between 250 and 400 hryvnia (£7–12) per performance in royalties. This seemed extraordinary to me: how can a project seek to promote respect to women across the country if they cannot respectfully pay the author of this autobiographical text. I do not mean to criticize Wild Theatre as they are one of the only theatres in Ukraine to take on New Writing at all, I purely wish to illustrate for the foreign reader the extent to which authors are viewed as 'support staff' and not 'leaders of ideas', to use the words of Maksym Kurochkin.

PostPlay theatre is an example of a rather different approach: one much less popular in the box office. The theatre was born in the months following the revolution and outbreak of war in the east. To this day, their repertoire, through the work of artists such as Den and Yana Gumennyi and Galina Dzhikaeva, attempts directly to address some uncomfortable realities of life in Ukraine. Dzhikaeva and Anton Romanov (both involved in founding PostPlay with the Gumennyis) worked together in an independent theatre in Crimea before 2014. While before the war they staged contemporary takes on classic authors (such as Marina Tsvetaeva) and other fictional works, the experience of the annexation of Crimea and the trauma of having to leave their homes had a profound effect on the way they both approached theatre. Neither has returned to working with fictional texts. The experiences that they are attempting to exorcise from themselves through their art can only find form in documentary or post-documentary texts or 'not-theatre' as Romanov labels his bold performance pieces. PostPlay's recent productions *Girls-Girls* and *Grass Breaks through the Soil* (Dzhikaeva/Gumennyi) are striking pieces of theatrical activism, provoking a conversation about the issues of women on the Donbas frontline and human-rights abuses in Crimea respectively. On the recent seventy-fifth anniversary of Stalin's 1944 forced deportation of Crimean Tatars to Central Asia, PostPlay responded with a one-off solemn performance in the central hall of the main Kyiv railway station. PostPlay has taken on a very difficult task of being the only hard-hitting, uncompromising theatre of critical thought in Kyiv. PostPlay's performances are temporary bandages for open wounds; they are a call to arms. It is perhaps a step too far to expect them to be the primary space for the playwright too but so far this is the only space in Kyiv where I have seen a writer's text duly respected.

'Zaporizhzhian New Drama'

There was one theatre where the playwright did achieve a dominant role: that theatre was 'Zaporizhzhian New Drama', and the playwright was Anastasia Kosodiy. I use the past tense because unfortunately the ZND team lost their venue at the beginning of 2018: when gas prices rose and grants dried up they could not afford to rent their underground space in a semi-derelict nineteenth-century mill in the industrial city of Zaporizhzhia. However, the company is still alive and is planning projects for summer 2019. Kosodiy founded the theatre with producer, activist and actress Viktoria Petrova in 2015. After the Maidan revolution and the beginning of the war, politically active young people across the country searched for likeminded people with whom to start businesses, charities or in this case an amateur theatre. Kosodiy had already received recognition for her writing before 2015, after her play was read at the Drama.UA festival and Moscow's Liubimovka festival in 2014. The theatre was at first a platform for Kosodiy's texts with *The Greatest Pain on Earth*, *The Ministry of Education and Science of Ukraine* and *Paradoxical Papa* all being staged, but soon the theatre began to stage works by other writers such as Andriy Bondarenko's *Interview with a Friend*, and held rehearsed readings of works by writers such as Olia Maciupa and Oles' Barlig. I spent a summer as a 'director in residence' at 'Zaporizhzhian New Drama' in 2017. At the time, I had not travelled so much around Ukraine's theatre scene, and had only had experience with Drama.UA in Lviv and Class Act in Kyiv. Only later did I realize that the set-up there was truly unique for Ukraine, and exactly the kind of theatre that should exist in more parts of the country. Aside from being playwright-led there were two other factors that made 'Zaporizhzhian New Drama' unique: a company of talented amateur actors untainted by 'old school' training, and fully fledged productions of the texts with all actors learning their lines, as well as basic set design and costumes. This final point may sound extraordinarily basic, but for the majority of playwrights their texts never leave the festival rehearsed-reading stage. I also differentiate between ZND and PostPlay, because while PostPlay is very welcoming to 'New Drama' it is still primarily associated with documentary and 'post-documentary' theatre, and not for original fictional texts. The vast majority of texts read at The Week of Contemporary Plays or at the Drama.UA festival are never staged in theatres. As discussed earlier, writers that are staged such as Natal'ia Vorozhbyt and Pavlo Ar'ye often have to sacrifice the integrity of their text to see it performed by a government theatre or a mainstream independent theatre such as Wild Theatre.

'Zaporizhzhian New Drama' was truly unique as a platform for staging contemporary texts. However, its loyal but small following in Zaporizhzhia was not enough to keep the theatre alive as a venue for longer than four years. Many new writers have emerged since 2014, Kosodiy, Maciupa and Natasha Blok being the most exciting in my opinion, but they lack a space where text is king. As a result of a period of artistic first aid directly following the war, documentary theatre in Ukraine is far more developed than fictional socially relevant playwriting, even though it is precisely the latter that will bring the 'high-quality breakthrough' that Maksym Kurochkin says Ukrainian theatre is waiting for. Now that Kosodiy has taken over from Den Gumennyi as the Chief-Dramaturg of PostPlay Theatre, and her play *Song* (2018/19) is a successful part of their repertoire, it is to be hoped that fictional 'New Drama' will have a space to develop and grow in Kyiv. Even if that space only seats around forty people, and actors often have to battle with neighbouring nightclubs to be heard. While Ukrainian playwriting has thrived despite adversity over the past five years it would be nice to believe that spaces such as PostPlay and 'Zaporizhzhian New Drama' will become bigger, more common and more financially viable. Without continued support from abroad and more interest from the Ukrainian theatrical mainstream, 'New Drama' will not have the scope that it needs to develop.

Ukraine has extraordinary writers that have emerged over the past five years. It is imperative that these voices, these stories and their independent institutions are supported before this movement fades away before it has truly begun.

11

A new 'dawn' in Ukrainian theatre

A conversation with Maksym Kurochkin (April 2019)

Jack Clover

> This conversation between Jack Clover and Maksym Kurochkin begins with some comments on a project they worked on in December 2018, together with two of the contemporary playwrights Kurochkin most admires (apart from Natal'ia Vorozhbyt), Natal'ia Blok and Anastasia Kosodiy. In the light of Russia's aggressive acts towards Ukraine since 2014, Kurochkin goes on to share with Jack his bitter regrets about the years he feels he wasted as a playwright within the orbit of Russian 'New Drama', and the challenges he has faced in redefining himself exclusively as a Ukrainian playwright who has resolved henceforth only to write in the Ukrainian language. Despite the difficulties faced by Ukrainian theatre-makers, they do at least enjoy far more freedom in the cultural sphere than their colleagues in Russia, and are not subject to the oppressive regulations and socially conservative attitudes which now constrain artistic freedoms there. Kurochkin comments on the 2018 visit by Teatr.doc to Kyiv at which the memory of Mikhail Ugarov and Elena Gremina was honoured, and also talks about what he would like to see happening in Ukrainian theatre in the next five years.

Maksym Kurochkin was one of the most instrumental playwrights in the beginning of the 'New Drama' movement in Moscow in the late nineties and early 2000s.[1] Being the only prominent and proud Ukrainian playwright to be living and working in Moscow at the outbreak of war in 2014, his experience of the cultural rift with Russia is a unique one. He now lives in Kyiv with his family.

Kurochkin and I met on the project *Theatre in Two Weeks: Silence Isn't Golden* in Kyiv in December 2018. The project was a co-production between my theatre company/format 'Theatre in Two Weeks' and the 'Theatre of Displaced People'. Three contemporary writers (Maksym Kurochkin, Anastasia Kosodiy and Natal'ia Blok) were paired with three directors (Dmitrii Zakhozhenko, Piotr Armianovsky and Daisy Hayes): each group was given four actors, and in the space of two weeks wrote, rehearsed and performed an original play from scratch. The purpose of the project was to create a democratic balance between writer and director, and to give writers a chance to see their work instantly performed and not written just for the desk-drawer.

Kurochkin's play *The Monastery* (*Lavra*) was a semi-autobiographical musing on the 'Tomos for autocephaly' (independence) from the Moscow patriarchy that the Ukrainian Orthodox Church had received only a week prior to the project. The play takes place in the early 1990s and is set within the historical Kyiv Pechersk Lavra Monastery of the Caves. In Kurochkin's version of history, the monastery (a museum during Soviet times, where Kurochkin worked as a recent graduate) was not sold to the Russian Orthodox Church but rather to the Cult of the Goddess Kali (as seen in *Indiana Jones and the Temple of Doom*). By the end of the play The Cult of the Goddess Kali ends up transforming into the Russian Orthodox Church all the same, because the financial rewards are just too tempting. While the performance was jolly and successful, Kurochkin and Zakhozhenko's team ended up being the most difficult to manage as a balance was not reached between text and direction.

Kosodiy's play *Song*, directed by Piotr Armianovsky, addressed the plight of Ukrainians in Poland. Kosodiy intertwined personal materials from her recent trip to Poland to find the stories of her ancestors (ethnic Ukrainians who lived on the territory of Poland until being forcibly relocated to Zaporizhzhia by Stalin after the war) with stories of contemporary economic migration to Poland. The text took the form of a '*poema*' (epic poem), a monologue in eight parts. Armianovsky's direction saw the actors each learning the text in its entirety so that each actor could choose when to share which lines, depending on the atmosphere created by the ensemble. As a work of literature, this was the strongest text in my opinion. The performance is still running as a part of the repertoire of PostPlay (May 2019).

Blok's *Bomb*, directed by Daisy Hayes, was a humorous Gogolian piece in which a female civil-rights activist finds that the anxious 'ticking' that she feels in her stomach is an actual bomb, and if she allows this bomb to be detonated – thus sacrificing herself – she will turn back the clock for the whole of Ukraine, and the nation will have a chance to start again in a reality where no 'Maidans' or war exist.

Being a curator of the project and a witness of the writing process was a great joy. Perhaps surprisingly Kurochkin's play was the only one written in Ukrainian. Kosodiy, who normally writes in Ukrainian, chose Russian for this subject matter. When I asked her why I was met with justified disdain, like Bob Dylan being asked what his songs mean. In her piece, Ukraine is an underworld, a Hades lurking under a field or a car-park in Poland: 'Orpheus descends into hell / And hell is Ukraine.' When the actors are speaking in Russian, their own voices are the products of two centuries of cultural oppression, and so their own 'Ukrainianness' lies beneath the surface.

I spoke with Kurochkin over Skype in April 2019. I initially tried to pose these questions to him in writing but he struggled to get back to me. He said that every answer he tried to write seemed somewhat imperfect. I have tried to translate and convey our conversation faithfully, though of course I have made some minor cuts and re-phrasings. So I would like the reader to appreciate this conversation as just that: imperfect. It is the start of a conversation that I hope will continue.

JC Does Ukrainian theatre, its institutions and systems, have the necessary tools effectively to react to the changes and traumas of the past five years?

MK What we're experiencing now is a new dawn. But not a dawn in the full sense. It's a stage of correcting some kinds of very [major mistakes]. This is the most difficult thing: it's not just correcting mistakes, it's addressing and neutralizing a blatant emergency. Crudely speaking, in my opinion, which not all agree with, it's a stage of liquidating the consequences of a long period of mindlessness. Let's use the example of the Chernobyl' nuclear disaster, where we're now seeing the thirty-third anniversary. In Ukraine we often have these heroic moments, with firefighters throwing themselves on the fire, and I suppose we're now using the stage to put out the fire in our own lives. Sorry, this is obviously a terrible over-exaggeration when talking about theatre, but [I see it as the] elimination of obvious kinds of disequilibrium, the removal of blatant restrictions on theatre as a place for intellectual training. For many years it has not operated either as a forum, nor as a place for complex emotions, nor as a place for intellectual discussion. Now it's starting to work, but of course what we lack is some major theoretical work.

Very often we end up trying to put out this fire using old techniques. It's a place where the right experience is needed, but often we throw in people who just try to chuck wheelbarrows of graphite off the roof of the reactor. Sorry for this metaphor. Just at the moment, it is hard not to read about [Chernobyl'] in the papers. There have been lots of documentary performances that are very good and necessary, but we need some kind of theoretical work to go alongside it. How does a documentary text work? What is a theatrical document, and how does it interact with society? I think that our efforts in this direction are often very naïve. That's much better than a situation in which they don't exist at all, but in any case there's a lot of work to be done. Technically speaking we're experiencing a 'dawn' but so far it has been extensive, not intensive. We're still waiting for a high-quality leap [in the right direction]. I think that now we're expecting a breakthrough of good quality. Who will do it we don't know, but at least now it's possible, and there are a lot of players on that playing field. Sorry, perhaps I've confused you.

JC No, it's okay, I understand. Olena Apchel said that there is a risk that everything that has developed in 'New Drama' over the past five years runs the risk of going stale, because directors don't understand how to work with these texts, or else they work with them using old tools.

MK In other words, they 'understand' how to work with [new texts]. They *think* they understand how to work with them, but actually we have to invent new tools. There is a sense that everyone has calmed down and has agreed 'this is how we're going to deal with this [i.e with old techniques]'. This is what scares me.

But at least no one is disturbing those people who do want to do more experimental theatre any more. Those who know how to [work with documentary and 'New Drama'] haven't calmed down. At least now we don't have constantly to justify our right to exist. However, we do need a breakthrough in terms of working with a play text. Because so far even the loud, successful theatrical events connected with 'New Drama' are in some manner compromised, due to the way in which directors work with writers. Your case is perhaps the exception [the Theatre in Two Weeks festival] because of the specifics of the world that was created. The approach was correct to the nth degree but, all the same, there were moments of conflict, because the balance between writer and director was still not found.

JC I think that in the other groups (Piotr Armianovsky/Anastasia Kosodiy and Daisy Hayes/Natal'ia Blok) there was a balance. Ironically the problem is with the directors that have had a Ukrainian theatre-director's education. The people who do understand [how to approach a text], they understand through experience, often a terrible experience, and discover the necessity of working with the text.

Let's move on to a different question. In what way have the geopolitical events of the past five years affected your self-identification as an author?

MK Look, Jack, I have always considered myself a Ukrainian writer. Considering my position, that has always been slightly wishful thinking. Bearing in mind my inadequate mastery of the Ukrainian language, and me being brought up in a Russian-speaking family, I feel a certain level of awkwardness.

After the start of the war, there were no longer any other options. Crudely speaking, I now don't want to have anything to do with Russian playwriting. If before it was possible to half turn a blind eye if your name was written with a slash, as some kind of Ukrainian/Russian author, since the winter of 2013 it is absolutely not. I'm so imperfect, but I have no alternative. I am a Ukrainian author and that is forever. Any other description of me is insulting.

JC In that sense there is often a mild failing of Western academia, because we study literature via the language, and if you write in Russian and you are from Georgia then we can study it as literature in the Russian language which is often, albeit through a slash, equated to Russian literature. Have you thought about what canon your work is adding to – Russian or Ukrainian? Or is it not important, because Ukrainian literature is bilingual? In other words, after Maidan, when lots of writers switched from Russian to Ukrainian, do you think it became a more conscious attempt to be adding to a Ukrainian literary canon?

MK Everyone has their own choice and their own motives. [Switching language] is always a deep and difficult choice. We are the transitional generation. We are the [last] generation that experienced direct discrimination [against the Ukrainian language], and who bear upon us the marks of this discrimination. As a result, my Ukrainian is weaker than my Russian to this day. Whether that will change within my lifetime, who knows.

They haven't given us any choice, we cannot fail to see how [the Russian language] works as a tool of imperialism, a tool for the absorption and annihilation of Ukrainian nationality. Purely artistic questions become somewhat secondary, such as the question of high literature. I understand what you're getting at. Dramaturgy as literature is a very complex question. For me, it is almost the height of literature. Yet even these considerations are secondary when the conversation is about genocide, and language as an instrument of genocide.

Even a few years ago it was still possible to laugh at or shrug off such extreme notions, but now it's perfectly evident that that is how it is. What used to be taken as snide jokes or irony has now transformed into a realization of, 'Oh yep, that's how it is'.

It has now been accepted that the Russian language is a weapon. The Ukrainian language, since the time of the Russian empire, has suffered 160 direct prohibitions. In reality, it was many more. I myself am a product of this process.

Please understand that this is extremely painful. It's very painful that I wasted such a vast amount of time being part of this process of Russification. It's a guilt that will always be with me. My personal fate as an artist is already not that important, because I will probably never reach the level of mastery of the [Ukrainian] language which my internal sense of truth will accept as sufficient, but what I can do is minimize the damage that I have already done. Minimize this misfortune that has befallen all of us.

Everything is now all so obvious, so clear, so transparent. All these mechanisms have been laid bare. Now there isn't even the tiniest excuse to have a conversation which says that language isn't guilty. It's not possible. Those who talk about the fair competition between the languages of Great Russian culture ... this is a continuation of direct aggression, because the forces are not evenly balanced and one of them for a long time was trying to destroy the other. A child cannot compete with a bodybuilder who for many years has been pumping himself full of steroids. In all this there is one positive thing: the Ukrainian language is experiencing a revival, Ukrainian culture is experiencing a revival, and it is a great thing to be a witness of this and being a partial participant brings great enjoyment. The sooner it becomes apparent in the mechanisms of academia, the better it will be for academia.

JC So, my next two questions: what were the difficulties of switching from writing in Russian to Ukrainian, and how did this switch affect the form of your work or the characters' voices? You said yourself that your aptitude with Ukrainian was somewhat unsatisfactory for you as a writer, do you think that will be forever?

MK Look, the point isn't even about how well you speak or write the language. It's about the fact that a huge part of life in Ukraine is conducted in the Russian language, by Ukrainian people and in Ukrainian texts. Just even describing a Ukrainian person we often, for the sake of precision, have to state 'he spoke in Russian'. But I hope that the more Ukrainian is heard [on the street] ... I mean we're all switching gradually, some correctly, some not, some suddenly, some not; my opportunities are growing every day because I'm describing people [and events] not exactly as they happen. Broadly speaking, the reality is chasing the dream. Therefore I think that this problem [of which language to write in] is already solved: Ukrainian language – full stop.

Ukrainian has the means to express any complex thought, any complex shade of character, any avant-garde or underground sense; they can all be expressed thanks to Ukrainian. Russian as a tool is no longer compulsory, and is in many ways unacceptable.

Russian missed its chance. It missed its chance for Ukrainian literature to exist in the Russian language. This will no longer be possible. It's already not possible.

JC Does the form of the plays have to change, in your opinion? If the surrounding environment is often in Russian and 'New Drama' should reflect how people speak on the street, how does [writing in literary Ukrainian] affect the form of the text, if people relatively rarely in Ukraine speak in pure literary Ukrainian? Have you noticed a transition in your form since you started to write in Ukrainian?

MK I think, Jack, that the problem was mainly a psychological one. It's possible to analyse the difference, to find some kind of trends. If some kind of crazy academic is interested in this at some point, then he'll find out, but for me, my principle remains the same. I've always tried to write not 'for money', to write plays that are written for myself, and to do what I find interesting. I think that there will come a time when we can write about the history of the Russian state, about Lenin or Stalin, in Ukrainian, because they are the rightful villains of our own national carnival. They are the characters that we'll want to write about. We probably will sooner or later have to write about them, and language is important of course. For my generation, writing about them in Ukrainian won't really be much of a problem.

JC So I suppose every author has their own answer to this, but as I understand you the most important element seems to be to switch to Ukrainian, and it's rather too early, or uninteresting in some ways, to over-analyse the artistic consequences of this switch at this stage.

MK You must understand that any perceived loss or any difficulty in expressing something [in Ukrainian] purely comes from the writer's lack of knowledge or lack of mastery of the language, not the language itself – therefore these difficulties can be solved. There are no ideas that cannot be expressed in Ukrainian. Either it's idleness, or this is a learnt part of one's upbringing [stopping us from writing only in Ukrainian], because we were very strictly conditioned to believe that some part of life has to occur in Russian. For lots of people, even now, when thinking about classical literature they can't quite grasp that Dickens didn't write in Russian, that Jules Verne didn't write in Russian and that even Salinger didn't write in Russian.

In this sense, I'm an optimist. Language is an influence on form, but it's like the outline of an aircraft on Earth or on Mars. The configuration of the wings may have to be a tiny bit different because the atmosphere is different on each planet, but a wing remains a wing and the plane still flies regardless.

Plus we can always use that custom of referencing the real language environment that is present in many contemporary plays, such as referencing '*surzhyk*' [a colloquial blend of Russian and Ukrainian], and we can remark upon and contemplate the existence of this transitional language because that is the legitimate role of the playwright. However, I think that even this practice will happen less often. As more and more people speak naturally in literary Ukrainian the popularity of such techniques [writing in '*surzhyk*'] will diminish.

JC Now for more personal questions. When we did the 'Theatre in Two Weeks' festival you spoke of how you have two Russian passports at home, of your wife and one of your daughters. How did the geopolitical shift in relations between Russia and Ukraine affect your personal relationships, and in turn how did that affect your work?

MK Considering that I am already a compromised and disappointed man, and rather indifferent to my own happiness, I won't allow myself to over-exaggerate my own situation, or take it too far to the extreme.

I do know other people who have lost contact with their children, or at least haven't spoken to them for years, as a result of this situation. It's all very tragic. I try to soften the reality but that's how it is.

I've lost a vast number of colleagues. I've lost a wonderful market, if you want to call it that, a market that appreciates playwriting and experimental theatre. It's not a market full of money or anything, but the playing-field of Russian theatre, of course, was a very interesting playing-field.

Plus I coincided with people who were real innovators. People who were deep and complex in their thinking, and who knew how to counteract the burdens and to oppose the inhumane instinct of their government. But I even lost them too. Despite the fact that they were on the side of everything good and liberal (I was lucky in the sense that the vast majority [though not all] of my Moscow theatrical friends around [Teatr.]doc were opposed to the war against Ukraine and against the annexation of Crimea and this whole nightmare), all the same they are still bearers of this imperial cultural tradition.

Playing on their playing-field, taking part in their joys, is to contribute to a foreign culture. If I could allow myself to do that a few years ago when we thought we would never fight each other, when we thought that the dark days between us were in the past, then it's certainly not possible now, because it's clear that those deepest instincts have not been switched off. Russia cannot accept the existence of Ukrainian culture, the existence of a real Ukraine not a 'Malorossiya' ['Little Russia', a term with Russian imperialistic connotations used to deny that Ukraine and Ukrainians have an identity that differs from Russia and Russians].

In this sense my loss is huge. I mean, in the cultural sense none of the Ukrainians (those who considered themselves Ukrainian) were as deeply involved as me [in the Russian theatre world], but in comparison to any person who has died or whose relatives have been killed in the war this is no loss at all. Only friends, idlers and alcoholics sympathize with me. This is nothing compared to those who have really experienced this horror: the horror of the war, the horror of the annexation, this betrayal by Russia. It's not even just a betrayal, it's Cain and Abel, it's Judas. It's such a classic, distilled, purified form of betrayal that it will be an example for ages to come of the very essence of betrayal.

My loss in this sense isn't big. I lost twenty-five years of my life. It's trivial. It's not as much as your whole life. If you compare it with someone who lost their life at seventeen or seventy. I'm just a witness of these processes. I enjoy contemplating. I came into this world to contemplate. Writing plays is secondary; it's just a means of dwelling in this state of contemplation in a more or less constructive manner.

JC   Okay, let's talk about the [November 2018] tour of Teatr.doc, visiting PostPlay [in Kyiv]: what was its significance in your opinion?

MK   There are two factors: there's the personal element, because in some way [with this tour] I recorded my involvement in this phenomenon, in this movement, in this theatre. It was important for me that no one here had any illusions with regards to Teatr.doc, that they saw them as they are with all their revolutionary practices. There is not enough of their kind of spirit of practice in Ukraine. This has now already been assimilated into a part of Kyiv's theatrical life, we have made it our own and it will make us stronger. For the development of theatre in Kyiv a tour from Teatr.doc should have happened much earlier and on a greater scale. We would have saved a lot of time spent on talking. It wasn't in any way a breakthrough in showing new ways of doing theatre but it was very important all the same, and that quality of work with documentary text, and the actor's manner of existing on the stage, in the best of [Teatr.]doc's performances, is still not always attainable in Ukrainian theatre. In this sense, it was important that they performed in Kyiv and it was very important that this tour happened.

JC   I spoke with Galina Dzhikaeva about this. She wasn't connected with the Moscow scene before the tour, unlike the Gumennyis (co-founders of PostPlay), and she seemed to think, and I agree with this, that the tour served as a positive end to an era [but an end all the same]. Not only an end for [Teatr.]doc, but also the end of the era of a Ukrainian theatre that looks towards Moscow. They saw these stars of contemporary theatre and understood that what we do is often more interesting, and here there is something more like democracy. The only interesting thing for me was the actors' approach. But the content of the tour was torn from its context, and only in Russia would it be powerful. In Ukraine, it didn't seem relevant. For me, it was Russian contemporary theatre losing its power over Ukrainian contemporary theatre.

MK   You're right. I completely agree with you. There were no idols. [Teatr.]doc is no longer an example to be followed. The period in which one could directly transfer the experience of [Teatr.]doc to Ukraine is over. Because, crudely speaking, they don't have the experiences that every person sitting in the audience has had. [We no longer] have the experience of that kind of opposition, [Teatr.]doc have their themes that are thankfully very far away from the Ukrainian experience. You can't write them off entirely though, because the kind of fighting that [the playwright and director Zarema] Zaudinova does, they're warriors, they address their own curses, well, torture, all this kind of cannibalism that they have to live within. However, [Teatr.]doc, unfortunately, is obliged [perpetually] to react. They don't send their own draft notices. They have to react to the draft notices sent to them by the state.

JC   Yes, I agree, in the artistic sense they are not free. They have to say what they say. I don't know. I saw that in Ukraine after this tour. I understood that here there is an extremely powerful playing-field. At least there are all the elements for one, but somehow they are not quite switched on yet. It is necessary to get rid of these idols, as you said.

MK Yes, Jack, but really what we definitely don't have is a place for documentary theatre as authoritative as [Teatr.]doc. It's without a doubt the leader of that movement. In Kyiv, there isn't any theatre space with the same authority, that would always be one step ahead of the rest in the realm of working with contemporary text. That's what we need to make. That's what I feel is lacking. That kind of centre that would work deeply with new writers, that would provoke them to write plays. Maybe it's not a bad trait that we're all more fixated on ourselves. But I think such a centre would help us. A theatre that is clear in its principles as a place for 'New Drama'.

JC Let's talk about when you were in Kyiv and when you were in Moscow. I'm a little confused. Did you live here after the Orange Revolution (2004)? Then went back to Moscow?

MK When the Orange Revolution started, Natasha [Vorozhbyt] and I were in America, at a writing programme at the University of Iowa, and we understood that we had to go back to Ukraine. Even a little earlier we had made that decision, not just because of the revolution but it was clear to us that we would return to Ukraine, and that's what we did until 2008. We lived in Ukraine, we didn't lose our connections with Moscow. What I could earn I earned thanks to Moscow. Generally speaking at that time I didn't have any work in Kyiv. Natasha did, however. I wrote for TV series, dialogues. Moscow of course in that sphere gives more possibilities to function and exist in this profession. Although serving the worst manifestations of this profession, knowingly writing TV series that are bad, that contributes to the reproduction of the myths and inferiority complexes of Ukrainians that they aren't fully fledged, that they are second-class citizens. I tied myself into the stereotypes of a Ukraine just like *The Milkmaid from Khatsapetovka* [a Russian soap romance with a stereotyped Ukrainian heroine, 2007–11]. A vast amount of TV series, even ones that they film today, revolve around labels. Where real Ukrainians are transformed into these stock characters, that as a rule are cynically re-conceptualised versions of reality. I didn't want to do this as a job. That was the only kind of work that there was here. Ukrainian theatre cannot feed a writer at the moment. It cannot promote the progress that is needed because in this sphere there is very little money. In Moscow they put a lot of money into the theatre, they understand the power of the theatre as a phenomenon. The powers that be understand how powerful the theatre is as a tool for masking their beastly grins.

JC Let's talk about Europe. You've taken part in projects at London's Royal Court Theatre, in Germany and the US. Do you now think that you're writing more for the European audience than for the Ukrainian one? What's changed in the past few years in terms of which direction your work is pointing?

MK No, I will always be writing for a Ukrainian audience, but at the same time this shouldn't distance me from the European or American viewer. What is categorically clear is that my audience is not in Moscow. But paradoxically, I am not much of a follower of the tendencies of European theatre. I'm not enamoured with even the most highly acclaimed idols of European contemporary theatre. I believe in my own internal voice and in the necessity to be as honest as possible with this voice. I don't construct myself according to the demands of a market. I do what I can. It's important for me first and foremost to do something that is absolutely my own; only then can I think about what audience it would be interesting for.

JC You said this is a period of a new dawn in Ukrainian theatre. But it's a difficult period. The realm of contemporary Ukrainian theatre that shows some form of empathy, that knows how to work with a writer, is still very small. What has been the most positive moment of the past five years, either in your career or in Ukrainian theatre as a whole?

MK You know, for me it is very important that a new generation of writers is emerging who are gaining a sense of their own worth, that they are gaining a voice not only in their plays – because plays are a refuge, a scream, a shout, it's an attempt to say 'I exist' – but often previously authors of uncompromising plays would accept some kind of awful compromise with a theatre, didn't refuse the most slave-driverish suggestions and sold out for pennies. I believe that now a process has begun where authors are becoming aware of themselves as authors, aware of their own strength, their own vision and their own mission: a mission not to serve as a member of a theatre's support staff, but rather as the leader of ideas.

JC These new writers are those who have, broadly speaking, appeared after the Maidan revolution: Kosodiy, Blok, Maciupa?

MK Before the Maidan they couldn't show themselves anywhere. Only in some narrow playwriting gatherings. Theatres were not interested at all.

You know these names: Natal'ia Blok, Anastasia Kosodiy. It probably wasn't an accident that [you chose them to be a part of your project], but they happen to be exactly the voices which I listen to. When I don't understand something in Ukraine I turn to the texts of these authors. They explain something to me. It is not only those two of course. I keep up with the work of [Evgeny] Markovsky, of [Pavlo] Ar'ye and many others. But these authors [Kosodiy, Blok] are especially important because they don't exploit Ukrainian themes, but rather attempt to unpack and understand them.

I respect them unreservedly, not in the sense of 'yeah, interesting, but ...' – no 'buts'. So I suppose I'll stick with those names [Kosodiy, Blok]. But of course I always follow everything that Natal'ia Vorozhbyt writes. She is for me the strongest Ukrainian dramatic writer, and probably the most uncompromising. The fact that she, an author of such standing, was not staged for a long time of course paints Ukrainian theatre in a terrible light. Even when her plays are staged it's never ideal, and it's never done with full trust of the text: the directors still allow themselves to be casual with these texts, and that is still the remnants of the old way of thinking. I think it will end sooner or later, but it's annoying all the same. Everything should happen at the right moment. The authors that we're talking about [Blok, Kosodiy] emerged at the right moment. A huge problem in Ukraine, despite it being hugely rich in talent, is to draw out new writers. We encourage a young person to attempt writing, and for many of them it works out well, but after that we have nothing to offer them. We then abandon them; we have abandoned so many talented new authors because we gave them no prospects for the next stage. Theatres don't invest. Theatres don't take a risk with authors. They don't put up with their mistakes and attempts. We need our own Royal Court. Our image of the Royal Court is probably not actually what the Royal Court is like, but we live with that dream.

We need such a theatre. A theatre for writers. It's essential. I'm trying to write a stupid thesis about what theatre we need. It's stupid. Vorozhbyt thinks I'm naïve, I'm almost fifty and still wanting to write a manifesto like a child, but I feel we're in the same place where we were fifteen years ago. We need to write a new manifesto. We need to agree on some kind of basic principles. This hasn't happened. Even though we've experienced a new dawn we still don't have the experimental theatre which we so need.

JC Yes, there is some kind of strange irony that there is no further step after people come to 'The Week of Contemporary Plays'. It's been running for nine years, and only a couple of times has a play ended up on a government stage after a reading there. (This is primarily the fault of the government theatres not of 'The Week…'.) It's shameful.

MK It's shameful, yes. [...]

JC In five years' time what are you hoping to see, and what do you think will be the reality in Ukrainian theatre?

MK I dream of theatre as a forum. I wish that theatre would be in the centre of Kyiv life, that there would be a building in the centre of Kyiv for modern experimental theatre that specializes in new plays, and that such a building should appear in all the main cities of Ukraine. I wish that across Ukraine the premiere of a new play would happen on one day in every region, that at last those people would go to the theatre who are at the moment forced to watch '95 Kvartal' and therefore vote for [Volodymyr] Zelensky ['95 Kvartal' is the new president's comedy production company]. I wish theatre would be *needed* and would grow into a part of the nation's body. I wish that theatre had the impudence to give answers, to castigate, to be a pulpit, to be a sermon, a theatrical sermon. I want a world where people of the theatre can influence what's happening in society. I want writers to hire directors. I want the merging of theatre and film: theatre as an experimental space, and film as the place for its realisation. I want TV dramas that are not only a quiet refuge for the playwright, but also an active space for art. We could have all of this. We could have wonderful television, uncompromising, challenging for our times, we could have all this in Ukraine. I hope that is what will happen and that it will all be in Ukrainian.

Translated from the Russian by Jack Clover

Note

1   See Chapter 9 by Noah Birksted-Breen for more on this background.

12

Stages of change

Ukraine's Theatre of Displaced People

Molly Flynn

> Molly Flynn examines the work of the Theatre of Displaced People, founded by Natal'ia Vorozhbyt and Georg Genoux in Ukraine in 2015. They ran over a dozen documentary projects in the following two years, in order to give voice to the experiences of those caught up in the ongoing hostilities between government forces and Russian-backed separatists in the east of the country. Through the process of sharing personal testimonies their projects have aimed to instigate a dialogue between people who find themselves in opposing camps. Another of their projects has been 'Class Act – East/West', an initiative developed under the 'Class Act' scheme described elsewhere in this volume by Maria Kroupnik. Molly's research is based on her experience of working with the Theatre of Displaced People as a volunteer between February and July 2017.

Living in Mykolaivka is like living on Mars – at least that is how it is described by one of the teenage protagonists at the centre of the 2016 documentary film *School # 3 (Shkola No. 3)*.[1] 'We don't know anything about the world except what we see on the internet', the speaker continues, 'and to see something online just isn't the same as seeing it with your own eyes.'[2] Filmed inside the local school, which had been severely damaged by shelling the previous summer, *School # 3* is an expanded screen adaptation of the 2015 documentary play *My Mykolaivka* (*Moia Mykolaivka*). Both the film and the play feature thirteen local teenagers who speak with striking sincerity about their personal experiences of love, loss and life during war.

In the summer of 2014, conflict erupted in this small city in the Donetsk region of Eastern Ukraine when the Ukrainian army clashed with Russian-backed separatists seeking to expand their control of Ukrainian territory. After four days of heavy shelling, Mykolaivka was secured by Ukrainian forces and the rebels began to retreat. Many of the stories shared by the protagonists of *My Mykolaivka* recount the details of those four days when the city was caught between two opposing forces. Other stories inadvertently reveal the lingering effects of the war on the speakers' day-to-day lives. Some of the other performers in the play cast the war in a peripheral role, focusing instead on intimate details about their hopes for the future and their regrets about the past. At one point in the play, fourteen-year-old Vladislav Shokin speaks to the audience as if to a friend, as he remembers one time when he found a small bug in a bunch of grapes and carried it to the window to fly away. 'I don't know why', Shokin says, 'I just didn't want to kill it. And that made me think, how could I kill a person if I can't even kill a bug? [...] I've stopped asking myself questions like that', he claims, 'I don't think about the war anymore.'[3]

Created in collaboration with the Ukrainian playwright Natalia Vorozhbyt and the German director Georg Genoux, *My Mykolaivka* was the first play produced by Ukraine's original dedicated documentary theatre company, the Theatre of Displaced People. The company was founded by Vorozhbyt and Genoux along with the Ukrainian military psychologist Aleksei Karachinskii in 2015. Together these three founders aimed to create a theatre that responded directly to the plight of the 1.6 million people who had been internally displaced in Ukraine as a result of the ongoing military conflict in the east of the country, an undeclared war that has claimed over 13,000 lives since spring 2014. Following the success of *My Mykolaivka*, the Theatre of Displaced People went on to stage over a dozen documentary theatre projects between 2015 and 2017 in which internal refugees, teenagers, soldiers, artists and activists speak their own stories onstage.

This essay considers the political, ethical and aesthetic valences of the company's work. It situates the significance of the Theatre of Displaced People's repertoire within its contemporary Ukrainian context and also considers the company's relevance to artists and activists working in conflict zones across the globe. My research on the Theatre of Displaced People's activities adopts an ethnographic approach known as participant observation, a method of qualitative data collection that involves a significant amount of time in the field conducting interviews and observing rehearsals and performances. In this way, I have sought to track the company's work in real time as the artists and participants involved react rapidly to the political and social changes unfolding around them. This research also draws on my experiences as a volunteer with the group between February and July 2017, during which time I contributed to the company's fundraising efforts and participated in several of the group's projects. My research on the company's work is still in development and, for that reason, I refrain from articulating any definitive conclusions at this time. Instead, I take this essay as an opportunity to introduce the company's repertoire to an English-language readership and to note certain preliminary findings that will continue to lead my ongoing research on social theatre practice in twenty-first-century Ukraine.

Since the start of Ukraine's country-wide opposition protests in 2013, documentary theatre has emerged as one of the most aesthetically innovative and socially relevant responses to the country's shifting cultural landscape. Commonly referred to as 'verbatim theatre' in the UK, the term 'documentary theatre' is used throughout the former Soviet region to describe a wide range of reality-based performance practices. It can be broadly understood as an umbrella term that includes any theatrical performance that draws on real-life events and incorporates documentary materials such as interviews, autobiographical narratives, trial transcripts, found texts, etc. As a form of political performance practice, documentary theatre is used internationally to explore what theatre studies scholar Carol Martin has called a 'global condition of troubled epistemologies about truth, authenticity and reality'.[4]

As I have argued in my previous research on the history of documentary theatre in twenty-first-century Russia, the form has proven of particular relevance in the post-Soviet context as a result of how it speaks to a series of core cultural anxieties in the region. These anxieties include tensions about the veracity of documents, the sincerity of testimony, the performance of justice and the region's complicated relationship to its Soviet past.[5] There are several essential differences between the way documentary theatre is commonly practised in Russia and the way it is currently developing in Ukraine. However, an investment and interest in these four key cultural anxieties are among the things the two culturally specific performance practices share.

One of the primary differences between the development of documentary theatre forms at Ukraine's Theatre of Displaced People and the way the form is practised in Russia is that the Theatre of Displaced People works nearly exclusively in a sub-style of the genre known as 'witness theatre'. The designation 'witness theatre' is used in both Ukraine and Russia to describe documentary performances in which individuals speak their own stories onstage. The word 'witness' appears often in international documentary theatre scholarship and practice, as it points to the way the form facilitates a collective process of recognition of both personal and cultural trauma.[6] In the case of the Theatre of Displaced People performances, individuals are invited to speak their actual experiences of war, displacement and social unrest. Participants share their stories onstage in a simple and straightforward manner without the theatrical trappings that are often associated with the theatre as an institution, documentary or otherwise. There are no costumes, there are no sets. Some of the plays in the repertoire include video components but, with this exception, the company adheres strictly to a 'poor theatre' aesthetic.

This bare-bones style of theatre-making is, in part, what the group is referring to when they say that the Theatre of Displaced People is 'a theatre without acting games',[7] a claim that echoes the motto of Russia's leading documentary theatre venue Teatr.doc, 'a theatre without acting'. In both cases, the stripped-down, straightforward and non-illusory style of performance is part of what makes the plays at Teatr.doc and at the Theatre of Displaced People effective as spaces for dialogue and civic engagement. One such example from the Theatre of Displaced People's repertoire is the play *Product* (*Tovar*, 2016). Written, directed and performed by Alik Sardarian, *Product* recounts some of the author's experiences working as a volunteer-medic on the front line and includes several harrowing stories about what he witnessed there. In the promotional materials for *Product*, Sardarian writes, 'Are you tired of depressing news stories? Don't want to hear or talk about the war anymore? Want to be distracted by something lighter? Then you can fuck off to another theatre.'[8] As this passage makes clear, the Theatre of Displaced People distinguishes itself from more traditional notions of what constitutes theatre. Set apart from the velvet seats and heavy curtains of Ukraine's academic state theatres, the Theatre of Displaced People performs in school auditoriums and former industrial buildings. Their plays defy conventional approaches to dramatic structure and shun the notion of theatre as a space for high art and heroic narratives. In fact, the rejection of heroic narratives is one of the central ways the Theatre of

Displaced People engages with the complex cultural and political territory within which the company was conceived.

The war in Ukraine continues to claim the lives of soldiers and civilians. Despite two internationally negotiated ceasefire agreements, the first in September 2014 and the second in February 2015, violations of these Minsk Protocol Agreements on both sides of the front line are relentless. As the violence and destruction continue with no apparent resolution in sight, the slogan 'Glory to the heroes' has returned to popular parlance in Ukraine. The contemporary repurposing of this contested phrase began during the Maidan revolution in 2013/14. As tens of thousands of people took to the streets in an historic act of civil unrest that led to the ousting of President Viktor Yanukovych, who was closely connected to Russia, the slogan 'Glory to the heroes' emerged as a rallying cry for Ukrainian activists seeking to raise the profile of their country's bid for transparency and independence. However, this patriotic repurposing of the slogan recalls an earlier and less inclusive use of the same phrase by Ukrainian nationalists in the first half of the twentieth century. The term 'hero', as the historian Olesya Khromeychuk describes, has often been deployed by state organizations and government representatives in Ukraine and internationally in an effort to narrativize, mythologize and justify the individual lives lost to war.[9] Perpetuating popular narratives about military heroes is in part, Khromeychuk suggests, a strategy employed by those in power in order to maintain public support during wartime.

The stories included in the Theatre of Displaced People's plays cannot be said to exist outside the structure of Ukraine's political divisions. However, by eschewing the concept of national heroes, the autobiographical stories shared in the plays run alongside those more prevalent and divisive narratives in such a way as to acknowledge their presence, while simultaneously resisting their ideological dominance. This is one way in which the company's aesthetic approach intersects with the cultural efficacy of their work. By focusing exclusively on the process of composing, speaking and listening to subjective stories of individual experiences, the company avoids the common tendency to mythologize the war and thereby simplify the complex experiences of those whose lives it affects.

The multilingual pluralistic population of twenty-first-century Ukraine is regularly misrepresented by mainstream media, politicians and policy-makers to create a streamlined narrative of Ukraine as a 'divided country', pitting east against west. As Ukrainian historians such as Yaroslav Hrytsak and independent journalists like Oksana Forostyna have clearly illustrated, this reductive reading of Ukraine's national identities serves to create a diversion, a marketable narrative that obscures the corrupt practices the country's network of power elites has been engaged in since well before the war in the east began.[10] Common cultural stereotypes about Russian-speaking Soviet loyalists and Ukrainian-speaking Euro-enthusiasts have become even more divisive in recent years as a result of the war. Furthermore, the propaganda disseminated on both sides of the conflict leads to increased resentment and violence across the country. The Theatre of Displaced People aims to dispel these stereotypes, counteract propaganda and bring seemingly disparate groups of people into dialogue with one another.

For example, the company's project *Children and Soldiers* (*Deti i voennye*) brought the Theatre of Displaced People team to several Ukrainian-controlled front-line cities where soldiers have been stationed since 2014. In previous visits to the eastern cities of Popasna, Shchastia, Slov'iansk and Mykolaivka, the theatre's directors noticed that local residents were often afraid of the soldiers who were living in their towns, while many of the soldiers suspected the locals to be separatist sympathizers. Working together with a team of professional playwrights, filmmakers and directors, the soldiers and students in each of these cities created a documentary play in which they recalled their experiences of the war and performed their stories for the public at the end of the week.

Following a week of work together in Popasna, Vorozhbyt recalls that one of the soldiers told the group how, before his participation in the play, he used to look across at the block of flats opposite the checkpoint where he worked. He noticed that the light was always on in one window on the ninth floor. He was sure someone inside was watching him with binoculars. Since his work with Theatre of Displaced People, however, this soldier had learned that that ninth-floor window belonged to Lyosha from the school, and that below his window was Marina's. Such a statement of recognition and personal connection speaks directly to the impact that work with the Theatre of Displaced People has had for the group's participants. By inviting individuals to share their stories with one another, the group engages participants in an important process of self-definition. The practice of speaking and listening to people's experiences of war and displacement offers new agency to those involved. Participants gain the opportunity to tell their own stories, to defy common stereotypes, and, in this way, learn to see themselves and each other as individuals.

Another important project initiated by the Theatre of Displaced People collective is 'Class Act – East/West', the playwriting workshop for teenagers. Based on a similar programme originally developed at the Traverse Theatre in Scotland in the 1990s, the 'Class Act' model has been restructured for the Ukrainian context. Each year between 2016 and 2018, the company brought ten students from a secondary school in Eastern Ukraine together with ten students from a secondary school in Western Ukraine, for two weeks of playwriting workshops in Kyiv. Under the mentorship of a professional playwright, the students worked together in pairs to write ten-minute plays which were subsequently staged by professional actors and directors in a gala performance at the end of the two weeks. 'Class Act – East/West' not only facilitated friendships between participants from different parts of the country, it also gave a voice to Ukraine's next generation and, through widespread media coveraged, encouraged a national audience and readership to listen.

As these two projects illustrate, the work taking place at the Theatre of Displaced People often resembles international instances of applied theatre practice in conflict zones. As James Thompson describes in his 2006 book *Digging Up Stories: Applied Theatre, Performance and War*, one use of theatre in places of crisis can be to 'create safe zones – places apart where participants feel comfortable expressing themselves'.[11] The creation of safe spaces is undoubtedly an important element of the Theatre of Displaced People's work. Additionally, the process of self-realization their work encourages and inspires in the Ukrainian context is similar to the practices Nandita Dinesh describes in her 2016 study *Theatre and War: Notes from the Field*.[12]

Both at the Theatre of Displaced People and in the applied theatre practices described in the two studies cited earlier, professional theatre practitioners work with non-professional participants to create spaces in which to process people's experiences of war through the practice of theatre-making. However, unlike these established studies of applied theatre in conflict zones, the Theatre of Displaced People collective are not intentionally drawing on the tradition of Augusto Boal's Theatre of the Oppressed, an important source of inspiration for most Western applied theatre practitioners. The process of speaking and listening that makes up rehearsals for a Theatre of Displaced People performance purposefully excludes the use of physical exercises and role-playing games that are essential to many forms of international social theatre practice. Instead, the creative process at the Theatre of Displaced People is focused exclusively on the remembering, composing and sharing of stories from the participants' real lives.

Here, it is important to note that the artists at the heart of the Theatre of Displaced People collective do not come from a background of Anglophone theatre education and therefore do not situate their work in relationship to an established history of applied theatre practice as it has come to be known in academic and artistic circles in the UK and the US. In fact, the personal nature of the stories told onstage in the plays and the non-illusory style of delivery their participants adopt has more in common with a mode of performance that has developed as a distinct characteristic of documentary theatre as it is practised in Russia and other post-Socialist countries. At the risk of perpetuating destructive cultural narratives about Ukrainian art and culture as always standing in some sort of relationship to Russian art and culture, it is important to note that the non-illusory style of performance developed by documentary theatre artists in Russia has been an influential factor in the way documentary theatre has come to be performed in Ukraine.

This line of influence should come as no surprise. Both of the company's co-founders were among the group of artists involved in founding Russia's first dedicated documentary theatre venue, Teatr.doc, in 2002. Both theatre-makers were completing their studies in Moscow at the time, Vorozhbyt at the Moscow Literary Institute and Genoux at Moscow's Institute of Theatre Arts (GITIS). Following the Orange Revolution in 2004, Vorozhbyt returned to her home city of Kyiv, although she continued to work in Moscow for several years. The playwright rarely worked in documentary forms before the Maidan uprising in 2013, when she and several of her Ukrainian colleagues began collecting interviews from activists which they later edited into a verbatim script that has since been performed in Kyiv, Moscow and London. Following his studies at GITIS in 2003, Genoux continued to work on the development of documentary theatre forms in Moscow, both at Teatr.doc and with his own company, the Joseph Beuys Theatre which he founded in 2008. In 2012, Genoux left Moscow to pursue a series of new documentary theatre projects in several European countries including Bulgaria, Germany and Ukraine.

In October 2014, Vorozhbyt and Genoux were both among a group of volunteers who travelled to Mykolaivka together with the charitable organization 'New Donbas' (Novyi Donbas). At that point the war had not yet lasted a year and volunteers from across the country were regularly travelling to Ukrainian-controlled cities in Donbas to assist local organizations repair schools, hospitals and other local facilities. Mykolaivka had come under attack only three months before and the volunteers were immediately put to work laying new linoleum in the school and replacing broken windows throughout the city. According to Vorozhbyt and Genoux, the two theatre-makers understood immediately upon arrival in Mykolaivka that, in addition to support in rebuilding the city's infrastructure, what local residents needed most was a forum in which to tell their stories. Moreover, as Vorozhbyt describes, she soon came to realize that what the volunteers needed most was to listen.

Vorozhbyt and Genoux soon began work on *My Mykolaivka* together with a group of thirteen teenagers from School No. 3, one of the buildings to have suffered the worst damage in the city during the shelling. Their conception of the larger Theatre of Displaced People project developed alongside their staging of this play. After returning to Kyiv, Vorozhbyt and Genoux began assembling a team of volunteers that included the psychologist Aleksei Karachinskii. The company's next major project was a series of performances grouped under the title *Where is East?* (*Gde vostok?*) in which people who had been internally displaced by the war shared their stories onstage. The Theatre of Displaced People soon began attracting national and international attention. The remarkable momentum of their initiatives attracted participation from many of Ukraine's most talented artists, journalists and activists. And, in a December 2016 article in the newspaper *Ukrayinska pravda*, the journalist Anastasia Haishenets wrote that the work taking place at the Theatre of Displaced People had done more to facilitate dialogue between East and West than all government programmes combined.[13]

Throughout these years, the Theatre of Displaced People has continued their work in Mykolaivka. Following the premiere of *My Mykolaivka* in 2015, Genoux began collaborating with the Ukrainian filmmaker Liza Smith on *School # 3*, an extended screen adaptation of the play that includes original footage of the protagonists in their everyday lives. In February 2017, *School # 3* was awarded the Grand Prix in the Generation 14 + category of the 67th Berlinale Film Festival. In her presentation of the award, the festival curator Maryanne Redpath announced that the jury had selected *School # 3* because of the remarkable sincerity and intimacy with which the teenagers shared their stories onscreen. The candid quality of the stories shared and the atmosphere of acceptance created through the Theatre of Displaced People's work were among the elements of the company's approach that I had the opportunity to witness first hand during my own visit to Mykolaivka in July 2017.

Together with Genoux and the Ukrainian documentary photographer Anastasia Vlasova, I spent approximately a week in the city of 15,000 people while working with a group of seven students between the ages of fourteen and eighteen to create a video installation entitled *What My Mum and Dad Should Never Know* (*Chto ne dolzhny uznat' mama i papa*). For the project, students from School No. 3 were invited to share stories about their relationships to their city, their families and their homes. The stories included in the video are varied. Several students share their memories of first loves and first kisses. Others reveal the darker sides of life as a teenager in small-town Ukraine. More than one student involved in the project spoke about the challenges of growing up in Mykolaivka, a city with extremely limited resources and virtually no indoor communal spaces in which to gather. There was once a cinema, one of the students explains in her monologue, but the building has been abandoned and boarded up for as long as she can remember.

Each monologue was recorded as an audio track that plays over a series of video portraits in which the speakers sit or stand in locations throughout the city that hold some significance to their lives or to the stories they share. The speakers stand relatively still, but the world around them continues to move at its usual pace. Mothers with young children are seen playing in the sandbox at the playground, local residents occasionally stroll across the frame carrying their groceries. This juxtaposition of stillness and movement results in an eerie dissonance that draws the viewers' attention to the details of the setting and frames the activities of everyday life in Mykolaivka as something worth pausing to observe, to consider. The video installation is approximately thirty minutes long and features either one or two appearances from each participant. The project premiered on 5 July 2017 with an outdoor screening. The video was projected directly on to the doors of the old boarded-up cinema. Without any advertising or PR, more than one hundred city residents showed up to watch the video, with several families arriving hours early just to ensure they would get a seat.

During the screening, audience members laughed at moments of humour and applauded stories they found particularly resonant or courageous. Though some of the teenage participants appeared nervous before the screening, it was clear that the stories they had chosen to share were not falling on especially critical ears. Residents from all across Mykolaivka's age and education demographics had come out to see what the fuss was all about. In the final story shared in the video, the speaker's voice is heard although he does not appear on camera. Instead, the image on screen is of a billboard that stands tall in the city's centre. On the left side of the billboard is written in Ukrainian 'The shop is open 24/7!' with a blue and yellow smile below, the colours of the Ukrainian flag. On the right side of the billboard there is an upside-down smile in the colours of the Russian flag, along with the slogan in Russian 'The shop is closed!'. Below the billboard, individuals stroll in and out of the frame going about their business on this hot summer day in July 2017.

The story the speaker tells is about a friend of his, a young woman from Mykolaivka whose older boyfriend from out of town occasionally comes to visit. Her boyfriend, the speaker explains, is very vocal in his pro-Ukrainian stance when it comes to politics and the war. One way that he expresses this view is by refusing to purchase any goods produced in Russia. The speaker of the story admits to finding such a choice puzzling, especially since, he argues, many of the suspected Russian-made products were actually made in Poland. The speaker refrains from passing judgement or expressing any political point of view of his own. He simply explains how this friend of his would never be able to introduce her boyfriend to her father, a man who lives and works in Russia and supports the separatist side of the conflict. In this seemingly simple narrative about the purchasing of pre-packaged croissants and chewing gum, the speaker encapsulates many of the intricacies of Ukraine's current cultural climate. Families are divided, the violence continues, and the everyday practice of buying groceries is a political act.

At the end of the screening, I joined Genoux, Vlasova and each of the project participants at the front of the crowd for a curtain call. Ol'ga Bakukha, director of School No. 3, distributed a flower to each of us and waited for the crowd to settle before opening up the floor for questions from the audience. A few of the students' peers asked clarifying questions about the stories included in the video, wondering if this or that detail was true. Seeing the students as the centre of attention, I was surprised when Bakukha addressed her next question to me. 'How', she began, 'would you say that the problems of children in Mykolaivka differ from those in the US?' It was probably the question I should have been expecting all along, although it came as a surprise on this evening as I stood in front of a crowd of one hundred local audience members. Stalling for time I replied, 'It's complicated', before pausing to compose my answer in Russian. 'Not that much', I finally settled on for better or worse. 'We also have first kisses in America. We also have towns without cinemas where teenagers complain that there's nothing to do. Of course, the problems of the two *countries* are quite different', I began to back track. 'But it seems to me teenagers have basically the same problems everywhere.' I regretted it as soon as I said it.

In that moment, I was recalling the conversations I had had the previous week with the teenagers from School No. 3, and I was reflecting on the ways in which those conversations resemble precisely the kinds of conversations young people are having all across the globe. I was caught by what we all have in common rather than what makes us all different. It is true that just like Ukrainian teenagers, Americans also clumsily fumble their way through early encounters with romance. It is also true that millions of American teenagers are living in difficult economic circumstances. Many of them live in towns with limited public resources and barely funded city initiatives, just like Mykolaivka. American kids are also growing up in single-parent homes, after one parent abandons their family, as one of the speakers in the video describes. These are problems we share. They are not culturally specific. However, what my well-intentioned answer failed to articulate is one important difference between the problems teenagers face in the US and those faced by the participants of our project.

In Mykolaivka, teenagers are growing up near the front line of a war zone. They have witnessed war on their doorstep. Some of them are approaching the age when they could be drafted. Others may join up voluntarily. Most of the young people I met do not want to have anything to do with the war at all, though the choice may be beyond their control. My failure in that moment to acknowledge this essential difference between the problems American teenagers face and those confronted by young people in Mykolaivka was unfortunate. However, in retrospect, I see that that oversight grew, in part, from my interest in the atmosphere of inclusivity and mutual understanding that work with Theatre of Displaced people is constructed to facilitate. By sharing our stories with one another both formally and informally, we had created a space in which that which we have in common, those experiences that connect us, became brighter in my recollection of the week than that which makes us different, those experiences that divide us. This, I would argue, is the primary component of what makes the work taking place at the Theatre of Displaced People so aesthetically generative and socially effective.

At a moment of extreme uncertainty for Ukraine particularly, and for Eastern Europe more broadly, it has become more important than ever for artists and activists to find ways for people whose lives have been touched by war to share their experiences with one another, and to know that others are listening. The act of speaking and hearing personal testimonies is at the heart of all the Theatre of Displaced People projects. The company's emphasis on recounting individual and subjective experiences allows us to see the human side of the conflict and consider how the violence and propaganda on both sides of the front line continues to shape people's day-to-day lives all over the country. The stripped-down non-illusory style of performance generates an attitude of accessibility that welcomes individuals to articulate the truths of their experiences, and to become open to hearing the stories of individuals who may have conflicting points of view. As divisions across class, culture and countries continue to lead to violence and hostility across the globe, the Theatre of Displaced People has found a way to facilitate dialogue and foster a sense of hope in the future of reconciliation. In this sense, Ukraine's Theatre of Displaced People can be said to work, not only on the front lines of Ukraine's cultural divisions, but also at the forefront of twenty-first-century political theatre practice.

Notes

1. This essay is partially adapted from a short piece about the film, 'School # 3: the Heartfelt Documentary Listening to the Kids of War-torn Donbass', *Calvert Journal* (29 March 2017). Available at www.calvertjournal.com/articles/show/7986/school-3-documentary-theatre-donbass-donetsk-ukraine (accessed 4 January 2018).
2. Directed by Liza Smith and Georg Genoux, *School # 3* was co-produced by Tabor Productions and Theatre of Displaced People (2016).
3. Ibid.
4. Carol Martin, 'Introduction: Dramaturgy of the Real', *Dramaturgy of the Real World Onstage* (London, 2010), 1.
5. See Molly Flynn, 'The Trial that Never Was: Russian Documentary Theatre and the Pursuit of Justice', *New Theatre Quarterly* 30, no. 4 (2014): 307–17; 'Show Us Your Papers: Performing Post-Soviet National Identities in Talgat Batalov's "Uzbek"', *Problems of Post-Communism* 63, no. 1 (2013): 16–26; and *Witness Onstage: Documentary Theatre in Twenty-first-century Russia*, (Manchester University Press, 2019).
6. See, for example, the work of director Teya Sepeniuk in Northern Ireland and director Emily Mann in the US.
7. Marina Litvinova, 'Teatr dlia pereselentsev i o pereselentsakh', *DonbassUA* (25 August 2016). Available at www.donbass.ua/news/ukraine/2016/08/25/teatr-dlja-pereselencev-i-o-pereselencah.html (accessed 2 January 2018).
8. Quoted here from the text included on the Facebook page for the production. Available at www.facebook.com/events/1713941832222253/ (accessed 22 December 2017).
9. Interview with Olesya Khromeychuk at a conference organized by Evangelische Akademie in Tutzing, Germany and shared online in December 2017. Available at www.youtube.com/watch?v=rceWOz8j9eE (accessed 28 December 2017); see also Khromeychuk's 2016 article, 'What Place for Women in Ukraine's Memory Politics?' in *Open Democracy Russia* (10 October 2016). Available at www.opendemocracy.net/od-russia/olesya-khromeychuk/what-place-for-women-in-ukraine-s-memory-politics (accessed 2 January 2018).
10. See, for example, Yaroslav Hrystak, *Strasti za natsionalizm – istorychni esei*, Kyiv: Krytyka, 2004 and Oksana Forostyna, 'Howl', *Krytyka* (April 2015). Available at https://krytyka.com/en/articles/howl (accessed 29 December 2017).

11 James Thompson, *Digging Up Stories: Applied Theatre, Performance, and War* (Manchester: Manchester University Press, 2005), 171.
12 Nandita Dinesh, *Theatre and War: Notes from the Field* (Cambridge: Open Book Publishers, 2016).
13 Anastasia Haishenets, 'Rik nezalezhnogo teatru: Naiguchnishi proekti, skandali ta osobistosti', in *Ukrayinska pravda* (22 December 2016). Available at www.life.pravda.com.ua/culture/2016/12/22/221840/ (accessed 3 January 2018).

Bibliography

Dinesh, Nandita. *Theatre and War: Notes from the Field*. Cambridge: Open Book Publishers, 2016.
Flynn, Molly. 'The Trial that Never Was: Russian Documentary Theatre and the Pursuit of Justice'. *New Theatre Quarterly* 30, no. 4 (2014): 307–17.
Flynn, Molly. 'Show Us Your Papers: Performing Post-Soviet National Identities in Talgat Batalov's "Uzbek"'. *Problems of Post-Communism* 63, no. 1 (2013): 16–26.
Flynn, Molly. *Witness Onstage: Documentary Theatre in Twenty-first-century Russia*. Manchester: Manchester University Press, 2019.
Forostyna, Oksana. 'Howl'. *Krytyka* (April 2015). Available at: https://krytyka.com/en/articles/howl (accessed 29 December 2018).
Haishenets, Anastasia. 'Rik nezalezhnogo teatru: Naiguchnishi proekti, skandali ta osobistosti'. *Ukrayinska pravda* (22 December 2016). Available at: www.life.pravda.com.ua/culture/2016/12/22/221840/ (accessed 3 January 2018).
Hrystak, Yaroslav. *Strasti za natsionalizm – istorychni esei*. Kyiv: Krytyka, 2004.
Khromeychuk, Olesya. 'What Place for Women in Ukraine's Memory Politics?' *Open Democracy Russia* (10 October 2016).
Litvinova, Marina. 'Teatr dlia pereselentsev i o pereselentsakh'. *DonbassUA* (25 August 2016). Available at: www.donbass.ua/news/ukraine/2016/08/25/teatr-dlja-pereselencev-i-o-pereselencah.html (accessed 2 January 2018).
Martin, Carol. 'Introduction: Dramaturgy of the Real'. *Dramaturgy of the Real World Onstage*. London: Palgrave Macmillan, 2010.
Thompson, James. *Digging Up Stories: Applied Theatre, Performance, and War*. Manchester: Manchester University Press, 2005.

13

'Ne skvernoslov', otets moy' ['Curse not, my son']

Anna Iablonskaia's *The Pagans* and the search for a language of authenticity

Molly Thomasy Blasing

> Molly Thomasy Blasing has written an essay to introduce the Ukrainian playwright Anna Iablonskaia, whose life was tragically cut short in a terrorist bombing at Moscow's Domodedovo Airport in 2011. She offers a close reading of her play *Pagans*, written in Russian, which was staged posthumously by Elena Gremina at Teatr.doc in Moscow, and which explores the clash of the sacred and the profane in contemporary life. The text is filled with religious language as well as obscenities. Molly goes on to consider how the 2014 law which banned the use of obscenities on the stage – as well as in the cinema and in print – has been defiantly ignored by Teatr.doc and by other leading contemporary theatres in Russia.

In July 2014, as the law banning obscenities in art and performance in Russia went into effect, Elena Gremina, then the director of Moscow's independent documentary theatre company Teatr.doc, gave a number of high-profile interviews announcing her intention to defy the ban.[1] The play she repeatedly cited as an example of a text that simply could not be altered was Odessa-based playwright Anna Iablonskaia's 2010 play *The Pagans* (*Iazychniki*). Iablonskaia died tragically at age twenty-nine in the Domodedovo Airport terrorist bombing on 24 January 2011, just six months before *The Pagans* was set to premiere at Teatr.doc.[2] While Gremina's impassioned argument against editing out the substantial amount of profanity in the play centred on authorial rights and Iablonskaia's personal tragedy, I argue in this essay that the play's unique resistance to censorship hinges on the interplay of sacred and profane that is thematically and linguistically woven into the text. It is this clash of two distinct expressive modes that allows this play to explore in depth the problem of how we seek spiritual meaning and human connection through struggles to find faith.

This article also aims to initiate a broader scholarly conversation concerning the dramatic works of Anna Iablonskaia (1981–2011), a figure whose work has received little critical examination in the English-speaking world, beyond a handful of obituaries following her tragic death.³ A playwright and poet from an early age, Iablonskaia was considered by those familiar with her work to be one of the most talented young writers of her generation.⁴ She authored more than a dozen plays and received numerous accolades, including awards in competitions such as *Evraziia* (Eurasia), *Svobodnyi teatr* (Open Theatre) and *Prem'era* (Premiere), and was long-listed for the 2004 'Debut' Prize for literary criticism. A native of Odessa, Ukraine, where she resided, Iablonskaia wrote primarily in Russian (though characters occasionally speak Ukrainian), and during her lifetime her plays were staged almost exclusively in cities in Russia. She received an especially warm reception in Moscow, a fact that – given her characteristic humility and provincial self-identity – continually surprised her.⁵

Anna Iablonskaia and transnational contexts

One of the remarkable things about Iablonskaia's creative life and legacy has to do with the fact that her works were composed entirely during a period prior to – indeed, on the verge of – a number of major social and political transformations that have fundamentally changed the way that Russian writing from Ukraine is approached and received. While Iablonskaia did not live to experience some of the more bitter recent conflicts between Russia and Ukraine – the Maidan protests in late 2013, the Russian annexation of Crimea in 2014, Black Sea naval confrontations in 2018 and the Ukrainian Orthodox Church's official 2019 split from the Russian Orthodox Church – she was nevertheless a writer who did not shy away from political themes. Indeed, Iablonskaia's position as a Russian-language writer from Ukraine in the post-Orange Revolution, pre-Maidan context means that her writing touches transnational themes and traverses borders unselfconsciously. Through dramas set in multiple Russophone and cross-linguistic spaces, Iablonskaia's political writings advocate for greater freedom of movement, expression and aspiration.

Transnational themes about the restrictions placed on human bodies caught in shifting geopolitical spaces are front and centre in Iablonskaia's play *Kiev-Moskva* (*Kyiv-Moscow*), which takes place on a train that travels between these two major post-Soviet cities.⁶ In this brief, one-act play each character describes their reasons for travelling to Moscow from Kyiv. Their stories of seeking employment opportunities in retail or filmmaking or travelling to visit family in Moscow are fuller and more complex than what they are allowed to report on the migration card that non-citizens must fill out at the Russian border. Iablonskaia makes use of profanity here in a fairly conventional way to evoke humour and absurdity, as the characters of *Kyiv-Moscow* suggest alternative answers to the standard 'reason for visit' prompt on the migration card:

> **Andrei** (*looking at the migration card*)   Do you know what we're supposed to write here? (*Reads.*) 'Purpose of visit'?
>
> **Petr**   So what's the purpose of your visit?

Andrei I . . . uh . . . well . . . I don't know.

Petr So write that. Write 'I'm fucking going for who the fuck knows why'.

Andrei Write that?

Petr Sure, do it.

[. . .]

Ania At the bottom there's a list you can choose from: 'Tourism; Commercial Business Trip; For Personal Reasons; Other' . . . So write 'For personal reasons' . . . that's the easiest thing.[7]

In this short dramatic work, Iablonskaia features characters from three distinct post-Soviet generations: there is twenty-year-old Andrei, who aspires to work in television and is heading to Moscow with dreams of working as an actor. His last acting gig in Ukraine was as a ditch digger for a short film; ironically, he subsequently gets a job digging graves at a cemetery (you have to actually dig, and the pay is a third of what it was in the TV show). There is forty-five-year-old Petr, who has been displaced from Ukraine by the decline of his rural town and lack of economic opportunity. He came to Moscow in search of a stable job. Returning on this train to Moscow from his mother's funeral in his hometown in Ukraine, he speaks of how there is nothing left for him there: no family, no beloved pet, a house in ruins. All that remains, he tells us, are 'alcoholics, old people, and Jehovah's Witnesses'.[8]

The drama reaches a cruel climax when the slumbering eighty-year-old Baba Nastia runs into problems at the border checkpoint because she attempts to use her Soviet passport; it seems she never updated it after the collapse of the Soviet Union. She tells us she is travelling to Moscow to visit her son, whom she hasn't seen in eighteen years. At the end of the play, she is pulled off the train at the border crossing and is apparently abandoned there by the border officials. The power of the document attesting to national identity overpowers any concern for the physical body or personal desires of the individual.

Iablonskaia succeeds here and elsewhere in problematizing the notion of the nation state and the sometimes overwhelming power of political institutions over individuals and communities. The ideological nature of this play is not one of nostalgia for the Soviet Union, although it recognizes the dissonance that threatens and disrupts the elderly woman's trip and her assumption about shared identity. At the same time, a character from the youngest generation, who shares the name and age of the playwright (Ania), speaks of being inspired by the Ukrainian national anthem sung by Orange Revolution protesters. Ania has abandoned her cynicism and quietly embraces a new national identity and the sense of community it affords. Like Iablonskaia herself, Ania is proficient in navigating the political borders and bureaucratic processes that have arisen along with the new post-Soviet nation states. She can move easily between these two worlds, carrying with her a sense of pride in her Ukrainian citizenship, while travelling comfortably between Kyiv and Moscow to visit relatives living in Russia's capital. The eighty-year-old Baba Nastia, on the other hand, has never fully accepted that the Soviet Union, the vast country in which she was born, came of age and raised a family, no longer exists. Her insistence that her Soviet passport should suffice as proof of identity and belonging is completely rejected by the government institution that controls the movement of people across borders.

Staging obscenities: *The Pagans* and the 2014 profanity ban

The fact that Iablonskaia's most famous play, *The Pagans*, has been performed on stages across Europe, Russia and Ukraine is emblematic of the way that theatres inside and outside of Russia that are committed to Russian 'New Drama' have found paths that converge more than they divide, something to which this volume certainly attests. As of this writing seven years after its premiere, *The Pagans* remains in the repertoire at Teatr.doc and at the Ermolova Theatre in Moscow. One of the earliest productions of the play was an adaptation entitled *Terroristy* (*The Terrorists*) staged in Russian at the Ukrainian Theatre in Iablonskaia's hometown of Odessa, as part of a larger memorial project, *Anna Iablonskaia: The Return*, organized in 2012 by Odessa-based director Sergei Proskurnia.[9] *The Pagans* has been staged at the Fifth Theatre in Omsk, the Russian Drama Theatre of Lithuania in Vilnius, in Tallinn, Kishinev, Warsaw, London and Kyiv as well as in large and small cities across Russia. The work has been recently adapted for the screen by its Teatr.doc director Valeria Surkova, who has won a number of domestic film festival awards for her cinematic directorial debut.[10] This seems to some extent to confirm what the long-time Russian theatre critic John Freedman observed in an interview with *Public Radio International* the day after Iablonskaia's death: 'I have a feeling that the impulse that Anna Iablonskaia gave with her life and her work is going to try to continue to have an effect on people.'[11]

The present essay works in particular to situate this play, *The Pagans*, within current debates about the linguistic and philosophical dimensions of Russia's 'New Drama', especially in the light of the 2013 and 2014 laws in the Russian Federation prohibiting material 'offensive to religious believers' and outlawing profanity in literature, mass media, film, theatre and other public performances.[12] The theatre critic Pavel Rudnev has called *The Pagans* – considered Iablonskaia's best play – 'a brutal drama about the contemporary crisis of faith, about our bewilderment in relation to problems of faith and about extremes in the search for individual salvation'.[13] The play serves as a strong vehicle for investigating the collision of political and artistic agendas in Russia today because of its sensitive religious subject matter and frequent use of obscenities. Furthermore, with the play's connection to a key documentary theatre company, Teatr.doc, which aims to inject authentic voices and experiences into contemporary Russian performance culture, Iablonskaia's drama offers readers and audiences a powerful case study of 'New Drama''s engagement with – and departure from – documentary modes. Perhaps most importantly, *The Pagans* presents a vision of what authenticity and falseness, connection and isolation look like in an environment in which the sacred and the profane collide. Indeed, it is the search for an unfiltered language of authenticity that underpins this story of a family both girded and torn apart by concealed emotional suffering. To begin, however, let us turn to the story of how this play became a lightning rod for debates about censorship of the arts in Russia today.

Early reactions in the Russian theatre community to the 2014 obscenity ban ranged from full and immediate compliance to tongue-in-cheek ceremonies 'bidding farewell to *mat*'.[14] While some theatres redacted profanity from scripts or removed plays containing offensive language from their repertoire, others – as was the case in the Moscow Art Theatre's 2014 production of Ivan Vyrypaev's *The Drunkards* – opted playfully to substitute euphemisms or neologisms for curse words, confident that audiences could deduce the intended meaning on their own.[15] Many directors appeared to shrug off the new restrictions, claiming that the obscenity ban would, in practice, have very little effect on their productions.[16] Others, such as Vyrypaev, a leading playwright, screenwriter and artistic director of Teatr Praktika at the time, expressed dismay at the law. However, he indicated his intention to comply, since his theatre benefited at the time from state-sponsored arts funding.[17] In one interview Vyrypaev characterized the law as unnatural and ineffectual:

> Well, it appears that we'll have to get by without [profanity]; I can write this way and my plays won't suffer for it. [...] This, of course, is an anti-cultural phenomenon: prohibiting language is a dysfunctional tactic that has no foundation in our culture. You won't accomplish anything with prohibitions. Fighting for morality and virtues should be done not with prohibitions, but with education. Profanity is a part of our lexicon. It would be better to ban profanity everywhere – on the streets, in everyday life – and leave it alone in art![18]

As the obscenity ban went into effect on 1 July 2014, Elena Gremina of the independent documentary theatre company Teatr.doc took to the airwaves, speaking to a number of prominent media outlets, including full-length interviews in the arts and culture websites Afisha Vozdukh and Colta.ru, in which she forcefully defended her decision to continue performing plays containing profanity. At the time, Gremina represented the lone voice of unabashed defiance within the theatre community:

> I am the director of Teatr.doc. I am an exceptionally law-abiding theatre director. I try never to break the law, even those ordinances that are commonly violated in the theatre community. [...] Everything our theatre does is completely above board. However, starting on 1 July 2014 I intend shamelessly to break the law. I enter into this with eyes wide open because to act any other way is simply impossible.[19]

The example of Teatr.doc and its stance on what Gremina called the 'law against the Russian language' is particularly illuminating in probing the intent of the law vis-à-vis the content of the performances that it would seek to alter. In particular, Teatr.doc's continued performance of Iablonskaia's popular play *The Pagans*, which contains more than a few of the outlawed obscenities, provides a striking example of the problems of intent and enforcement in the law's application. In interviews about the obscenity law, Gremina repeatedly discussed *The Pagans* as an example of a text that cannot, indeed must not, be altered. At times, her argument reads as an emotional plea for sanity in the face of a terrible loss:

It has come to my attention that some theatres in Russia are going to pull Anna Iablonskaia's play *The Pagans* from their repertoire. [...] She entrusted us with the first production of her play, she dreamed of a production at [Teatr.]doc ... but she never made it to the premiere. So let them do what they will – fine us, put us on trial, shut us down. This play *The Pagans* by Anna Iablonskaia will be performed at Teatr.doc exactly as Anna wrote it and as Lera [Valeria] Surkova directs it. Dixi![20] It is my responsibility as the director of this theatre. It is the theatre itself that is accountable, not the actors or the director. Ania, I will never betray you.[21]

In both of her major interviews on this subject, Gremina challenged Duma deputies and other supporters of the ban to attend a production of *The Pagans*. She expressed confidence that 'they would find nothing pernicious or offensive in it', and would realize that the language of the play simply adds a particular expressiveness to the work, which by and large is about the importance of family and mutual understanding.[22] According to Gremina, the overarching message of Iablonskaia's play is very much in line with the kind of ideology of 'defending values' that the authors of the obscenity law are trying to preserve and promote: 'This is an inspiring play in defence of true family values, in defence of family love and mutual understanding.'[23]

Language, religion and authenticity

The critic Andrei Desnitskii, in reviewing *The Pagans* for Gazeta.ru, cautions viewers that the play is not for the faint of heart: 'Fair warning: you shouldn't see this play if your religious feelings are easily offended or if you don't want to hear the full richness of the Russian language.'[24] Indeed, the struggle to define the role of religious faith in contemporary society occupies the heart of Iablonskaia's play. In addition, the play is about a search for a language of authenticity. The humorous interplay of sacred and profane registers serves to illuminate the larger failure of language and communication between the characters to express the authentic self. Iablonskaia's characters struggle to be true to themselves, to communicate their needs and desires, their hopes and aspirations, their memories and traumas.

The central characters include Marina, a forty-year-old estate agent; her husband Oleg, a meek, downcast classical musician who is repeatedly shamed by his wife for not having a proper job; their daughter Kristina, a college student who struggles with depression and engages in various destructive behaviours that culminate in a near-fatal suicide attempt; Botsman, the alcoholic handyman who has been to Africa and witnessed the pagan tribal rituals to which the play's title, in part, refers; and Natal'ia Stepanovna, Oleg's estranged mother who, sensing she is nearing the end of her life, returns to the family following decades spent serving God as a helper in a number of monasteries. Propelling the family's struggle is the clash of sacred and profane language in the play's script that animates the characters' search for faith and its place in their lives. As we will see from close readings of excerpts from the script, some of the most powerful – and most humorous – moments from *The Pagans* hinge on the range of expressive means the characters employ in their struggle to define religious faith and to achieve sincerity in their individual spiritual pursuits.

The centrality of language here must also be contextualized within the broader aesthetic philosophy of Russia's 'New Drama', which is itself heavily rooted in debates about whether and how theatre should capture contemporary speech culture and transpose it for the stage. If Russian 'New Drama's origins lie in the verbatim method, which, in its purest form, requires that the text of a performance be drawn entirely from direct speech, how then do we understand Iablonskaia's link to Teatr.doc, a key locus of documentary theatre, if her play is not a work of verbatim or witness theatre?[25]

It is important to emphasize that verbatim theatre has evolved in a way that allows for a good deal of creative adaptation of the stories that unfold therein. In writing about the problem of translating the voices of Russian 'New Drama' into English, Sasha Dugdale notes that while the theory behind verbatim theatre calls for staging only direct speech, its practice in Russia is more fluid, and more complex. Instead of a polyphonic pastiche of direct transcriptions of interviews, today's scripts more often than not present 'a balance of documentary and theatrically constructed text'.[26] In fact, this approach that blends empirical interview data and imagined subjectivities is not unique to Russia's 'New Drama'. Verbatim theatre is traditionally defined in opposition to fictional drama, yet critics of the genre in transnational perspective have noted an important shift in the way that fictional drama and verbatim methods are blended in recent writing for the stage, particularly with regard to plays that aim to inspire political engagement and action.[27]

While Iablonskaia's link to Teatr.doc might suggest that *The Pagans* comes out of this tradition, the play offers a more nuanced combination of contemporary vernacular and a moral framework somewhat reminiscent of 1980s *chernukha*.[28] Iablonskaia's play revolves primarily around the moral and spiritual struggles of a family in a middle-class, post-Soviet, urban setting. In this sense, it is a kind of inheritor of the theatrical projects of the 1980s and 1990s in the way that it interrogates the moral compass of a broader swathe of society, instead of aiming to capture the experience of a particular social 'type' or 'ecolect', to use Beumers and Lipovetsky's term.[29] Rather, *The Pagans*, with its clear arc of plot and character development and its internal debates about the place of religion and spirituality in contemporary society, is perhaps more comparable to the work of Ivan Vyrypaev than it is to most other plays in the repertoire of Teatr.doc in 2016–17, which were nearly all documentary productions.[30]

However, let us return to the main point. One way to understand the place of *The Pagans* in the realm of 'New Drama' is in its use of language as theme and motif in the play. What precise function, then, does *mat* serve in *The Pagans*? The interplay and inversion of sacred and profane language mirrors Iablonskaia's larger goal of privileging moments of interpersonal connection over larger dogmatic systems of belief – whether pagan or Christian. The inversion of the sacred and the profane that develops as the play unfolds recalls Uspenskii's writings on the origins of obscenities in Russian, in which the taboo against profane speech elevates it to the place of the sacred.[31]

> In any context the [obscene] words in question retain as it were a *direct* connection with their content, and consequently whoever utters them is in every case directly responsible for them. But this sort of attitude toward the linguistic sign is

characteristic first and foremost of sacred lexis: indeed, this specific sense of the non-arbitrariness of the linguistic sign is characteristic precisely of the sacred, and is responsible for the taboo attaching to expressions within it; hence, paradoxically, the vocabulary of degradation approaches that of religion.[32]

The play opens with dialogue that places obscenities front and centre as Botsman, the alcoholic handyman and family friend, begins to argue with Marina. He asks her for money for cigarettes. She explodes, accusing him of being a lazy, incompetent drunk who's doing a shoddy job renovating her kitchen, while she works tirelessly to put her daughter through school. Botsman fires back, suggesting that Marina has been blind to the reality of her daughter Kristina's situation and that the daughter isn't studying, but has essentially become a substance-abusing prostitute.

> **Botsman** Who's jerking off? Me?! You won't even give me a couple of bucks, and now you're bitching about your daughter. We know what kind of 'studying' she does! We've seen how she gets in and out of fancy cars, drunk off her ass! A student from the Department of Delinquency. Don't study hard, study smart ... fucking bullshit!!
>
> **Marina** What did you say, you half-wit drunk?!
>
> **Botsman** What you heard! She'll certainly never find a husband. And you! Well we could set you up in the nicest fucking kitchen in the world with the best fucking appliances and the best dishes and all that fucking non-stick shit and you ... I mean, holy shit, you can't even fucking boil an egg! How many times has Oleg come to me saying he's hungry, there's nothing to eat, and his wife never fucking cooks, but from morning to night it's Doctor Fucking House and all that other bullshit!
>
> **Marina** What did you ...?!
>
> **Botsman** What you heard!![33]

The explosive argument in this opening scene is made all the more forceful by its relentless use of obscenities, and it sets the stage for the stark contrast in registers that emerges when Oleg's mother, Natal'ia Stepanovna, appears in the apartment, bearing gifts of water from holy springs, honey bottled by monks, healing salves and a constant stream of blessings and appeals to the Almighty. Natal'ia has spent most of her son's life away from him, travelling from monastery to monastery devoting herself to the Church, expiating a sin, the nature of which is revealed only very late in the play; she has made no contact with the family until now. The speech patterns of the devout grandmother alternate between a sweet, nurturing sing-song in her role as nurturer ('Why aren't you eating more? Eat! Have some tasty *blini* [pancakes]!') and her incantatory cries of 'Lord save us and have mercy!' and reassurances of 'It's okay, it's okay, God will show the way, He will guide us'.

Iablonskaia has written into the script a number of key moments when these linguistic registers collide or are exchanged between characters in unexpected, and often humorous ways. For example, after Marina slaps Kristina hard, drawing blood,

Marina and Natal'ia – in a series of *ogovorki* [slips of the tongue] – confuse '*spasatel*' (ointment, salve) and '*spasitel*' ([S]aviour) – each from the root 'to save'. This linguistic play adds light humour to a scene that sets up a key problem that re-enters later in the play: how and whether to turn to medicine or prayer when Kristina is severely injured following a suicide attempt.

The arrival of Natal'ia Stepanovna has the most overt effect on Botsman. Over the course of the play – inspired by Natalia's prayer and proselytizing – his character undergoes a transformation from a non-believer struggling with alcohol and unemployment to a reformed believer who chooses faith over vodka. Later, however, he becomes disillusioned with the fetishizing of suffering he sees in Natal'ia's Orthodox Christian worldview and embraces a wholly different system of beliefs, the tribal rituals he observed while travelling in Africa, which he interprets through the lens of a kind of 'noble savage' paradigm. The stages of Botsman's spiritual transformation are marked by an evolution in his language use; in particular, this involves a mysterious curse that afflicts him with intense pain each time he utters an obscenity.

This bizarre ailment begins shortly after Natal'ia's arrival. Botsman explains that death has appeared to him, embodied in the vodka that Natal'ia had encouraged him not to drink. He immediately quits drinking and devotes himself intently to completing the renovation project in Marina and Oleg's apartment. When Oleg confronts him about his unexpected change in behaviour, Botsman angrily responds in a barrage of obscenities. As Natal'ia scolds him for this language, Botsman ends up quite literally biting his tongue, which Natal'ia interprets as a sign from God, punishment for his cursing:

> **Natal'ia** That's a sign from the Good Lord, young man ... Take not the name of the Lord in vain ...

Punishment for obscene language escalates in Act One, Scene Eight, when Botsman is afflicted with intense pain each time he utters a curse word. Oleg, who later on insists that his faith lies in 'higher reason' (*vysshii razum*), argues that Botsman's pain must be only in his mind. However, the intervention of whatever force afflicts Botsman in response to his profanity is clearly more powerful than reason and rationality can explain.

> *The entryway of the apartment. Botsman is by the mailboxes, fixing Oleg's mailbox door. Oleg comes down the stairs with a big checkered shopping bag and looks around suspiciously.*
>
> **Oleg** What are you ...? Why are you doing that?
>
> **Botsman** What? I was walking by anyway ... I thought I'd try to fix it ... I mean, your box is totally stuffed with all kind of ... with papers and ... fucking cat shit and ... ow!
>
> *Grabs his skull.*
>
> **Oleg** What is it?
>
> **Botsman** Ow, it hurts! Like I got shot in the head. I've noticed if I say ... those words ... it's like I get shot.

Oleg   Which words?

Botsman   Any kind of curse word ... I get this awful spasm ...

Oleg   Yeah, right, whatever!

Botsman   Seriously!

Oleg   Sounds like it's all in your head!

Botsman   What the fuck do you mean in my fucking head! OW! OW! OW-ow-owww!

In a subsequent scene, Iablonskaia subverts our expectations for profane speech by inserting obscenities into the devout Grandmother's text. When Marina confronts Natal'ia about how long she intends to stay with them, Natal'ia assures her that she will stay only as long as it takes to get Kristina to repent her sins and change her ways. Marina presses her mother-in-law for clarification in an exchange that typifies the kind of talking past one another that occurs frequently among the play's characters. The miscommunication here is so extreme, it prompts Natal'ia – the pious grandmother – to use perhaps the most graphic of the forbidden obscenities against which she prays and preaches. Her linguistic register undergoes a tripartite shift as she attempts to be understood:

Natal'ia   She's a loose woman, Marina. She needs to be saved. We must take her to Father Vladimir for confession. I've already arranged it.

Marina   What is she?

Natal'ia   A loose woman. You know, a prostitute.

Marina   WHAT???

Natal'ia   She's a fucking whore, that's what ... Oh, goodness! (*Crosses herself.*) Forgive me, oh Lord!

In the play's second act – and in another inversion – it is Kristina who enlists the language of the Bible and the texts of Saints' Lives to complicate and counter her grandmother's beliefs, and to challenge her parents' understanding of faith and piety and its broad application in contemporary culture. When Kristina appears in her underwear and her grandmother, aghast, orders her to get dressed, Kristina quotes Matthew 6:28–29, a passage in which Christ urges his followers to concern themselves less with food and clothing and more with their body and soul. Kristina's invocation of this text is meant to draw attention to the hypocrisy inherent in the Church's attitudes towards the female body and society's persistent Lapsarian narratives of shame and 'loss of innocence'.

This scene, in which Kristina quotes the Bible, but in the very next breath provokes her mother with obscene suggestions about Botsman's sexuality, is one that sparks a violent physical response. It is as if all of the play's verbal and emotional tension to this point finally reaches a peak, exploding into Marina's angry slap that draws her daughter's blood. Yet the stage directions indicate a deflated response: the others in the scene '*do not react to the blow in any way. A crooked smile comes across Kristina's face and she touches her cheek.*' Natal'ia then proceeds to greet Botsman and invite him to join them for porridge (*kasha*), the appropriate morning dish for the Palm Sunday fast.

The rejection of the sanctity of the body here – the insistence on clothing and the indifference to pain – is important; Kristina's family finds out almost too late that her erratic and destructive behaviour is closely tied to a sexual encounter with a university instructor – a painful, unrequited love – that has brought her shame and rejection, fuelling Kristina's deep depression and suicide attempts. The muted response to physical violence is representative of a larger communicative breakdown that has infected the characters in the play and, arguably, much of broader contemporary society. Each member of the family constructs an externalized performance, rituals that mask a deep, private suffering. Oleg's crushed hopes of being a professional musician mean that he closets himself in the bathroom late at night, listening to music in private. Marina reflexively shifts to an upbeat tone of voice when speaking to real estate clients on the phone, but she is deeply dissatisfied that her round-the-clock work activities have not brought her financial stability or fulfilment. Botsman's alcoholism masks his grief over the death of his spouse from cancer, and Natal'ia's abandoning her family and turn towards service in the Church, we learn late in the play, is penance for getting an abortion when she was a newly single mother with a young child, in a desperate situation. In each case, these external performances mask suffering and disrupt any sort of authentic connection between the family members.

Throughout the play's second act, the author works to dismantle a number of seemingly sacred tropes to reveal them as profane illusions. For example, Act 2 exposes corruption within the Church: the priest has been smuggling goods as part of a business on the side. Characters in the play invert the sacred and the profane in other places as well. Marina believes that happiness is found in financial gain; Kristina's first suicide attempt – jumping off a pier – is figured as a kind of baptism; after giving up vodka and obscenities to save himself from death, Botsman's change of heart at the conclusion of the play means that he rejects the narrative of suffering and sacrifice and returns to drinking, and finds joy and release in embracing obscenities once again.

Sacred and profane registers vie for dominance but, in the end, neither proves sufficient. Natal'ia and Botsman in some ways take on qualities of caricature or parody, and neither is given a final confessional monologue, such as is afforded to the other characters. As the play resolves, we find that while each has made changes and shifted their lives and their focus in different directions, their suffering is only slightly relieved and abated; the author does not offer a clear solution to the problem of how to achieve authenticity and connection.

Kristina, Marina and Oleg each speak at length, as if answering interview questions from the audience – a nod to verbatim – about their paths towards resolution and greater peace following the traumatic events that have come before. Natal'ia Stepanovna has died, Marina and Oleg have separated, Botsman has evidently gone to live in Africa, and Kristina is slowly recovering from her traumatic injuries. For those who remain, their emotional scars are still evident. Yet each of the characters has undergone a shift from the rituals of isolation and self-destruction to rituals of connection with one another, or with a more authentic, if still imperfect version of their true selves. Kristina is intent on pursuing physical rehabilitation and completing her studies. Marina regrets her past obsession with her career and is working to repair her relationship with her daughter and prepare for a new job that will be more suitable to her personal interests and aspirations. She has also begun to go to church, finding a renewed sense of peace and comfort in God. Oleg has given up his dream of being a professional musician and has settled into steady employment in sales. Though he visits Natal'ia's grave and occasionally visits a church to light a candle in memory of his mother, it is only as a way to honour her memory: for him it is not an act of devotion to God:

> **Oleg**   To church? You'll probably laugh, but sometimes I do stop by. What do I do there? I just stand there, light a candle, do some thinking . . . Yes, of course I visit her grave. She's my mother after all. I'm certain that she . . . that her role in all of this . . . it's possible that without her, everything might have turned out worse . . . Blame? I find only one person to blame. You know who.

This final line leaves open the question of who is to blame for suffering and who is responsible for the other characters' rehabilitation and recovery. The open-ended nature of the conclusion enhances the dialogic power of the text, for each person viewing the play must decide for him/herself, just as each character in the work settles on his or her own conclusions about what role religious faith has in their lives and how they will choose to define it.

Anna Iablonskaia's *The Pagans* is a play that employs profanity for purposes that go beyond the expression of emotional intensity or vulgarity. Profane language in this work is juxtaposed with sacred speech and the language of everyday life to call into question the equivalence of words and moral character. The play argues, through the clash of two powerful linguistic registers, that sacred speech and the pious rituals of (Orthodox) Christianity do not necessarily imply moral virtue.

Conclusion

'Worst of all is that self-censorship is infiltrating our heads. It's impossible to know about the new laws and not think about the consequences if you plan to create work about something that really matters to you', graphic artist Viktoria Lomasko said.[34] An important consideration, as we continue to explore the impact of the 2014 obscenity law on Russian performance culture, is that the law has not been actively enforced in the theatre community since it went into effect. While a number of theatres, including Teatr.doc, are now operating in a climate in which they are subjected to other forms of pressure, threats and harassment, the reasons for this treatment tend to be viewed as more political than linguistic. For example, Teatr.doc, after showing a documentary film about the atrocities in Ukraine and staging a play about the Bolotnaia Square protests and arrests, has three times been evicted from its performance space since October 2014. Gremina maintained at the time that this had nothing to do with their performances of *The Pagans* or the obscenity law at all. At the same time, she agreed that other theatres are practising self-censorship; while Teatr.doc will not censor their plays, she refrains from judging other directors:

> As far as I know there haven't yet been any prosecutions of those violating the law. Of course it's self-censorship. But whether it is cowardice or prudent caution, only future developments will tell.
>
> With regards to us, we have no intention of redacting obscene language now or in the future.[35]

Thus far, it appears by all indications that the law is not being directly enforced in theatres or in literature. Not only does *The Pagans* run uncensored at Teatr.doc, but more than half of the plays at the time of the writing that are in repertory at Kirill Serebrennikov's Gogol' Centre are labelled 18+; one can also easily purchase books in major Moscow bookstores labelled 18+ due to the use of profanity. However, the film industry is feeling the effects of the ban in a much more profound way because of the stipulation concerning distribution licences for films. A group of prominent filmmakers, including among others Nikita Mikhal'kov, Fedor Bondarchuk and Karen Shakhnazarov, mounted an unsuccessful campaign in January 2015 to try to encourage the Duma to adapt the law in such a way as to make it possible for directors to make and distribute films containing profanity under strict '18+' labels.[36] Such an option could have protected the integrity of Iablonskaia's text in its newest incarnation; at the time of this writing, Valeria Surkova's film adaptation of *The Pagans*, which features the same actors who star in the production at Teatr.doc, was released widely on 15 February 2018. The film is rated 16+ and the obscenities are bleeped out in most public screenings of the film.

The pressure has persisted. In an interview with Japanese journalist Satoko Kosugi in April 2018 after the release of his film *Loveless*, acclaimed Russian filmmaker Andrei Zviagintsev explained how he balances the need to maintain authentic speech with the restrictions:

> I am completely indifferent to this law. I want the characters in my films to speak naturally, so, as a rule, I don't limit myself in any way. Nevertheless, it's dangerous to get caught by the censor, so I remove the sound in the moments when the characters use profanity. In those places people's mouths open such that it is clear to the viewers what the characters are saying. I don't like when the censor insists on bleeping out obscenities, so we remove the sound ourselves. Russian speakers still can tell what the characters are saying, even without the sound. [...] British and French dictionaries contain all kinds of words, it's just in Russian dictionaries that there are no obscenities. It's precisely because of this, I think, that the Russian equivalents of the English F*-word are so much stronger. These words become stronger precisely because they are banned.[37]

For the time being it seems that the censorship is affecting the film industry more than the theatre, but the threat of crackdowns is nevertheless ever-present. Indeed, the Minister of Culture Vladimir Medinsky in July 2017 answered questions from the

TASS news agency about the profanity ban and suggested that theatres too will eventually be made to conform:

> **TASS** But is there any hope that the law will be reconsidered?
>
> **VM** I am categorically against that. This lexicon is called 'non-normative' because it is *not the norm*. I don't want my kids or your kids to go to movie theatres and hear profanity flowing from the screen. Or in the theatres. By the way, some of our theatre institutions continue to violate this law. I promise you that in the future we are not going to tolerate this.
>
> **TASS** Do you know of specific cases?
>
> **VM** Yes, we do.
>
> **TASS** What are you preparing to do about it?
>
> **VM** I'm not going to answer that question.[38]

The recent legislative moves to control various aspects of verbal expression are not the only time contemporary Russia has considered such restrictions on profanity,[39] but it is the first time in recent history that such restrictions have been put in place with legal force. Thus, in the wake of the passage of the 2014 ban, a crucial question emerges as the country moves forward creatively: to what degree will the obscenity ban – whether enforced actively or simply through the psychological pressure of self-censorship – alter the shape of artistic expression in Russia?

One indication comes in Ivan Vyrypaev's statement in a 21 September 2015 interview with *Novaia Gazeta* on the occasion of the release of his film *Spasenie* (*Salvation*). If Vyrypaev stated in June 2014 that he would be able to continue to write plays successfully in accordance with the ban ('I can write like this [without profanity] and my plays won't suffer for it'), in an interview just over a year later, he characterized the obscenity ban as the greatest impediment to his creative work:

> The only prohibition that I'm really suffering from, the thing that really puts pressure on me, is the profanity ban. It's just killing me. Right now I'm doing a reading of my play about two people called *Solar Line*. I can't just take out the 'bad words'. If I have to, I just won't stage it here. I'll stage it in Poland. I'll wait until they change the law. [...] My characters are mostly freaks, lost souls. And they use profanity – beautifully, I might add, because that's how I use it – beautifully. [...] For me, Bakhtin's principle of the carnivalesque is extremely important. When you contemplate some sort of serious ideas ... For example, the heroine says: 'Oh, f**k! The Universe is expanding!' If she says 'Oh, fudge!' it's like we're at the playground. Or if she says 'How incredible! The Universe is expanding!' then the poetry is lost. I'm not a vulgar person. I want for there to be rhythm and poetry in speech.[40]

Just as in the case of Iablonskaia's *The Pagans*, Vyrypaev frames the language of obscenities as one of the key tools for contemporary artistic expression. It is a central device in capturing the carnivalesque and the poetry of everyday life, and it offers a means to achieve the most profound and most sincere forms of expression of the struggles inherent in the human condition.[41]

When asked about the problem of obscene language in *The Pagans*, Iablonskaia herself responded that profanity is not only commonplace in everyday speech, but it is forceful enough to alter mindsets and change people and circumstances, ideally, for the better:

> In terms of profanity in contemporary plays, there is as much there as there is in life. Everyone uses obscenities, but it's only in the space of the theatre that people start to worry about the loss of morality. The point of having real living language in plays is not to drag the audience through mud and shit, but just to show them life as it is. And then, if they have it in them to absorb what they've seen and heard, to try to make this life better. After all, what is theatre for?[42]

Iablonskaia suggests here that employing contemporary vernacular is a key aspect of the theatre's mission to harness authentic stories, told in familiar language, that will resonate with audiences and lead to social action. As this statement makes clear, Iablonskaia's stated goal is not far removed from what pure verbatim theatre works to achieve.

Notes

1. Tragically, the intrepid Elena Gremina died of heart failure on 16 May 2018. She was sixty-one. Her partner and Teatr.doc co-founder, the playwright, director and teacher Mikhail Ugarov, had died of a heart attack the previous month, on 1 April 2018, at age sixty-two.
2. At the time of the attack, Iablonskaia was arriving in Moscow to receive a 'New Voices in Russian Drama' award from the journal *Iskusstvo kino* (*Film Art*). The award was to celebrate the screenplay adaptation of her play *Iazychniki* (*The Pagans*), the stage version of which premiered at Teatr.doc in 2012 under the direction of Valeria Surkova.
3. Anna Iablonskaia is the pen name of Anna Mashutina. See, for example, Sasha Dugdale's moving tribute 'Playwright Anna Iablonskaia: a Tribute', *Guardian*, 25 January 2011, https://www.theguardian.com/stage/theatreblog/2011/jan/25/anna-yablonskaya-playwright-tribute
4. Theatre director and producer Sergei Proskurnia places Iablonskaia among the most important Russian playwrights of all time. In an interview, he said, 'I've conceived of a dramaturgical lineage: Chekhov, Arbuzov, Vampilov, Iablonskaia', in A. G. Iablonskaia, *Teatr i zhizn': Dramaticheskie proizvedeniia*. (Odessa: Bakhva, 2014), 7.
5. Pavel Rudnev, 'Angel novoi p'esy', *Open Space*, 25 January 2011, http://os.colta.ru/theatre/events/details/20111/ (accessed 15 July 2015).
6. Discourse on borders and the nation state is also present in Iablonskaia's play *Kosmos* (*The Cosmos*), though in this work the transnational theme is somewhat more metaphorical, since a central *topos* in this play is the border between earth and outer space. At the same time, the theme of borders arises in the play's discourse about human aspirations, potential to engage other civilizations, and even the border

between madness and sanity. *The Cosmos* and *Kyiv-Moscow* are published in Iablonskaia, *Teatr i zhizn'*, pp. 489–512.
7   Iablonskaia, *Teatr i zhizn'*, 491–2. All translations, unless otherwise noted, are my own.
8   Ibid., 491.
9   On the decision to change the name of the play from *Pagans* to *Terrorists*, Proskurnia explained that it had less to do with Iablonskaia's death and more to do with each individual's potential to inflict harm on others: 'The terrorists – that's you and me. Because terror inflicted by humans is one of the most terrible features of the human personality. The absence of mercy towards another person.' Sergei Proskurnia, 'Eto my terroristy!', 23 January 2012, http://reporter.com.ua/interviews/c83/ (accessed 31 January 2018).
10 The film premiered on 8 November 2017 and had its domestic opening in cinemas in the Russian Federation on 15 February 2018, followed by its digital release in March of that year. The film has received a number of awards at film festivals across Russia, including the prize for 'best debut' at the Smolensk Golden Phoenix Festival. https://www.facebook.com/yazichniky/posts/996312327176399
11 John Freedman and Marco Warman, 'Remembering Anna Iablonskaia', *The World on PRI*, 25 January 2011, https://www.pri.org/stories/2011-01-25/remembering-anna-yablonskaya (accessed 25 January 2018).
12 The regulations understand profanity (*netsenzurnaia leksika*) to be any morphological variation on four or five key obscenities in Russian known as *mat*: 'khuy' (cock), 'pizda' (cunt), 'ebat" (to fuck) and 'bliad"' (whore) (Marina Mikhneva also lists 'mudak' (dickhead)). See Victor Erofeyev, 'Dirty Words: The Unique Power of Russia's Underground Language', *The New Yorker*, 15 September 2003: 42 and Marina Mikhneva, 'The Five Forbidden Russian Words on Stage and Screen', *Open Democracy*, 26 August 2014, https://www.opendemocracy.net/od-russia/marina-mikhneva/five-forbidden-russian-words-on-stage-and-screen (accessed 31 January 2018). The obscenity law, known commonly as the *zakon o mate*, stipulates a number of punitive measures for individuals and organizations found in violation of it, from a series of fines to possible suspension of activities. This legislative measure, along with the 2013 changes to the Criminal Code to punish those who 'offend the convictions and feelings of religious believers', represents part of a broader series of government-sponsored initiatives that aim more closely to regulate speech and protect conservative national values in the Russian Federation. The laws have enjoyed broad public support in many parts of Russian society, but have also drawn criticism from champions of freedom of expression within Russia and around the world.
13 Pavel Rudnev, 'Angel novoi p'esy', *Open Space*, 25 January 2011, http://os.colta.ru/theatre/events/details/20111/ (accessed 30 January 2018).
14 Moscow's experimental Meierkhol'd Centre held a ceremony to bid farewell to *mat* on 6 June 2014, during which participants performed texts with obscenities by authors and playwrights ranging from Sorokin and Erofeev to Kurochkin and Klavdiev. 'V TSentre im. Meierkhol'da ustroyat aktsiyu Al'maNAKH – proshchanie s matom na stsene', http://calendar.fontanka.ru/articles/1620/ (accessed 15 August 2015). The event's Facebook page can be found at https://www.facebook.com/events/634903289935467/permalink/639343066158156/
15 Mikhneva, 'The Five Forbidden Russian Words on Stage and Screen'.
16 For instance, Maria Koziar, head dramaturge at the Petr Fomenko Workshop, downplayed the significance of the ban: 'Obscene language is used only in one play, *Summer Wasps Sting Us Even in November* [by Ivan Vyrypaev], and only once, in an

actress's improvised monologue. Nothing will to happen to *Summer Wasps* after July 1. I think that if that single "non-normative" [obscene] interjection is removed from the play, or if it is changed to a suitable "normative" alternative, it won't be any better or worse for it.' 'Kak moskovskie teatry gotoviatsia k zapretu netsenzurnoi leksiki', *Interfax*, 23 June 2014, http://www.interfax.ru/culture/382199 (accessed 31 January 2018).

17 Vyrypaev stepped down from the position of artistic director of Praktika in 2016 and now lives full time in Poland. Larisa Maliukova, Ivan VYRYPAEV: 'You act slyly, but you tell your son "Be a good boy, be open!"', *Novaya Gazeta* (20 September 2015), https://www.novayagazeta.ru/articles/2015/09/21/65693-ivan-vyrypaev-171-sami-hitrite-a-synu-govorite-171-bud-horoshim-otkrytym-malchikom-187 (accessed 31 January 2018).

18 Tatiana Pod'iablonskaia, 'Ivan Vyrypaev v Voronezhe', *Komsomol'skaia Pravda*, 20 June 2014, http://www.kp.md/daily/26245/3126547/ (accessed 15 January 2018).

19 Gremina, Elena, 'Pochemu ia sobiraius' narushit' zakon', *Colta*, 4 June 2014, https://www.colta.ru/articles/society/3443 (accessed 28 January 2018).

20 'I have spoken!' (Latin).

21 Elena Gremina, 'Pochemu ia sobiraius' narushit' zakon', *Colta*, 4 June 2014, https://www.colta.ru/articles/society/3443 (accessed 28 January 2018).

22 Elena Gremina, 'K sudam ia gotova. Ia ne boius'', *Afisha Vozdukh*, 3 June 2014, https://daily.afisha.ru/archive/vozduh/art/k-sudam-ya-gotova-i-ya-ne-boyus/ (accessed 31 January 2018).

23 Ibid.

24 Andrei Desnitskii, 'Teatr religioznykh deistvii', *Gazeta.ru*, 10 March 2014, http://www.gazeta.ru/comments/column/desnitsky/5943025.shtml (accessed 31 January 2018).

25 Birgit Beumers and Mark Lipovetsky, *Performing Violence: Literary and Theatrical Experiments of New Russian Drama* (Bristol: Intellect, 2009), 15–25.

26 Ibid., 20.

27 On the example of contemporary English-language drama, see Stephen Bottoms, 'Putting the Document into Documentary: An Unwelcome Corrective?', *TDR/The Drama Review* 50, no. 3 (2006): 56–68; M. Andersen and L. Wilkinson, 'A Resurgence of Verbatim Theatre: Authenticity, Empathy and Transformation', *Australasian Drama Studies* 50 (April 2007): 153–69.

28 *Performing Violence*, 37–8. *Chernukha*, with its root in the Russian adjective *chernyi* ('black'), is a term for representational art that focuses on the bleakest, darkest parts of human experience. It came into being in the late 1980s, during *perestroika*, and was applied in particular to prose and drama by Liudmila Petrushevskaia, but has since been used more often with reference to cinema. See Seth Graham, '*Chernukha* and Russian Film', *Studies in Slavic Cultures* 1 (January 2000): 9–27.

29 *Performing Violence*, 215–16.

30 The Teatr.doc event archive is at http://www.teatrdoc.ru/events.php (accessed 15 July 2017).

31 Indeed, in the play's somewhat reductive positioning of 'pagans' against Orthodox Christian practices, Iablonskaia's interest in religious discourse seems to align with a Durkheimian approach to systems of faith. Durkheim, who studied the religious practices of indigenous Australian totemic societies at the turn of the twentieth century, argued in *Les formes élémentaires de la vie religieuse* (1912) that all religions – pagan or Christian – are characterized by 'a unified system of beliefs and practices relative to sacred things, that is to say, things set apart and forbidden'. Durkheim's

sacred–profane dichotomy suggests that it is simply the habitual, the everyday, the mundane that constitutes the profane, while the sacred is that which is kept at a distance. Furthermore, rituals reaffirm the meaning of the sacred by acknowledging its separateness. The very definition of sacred as that which is 'set apart and forbidden' certainly calls into question the absurd logic of a profanity ban, which can only have the effect of sanctifying obscenities by setting them apart.

32 B. A. Uspenskij, 'On the Origins of Russian Obscenities', trans. Ralph Cleminson (in Lotman and Uspenskij, *Semiotics of Russian Culture*, ed. Ann Shukman (Ann Arbor: Department of Slavic Languages, University of Michigan, 1984), 295.

33 The full text of *Iazychniki* was published in the journal *Iskusstvo kino* in January 2011, shortly after Iablonskaia died: http://kinoart.ru/archive/2011/01/n1-article5. A volume of her complete works, including *Iazychniki*, was published in 2014. Iablonskaia, *Teatr i zhizn'*, 149–92.

34 Viktoria Lomasko, Graphic Artist. Elena Kryzhanovskaia, 'Rossiia protiv Rossii: ot tsenzury do samotsenzury', 4 April 2015, http://dw.com/p/1F6s7 (accessed 7 August 2015).

35 Elena Gremina, personal correspondence with the author, 2 September 2015.

36 Nikolai Kornatskii, 'Minkul'tury otkazalos' vozvrashchat' mat v shirokiy prokat', *Izvestiia*, 9 July 2015. http://izvestia.ru/news/587495 (accessed 28 January 2018).

37 Andrei Zviagintsev and Satoko Kosugi, 'Zakon o mate prepiatstvuet svobode slova v Rossii', *Inosmi.ru*, 14 April 2018. https://inosmi.ru/culture/20180414/241950207.html

38 'Vladimir Medinsky: ia kategoricheski protiv peresmotra zakona o zaprete nenormativnoy leksiki v kino', *TASS Information Agency*, 14 July 2017, http://tass.ru/opinions/interviews/4335663 (accessed 28 January 2018).

39 Viktor Erofeev, for example, details legislative attempts led by Duma Deputy Kaadyr-ool Bicheldei that were under way earlier this century to ban the words. See Viktor Erofeev, 'Dirty Words', *The New Yorker*, 15 September 2003: 42–8 (42).

40 Maliukova, 'Ivan VYRYPAEV'.

41 Worthy of further scholarship would be analysis comparing *The Pagans* with Vyrypaev's *Oxygen*, given that Iablonskaia's play is set against the backdrop of Holy Week, a framing device like Vyrypaev's Ten Commandments, that adds an additional layer of subtext to the story that unfolds therein.

42 Iablonskaia, *Teatr i zhizn'*, 7.

14

Natal'ia Vorozhbyt's *Viy*

Autoethnography through a Gogolian lens

Jessica Hinds-Bond

> Jessica Hinds-Bond considers a play by Natal'ia Vorozhbyt, one of the first works she wrote in Ukrainian rather than Russian, which is based on an 1835 story by Nikolai Gogol' called *Viy*. Gogol's story, written in Russian for a St Petersburg audience, was a pastiche of Ukrainian folk tales, in which he invented a monstrous creature called Viy, who brings about the hero's death. Vorozhbyt, in transposing the events to modern-day Ukraine and including visitors from France in the plot, plays on foreigners' views and preconceptions of the Ukrainian nation, much as Gogol' had done with Russian views of Ukraine in the nineteenth century. Jessica also looks at how these stereotypes have been handled in the different productions of the play in Russian and in Ukrainian.

The Ukrainian playwright Natal'ia Vorozhbyt (b. 1975) reimagines Nikolai Gogol's 1835 Ukrainian tale *Viy* (written in Russian) in her 2011 play *Viy: A Docudrama*. She uses her play and its source material largely as a pretext to open a dialogue between Ukraine and the West – or between the periphery and the centre – subverting state-authored Ukrainian nationalistic discourse and addressing contemporary Ukrainian concerns before a transnational audience. *Viy: A Docudrama* reimagines Gogol's story for a disbelieving and globalized age. The play exists at a transnational crossroads: thematic elements of linguistic and cultural confusion echo both its genesis and its production history.

Vorozhbyt originally wrote her play for a Western audience: she was commissioned by Vlad Troitsky (b. 1964), artistic director of Kiev's DAKh Contemporary Art Centre, to create a Ukrainian-language adaptation of Gogol's *Viy* for performance at the Théâtre Vidy-Lausanne in Switzerland.[1] This project was among the first three plays that Vorozhbyt drafted in Ukrainian, after having written in Russian for most of her career. It was translated into Russian almost immediately upon completion, so that it could be performed in a rehearsed reading at the Liubimovka Festival in Moscow. The play was anomalous for Vorozhbyt, who explained, 'I was asked to write *Viy*. Never in my life would I have written it myself; I don't like adaptation.'[2] Ultimately, Troitsky never took Vorozhbyt's play to Switzerland. And so *Viy: A Docudrama* received its first reading – in Russian – at the Liubimovka Festival in 2011, before winning first place in Russia's 2012 Golden Mask Festival 'New Play' competition, and it has since been performed in both Russian and Ukrainian in multiple cities across the two countries.

Vorozhbyt retains Gogol's basic plot about a student travelling through the Ukrainian countryside – but she transplants the events to today and recasts her student as Lukas, a non-Ukrainian-speaking, atheistic Frenchman who is vacationing in Ukraine. Gogol's *Viy* follows the misadventures of Khoma, the Ukrainian seminary student travelling home from Kyiv who encounters and kills a witch, an old woman who transforms into a beautiful young maiden as she lies dying. Khoma soon finds himself summoned back to the countryside to spend three nights in prayer over the body of the young maiden. He protests but holds vigil, and each night he is visited by stranger and scarier wonders, culminating in the fatal visit of the monstrous 'Viy', a 'squat, hefty, splay-footed man ... covered all over in black earth'.[3] Notoriously, Gogol quite falsely claimed folk authenticity for his story in the author's note to *Viy*:

> Viy is a colossal creation of the folk imagination. This name is applied by people in Little Russia [a term used at the time to designate Ukraine] to the chief of the gnomes, whose eyelids reach to the ground. The whole story is a popular legend. I did not wish to change it in any way and tell it almost as simply as I heard it.[4]

As multiple scholars have concluded, no such legend ever existed.[5] Gogol published *Viy* in *Mirgorod*, his second collection of Ukrainian tales – stories that he set in his native Ukraine but wrote for a Russian audience after he had moved to St Petersburg. Yulia Ilchuk argues that part of Gogol's project in writing these Ukrainian tales was 'to gain inclusion into the diverse imperial and national spaces of Russia' by 'appropriat[ing] the performative identity strategies of mimicry'. As she explains, 'His hybrid identity [of Ukrainian and Russian] was fashioned as the colonial/ethnic Other through discourses and practices of transgression and imposture'.[6]

Vorozhbyt enacts her own act of appropriation in her play, using Gogol's Ukrainian story to construct an imagined Ukraine that is geographically, culturally and financially isolated from the world. In so doing, she engages in a process of Ukrainian autoethnography, contesting and playing on non-Ukrainian images of Ukraine, much as Gogol did before her.[7] I scaffold my reading of Vorozhbyt's play on the work of Mary Louise Pratt, who defines an autoethnographic text as:

> A text in which people undertake to describe themselves in ways that engage with representations others have made of them ... They involve a selective collaboration with and appropriation of idioms of the metropolis or the conqueror. These are merged or infiltrated to varying degrees with indigenous idioms to create self-representations intended to intervene in metropolitan modes of understanding. Autoethnographic works are often addressed to both metropolitan audiences and the speaker's own community. Their reception is thus highly indeterminate.[8]

Vorozhbyt raises the question of what images a periphery might (or should) project to the centre. Her play stages a confrontation between Westerners and Ukrainians to invite transnational dialogue about the lived reality in the 'borderland' state of Ukraine.[9] It might be said to be not so much about allowing the world to see the unknown *Ukrainian nation*, as fostering contact with real-life, present-day *Ukrainians*. Pratt locates autoethnographic texts within *contact zones*, or 'social spaces where cultures meet, clash, and grapple with each other, often in contexts of highly asymmetrical relations of power'.[10] As I will show, Vorozhbyt structures her play as a series of encounters across contact zones, both within the play – including the real (face to face) and the virtual – and outside it, with the production itself becoming the ultimate contact zone.

The subtitle of Vorozhbyt's play, 'A Docudrama', directly references the verbatim methods that underpin so much of contemporary Russian drama and alerts the audience to the possibility of real-life resonances, even as it subtly echoes Gogol's own spurious claims of authenticity in the original story. Her play centres on a group of bored, broke and shiftless Ukrainian millennials who chafe at the lack of prospects in the village: 'They drink *horilka* [Ukrainian alcohol] to the point of memory loss, cuss and practice witchcraft out of boredom.'[11] Why show this side of Ukraine to a non-Ukrainian audience – either the Western audiences for whom Vorozhbyt initially wrote, or the Russian audiences for whom this play has frequently been produced? Complicating this question is Vorozhbyt's avowal that she speaks to a *Ukrainian* audience: 'As a playwright, I am interested in investigating why our people drink so much. I want the theatre spectator to see himself drinking on the stage. [To see himself as] pathetic, destroying himself, his family, his country.'[12] These words suggest that the transnational audience for whom Vorozhbyt wrote *Viy* is extraneous. And yet the majority of Vorozhbyt's plays have been performed for Western or Russian audiences before (or to the exclusion of) Ukrainian ones. Take, for example, her 2002 breakthrough play *Galka Motalko*, whose premiere production took place in the Russian city of Togliatti in 2003; or her 2009 historical epic *The Grain Store* (*Zernokhranilishche*), which was commissioned by Sir Michael Boyd of the Royal Shakespeare Company and first performed in English. Her production history aside, Vorozhbyt identifies as first and foremost Ukrainian, an identity that, in her words, links her to Gogol: 'I am a Ukrainian writer. It seems to me that language is not the main indicator of a "national writer". If I was to write in English (I won't, of course), I would not stop being a Ukrainian writer. Nabokov never stopped being Russian, and Gogol – Ukrainian.'[13] Such a sentiment suggests that Vorozhbyt speaks to (or for) Ukrainians in her plays, regardless of the expected nationality of her spectators.

For Vorozhbyt, I argue, the transnational audience is a *necessary* witness to a narrative of the continuing and multifaceted existence of the twenty-first-century Ukrainian subject. A similar role awaits the foreign Lukas in Vorozhbyt's play, who faces seemingly insurmountable intercultural and interlinguistic conflict with the Ukrainian villagers. Lukas's arrival catalyses the events that unfold. And yet, if these events take place *because* of Lukas, they are most assuredly not *for* him. The Ukrainians all need something from him, urgently even: a kind ear, a good lay, a sincere and well-worded prayer, an admission of fear. But Lukas is not the subject here, merely the empty, uninformed object that allows the Ukrainian subject to (re)locate itself.

The play concerns two Frenchmen. Lukas arrives in Ukraine with his friend Damian, who has Ukrainian roots and speaks some of the language – although he cannot understand all the villagers' colloquial Ukrainian. Damian met local girl Oksana online and has been invited to her wedding, bringing Lukas along. At the bachelor party, Lukas meets another girl named Dren'ka, and the two eventually have sex in the cellar. Unfortunately, when the lights flick on, Lukas finds not Dren'ka but – in a reverse Gogolian twist – the elderly granny. In confusion and horror, he attacks her. He wakes the next morning sure that he has killed Dren'ka but soon realizes – at a wedding scene that turns funereal – that he has killed the bride Oksana, apparently a shapeshifting witch. Just like in Gogol's story, Lukas is informed that Oksana's dying wish was that he should pray over her body for three nights. After downloading some prayers from the internet and spending two uneventful nights, however, Lukas returns to France, leaving the final night unattended.

The cellar scene: locating the Ukrainian subject

The cellar scene is a flashpoint of the concerns that permeate Vorozhbyt's play. It presents a prolonged one-on-one exchange between a Ukrainian and a Westerner across a barely penetrable linguistic barrier and establishes the Gogolian plot, culminating in the murder that precedes the three nights of prayer and the (anticipated, but unfulfilled) arrival of the monstrous Viy. Lukas accompanies Dren'ka to the cellar to fetch more pickles for the party. She names various provisions, but he responds, in what is understood to be French,[14] that he cannot understand her. Exasperated, she responds:

> I honestly don't believe that you can't understand Ukrainian ... It seems to me that all these foreign languages were thought up specifically to make it seem like they don't understand Ukrainian ... That's so convenient. I tell you: lend me money, and you respond – croak, croak, croak. I can speak foreigner too. Karabarabaka.[15]

Humorous as this line is – particularly as Dren'ka's words are utterly lost on Lukas – it speaks to a deep frustration at the disconnections between characters and worlds in this play. As it turns out, however, Dren'ka and Lukas find some common linguistic ground when the subject of obscenities arises:

Dren'ka   And do you have *mat* [profanity]? We do. *Bliad'* [whore], for example. Repeat after me. Well, *bliad'*. Blia-iad.

Lukas   Bliat.

For some reason they are both overcome by shyness.

Dren'ka   And now say *palianytsia* [Ukrainian bread].

Lukas   Pa-lia-ni-tsa. Oh, fuck off.[16]

As Dren'ka attempts to get Lukas to curse in Ukrainian, the stage directions indicate that both characters become shy, revealing a growing attraction or closeness between them. It is only through this youthful, shared language of obscenities that Dren'ka and Lukas can bridge their intercultural divide, which soon widens again. In a heartrending moment, Dren'ka begins to pour out her despair at rural life: 'I hate this village, this life. It's hard labour, not life. Everyone comes from the city in the summer, they say – beautiful, romantic, nature ... You try living here. In the winter, for example. Walk to the toilet on the street. Shit freezes before it hits the ground. Like in outer space.'[17] Dren'ka lets loose this torrent of words to a Frenchman whose only interjection is to ask about the pickles, wanting to go back upstairs. She is seemingly desperate for a human connection that Lukas is unable to reciprocate. And yet, she delivers this monologue *after* reconfirming that he cannot speak Ukrainian. He is a safe sounding board: he cannot understand what she is telling him or ever repeat her words. Further, when Oksana's sorcery is later revealed, this confessional moment in the cellar comes into full relief. It is not Dren'ka who has poured out her soul to Lukas, but rather Oksana, who on the eve of her own marriage is so vastly unhappy that she is desperate for any escape.

The scene in the cellar is not, in the end, about Oksana's need to find a human connection, even if we witness a tentative, growing intimacy between her (as Dren'ka) and Lukas, an exchange that culminates in sex (and, ultimately, in Lukas's murder of the girl). Rather, Oksana needs to vent to someone at a safe remove, and Lukas's foreignness makes him ideal for this purpose.[18] As Vorozhbyt later reveals, Oksana has much to lament about a rural life so lacking in prospects that her brother had to sell his kidney after their parents died. How can Oksana complain to her fellow villagers when she now lives in the best house in town (never mind that it was funded by the organ sale, or that her once strong brother now uses a cane)? In the contact zone of the cellar, it is only the absolute language barrier that frees Oksana to express her despair.

The interrogation scene: autoethnographic storytelling

Oksana is far from being the only Ukrainian character who needs something from Lukas. The next morning, before everyone learns of Oksana's murder, the groom Kolia asks Lukas to stand in as his best man because the real groomsman has passed out drunk. Lukas is linguistically and culturally out of his element. He is given a traditional Ukrainian costume to wear, and he must participate in the morning's folk wedding rituals: the procession to the bride's home and the riddles and games in her yard, in which the best man plays a significant role.[19] Lukas's obvious discomfort and unfamiliarity with the wedding rituals is a source of delight for the other guests in this scene, Damian included.

It is only later, however, in the interrogation scene following Lukas's first night in the church, that his utility for this village becomes clear: Lukas's presence allows the Ukrainians to (re)connect with each other. If earlier, Oksana (as Dren'ka) needed Lukas *because* he was a silent sounding board, unable to communicate with her, then later, Lukas's presence – as mediated by Damian's interpretive efforts – enables a ritualistic storytelling session between *and for* the Ukrainian villagers. In one of the play's most memorable scenes, the local villagers question Lukas about his vigil. The interrogation is disjointed, the questions filtered through Damian, and the emotional register of the scene broken. The old woman Baba Son'ka initiates the questioning:

Baba Son'ka   Well?

Lukas   What?

Baba Son'ka   Was there an evil spirit?

Lukas   What?

Damian   Was there an evil spirit?

Lukas   There was.

Damian   There was.

All are excited and rejoice.

Baba Son'ka   Was it frightening?

Damian   Was it frightening?

Lukas   Frightening? No.

Damian   No, it wasn't frightening.

Baba Son'ka (*disappointed*)   How could it not be? Phoo...

All are indignant and start to grumble noisily.[20]

The locals quiz Lukas about a red-eyed witch, fire-breathing goats, *rusalki* [seductive female water sprites][21] – and in each case Lukas confirms that he saw them but was unafraid. The emotional pitch of the Ukrainians continues to rise, and Vorozhbyt writes that they are 'disappointed, humiliated'[22] at the foreigner's lack of terror. Only when Lukas states that he did not see the Viy do they relax, exhibiting 'relief and joy':[23] they are convinced that if he *had* seen the Viy, he would not have lived through the night.

This scene suggests a deep cultural divide and a dual critique of both the Ukrainians and the Westerners, the former for their provincialism and the latter for their jadedness and indifference. The local villagers are mortified to discover that their foreign visitor is unaffected and even bored by the folkloric demons and stories that so terrify them. Conversely, Lukas is perhaps so jaded by contemporary Western culture that he feels nothing when in the presence of real mystical beings. He tells Damian that the demons were no different from the cartoons and music that he consumes daily through digital media,[24] and in the play's final scene he reveals that he believes everything he encountered in Ukraine, even the murder itself, to have been a well-executed hoax – a sentiment that perhaps comes a bit too easily to him, delivered as it is from the safety of France.[25] If it is true that Lukas's Gogolian predecessor dies 'because he got scared',[26] as is claimed in the story, then perhaps it is

Lukas's lack of religious faith and resultant immunity to fear that saves his life in Vorozhbyt's play.

More significantly, the interrogation scene reveals once again that the Ukrainian villagers *need* something from their French visitor. The weight that the villagers place on Lukas's answers suggests that they may not ever have seen the horrific creatures themselves, but rather depend on the odd visitor to confirm the continued existence of the demons from their lore. Further, they appoint Lukas to enact the sacred prayer rituals despite his lack of Ukrainian language or any religious belief. Lukas – who has already been conscripted as best man – is thus doomed to be drafted into the role of key witness of (and key actor in) the ritual at hand, whether that ritual is celebratory or mournful. To understand what this foreign visitor has to offer to the life-cycle rituals of the Ukrainian village, we must examine what happens after Lukas denies having seen the Viy.

The scene quickly morphs into one of ritualistic storytelling between the villagers, their flowing monologues delivered for each other rather than for Lukas. Indeed, although Baba Son'ka cursorily instructs Damian to interpret,[27] the audience no longer witnesses this choppy process taking place. It does not matter to the villagers that this foreigner cannot understand them – the stories are not for him – and yet, his presence is crucial in triggering the storytelling, as they only begin the ritual because they ostensibly have a new audience.[28]

The villagers tell stories of famine, war and nuclear contamination rooted in the horrors of the twentieth-century Ukrainian past, sharply different from the listing of folkloric creatures that formed the crux of the earlier interrogation. The play thus achieves a blending of the nineteenth-century world of Gogol's tale with contemporary modernity. The excitement rises as villagers interject and cheer the speakers. The first three stories evoke Ukrainian traumas of epic scale and unquantifiable devastation, traumas that had – and continue to have – an overwhelming impact on the Ukrainian people. Baba Son'ka tells of cannibalism during 'the hunger',[29] euphemistically referencing the genocidal famine of the early 1930s in Ukraine, known as the 'Holodomor'. 'One of the defining events of twentieth-century Ukrainian history', the Holodomor is for Ukrainians, according to the scholar Catherine Wanner, 'the Ukrainian holocaust, a national symbol of oppressive Soviet rule, Ukrainian suffering, and a justification for independent statehood.'[30] Scholars estimate that between five million and eleven million souls perished in an event apparently orchestrated from Moscow by Stalin,[31] and the Ukrainian countryside was left 'irreversibly sapped of life'.[32] Notably, the Holodomor was also the subject of Vorozhbyt's *The Grain Store*. As Vorozhbyt explained, 'the topic of the Holodomor became immediately irrelevant' upon the 2010 election of President Viktor Yanukovych, who returned Ukraine to closer relations with Russia. *The Grain Store* had been in rehearsals in Ukraine at this time, but 'was banned a week before its premiere', evidently so as not to offend the Russians.[33]

Dren'ka speaks of Ded Gavrilo, a soldier who wanted so badly to return home from the war – presumably the Second World War – that he allowed his hand to be shot off in order to obtain a medical release. Unfortunately, the bloody appendage followed him home, reappearing in his firewood or his boots or a wine bottle. Wilfried Jilge explains that the war – which took the life of five million Ukrainians and left twice as many homeless[34] – was 'an existential matter for the Ukrainian state and Ukrainian society, [and] is still directly felt by Ukrainians today, as is reflected in eye-witness accounts and stories passed down from one generation to the next.'[35] Perhaps no stronger evidence exists of this continued impact – and contemporary reassessment – of the war than Ukraine's 2016 signing of the 'Declaration of Remembrance and Solidarity', which stated that the Soviet Union had been as responsible as Germany for its outbreak.[36] This declaration directly contests the Soviet Union's 'heroic narrative of the "Great Patriotic War" . . . one of the Soviet Union's basic legitimizing myths'.[37]

Kolia tells of a fisherman from Chernobyl, evoking a more recent national trauma. His story is particularly harrowing because the trauma that it conjures is so recent – 'not a historical event . . . but a living reality'[38] – and yet still so obscured, its true human impact largely unknown.[39] And yet, again, the trauma of the nuclear disaster at Chernobyl is not merely one of lives lost. Rather, as Will Englund writes, 'Ukrainians, who achieved independence five years after the disaster, remember the fear of radiation and of the unknown – but more pointedly, they remember their sense of betrayal . . . It wasn't just the authorities' silence in the first two weeks. Official indifference became an enduring part of the Chernobyl story.'[40]

Finally – just as Dren'ka is suggesting a story about a villager who froze to death on the walk home from a Soviet gulag – old Ded Iavtukh interjects with what is sure to be the village's newest legend: 'And this . . . The other day . . . A newly arrived student raped and killed our witch!'[41] The mood plunges: 'Everyone hushes Ded, then they guiltily look at Lukas, embarrassed.'[42] In this moment, Lukas's presence is abruptly remembered. Baba Son'ka tells Iavtukh to shush, announcing that it is about time for Lukas to head back to the church for the second night of prayer. If the earlier stories point to national traumas from the past century, each of them wrought by Ukraine's fraught relationship with the USSR/Russia, then this kernel of a story points to the potential for new national traumas to arise as Ukraine goes its own way with the West. Such a story suggests that Ukraine's history is still being written, actively negotiated as Ukraine finds its way as a sovereign nation.

This storytelling scene and sharing of national traumas marks the centre of Vorozhbyt's autoethnographic project in *Viy*. The village square becomes a true contact zone, facilitating an encounter between Ukrainians and Westerners, allowing the locals the chance to tell their own stories. Moreover, the villagers relate their narratives through a form that is expressly theirs, contesting dominant/official narratives of these traumas – narratives that so often enact their erasure – through storytelling and folkloric performance. In this scene, the Ukrainian characters use storytelling to take control of their historical narratives and of Ukrainian/non-Ukrainian interactions.

But it is only through the production realm that Vorozhbyt ultimately fulfils her mission. Although Lukas cannot understand the stories being told, the theatre audience (whether Ukrainian or not) certainly can, and Vorozhbyt has successfully found a venue in which to discuss these traumas. Indeed, in contrast with her earlier play *The Grain Store*, and despite its similar airing of unwelcome memories, Vorozhbyt's *Viy* has played quite successfully in Kyiv, its historical truths wrapped in a familiar, and palatable, Gogolian narrative. As the Ukrainian characters share their memories of trauma before the unperceiving Lukas, Vorozhbyt synecdochally shares with the audience Ukrainian memories of trauma that may be unwelcome, regardless of the listeners' identities. Moreover, Vorozhbyt's project of autoethnography wrests these narratives of trauma not just from a Western or Russian 'other', but from the Ukrainian state itself. As Wanner explains, 'New historical myths and a revised historiography encapsulated in historical representations are now the cornerstone of the new Ukrainian state's efforts to expand a sense of nation based on common historical experiences among an otherwise highly diverse and disenfranchised population.'[43] Vorozhbyt's play – and this scene in particular – suggests that these historical narratives should not belong to the Ukrainian state, but rather to the Ukrainian people.

Lukas's return home: intercultural acts of kindness

The play's final scene represents a real moment of intercultural connection, unlike anything else in Vorozhbyt's play. The dead Oksana and Lukas speak, meaningfully and directly, if only through the medium of the internet and their computers – a modern-day magic. She contacts him over Skype, and the language barrier disappears:

Oksana Hello.

Lukas Hello.

Oksana How was the flight?

Lukas Fine. I was able to change the ticket immediately, so I only lost 30 euros.

Oksana That's not much.

Lukas Stop. You speak French?

Oksana Of course not. You're speaking Ukrainian.

Lukas How can that be? . . .[44]

This is the only scene in which Lukas shares something real about himself. His brother was beaten to death two years prior, and Lukas has watched a video of the beating, despite it being 'long and degrading'.[45] He offers to send Oksana the video, and she accepts. Oksana asks him to complete his vigil, to release her into the next world: 'Please. The ritual is idiotic. I didn't think it up. It's a trifle you can do for another person. A trifle. And I'll say hi to your brother for you.'[46] Lukas retrieves the computer printouts of the prayers, lights a candle and begins to pray. As the lights fade, there is no indication that this evening will resemble the final, fatal night of prayer in Gogol's story. It is not out of fear or religious devotion that Lukas prays. Rather, it is an act of kindness freely undertaken, facilitated by twenty-first-century technology. Oksana once again needs something from Lukas: the ritual (however 'idiotic') and the interpersonal act of kindness that underlies it. If earlier she needed Lukas because he was different, then in this final moment she needs the real connection with him. She offers in return to say hello to his deceased brother. This, then, is a moment in which she also finds the strength to give back to another human being. Paradoxically, the two find this connection only through the distance that separates them.

Vorozhbyt's play traces a progression of the Ukrainian characters' developing relationships with Lukas and, by extension, the West. Lukas's presence, despite the varying levels of linguistic barriers, facilitates moments of emotional outpouring, the ritualistic storytelling of national traumas, and expressions of human intimacy for the Ukrainian characters. Yet, although Lukas's arrival catalyses the chain of events and encounters, they are not about him: whether Lukas is changed by his visit to Ukraine is not the point. Rather, Vorozhbyt is concerned with how the Ukrainians are shaped by these meetings with Lukas, and how they might develop – or prove themselves – as subjects through their encounter with the Western 'other'.

Viy in production

As an autoethnographic work, *Viy* (to quote Pratt) has had multiple audiences and a 'highly indeterminate' reception. We cannot examine this play as a work of autoethnography without also considering its transnational production history and the diverse set of meanings that this history reveals in Vorozhbyt's text. What happens to this Ukrainian play when it is performed in Russian, by Russians and for Russians, as a representative sample of contemporary Russian drama (at a theatre associated with Russian 'New Drama')? What happens to the same text when it is performed in Ukrainian, by Ukrainians and for Ukrainians (or by these same Ukrainians directly for a Western audience), as a work related to a classic author (Gogol), long co-opted by Russia, who has lately been reclaimed as canonically *Ukrainian*?[47]

Despite being unperformed for its originally intended Swiss audience, *Viy* has received several key productions in Russia and Ukraine, two of which I discuss here.[48] The first Moscow production opened in 2013 at the Centre for Playwriting and Directing (TsDR; Tsentr dramaturgii i rezhissury) and was directed by Denis Azarov (b. 1986), a Moscow theatre director who got his start as a director in opera and musical theatre.[49] Vorozhbyt herself has commented that the production that most 'got' her text was the Ukrainian-language production directed by the then-unknown Ukrainian director Maksim Golenko (b. 1978). That production, which was entitled *Viy 2.0*, premiered in 2014 at Kyiv's Bilyts Art Centre and was remounted in 2016 by Kyiv's Wild Theatre (Dikiy Teatr).[50] The Russian TsDR and the Ukrainian Bilyts/Dikiy productions each expanded on the themes of intercultural and interlinguistic conflict in the play.

A Russian audience of *Viy* – such as the play received in its staging at Moscow's TsDR – necessarily encounters in it two groups of others: the Frenchmen and the Ukrainians. Thus, while Vorozhbyt engaged in autoethnography in writing her play – writing from the periphery to the centre – the TsDR production risked undoing this autoethnographic element, hindering transcultural dialogue in its co-opting of Vorozhbyt's language and images. In production, the play became a lark on the crazy superstitions and habits of the Ukrainian villagers. Despite Russia's geographical and cultural proximity to Ukraine, the TsDR staging of *Viy* emphasized the greater comparative foreignness of the Ukrainian characters to their French counterparts through both linguistic and staging choices.

The most significant 'othering' of the Ukrainians took place linguistically. Although the entire play was performed in Russian, the 'French' lines and 'Ukrainian' lines were separated. 'Ukrainian'-speaking characters delivered their own lines, while the two Frenchmen were dubbed by an actress sitting at a downstage café table. As the scenes played out in the back half of the stage space, the actress read the 'French' lines from the script in Russian in a crisp, calm voice, as if it were a dubbed foreign film. The actors moved and gestured as normal, but their lips did not move. Dissonance ensued: the back-and-forth conversation with the local villagers resulted in two separate planes of speakers and two disparate emotional pitches. The villagers and the Frenchmen became more and more excited, while the actress continued to read the lines in an even tone. Thus, the spoken 'Ukrainian' tended to be excited and frantic in pitch, while the spoken 'French' (as voiced by the only person in the staging marked as 'Russian' – a representative of the civilizing centre in contrast with the barbarities of the periphery) was always calm and collected.

Costuming and characterization choices exaggerated the unsophistication of the villagers, who were described in the programme as 'the wild inhabitants of the modern Ukrainian interior'.[51] Men and women drank to exhaustion, wore black-and-white track pants with white sleeveless undershirts (or, for the wedding, gaudy and risqué attire), and frequently positioned themselves in 'squats', thus playing on the *gopnik* stereotype in Soviet and post-Soviet culture.[52] In contrast with these stereotype-laden portrayals of the Ukrainians as boorish and provincial, the Frenchmen in the TsDR staging wore suit jacket or button-down shirt and appeared suitably bewildered by the mannerisms in the village.

Unlike the TsDR production, which was performed by a Russian theatre for a Russian audience (thus subduing Vorozhbyt's act of autoethnography by removing an element of the Ukrainian from her Ukrainian play), the Ukrainian Bilyts/Dikiy production was performed by a Ukrainian theatre for Ukrainians. The linguistic soundscape could only be fully legible to a Ukrainian audience dually fluent in the Ukrainian and Russian languages. Whereas the TsDR production used dubbed Russian for the Frenchmen, allowing the entire play to be rendered in a single language, the Bilyts/Dikiy production rendered the play's internal language barrier visible through a mix of French, Ukrainian and Russian. The Ukrainian characters spoke Ukrainian. The Frenchmen, conversely, spoke either French or Russian. In the opening scenes, they spoke French, and then a woman sitting offstage repeated their lines in Russian. Later, the actors playing Frenchmen reverted to simply speaking Russian (the offstage female interpreter no longer participated). This production thus reproduced a pattern common to language politics in contemporary Ukraine, in which 'Ukrainian language and culture [is associated] with the rural sphere and Russian with the urban sphere'.[53] Crucially, however, the production's use of Russian for the Frenchmen served subtly to overlay on to the play a Ukrainian/Russian dichotomy (in which Ukrainian/Ukraine is central and Russian/Russia is the 'other'/periphery, a direct inversion of the historical pattern), despite the fact that Vorozhbyt's written play text does not deal with Russia at all.

If Vorozhbyt's primary concern in this play is interlinguistic and intercultural conflict in the contact zone of a contemporary Ukrainian village, then these two productions suggest different ways in which these conflicts can play out. For the Russian (TsDR) production, the language barrier was rendered mute, the French words dubbed into Russian like a badly imported film. The intercultural conflict was more caricatured than terrifying or mystical, as Ukrainian characters seemed at points merely embodiments of common stereotypes. And yet, poking fun at Ukraine or at Ukrainians was hardly the point of this production. Rather, staged as part of a larger tradition of 'New Drama' and contemporary playwriting in Russia, the play as it was brought to life in this production might be read as a commentary on the poor prospects of today's youth (of Russia as much as of Ukraine), who idle away their lives with alcohol, drugs, sex, parties and technology. In contrast, the Ukrainian (Bilyts/Dikiy) production rendered the language barrier paramount, suggesting that one's spoken language and one's worldview are inextricably connected. And yet, just as the TsDR production was hardly all negative in its portrayal of Ukrainians, this production was not solely positive. Rather, real social ills – drinking, violence, hopeless prospects – were portrayed, in a staging so much in proximity to the audience that, as Vorozhbyt hoped, the spectator could not help but 'see himself' on the stage.

Conclusion

Vorozhbyt constructs her play as a vehicle for intercultural communication between Ukraine and the outside world. Her play calls for – and assumes – the presence of a transnational witness to its addressing of contemporary Ukrainian concerns, but she very much writes for a Ukrainian audience, wanting them to see themselves embodied on the stage. The play offers a space of mourning for the losses of twentieth-century Ukrainian history and also one of celebration for the country's cultural traditions. Her project might thus be considered in dialogue with Gogol's own in writing *Viy*: she uses opposing tactics to achieve what is arguably a consonant purpose. Bojanowska contends that although Gogol directed *Viy* and his other Ukrainian stories towards a Russian audience, his objective in writing them was to foster a Ukrainian nationalism in dialogue with the Russian nationalism of the era. As she explains, Gogol's Ukrainian stories do a fair amount of 'pandering to the Russians' assumptions about Ukraine' in order to make the subject matter 'palatable and attractive', but Gogol simultaneously 'undermines the imperial project' of Russia by highlighting 'the preimperial glory' of its past, thus advancing his own purposes.[54] Vorozhbyt is uninterested in pandering, but she is absolutely invested in fostering a Ukrainian nationalism and in doing so before the captive, transnational audience of her theatre space.

Notes

1   I base my analysis on and quote from the Russian-language text that was read at the Liubimovka and later made available on the website of Russia's Golden Mask Festival.

This script includes songs and some early, atmospheric dialogue in Ukrainian. The haste with which this translation was produced is evidenced from the scattered Ukrainian words that remain in the text as obvious errors, as in a late scene in which a line of dialogue from the inspector (*sledovatel'*) is randomly labelled with the Ukrainian-language word *slidchii* (p. 23), or the sporadic use of the Ukrainian *vsi* instead of the Russian *vse* to indicate that everyone is speaking (p. 29). Natal'ia Vorozhbyt, *Viy. Dokudrama*, GoldenMask.ru, http://download.goldenmask.ru/doki/konkurs_konkursov/Vorojbit.doc (accessed 1 December 2014).

2   Ekaterina Sergatskova, 'Natal'ia Vorozhbyt: Segodnia p'esy zachastuiu osnovyvaiutsia na real'nykh sobytiiakh', *Ukraïns'ka Pravda*, 4 April 2016, https://life.pravda.com.ua/

3   Nikolai Gogol, *Viy*, in *Vechera na khutore bliz Dikan'ki. Mirgorod* (Khar'kov, 1989), 348. Translation quoted from Nikolai Gogol, *Viy*, in *The Collected Tales of Nikolai Gogol*, trans. Richard Pevear and Larissa Volokhonsky (New York: Vintage, 1998), 192.

4   Gogol, *Viy*, 317; translation quoted from Pevear and Volokhonsky, 155.

5   Although the events that Gogol narrates in *Viy* do bear some resemblance to extant folk stories (particularly when the witch rides Khoma across the countryside), the story's feared namesake bears no resemblance to any known legend. Daniel Rancour-Laferriere offers a summation of scholars on this point, before concluding that 'The footnote is thus likely to be a pseudo-documentary device designed to build up certain expectations'. Rancour-Laferriere, 'The Identity of Gogol''s Vij', *Harvard Ukrainian Studies* 2, no. 2 (1978): 214–15.

6   Yuliya Ilchuk, 'Nikolai Gogol's Self-Fashioning in the 1830s: The Postcolonial Perspective', *Canadian Slavonic Papers/Revue Canadienne des Slavistes* 51, no. 2/3 (2009): 204.

7   On Russian imaginings of Ukraine, see Myroslav Shkandrij, *Russia and Ukraine: Literature and the Discourse of Empire from Napoleonic to Postcolonial Times* (Montreal: McGill-Queen's University Press, 2001), especially chapters 2 and 3. Shkandrij argues that Ukraine and its people have historically been portrayed in Russian culture as backward and in need of the civilizing influence of Russian: 'a people who have not progressed, who, in contrast to Russians, have preserved a patriarchal style of life' (p. 77). On Western imaginings of Ukraine, see for example Giulia Lami, 'Ukraine's Road to Europe: Still a Controversial Issue', in *Contemporary Ukraine on the Cultural Map of Europe*, ed. Larissa M. L. Zaleska Onyshkevych and Maria G. Rewakowicz (Armonk, NY: M. E. Sharpe, 2009), pp. 29–39. Lami writes that 'common knowledge about Ukraine' is scarce in Europe (and specifically in Italy), 'because of old attitudes that Eastern countries are the Soviet Union's territory, worthy of consideration only when something happens' (p. 36).

8   Mary Louise Pratt, 'Arts of the Contact Zone', *Profession*, 1991, 35. I come to Pratt through Edyta M. Bojanowska, who scaffolds her reading of Gogol on Pratt's theory. Edyta M. Bojanowska, *Nikolai Gogol: Between Ukrainian and Russian Nationalism* (Cambridge, MA: Harvard University Press, 2007), 40–5.

9   Orest Subtelny writes: 'Ukraine means borderland. It is an appropriate name for a land that lies on the southeastern edge of Europe, on the threshold of Asia, along the fringes of the Mediterranean world, and astride the once important border between sheltering forest and the open steppe.' Orest Subtelny, *Ukraine: A History*, 3rd edn (Toronto: University of Toronto Press, 2000), 3.

10 Pratt, 'Arts of the Contact Zone', 34.

11 TsDR; Tsentr dramaturgii i rezhissury, *Viy*, production programme, 2013.

12 'Natal'ia Vorozhbyt: Zriteliu nuzhno delat' bol'no', *Ukraïns'ka Pravda*, 13 May 2011, https://life.pravda.com/

13 John Freedman, 'Russko-Ukrainskaia granitsa: Kievskie dramaturgi Maksym Kurochkin i Natal'ia Vorozhbyt o protivorechivykh otnosheniiakh s russkim iazykom', Teatral-online.ru, 24 June 2014, http://www.teatral-online.ru/news/11827/
14 In the Russian-language version of Vorozhbyt's *Viy*, Lukas's lines in this scene and through much of the play are written in Russian, just as the Ukrainian characters' lines are. We are meant to understand, however, that the characters are speaking variously French and Ukrainian. Productions in Ukraine and Russia have tackled the language divide in radically different ways, as I will discuss.
15 Vorozhbyt, *Viy*, 12.
16 Ibid., 12–13. I have made a distinction between transliterating *bliad'*/whore and translating 'fuck off' to indicate that, presumably, Lukas reverts to his native language for the latter obscenity.
17 Ibid., 13.
18 Conversely, Oksana (as Dren'ka) rebuffs the advances of Damian, who does speak Ukrainian and whom she personally invited to Ukraine.
19 Kolia dons his own suit of national Ukrainian dress (ibid., 15), stating that when he proposed to Oksana, he had suggested a modern white dress and veil, but she had insisted on wearing 'what my granny wore' (ibid., 17). The Ukrainian folklorist Natalie Kononenko suggests that such a practice is not uncommon today in the former Soviet republics, 'as a way to express . . . anti-Soviet sentiments'. Natalie Kononenko, *Slavic Folklore: A Handbook* (Westport, CT: Greenwood Press, 2007), 54. On the role of the best man (*druzhko* or *boiaryn*) in a traditional Slavic wedding, see ibid., 52.
20 Vorozhbyt, *Viy*, 27.
21 On *rusalki*, see Kononenko, *Slavic Folklore*, 18–19.
22 Vorozhbyt, *Viy*, 28.
23 Ibid.
24 In response to a question about whether he saw *rusalki*, Lukas responds affirmatively if dismissively: 'Yes, like a cartoon.' To a follow-up question about the malevolent *mavki*, Lukas responds, 'Like the Moulin Rouge in the 1930s, or comics'. And to a final question from Damian, asking if he was really not afraid of anything – a question that immediately precedes the question about the Viy – Lukas responds, 'I've heard scarier things on my MP3'. Ibid., 28.
25 He tells Oksana in the final Skype exchange that 'It was a great show'. He elaborates: 'You guys pulled off a terrific trick. Your country has a great future with 3-D animation like that.' Ibid., 33.
26 Gogol, *Viy*, p. 349; translation quoted from Pevear and Volokhonsky, 193.
27 Vorozhbyt, *Viy*, 29.
28 My observation about Lukas's necessity in this scene resonates with Kononenko's reflections on her data collection in rural Ukraine. Musing on her role as external witness to villagers' storytelling sessions, Kononenko writes: 'If the women whom I was interviewing could involve me emotionally in their lives through performance, as they did, if they could control the interaction between us through their assuming the role of performer instead of respondent, as they did, then perhaps they could take control of their lives in the very turbulent and confusing post-Soviet world. If in some small way I facilitated their dealing with Ukrainian independence, then I can be proud that I gave something in return for the powerful religious stories that my respondents shared with me.' Natalie Kononenko, 'How God Paired Men and Women: Stories and Religious Revival in Post-Soviet Rural Ukraine', *Canadian-American Slavic Studies* 44 (2010), 140.
29 Vorozhbyt, *Viy*, 29.

30 Catherine Wanner, *Burden of Dreams: History and Identity in Post-Soviet Ukraine* (University Park, PA, 1998), 40.
31 Ibid., 214, n. 16.
32 Ibid., 43.
33 Molly Flynn, '*Maidan: Voices from the Uprising*: Molly Flynn Interviews Natalya Vorozhbyt about Her New Documentary Theatre Piece', *CEEL*, 19 May 2014, http://ceel.org.uk/
34 Wanner, *Burden of Dreams*, 191.
35 Wilfried Jilge, 'The Politics of History and the Second World War in Post-Communist Ukraine (1986/1991–2004/2005)', *Jahrbücher für Geschichte Osteuropas* 54, no. 1 (2006): 50.
36 Poland also signed this declaration. Damien Sharkov, 'Ukraine and Poland Point to Soviet Culpability for World War II', *Newsweek*, 21 October 2016, https://www.newsweek.com/ukraine-and-poland-point-soviet-culpability-wwii-512449
37 Jilge, 'The Politics of History', 50.
38 Tom Burridge, 'Chernobyl Disaster: Ukraine Marks 30th Anniversary', BBC News, 26 April 2016, https://www.bbc.co.uk/news/world-europe-36136286
39 The most widely cited estimate of Chernobyl's human cost is a 2005 report from the UN's Chernobyl Forum, which suggested that upwards of 4000 people will eventually die from Chernobyl-related cancers. John Bohannon, 'Panel Puts Eventual Chornobyl Death Toll in Thousands', *Science* 309, no. 5741 (2005): 1663. But see also Greenpeace, 'Chernobyl Death Toll Grossly Underestimated', 18 April 2006, https://wayback.archive-it.org/9650/20191115144840/http://p3-raw.greenpeace.org/international/en/news/features/chernobyl-deaths-180406/. Wanner noted in 1998 that Chernobyl had been largely erased from post-Soviet Ukrainian discourse. See *Burden of Dreams*, 100, 151. Although the situation has changed in the past two decades – with Ukraine hosting a thirtieth anniversary commemoration at the local and national level in 2016 – Chernobyl is still not given a regular day of commemoration on the official calendar.
40 Will Englund, 'Chernobyl a Milestone on the Road to Ukrainian Independence', *The Washington Post*, 24 April 2011, https://www.washingtonpost.com/world/chernobyl-a-milestone-on-the-road-to-ukrainian-independence/2011/04/22/AFRghNdE_story.html
41 Vorozhbyt, *Viy*, 30. Ded Iavtukh is the village's oldest resident and the only character in Vorozhbyt's play who shares a name with one from Gogol's story.
42 Ibid.
43 Wanner, *Burden of Dreams*, xxiv.
44 Vorozhbyt, *Viy*, 33.
45 Ibid., 34.
46 Ibid.
47 On the question of Gogol's nationality, see, for example, Uilleam Blacker, who writes that 'for a long time, Gogol was not fully accepted into the Ukrainian cultural canon. He had sold out to the empire, in contrast to the great Taras Shevchenko, Ukraine's national poet, who not only founded a Ukrainian literary language, just as Pushkin did for Russian, but also suffered for it ... In the popular imagination, both writers' reputations were coloured by imperial and anti-imperial politics: Gogol became a villain for some in Ukraine for embracing Russia, while Shevchenko was a hero for rejecting it.' However, Blacker concludes, 'Things change: Gogol is accepted by many today as a figure who spans two cultures' ('Blurred Lines, Russian Literature and Cultural Diversity in Ukraine', *Calvert Journal*, 17 March 2014, https://www.calvertjournal.com/articles/show/2176/russian-culture-in-ukraine-literature). Cutting

through debates over Gogol's nationality, Bojanowska argues that '*Whether* Gogol was a Russian *or* a Ukrainian is ... the wrong question to ask'. Rather, she suggests that we consider '*how* Gogol's writings participated in the discourses of *both* Russian and Ukrainian nationalism' (p. 6).

48 The premiere production of *Viy* (which I do not analyse here) was in Russian and opened in February 2013 at the Volkov Theatre in Yaroslavl'. This production, which was widely recognized in Russian theatre festivals, was directed by the St Petersburg director Semyon Serzin (b. 1987).
49 I attended a performance of *Viy* at TsDR in September 2013. This production, which premiered on 22 June 2013, was listed by the Russian literary journal *Snob* as one of the twenty-five must-see productions of 2013. See Vadim Rutkovskii, 'Itogi-2013: 25 spektaklei, radi kotorykh stoit priekhat'' v Moskvu', *Snob*, 8 January 2014, https://snob.ru/selected/entry/69958/
50 The remounted production was invited to a 2016 Ukrainian theatre festival in Germany. Vorozhbyt lauded the production: 'I myself watched the production in Magdeburg as if through their eyes, and realised that they had got a really cool director, and that there were people to write for'. Oleg Bergelis, 'Natal'ia Vorozhbyt: Zhanry nashei zhizni ne razgrebet dazhe Aristotel'', *Zerkalo nedeli: Ukraina*, 4 June 2016, http://gazeta.zn.ua/. *Viy 2.0* can be viewed on YouTube
51 Tsentr dramaturgii i rezhissury, *Viy*, production programme, 2013.
52 The stereotype of the lower-class *gopnik* subculture of Russia and other post-Soviet states implies 'poorly educated young people without any special interests or prospects in life' who wear tracksuits and '"hang out" by squatting, drinking cheap beer and vodka, eating sunflower seeds and swearing at each other'. Oleg Yegorov, 'Criminals or Just Misunderstood: Who Are Russia's "Gopniks"?', *Russia Beyond*, 29 March 2016, https://www.rbth.com/politics_and_society/2016/03/29/criminals-or-just-misunderstood-who-are-russias-gopniks_580121. The image of the Ukrainian in a tracksuit is particularly ubiquitous in Western culture, as, for example, with the character Alex in the 2005 movie *Everything Is Illuminated*. See also: Ciarán Miqeladze, 'What Westerners Get Wrong about Ukraine', *PostPravda*, 11 July 2016, http://www.postpravdamagazine.com/westerners-opinions-of-ukraine/; and Sophie Pinkham, *Black Square: Adventures in Post-Soviet Ukraine* (New York: Norton, 2016), 85.
53 Laada Bilaniuk, *Contested Tongues: Language Politics and Cultural Correction in Ukraine* (Ithaca, NY: Cornell University Press, 2005), 38.
54 Bojanowska, *Nikolai Gogol*, 42.

Bibliography

Bergelis, Oleg. 'Natal'ia Vorozhbyt: Zhanry nashei zhizni ne razgrebet dazhe Aristotel''. *Zerkalo nedeli: Ukraina*, 4 June 2016. http://gazeta.zn.ua/.

Bilaniuk, Laada. *Contested Tongues: Language Politics and Cultural Correction in Ukraine*. Ithaca, NY: Cornell University Press, 2005.

Blacker, Uilleam. 'Blurred Lines, Russian Literature and Cultural Diversity in Ukraine'. *Calvert Journal*, 17 March 2014. https://www.calvertjournal.com/articles/show/2176/russian-culture-in-ukraine-literature

Bohannon, John. 'Panel Puts Eventual Chornobyl Death Toll in Thousands'. *Science* 309, no. 5741 (2005): 1663.

Bojanowska, Edyta M. *Nikolai Gogol: Between Ukrainian and Russian Nationalism.* Cambridge, MA: Harvard University Press, 2007.
Burridge, Tom. 'Chernobyl Disaster: Ukraine Marks 30th Anniversary'. BBC News, 26 April 2016. https://www.bbc.co.uk/news/world-europe-36136286/
Englund, Will. 'Chernobyl a Milestone on the Road to Ukrainian Independence'. *The Washington Post*, 24 April 2011. https://www.washingtonpost.com/world/chernobyl-a-milestone-on-the-road-to-ukrainian-independence/2011/04/22/AFRghNdE_story.html
Flynn, Molly. '*Maidan: Voices from the Uprising*. Molly Flynn Interviews Natalya Vorozhbyt about Her New Documentary Theatre Piece'. *CEEL*, 19 May 2014. http://ceel.org.uk/
Gogol, Nikolai. *Viy*. In *Vechera na khutore bliz Dikan'ki: Mirgorod*, 317–49. Khar'kov: Prapor, 1989.
Gogol, Nikolai. *Viy*. In *The Collected Tales of Nikolai Gogol*, translated by Richard Pevear and Larissa Volokhonsky, 155–93. New York: Vintage, 1998.
Greenpeace. 'Chernobyl Death Toll Grossly Underestimated', 18 April 2006. https://wayback.archive-it.org/9650/20191115144840/http://p3-raw.greenpeace.org/international/en/news/features/chernobyl-deaths-180406/
Ilchuk, Yuliya. 'Nikolai Gogol's Self-Fashioning in the 1830s: The Postcolonial Perspective'. *Canadian Slavonic Papers/Revue Canadienne des Slavistes* 51, no. 2/3 (2009): 203–21.
Jilge, Wilfried. 'The Politics of History and the Second World War in Post-Communist Ukraine (1986/1991–2004/2005)'. *Jahrbücher für Geschichte Osteuropas* 54, no. 1 (2006): 50–81.
Kononenko, Natalie. 'How God Paired Men and Women: Stories and Religious Revival in Post-Soviet Rural Ukraine'. *Canadian-American Slavic Studies* 44 (2010): 118–50.
Kononenko, Natalie. *Slavic Folklore: A Handbook.* Westport, CT: Greenwood Press, 2007.
Kurochkin, Maksim, and Natal'ia Vorozhbyt. 'Russko-Ukrainskaia granitsa: Kievskie dramaturgi Maksim Kurochkin i Natal'ia Vorozhbyt o protivorechivykh otnosheniiakh s russkim iazykom'. By John Freedman. Teatral-online.ru, 24 June 2014. http://www.teatral-online.ru/news/11827/
Lami, Giulia. 'Ukraine's Road to Europe: Still a Controversial Issue'. In *Contemporary Ukraine on the Cultural Map of Europe*, edited by Larissa M. L. Zaleska Onyshkevych and Maria G. Rewakowicz, 29–39. Armonk, NY: M. E. Sharpe, 2009.
Miqeladze, Ciarán. 'What Westerners Get Wrong about Ukraine'. *PostPravda*, 11 July 2016. http://www.postpravdamagazine.com/westerners-opinions-of-ukraine/
'Natal'ia Vorozhbyt: Zriteliu nuzhno delat' bol'no'. *Ukraïns'ka Pravda*, 13 May 2011. https://life.pravda.com/
Pinkham, Sophie. *Black Square: Adventures in Post-Soviet Ukraine.* New York: Norton, 2016.
Pratt, Mary Louise. 'Arts of the Contact Zone'. *Profession*, 1991: 33–40.
Rancour-Laferriere, Daniel. 'The Identity of Gogol's Vij'. *Harvard Ukrainian Studies* 2, no. 2 (1978): 211–34.
Rutkovskii, Vadim. 'Itogi-2013: 25 spektaklei, radi kotorykh stoit priekhat' v Moskvu'. *Snob*, 8 January 2014. https://snob.ru/selected/entry/69958/
Sergatskova, Ekaterina. 'Natal'ia Vorozhbyt: Segodnia p'esy zachastuiu osnovyvaiutsia na real'nykh sobytiiakh'. *Ukraïns'ka Pravda*, 4 April 2016. https://life.pravda.com.ua/
Sharkov, Damien. 'Ukraine and Poland Point to Soviet Culpability for World War II'. *Newsweek*. 21 October 2016. https://www.newsweek.com/ukraine-and-poland-point-soviet-culpability-wwii-512449

Shkandrij, Myroslav. *Russia and Ukraine: Literature and the Discourse of Empire from Napoleonic to Postcolonial Times*. Montreal: McGill-Queen's University Press, 2001.
Subtelny, Orest. *Ukraine: A History*. 3rd edn. Toronto: University of Toronto Press, 2000.
Tsentr dramaturgii i rezhissury. *Viy*. Production program. 2013. Author's collection.
Vorozhbyt, Natal'ia. *Viy. Dokudrama*. GoldenMask.ru. http://download.goldenmask.ru/doki/konkurs_konkursov/Vorojbit.doc (accessed 1 December 2014).
Wanner, Catherine. *Burden of Dreams: History and Identity in Post-Soviet Ukraine*. University Park, PA: Pennsylvania State University Press, 1998.
Yegorov, Oleg. 'Criminals or Just Misunderstood: Who Are Russia's "Gopniks"?', *Russia Beyond*. 29 March 2016. https://www.rbth.com/politics_and_society/2016/03/29/criminals-or-just-misunderstood-who-are-russias-gopniks_580121

Part III

Belarus

15

The transformation of the language of 'New Drama' in Belarus, as a reflection of a new model of identity

Tania Arcimovich

> The cultural commentator Tania Arcimovich considers the evolution of 'New Drama' in Belarus since the early 2000s, and the opportunities which Russian theatres have offered to Belarusian authors during this period. She notes the phenomenon of 'bilingualism' (mixing Russian with Belarusian), as well as plays which additionally use the hybrid Belarusian/Russian dialect known as 'trasianka'. Tania reflects specifically on the switch away from the use of Russian by playwrights towards using the Belarusian language in recent years, seeing this as a response to international political events, and also as a step towards a redefinition of Belarusian national identity.

'New Drama' emerged in Belarus at the beginning of the 2000s as a purely Russian-language phenomenon. Due to the power of its documentary effect in a country where the majority of the population speaks Russian, the Belarusian language simply did not seem appropriate for the writing of such plays – this is something which Belarusian playwrights have themselves spoken about. But the annexation of Crimea by the Russians in 2014 and the beginning of the conflict in Ukraine became, in their own way, 'triggers' for a new generation of writers: suddenly 'New Drama' spoke out here in the Belarusian language. And it then turned out not only that its documentary effect was not lost, but that on the contrary it became even stronger: the use of the Belarusian language simply extended the range of instruments at the playwrights' disposal, allowing them to describe everyday life in Belarus at different levels of society, and thus enabling them to reveal the unique social and cultural features of this land.

This essay describes and analyses this process of the transformation of the language fields of 'New Drama' in Belarus, focusing on their political power. I suggest that this turning away from Russian-language plays towards Belarusian ones constitutes a new model of Belarusian identity, and makes visible some of the political processes that have taken place in the post-Soviet space in general.

'New Drama' in Belarus: the early 2000s

There are numerous definitions of 'New Drama', and they range from the rather broad, as in 'it just means new plays' (Kirill Serebrennikov),[1] or 'any play written by modern people about their contemporaries' (Pavel Rudnev),[2] to the more specific, as in 'a theatrical movement' and 'a distinct socio-cultural phenomenon, and the most typical segment of contemporary Russian drama' (Il'mira Bolotian).[3] In this instance 'Russian drama' stands automatically for 'Russian-language drama'. Most researchers define 'New Drama' simply as being a post-Soviet phenomenon across the whole region, and therefore the author's nationality has not been held to reflect any separate strand within the movement.

Scholars believe that the main reason for the rise of 'New Drama' in the post-Soviet region lies in historical circumstances: the collapse of the Soviet Union and, consequently, the crises (economic, political and intellectual) of post-Soviet society. Mark Lipovetsky and Birgit Beumers describe New Drama as 'a reaction to the identity crisis'.[4] Theatre in the post-Soviet region found itself in stagnation. Not only did a total need for renewal become obvious, but also the need to have contemporary heroes on stage, especially ones who previously had had no voice and who found themselves facing new identity challenges; that is, the challenges of their new, post-Soviet identities.

In Belarus the 'New Drama' movement was closely related at first to the Russian drama festivals of the 2000s. At that time, the Liubimovka Festival in Moscow and the May Readings in Togliatti were actively establishing themselves, the 'New Drama' Festival and the Eurasia Contest were launched, and in 2002 Teatr.doc opened. Winners from Belarus began to appear on their shortlists more and more often, playwrights such as Andrei Kureichik, Nicolai Khalezin, Pavel Priazhko, Konstantin Steshik and others. The period of 2002–4 saw the emergence of several new Belarusian authors, although not all their plays would later be categorized as 'New Drama'. And right up until the present, every year, almost every Russian competition and festival programme includes the names of Belarusian playwrights. Thus, for example, there were plays by Aleksandr Savukh, Maksim Dos'ko and Konstantin Steshik as well as Dmitry Bogoslavsky in the shortlist of the 2017 Liubimovka Festival.[5]

However, the theory of 'New Drama' is problematic for the Belarusian context. Quite apart from the general questions of definition, we have two completely separate linguistic registers of modern drama here – Russian and Belarusian. Plays written in Belarusian represent only a small segment of Belarusian modern drama: one reason for that is the limited market for those plays within the country. Moreover, the plays that are written in Belarusian could mostly be categorized as literary theatre, where the author creates an autonomous, rather than a documentary theatrical reality.

In her analysis of plays by Konstantin Steshik, Pavel Priazhko and Andrei Kureichik, the Belarusian scholar Svetlana Goncharova-Grabovskaia describes them as examples of modern Russophone Belarusian drama, which is 'a part of Belarusian drama', with an inherent link to Russian drama.[6] But her argument that Belarusian authors write in Russian under the influence of Russian 'New Drama' seems controversial to my mind. Firstly, the reasons for their common intonations and forms should be sought not in the influence of one geographical and cultural space upon another, but in the phenomenon of post-Sovietism in general, which is what replaced the Soviet paradigm. This interpretation can be supported, for example, by the fact that one playwright from Belarus, Pavel Priazhko, has himself had a strong influence on the evolution of 'New Drama' within Russia.

Secondly, one of the reasons for the emergence of Russian-language 'New Drama' in Belarus was its orientation towards documentary theatre. As the Belarusian literary critic and playwright Siarhiej Kavaliou notes:

> This kind of drama is based on the language of the streets. Most Belarusians speak in Russian or in *trasianka* (a mixed form of speech in which Belarusian and Russian elements and structures alternate in rapid succession). And so, if a playwright wants to reflect the language of the streets and the mentality of the people around him, he has to write in Russian.[7]

Another reason for the domination of the Russian language in Belarusian theatre is what Kavaliou describes as the way in which young authors can be influenced: 'Theatre is not only about creativity, but also about production. An author who writes in Russian can offer his works not just to three Belarusian-speaking theatres, but to three hundred theatres.'[8] According to the statistics, in 2016 there were twenty-eight state theatres in Belarus, only four of which work using Belarusian, while the rest are Russian-speaking, with only a small number of bilingual theatres. My essay focuses on the Belarusian 'New Drama' that works with the spoken language of the street to achieve a representation of the social and political processes in our society.

Language as the main mechanism of representation is still a key tool in Belarusian theatre and, I would argue, in the post-Soviet space in general. Perhaps that is why 'New Drama', based on a novel use of the language, became so popular here at the beginning of the 2000s. Kirill Serebrennikov notes that 'text plays a decisive role in 'New Drama' [...] One of its triumphs is the recording of a new linguistic reality [...] The relationship between language and reality had previously become monstrously and absurdly distorted.'[9] I wonder whether the group of theatre-makers from the Royal Court who in 1999 held seminars in Moscow about documentary theatre could ever have guessed that this tool would determine the direction of all modern post-Soviet drama and theatres for decades to come. It seems to me that 'New Drama' was not only a reaction to the state of stagnation and crisis in theatre, but it has also become the vehicle for the representation of often hidden practices of everyday violence in the post-Soviet space. And its main instrument became the Russian language.

Historical context: language as a political field

The formation of the Belarusian language took place during the fourteenth to sixteenth centuries, when the territory of modern Belarus formed a part of the Grand Duchy of Lithuania. At the end of the sixteenth century the territory became part of another political formation – the Commonwealth of Poland – and then in the late eighteenth century most of its territory was transferred to the Russian Empire. In fact, the Russian

Empress Catherine II promptly issued a decree according to which all legislative activity in the North-West Territory, as Belarus was then called, was to be conducted in Russian. Gradually the Belarusian language was displaced to the periphery of political, social and cultural life, remaining the language of communication only for mundane, everyday interactions. In 1905, after the First Russian Revolution, the Russian Imperial authorities officially permitted the use of the Belarusian language in printed publications. In the 1920s, this time under the Soviet Empire, there was a period called Belarusization, when the Belarusian language officially became one of the state languages (alongside Russian, Polish and Yiddish, which reflected the multicultural situation in Belarus at that time).

At the end of the 1920s Belarusization was halted. In 1933 a decree 'On Changes and the Simplification of Belarusian Spelling' was signed. It was the start of a process of standardization of the Belarusian language. Most of the leading figures of Belarusian culture, as well as writers and poets whose names had been associated with the revival of Belarusian culture and language, were persecuted during the Stalinist Terror in the late 1930s (shot or exiled to camps). According to the Belarusian researcher Leanid Marakou, 90 per cent of all writers, and 25,000 intellectuals in general, suffered repressions in this way.[10] A similar scenario was implemented in Ukraine during this period. After the Second World War, a campaign of 'ideological struggle against any manifestations of nationalism' unfolded in the Belarus Soviet Republic, provoked by the anti-Soviet nationalist partisan movement which arose there during the Nazi occupation. That movement was eliminated by the mid-1950s (its members too were shot, or exiled to labour camps). The homogenization of education, and a specific language policy, became the priority for the Soviet authorities. In 1952, the Central Committee of the Communist Party limited the teaching of the history of Belarus and culture at the Belarusian State University; the Belarusian language was soon displaced, and the Department of Belarusian History was closed down. Gradually, Russian began to be perceived as the language of the city and of nomenclature elites; at the same time Belarusian was becoming more and more the language of the villages, and of the suburbs. According to statistics, in 1946 the circulation of magazines in Russian in the Belarus Soviet Republic was 1 per cent; but by 1955 it reached 31 per cent. In 1970 the total circulation of Belarusian-language books was 9 million copies, whereas Russian-language books were about 16 million.[11]

From 26 January 1990 to 14 May 1995 (five years, three months and nineteen days) the Belarusian language was declared to be the only state language of the Republic, and this was confirmed in its new, post-Soviet Constitution. In 1995 a Republic-wide referendum initiated by the new President Alexander Lukashenko was held, and the Russian language was granted the status of the second state language. But obviously, this was not a question of real equality. The leftist and feminist researcher Heidi Hartmann has compared the union of Marxism and feminism with a 'marriage' which is in reality one thing only, and that one thing is Marxism. We can say the same about the 'marriage' of the Russian and Belarusian languages, when that always really means that Russian prevails. According to the statistics, in 1999 about 73 per cent of the population reported that Belarusian was their native language, but only 37 per cent of inhabitants spoke it in everyday life. We can compare this with the data from 2009, when 53 per cent of the citizens still marked Belarusian as their mother tongue, but only 23 per cent really used it.¹² In 2009, UNESCO listed Belarusian as an endangered language.

In her article 'The Nation in Between; or, Why Intellectuals Do Things with Words', Elena Gapova tells the story of a doctor of her acquaintance, who in the late Soviet period came to Minsk from the countryside, where he had been to school and had spoken Belarusian in his everyday life, in order to enter an institute. During the entrance examinations the board of examiners listened to his replies in Belarusian with a smile: for them, he was 'a village boy'. He began to study, gradually switching over to Russian. By the time the doctor was telling Gapova this story in the mid-1990s he knew Russian and French, but could no longer speak Belarusian: 'The doctor is sure that there was no external force that made him drop his native (village) tongue; it just happened "naturally".'¹³

Could we argue that 'New Drama', which typically uses the language of the streets, is a reflection of the socio-political situation that has developed in Belarus over these decades of Russian cultural expansionism?

Representation as a way to produce meanings

In 2013 a discussion about the language of 'New Drama' was held in Minsk. Playwrights and translators alike agreed with the above hypothesis. Thus, the Belarusian translator Iryna Hierasimovich stated 'that the milieu speaks through both protagonists and the authors. It is a fact that we have a limited Belarusian milieu [...] But it is necessary to see the truth of this language situation, and not to manufacture a schizophrenic reality which does not exist.'¹⁴ There was a reading of Andrei Sauchanka's play *Bilingua, or Chicken with Heart* within the framework of the discussion day. The author presented it himself. The play takes place in modern Belarus; a main protagonist who speaks Belarusian is placed in various everyday situations (in shops, at a market, on the streets). Often the people don't understand his Belarusian, or it arouses suspicion and aggression (under President Lukashenko the Belarusian language became identified for a long time with opposition parties, whose image was rather negative and deemed to be destructive by the majority of the population). Thus, a certain conflict between different language registers in the country became apparent, and in fact Belarusian here starts to seem like a foreign language:

In the shop of the meat factory in Orsha.

Saleswoman *(speaks in 'trasianka' [a local dialect blend of Russian and Belarusian] and Russian)*   Hey, you men, what do you want?

Main protagonist *(speaks Belarusian)*   Good afternoon!

Saleswoman   Hi!

Main protagonist   You have a wide range of tinned products. I would like … 2 tins of pork with vegetables, and 2 tins of chicken with heart.

Saleswoman   There are about 30 varieties here. Can you speak more clearly?

Main protagonist But didn't I do that? Pork with vegetables and chicken with heart, two of each.

Saleswoman So I should leave everything here and go and look for those, specially for you? Say it in Russian.

Main protagonist Let's try to find them together. They're in the shop window, third row from the bottom, fourth from the left . . .

Saleswoman But can you speak Russian?

Main protagonist No, I can't, and I don't want to.

The first woman in the queue *(speaks Russian)* Hey, you do know that there are two state languages in this country?

Main protagonist Yes, I do know, and . . . ?

The first woman in the queue Teach Belarusian to your children at home if you want.

Main protagonist Thank you kindly for the permission . . .

The second person in the queue *(speaks in Russian)* He's asking for pork with vegetables, and chicken.[15]

Andrei Sauchanka uses the original languages for all the characters in the play, and these are not just two languages but, as we might say, two and a half languages, if we include the *trasianka*. And suddenly the mere use of this *trasianka* shows that it can be a real instrument for coming closer to Belarusian everyday reality. Belarusian playwrights of the 2000s, when they were recording the language of the streets, actually missed this unique characteristic of the local context, conducting their experiments within this framework exclusively in Russian, and only for Russian-language theatre spaces. Pavel Priazhko works in this way. He notes that language provides the most significant sphere for him, and he listens attentively to reality. Pavel Rudnev has stated that Priazhko transformed 'New Drama' 'from the drama of subject-matter into the drama of language'.[16] The language referred to in this instance is Russian, but I would argue that there is a broader issue about post-Soviet language(s). In this sense the play *Bilingua, or Chicken with Heart* became a talking point for modern Belarusian drama, because it provoked reflections around the Belarusian language situation. This, as it turned out, provides scope for the creation of new semantic possibilities, and allows people to consider how playwrights can take advantage of the unique language situation that we have.

There were numerous campaigns and discussions around the Belarusian language that took place at that time (for example, about using the Belarusian language in public spaces, and in commercial sectors). The annexation of the Crimea in 2014 and the subsequent conflict in Ukraine played a particular role in this process, prompting the younger generation to feel a new need for an additional public instrument to mark their own cultural autonomy. Even President Lukashenko, in various speeches, and after many years when the Belarusian language had been suppressed, suddenly began to talk about the importance of the country's native language, and in 2016 for the first time he spoke in public in Belarusian. And in this way he inaugurated a process called *soft Belarusization*. We may wonder how long this process will last, but currently it is still ongoing.

During this period more and more new plays depicting everyday life in Belarus have been emerging, either in Belarusian, or else using the full two and a half languages – for example, texts by Liokha Chykanas, Kacia Chekatouskaya, Volha Prusak, Maryya Bialkovich and others. Volha Ramanava's play *Do You Want Me to Blow Up Kempinski?* starts with this introductory explanation: '*This is a film told and partly shown by actors. The characters speak Belarusian, Russian and trasianka. The audience imagines all the details using their own visual and life experiences.*'[17]

Volha Prusak's play *Sikulakubuzuka* is based on the story of the Belarusian musician and poet Andrus Takidang, who is an Afro-American. He was born in Belarus; he has a strong sense of Belarusian self-identification, and he speaks Belarusian. In Act 3 he is coming back home in the evening, and meets a local:

Local man *(speaks in Russian)* Hey, black man!

Gabriel *(the main protagonist, he speaks in Belarusian)* Sorry, am I disturbing you in some way?

Local man Russia is for the Russians!

Gabriel I agree, and Belarusians live in Belarus. But I guess you want to ask me something?

Local man Hey, are you an antifascist?!

Gabriel Mister, don't be angry. You can have your own opinions. Let's go our own ways if you don't need any help from me.

Local man Hey, what on earth are you? Can you speak in Belarusian? You know Belarusian?

Gabriel One day in Belarus one Belarusian is amazed that another Belarusian speaks Belarusian . . . Are you kidding? But my writing is not so good, unfortunately.

Local man Who are you?

Gabriel A Belarusian of course!

Local man Ummm . . .

Gabriel Would you maybe like to try and remember where it is that people speak Belarusian? It's only here.

Local man Are you from Minsk?

Gabriel Yes, from East district.[18]

Often in these plays there is no clear boundary between the language registers. Sometimes it is only the author's stage directions and notes that are written in the

Belarusian language. Sometimes, after the Belarusian version appears, the authors translate the plays into Russian – this is once again a question of marketing. Nevertheless, using the Belarusian language begins increasingly to look like a means of underlining the author's civic position, where they talk about discrimination by using a language that is discriminated against. These 'New Drama' plays written in Belarusian describe various social situations and groups, but on the whole they do not create a schizophrenic reality, a reality that does not exist. And this has happened not only because the scope of the Belarusian language has expanded. In the wider context of the country as a whole, it still does not really play a significant role. Nevertheless, the Belarusian language has been naturally integrated into everyday life in these plays, and it serves precisely as an instrument of documentary theatre.

In describing the socio-political context at the moment in the country (soft Belarusization), I am not setting out to show Belarusian 'New Drama' as a passive, reactive force. In my opinion, it is true that culture both reacts and represents, but it also has the potential to develop (as an avant-garde phenomenon) in advance of social and political processes. Take, for example, the premiere which took place in December 2017 at the Centre for Belarusian Dramaturgy in Minsk of the show *Collective Farm Workers*, based on Pavel Priazhko's *Three Days in Hell*, directed by Cimafiej Tkachou. The play is written in Russian with elements of *trasianka*, which is the language in which all the characters whom the protagonist encounters in everyday reality speak. The original author's text of the play (*Three Days in Hell* was first written in prose) is spoken by the main character in Russian. Given the context of the provocative, Soviet-era name of the show – *Collective Farm Workers* – it would appear that by using a language marker (*trasianka* primarily characterizes citizens of a low social status and culture), the director was interpreting the play precisely in the context of class relationships, where the collective farm workers turn out to be those who do not speak Russian. But in the course of the show the main character somehow naturally switches to the Belarusian language – at first using odd words and snatches of phrases, and then suddenly the finale of the play is performed by him in pure Belarusian (the language adaptation was by Marya Pushkina). A linguistic transformation of this kind completely alters the meaning of the title as well: the use of the Russian term tends to conjure up a nostalgia for the USSR, whereas the use of Belarusian becomes a manifestation of a new *project* for Belarusian identity, which differs from the model which used to be proposed by Belarusian intellectuals during the 1990s.

Thus Elena Gapova notes that, after the collapse of the USSR, Belarusian-speaking intellectuals became the chief exponents of a 'national' project, in which city intellectuals – whose symbolic instrument became the Belarusian language – were contrasted with the less educated city working people, who came originally from the countryside and who spoke *trasianka*. 'From the very beginning "the language issue" (Belarusian versus Russian) has been at the very core of pro-independence discourse, and the *locus* of controversy: intellectuals champion it for the sake of "the people", while the ordinary folk very firmly reject it,' notes Gapova.[19] It might seem that the choice of languages in the show *Collective Farm Workers* precisely illustrates this account of the 'national' project. But Cimafiej Tkachou, just like Pavel Priazhko, deliberately chooses to remove the tensions of social class: in the finale the speakers of all the two-and-a-half languages that are prevalent in Belarus come together in a single space, thereby, as it seems, challenging the overdetermination of the national project in the terms in which 1990s intellectuals had proposed that this should be understood.

To summarize: Stuart Hall calls language a privileged medium, through which values are produced. He raises questions about how language, in the broad sense, being a system of representation, constructs meanings.[20] I would argue that the language transformations that are taking place in the linguistic field of Belarusian 'New Drama' demonstrate something more than a transition away from understanding 'New Drama' as a category of hyperrealism, and become a shift towards a system of representation. The point is that 'New Drama' does not just reflect, but can construct a new reality: in this specific context I understand this primarily as a perspective produced by the dominant discourse or ideology. In other words, returning to the story of the doctor, it is that reality which we are confident in, and which feels 'natural'. Often we expect that such art forms as 'New Drama' might somehow represent social and political reality, being an instrument for ethnography or autoethnography. My argument is that 'New Drama' is capable on its own of producing the reality that will be true, because of its representative power.

It would also be important to say that all these processes are closely related to the crisis of post-Soviet identity that is taking place right now, when in countries such as Belarus and Ukraine new identities have been starting to claim their positions. 'New Drama' has the privilege of bearing witness to reality. That is why it has a strong political potency, reflected by a new generation of Belarusian authors.

Translated from the Russian by J. A.E. Curtis

Notes

1 Kirill Serebrennikov, in Birgit Beumers and Mark Lipovetsky, *Performing Violence: Literary and Theatrical Experiments of New Russian Drama* (Intellect Books, 2009), 9.
2 Pavel Rudnev, 'Novaia drama: Punktirom' (Moscow, 2008), available at http://teatre.com.ua/modern/novaja_drama_punktyrom/ (accessed 10 October 2017).
3 Il'mira Bolotian, *Zhanrovye iskaniia v russkoi dramaturgii kontsa XX – nachala XXI veka*, (Moscow, 2008).
4 Beumers and Lipovetsky, *Performing Violence*, 34.
5 For details see Tatiana Arcimovič, 'Independent Theatre in Belarus (1980–2013)', in *Platform: East European Performing Arts Companion*, edited by Joanna Krakowska and Daria Odija, (Lublin and Warsaw: Adam Mickiewicz Institute, Centre for Culture in Lublin, 2016), pp. 176–87.
6 S. Ia. Goncharova-Grabovskaia, 'Khudozhestvennaia paradigma russkoiazychnoi dramaturgii Belarusi na rubezhe XX–XXI vv.', in *Russkoiazychnaia literatura Belarusi kontsa XX – nachala XXI veka: Sbornik nauchnykh statei* (Minsk: RIVSH, 2010), 157.
7 *Galina Bagdanava i Siarhej Kavaliou u Shkole maladoga pis'mennika* (Minsk, 2013), available at http://lit-bel.org/by/news/3655.html (accessed 12 October 2017).
8 Ibid.
9 Beumers and Lipovetsky, *Performing Violence*, 11.

10 Leanid Marakou, *Akhviary i Karniki: Davednik* (Minsk: Minsk, 2002).
11 For details see Mazanets, 'Valiantsin. Tendentsyia natsyianal'naia dziarzhaunay palityki y BSSR y 1950-ia gady', *ARCHE*, 10 (2011): 68–85.
12 For details see *The Databases of the National Statistics Committee of the Republic of Belarus*, available at: http://www.belstat.gov.by (accessed 15 October 2017).
13 Elena Gapova, 'The Nation in Between; or, Why Intellectuals Do Things with Words', in *Over the Wall/After the Fall: Post-Communist Cultures through an East–West Gaze*, (Indianapolis, IN: Indiana University Press, 2004), 69.
14 'Pra movu suchasnay belaruskay p'esy: kantekst al'bo shyzafrenichnasts'?' Discussion on 14 June 2013.
15 Andrei Sauchanka, *Bi-lingva, al'bo Kurania z sertsam* (2010). In author's private collection.
16 Rudnev, 'Novaia drama'.
17 Volha Ramanava, *Khochash, padarvu 'Kempinski'?* (2015). In author's private collection.
18 Volha Prusak, *Sikulakabuzuka* (2015). In author's private collection.
19 Gapova, 'The Nation in Between', 68.
20 Stuart Hall, *Representation: Cultural Representations and Signifying Practices* (London, 1997).

Bibliography

Beumers, Birgit, and Lipovetsky, Mark. *Performing Violence: Literary and Theatrical Experiments of New Russian Drama*. Bristol: Intellect Books, 2009.

Bolotian, I. M. Zhanrovye iskaniya v russskoy dramaturgii kontsa XX – nachala XXI veka. Candidate dissertation, Moscow, 2008.

Sauchanka, Andrei, *Bi-lingva, al'bo Kurania z sertsam* (2010 play, text in author's private collection).

Galina Bagdanava i Siarhej Kavaliou u Shkole maladoga pis'mennika (report dated 22 March 2013 about talks given at the Belarusian Union of Writers in Minsk), available at http://lit-bel.org/by/news/3655.html (accessed 12 October 2017).

Gapova, E. 'The Nation in Between; or, Why Intellectuals Do Things with Words'. In *Over the Wall/After the Fall: Post-Communist Cultures through an East–West Gaze*. Indianapolis, IN: Indiana University Press, 2004.

Goncharova-Grabovskaya, S. Ia., 'Khudozhestvennaya paradigma russkoiazychnoy dramaturgii Belarusi na rubezhe XX–XXI vv.' In *Russkoiazychnaya literatura Belarusi kontsa XX-nachala XXI veka. Sb. Nauchn, st*. Minsk: RIVSH, 2010, pp. 156–68.

Hall, Stuart. *Representation: Cultural Representations and Signifying Practices*. London: Sage, 1997.

Hartmann, Heidi. 'The Unhappy Marriage of Marxism and Feminism: Towards a More Progressive Union', *Capital Class* 3, no. 2, 1 July 1979: 1–33.

Ramanava, Volha, *Khochash, padarvu 'Kempinski'?* (2015 play, text in author's private collection).

Prusak V. *Sikulakabuzuka*. 2015. In the author's library.

Rudnev, Pavel. *Novaya drama: Punktirom*. Moscow, 2008, http://teatre.com.ua/modern/novaja_drama_punktyrom/ (accessed 10 October 2017).

16

Conversation with Natalia Koliada, Belarus Free Theatre (London, March 2019)

J. A. E. Curtis

> Natalia Koliada speaks about the history of the Belarus Free Theatre (BFT), whose founders were forced to leave Belarus and seek political asylum in 2011. She and her husband Nicolai Khalezin, together with Vladimir Shcherban, continue to train theatre students, stage events and even mount productions in Minsk, communicating with them by Skype from London. Koliada emphasises that the BFT has always been a theatre with an international outlook, speaking out about human rights issues and freedom of speech across the world as well as in Belarus, Russian and Ukraine. She also talks about the pressures and challenges facing the BFT at present.

JAEC   What was essentially a fairly free and open 'New Drama' movement across Russia, Ukraine, Belarus and the Russian-speaking countries of the post-Soviet space has become much more problematic in the last five or ten years, for obvious political reasons. You arrived in London in May 2011, and I was wondering whether you think the Belarus Free Theatre has changed in character in that time, in the last eight years? I'm thinking about the kinds of projects you do, and the kinds of audiences you're hoping to reach.

NK   That's a question I've heard many times here, since people assume that we started to tour the world after we arrived in London; and that's a major mistake, because we had already been touring to many countries before we came to London. It's interesting how people here associate our international success with our move to London, which is absolutely not true. We first discussed plans for the company in September 2004, and gave a press conference about it on 31 March 2005; and soon we were touring in Lithuania, Latvia, Finland, and then Sweden. Within a year of being established we were already touring.

JAEC   So would it be correct to say that in some ways the Belarus Free Theatre is more of an international theatre, rather than being focused mostly on Belarus?

NK It's the name ... There's a very interesting conversation that we are having with several people who are advising us at the moment, about how to establish ourselves here, how to stabilize the funding stream, and there is a suggestion that we really need to remove 'Belarus' from our name.

JAEC Really? That would be quite a dramatic step! Are you unhappy about that idea?

NK Firstly, I think it would send a very strong message to the Belarusian regime. And secondly, we should continue to fight back, pointing out that the Belarus Free Theatre is a major symbol of artistic resistance, not only for Europe and Eastern Europe, but we've been working with people in Brazil, in Ghana, Uganda, Rwanda, Nigeria and India, we were working with refugees in illegal camps in Morocco when Europe didn't even know about the European refugee crisis, because this was two years before the European refugee crisis began. And for people in those countries we're a major symbol. But they don't think about that in the organizations that provide funding streams: they just think about a group of people who are located underground in Belarus, and who continue – next year it will have been fifteen years – to resist the authorities there. So for us it's absolutely major ...

JAEC ... that you should carry on remaining involved with the Belarusian situation, you mean?

NK It's major for us to stay and work in Belarus on a daily basis, and of course we also continue to do shows and work with international audiences and with individuals from different parts of the world – but that was always part of our job.

JAEC It does seem to me that you've become spokespersons for that entire region of post-Soviet Russia and Ukraine, as well as Belarus. I was thinking, for example, about your shows *Burning Doors* (2016) and *Counting Sheep* (2019), and the fact that you feel completely comfortable speaking out on behalf of Ukraine and of Russia.

NK We feel comfortable speaking about everything!

JAEC So that's not a special role that you feel you have?

NK With the *Burning Doors* and *Counting Sheep* shows, for example, that was precisely the responsibility which we felt, that we must do something about it, because every single day when the war started people over here would ask: 'What's going in Ukraine? What's going on in Ukraine?' And this had been happening probably for a year after the Maidan started in Kyiv, and then suddenly we began to feel that this topic was disappearing from people's conversations; and it was at that moment that it became clear to us that we had to raise it, we needed to put it back on the agenda. Because there is something about all this that we understand: this year it will have been twenty-five years since the dictatorship was established in Belarus and I think everyone is missing this point – I don't know if they are simply ignoring it – but it was Aleksandr Lukashenko, better known as the last dictator in Europe, who initiated every single step in terms of human rights violations and repressions, that has been repeated by Putin, every single step that Lukashenko devised has also been taken by Putin.[1] He's just echoing what he did: so Lukashenko created the blueprint for subsequent tyrannies. And what is very upsetting is that nobody seems to want to talk about that. It's as if Belarus doesn't exist: it exists in people's minds only in the Minsk agreements [negotiated in Belarus under the auspices of the OSCE in September 2014 and February 2015, in an attempt to resolve the hostilities between Russia and Ukraine] – and that's another big conversation, about how you could have so-called peace talks in a country where a dictator has been kidnapping and killing people. But in terms of Belarus: he provided the blueprint, Putin repeated all of it, then there was Putin's puppet President Yanukovych in Ukraine, and Paul Manafort was his political consultant, then we got Brexit, and then we got Trump!

So that's why we're very interested in the wider world, and have been from the very first day of our existence.

JAEC And nothing is going to change in the Lukashenko situation for the moment?

NK No, I don't think so. And of course that's why we continue to try and draw attention to Belarus – we always still have this hope – but it's clear that there are never enough people inside the country doing anything, and there is no joint international position on the country. Nothing has ever happened in the history of mankind if there is no joint position . . . look at Brexit!

JAEC And you're still managing to stage some of your shows in Minsk, and perhaps in other towns in Belarus?

NK Last week we had the opening there of a new show, which was Beckett's *Waiting for Godot*. What has really changed, and this is beautiful, is that we have really encouraged our young actors to become directors.

JAEC This is a part of the Fortinbras Theatre Laboratory which you run in Minsk?

NK Yes, and this is a big job done by our managing directors, Nadya Brodskaya and Svetlana Sugako, who operate underground in Belarus. Because Nicolai Khalezin is working with them 24/7 on Skype, but there is this couple, Nadya and Sveta, who operate all activities on a daily basis back in Belarus. It's also they who see the situation from inside, and so we discuss with them what will be the best way to proceed. Already three or four years ago our actors, with whom we started out, began to direct their own shows. And we've seen *Waiting for Godot*, it was brilliant, and we just enjoyed it.

JAEC So where are they performing it?

NK In a secret location in Minsk.

JAEC That's still what happens ... and they're managing to do that without getting arrested?

NK No, they got arrested most recently in December, but that doesn't stop them. It was in June, and then again in December 2018, and then there was also a special visit from the Ministry of Emergency Situations, who usually deal with terrorists, but in our case it was us.

JAEC But presumably they could if they wanted close the whole thing down? And they're not doing that. Is it equivalent to the Russian authorities allowing a little bit of fringe theatre – if you can call it that – just to allow some people to let off steam, and it's simply more trouble than it's worth to close it down completely?

NK We had one place where we could work, but then the owner of that house was contacted many, many, many, many times, and then the final time it was – 'If they don't move out overnight, then we will just bulldoze the house'. It was just the same for Ai Weiwei in China. So it's different from Russia .... Even when Maria Alyokhina from Pussy Riot shared with us the conditions she suffered in jail, we were saying – 'that's paradise!', when we compared it to Belarus. Obviously it wasn't paradise, but you do think OMG, you could achieve so much, even when you were in jail?! It's simply impossible to imagine what it's like in Belarus for our political prisoners.

JAEC In the past, when I asked you once whether you had an archive of the playwriting competition [ICCD] which you run, you told me that as far as you could see it had been wiped by hackers – presumably government hackers – who had wiped your website so that you no longer have the archive of the competition's history. So you do still experience harassment of that kind?

NK Even here Nicolai Khalezin is still getting different threats over email. My computer was completely hacked, completely. We created the show against capital punishment, *Trash Cuisine*, and we had the opening in New York in 2015; and on that particular day when we had the opening, our website was completely hacked and no trace was left. We asked advice from some specialists, and they told us: 'It's unbelievable how you've been hacked ...', i.e. it was so professionally done.

JAEC So from that point of view things haven't really changed that much in the last eight years at all, as to how you are regarded by the authorities in Minsk and so on?

NK We always find the important topics, and we see our job as being that, to provoke them, all the time. So our previous campaign was with disabled people, and we created a show with disabled people. It was the first ever show with disabled people there, and also we campaigned together with them, and for the first time we even had some photos because some guys were streaming it, and I took photos of the moment when the riot police arrived: they arrested one guy ...

JAEC So where was this that you were taking photos?

NK I was photographing the streaming on the phone, and I took a photo of the moment when I saw the police coming in ... We worked on that issue for three or four years, and we have made some systemic changes. It's incredible what you can achieve when you are provoking people and highlighting issues, especially when a dictator is trying to show how liberal he is to the West. And we are able to achieve some incredible results.

JAEC You can change people's attitudes and so on?

NK Yes ... there were no public toilets for the disabled, but we organized simple artistic stunts, with twenty people in wheelchairs demanding the right to disabled toilets for the general public. They positioned themselves near the Palace of Sport, with a simple placard saying 'I want to use the toilet', and next thing there were police paddy wagons, and straight away you've got disabled people and riot police there ... and within a year we had managed to secure the first public toilets for the disabled. Then, for example, we surrounded a cinema with what the police use, yellow crime scene tape, so we did the same, with placards saying 'We want to go and watch the film' – because if you have the audio equipment for deaf people you are able to do that. Within a year they got that equipment in place, and it's the least of the things that we've been able to change.

JAEC So you're looking at every aspect of human rights, along the spectrum from extreme brutality and corruption down to minority rights and issues in people's everyday life. Last December I saw that you had staged a stunt in Minsk where the young people sang what sounded like traditional folk ditties (*chastushki*), but they were on LGBTQI issues, and that was very funny. To what extent are LGBTQI issues one of your themes in your shows?

NK Oh yes, they are present in many, such as *Minsk 2011: A Reply to Kathy Acker*, a response to her story *New York City in 1979*, directed by Vladimir Shcherban and produced by Nicolai and me as executive producers. One of the main texts in *Minsk 2011* was written by me, together with Nicolai.

JAEC But it's not a particular theme at the moment?

NK Our guys got arrested precisely for that! Those June and December 2018 arrests were connected to LGBTQI issues.

JAEC Because they were themselves gay, or because they were putting on plays that were presenting those issues?

NK I think it's exactly the same as the way we were provoking the authorities about disabled rights, or any other group or stratum of society whose rights have been violated. Knowing that it is a very bad situation with LGBTQI in Belarus, we've been highlighting specific issues, and the authorities just reacted. Those artistic stunts, what they did, were so innocent, nobody would even notice them in London, you'd just pass by and that's it. But over there guys get arrested, and one of them went to jail . . . .

JAEC One of the other themes that we are interested in are the very considerable tensions that have entered into the relations between Russia and Ukraine, and the impact that that has had on all sorts of playwrights like Natasha Vorozhbit or Maksym Kurochkin, and people like that, who not only have a real problem now about whether to participate in festivals or undertake collaborations in Russia, but even whether to write in Russian. I imagine that one sort of advantage of the Belarus Free Theatre is that your relations with Ukraine are unchanged in that respect, is that right? Your communications and your contacts and your collaborations are affected by the events, of course, but they are not damaged?

NK They have only become stronger, and also over the last three to four years we have received a huge number of requests to work with Ukrainian theatres. To help them and change their way of thinking.

JAEC So have you done that at all, and if so, where?

NK We were in Kyiv, and at the European Theatre Convention, they asked us to come to Kyiv and work with sixty-one representatives of theatres. We go to Ukraine probably five times a year, me and Nicolai Khalezin.

JAEC Have you built up particular links with any of the individual theatres or playwrights or directors there?

NK It's such a big country that we need to identify who to work with . . . And lots of things that we do are on a voluntary basis, and meanwhile our own situation in terms of funding is a complete disaster, and the very existence of the company is in question every month, financially. So we really need to prioritize what we are able to do on a charity basis, as volunteers. We have done a lot of training on Skype as well, so Nicolai Khalezin worked with people in Kharkiv, again with about sixty representatives of different theatres, giving coaching. In Kyiv in late 2018 we had *Burning Doors* being performed in the Franko National Theatre. Four prime ministers came, and around fifty journalists, we spoke at the parliament, it was huge. We have a big collaboration with BoomBox, their main music band, and it's because of their lead singer [Andriy Khlyvnyuk] that it was possible to bring *Burning Doors* to Kyiv.

JAEC The projects that you do are almost entirely written by yourselves, or people that you bring in. So do you have any connections with the established Belarusian playwrights like Pavel Priazhko, Dmitry Bogoslavsky and Konstantin Steshik?

NK We published them when we were still in Belarus. We were the first who did that. In Germany they started to record audio plays, for example, much later than we started to do that underground in Belarus. So in terms of innovative ideas we're always ahead of any very well-funded companies in the world. The only thing is that we're not able to sustain things, because we don't have those funding streams that other companies can rely on because their countries are behind them. We don't have a country where we belong, where the country will be proud to have us as their citizens and creative artists.

JAEC   And the funding that came from Britain, is that drying up?

NK   Britain was always very greedy, Britain funding-wise is the worst – it's really amazing in terms of human, personal support, we only exist as humans because of our friends' support here, but in terms of funding ... Again, probably this whole situation that we have the word Belarus in our theatre's name, this is something that is putting people off, even though we're registered as a charity, we have a board of trustees, but still it's like this.

JAEC   Where does your funding mostly come from?

NK   From America.

JAEC   So do you still have support from people like Ai Weiwei and Tom Stoppard?

NK   Yes, and David Lan and Michael Attenborough, all those people are there, we get incredible moral support.

JAEC   So what's happening to the play competition, is that still running?

NK   Again, because of funding we can't do it.

JAEC   You published those two volumes not very long ago ...

NK   No, we published much more! I mean while we were in Belarus, then we were publishing every year ... I need to check the details with Nicolai Khalezin, he will be the best person to tell you how many volumes we published, as it was his 'baby', as well as serving as an alternative system of education that led to Fortinbras.

JAEC   I was thinking about the two translated volumes that came out here.

NK   Yes, but before that every year we were publishing an edition of the competition in Belarus, so I think we have around ten volumes ...

JAEC   Were they actual books, or were they online?

NK   They were actual books, but again, when we left the country ... lots got lost.

JAEC   So the competition is suspended indefinitely, until or unless you get some more funding?

NK Not indefinitely... but we need to get funding to keep doing it...

JAEC The last one was probably... two years ago?

NK Two years ago... It is a shame, because we really discovered some new names from Belarus, Ukraine and even Russia and revealed them to the West, including to the Royal Court.

JAEC And people could submit plays written in Russian, Belarusian, and...?

NK Oh, we were getting plays from about twenty-two countries of the world, and we were translating even from French and German, and from American English. So now there are American playwrights... one of the American playwrights was the winner of our competition, so now he mentions it in his CV when he is writing for Broadway. It's very exciting that we discovered so many names who then got staged here.

JAEC So that alongside certain festivals in Moscow and in Kyiv, like the Liubimovka and The Week of the Contemporary Play, your competition was still very open to plays from all over the world, and that's now an opportunity that's closed down. And in your own work, is the issue of using Russian rather than Belarusian at all important, the choice of language? Or are you essentially a Russian-speaking writer?

NK For example, my father, who teaches the students of our school, he speaks Belarusian, and many of our actors, they speak Belarusian. I speak Belarusian when I give interviews, if it's necessary. In terms of shows, it really depends. In the early days, we felt it was necessary for us to think more broadly and on a larger scale, and then also we knew 100 per cent that those people who speak Belarusian, well, you don't need to convince them that dictatorship is bad! We had to convert our Russian-speaking audiences into free-thinking people.

JAEC So it's actually become a sort of intellectual marker...

NK Yes, the Belarusian language, it's a sign... a symbol of resistance. So now, with the younger generation, a very beautiful thing is happening. When they speak Belarusian it's a major symbol that they are first of all different from the authorities, and secondly, particularly with the Russian invasion of Ukraine, it's very important to show that we have our own language. Even Nicolai Khalezin and me sometimes (it's very sad that this happens), but when we get on a plane and people are speaking Russian, then we start to speak in Belarusian...

JAEC I can see why you might want to do that, to mark yourselves off.

NK You want to be different from that horrible culture, and then you think, OMG!

JAEC It's a very interesting phenomenon, that the Belarusian language is being preserved and resurrected in Belarus in this very specific political and cultural sense – I think it's an unusual phenomenon...

NK Also, when we did *King Lear* in 2012 at the Globe Theatre in London, we spoke about the show and they said, well of course for a big audience we need to have it in Russian – and I said: 'Then you will not have our show, we will do it only if we do it in Belarusian', because it was a very big political statement in terms of being part of the cultural Olympiad. So we opened at the Globe, and then the Belarusian ambassador arrived to say: 'These people can't represent Belarus as part of the Olympic Games, for the cultural Olympiad', and the Globe people replied: 'Our government doesn't tell us what to do, so obviously you will not tell us what to do! The only thing we can recommend you to do is to go and watch their shows!' I think many of them did come ... Security was increased here at the Young Vic when we performed one of our shows soon after we arrived, because there were a lot of 'infiltrators', who came to see the show, and who brought eggs and tomatoes, and so on. And because we spotted them – we know them, how they look – so we went to talk to security and they ceased.

So, the language: for us, we understood when we started that it was necessary to continue to use our shows also as a public awareness campaign, and to give accessibility to people.

JAEC But the shows you're doing at the moment are they ... *Counting Sheep* included songs in Ukrainian – it was not all in English ...

NK *Counting Sheep* is an English-language show with Ukrainian folk music and songs ... but the whole show is in English, so as to have a direct connection with the audience. The other current show that we have is about the controversial history of Belarus, because Belarusians have always wished that everyone, whether it would be Russians, or Poles, or Germans, would just leave us alone! It's called *The Master Had a Talking Sparrow*, directed by Nicolai Khalezin (2017).

JAEC This is what you're working on at the moment?

NK The show exists: it's running in Minsk, and it's in Belarusian and Ukrainian.

JAEC Is it about Ukraine as well?

NK It's about a part of the population of Belarus that lives on the border with Ukraine, in an area called Poles'e. A journalist, our friend, went to visit villages in Belarus, and he spoke to people who are still alive but who are very old, about their memories of when the war started, and right after the Second World War, and those memories ...

JAEC ... are probably horrendous, unbearable?

NK They're both. You listen to it and some of them will say that it was the partisans who were awful, but the Germans saved us, or they say the Germans came to us and said hide your cow, because the partisans are coming at night ... And you just listen and understand about the myths of Soviet propaganda. So for example we have

Kurapaty, this is a place where hundreds of thousands of people were killed by the NKVD, but the Soviets said that it was the Nazis who did it: but that's not true, it was they who did it. Or again, in Belarus we have the deliberate blurring of the names of the villages of Khatyn and Katyn [the small village of Khatyn was chosen to commemorate all Nazi atrocities against Belarusian civilians, partly in order to confuse people's recollections about the Soviet atrocities against Polish officers committed at a place called Katyn]. So everything always used to be propaganda, and therefore when they start to talk here about 'fake news', I feel that people here are simply like children ...

JAEC And these shows, like for example *The Master Had a Talking Sparrow*, will that be seen abroad? Do you have a lot of shows that are staged inside Belarus and don't then travel abroad?

NK Yes, because we feel that we need to create something that will give intellectual nourishment for our audience there as well.

JAEC So they are still, in some sense, your primary audience: your immediate audience are your compatriots really, and then there's a wider audience too.

NK We don't really make the distinction, it's like it's all one, we really don't think in those ways.

JAEC I get a very strong sense, particularly coming to see *Burning Doors* and *Counting Sheep*, that you have some very important messages for the Anglo-American world to absorb, that we are very innocent and very naïve about all sorts of things – and lucky us! We haven't had these experiences, but I have a feeling that with *Counting Sheep* you're saying, 'Let's make a revolution! This is what it might be like if you ever have to do it, this is what it feels like ...'. It's a very strong moral message, although I'm not sure that everyone will listen to it or hear it.

NK With every single show, when we think about it, when we try to build up a strategy for the show, it will be about its relevance for *everyone*. Very often people ask, 'Do you rework your shows to travel?' – No. If that show challenged me personally, if the topic of the show challenged our actors, then it will challenge everyone, because all of us are just human beings inside, and for us that's a major point: it's not about politics, it's about humanity.

JAEC It's about whether – and how – we can confront violence or threats to our sense of independence, yes ...
 The Ministry of Counterculture [an online news service which reports on cultural and human rights issues across the world], is that entirely organized by you?

NK We have been thinking maybe about separating them, but ... The idea started for diversification of funding! In our school, the Fortinbras Theatre Laboratory, we teach the subject of theatre-making, but also we teach – I teach – 'artivism'. That is, how to take a social or political issue and frame it into an art form and do it on the street. So those artistic stunts, when the students got arrested, unfortunately they were passing my exam! When we get new students we always say that they have to be prepared for the fact that they might lose their jobs or education, get beaten, get arrested... This is unfortunately part of our life as the BFT. Most of us went through it... Of course we have never planned for them to get arrested... but you know, it is all in order for me to be able to understand whether they can learn how to match art and activism, but also on top of that marketing and management, because we are also talking about target audiences, like all marketing companies, and so on. So that final event, the artistic stunt on the street, this is when I can evaluate whether they have managed to deliver that; but also, after they have done an artistic stunt, they need to do a debriefing in terms of... they need to write articles, they need to approach journalists, so that that particular topic will take root in public awareness.

JAEC So it's about using media and social media.

NK It's all the theatre subjects, plus activism, and Nicolai Khalezin teaches them citizen journalism. So now when we talk about the Ministry of Counterculture, that's also become a mechanism for our students to write those articles that will be worth publishing. Some of their articles – for example, I think they came out in January, but they were working on it last year – were on refugees, because we have lots of Chechen refugees in Brest [a town on the Polish border].

JAEC How many people come into the Fortinbras Theatre Laboratory every year?

NK Twenty people, and we give them a two-year education. By now up to 200 people have gone on to become multipliers, and they have started to change society through their own initiatives.

JAEC So does that have a formal structure, even though it's unofficial?

NK Everything is unofficial... we don't give diplomas! We have an open call, and then we have interviews with our teachers, for example Maryna Yurevich and Pavel Gorodnitsky who have been praised by *The New York Times* for their performances, Svetlana Sugako, who runs BFT's underground activities, and my father, who was vice-chancellor of the only Academy of Arts in Belarus, in Minsk, and who lost his job because of Nicolai Khalezin and me. He was told that he was a disgrace to the Academy of Arts because his children were a disgrace to this country. He was the person who converted the Academy of Arts to having 65 per cent of all subjects taught in Belarusian.

JAEC When did he do that?

NK He lost his job in 2008.

JAEC It was even more astonishing to do that at that time than it would have been more recently.

NK It was unbelievable what he achieved, really unbelievable.

JAEC He chose to do that as a sort of anti-Russian gesture? Or as an affirmation of something else?

NK He was a major translator of Dostoevsky and Chekhov, so obviously he was very confident about the quality of the literature, because he thinks that they are incredible – but he was translating them into Belarusian in order for people to have the best of Russian literature in the Belarusian language as well, so all people could share that.

JAEC So in a sense it's transforming Belarusian into a language of high culture?

NK Yes ... And when he was dismissed he was severely beaten up, he and Nicolai Khalezin were beaten by the police very badly. And again it was specifically because he was my father, and because he was working with us. But since then he has been teaching our students all the time, so when we have this new intake, it will be him and our older generation of actors – who are aged thirty or so – they will conduct the interviews, and we will get on Skype and interview those potential students too. We will scare all of them badly, and we will say: if you want to be part of the Belarus Free Theatre school, you need to understand that you will get arrested and beaten up, you'll even lose your job; and if they're still in higher education, they will lose their education ... So after all those interviews we'll get about twenty people, and then we have a very intense programme. If you look at our calendar, it's from morning until late evening, and we have a place where we perform, in a former American embassy garage for two cars, where we are able to accommodate seventy people, and that's where we have the school – so it's a bit tricky ... Nobody would ever allow this here, because of health and safety!

JAEC How often do the shows actually happen?

NK Three or four times a week. And in terms of the number of students, then by the end of the year we will have around ten people, because the moment people start to get arrested, or receive threats, even though we told them – everyone is always like 'yeah, yeah, yeah, this is exactly why we came' – but when you face that reality it's different ... But then you're left with exactly those people who do understand what they are doing, and then maybe from those twenty people we will invite two or three to be part of the theatre. But again, in different roles, so it could be management, it could be stage-managing, it could be Ministry of Counterculture journalism. And somebody who is very talented could do acting and performing and directing and writing, everything – there are such people.

JAEC It's like a wonderful, positive virus in Belarusian society that you're creating ...Is your father allowed to travel, is he able to come and see you?

NK Yes he can travel, but sometimes when I say, 'Dad, come to see us', he will say, 'Oh, but I can't leave my children!' And I'm thinking 'They are not your children, *we* are your children, just to remind you!' – and so I will have to travel to Vilnius [in Lithuania] to see him, and that's where he'll come. My family lived for many generations in one house, all together. My great-grandmother lived with my grandmother, with my mother, her sister and their families. I don't myself remember that moment, because my brother was born and I wasn't yet there, but then we lived together with my parents and our kids, so we were the first who broke the tradition, unfortunately, after hundreds of years – because the family goes back to the eleventh century, from what we know and what we managed to find in the family tree. My parents have been together for sixty years, and my mum is now here. It's difficult, with everything that's happened to us – in reality we have destroyed this generational tradition, and although they never blame us for it, we have this feeling of guilt. My mother spends half the year with us, and then she goes back to him, so she can balance things; our kids are now adults, but having her looking after us as though we were small kids is such a beautiful thing.

JAEC You've explained that the financial situation is worrying, and the future of the company is problematic – as it often has been – but do you have a clear sense of new directions or future plans?

NK We have our performance methods that we have been developing for fifteen years, and we are looking to see how we could create some sort of manual, so that our method could get licensed. We've also been thinking about doing a summer school in Belarus, in order to bring in foreign students, so our teachers could work with them.

JAEC You'd have to decide which language you were going to work in, then?

NK It was one of my main things, even ten years ago – I paid an English teacher to teach our actors English: you need to communicate with the world, and now many of them are doing pretty well ... We did manage to secure one educational partnership with an Australian university, Monash University.

JAEC When I spoke to you earlier in the year, you said you were also making a film?

NK Yes, and it's about Ukraine again. I mentioned Boombox previously. So it's about this musician who is very, very big in Ukraine, and him understanding how he could use himself and the stage as an opportunity to appeal to people and ask them to be active within society. And also in the film he is campaigning for the release of Oleg Sentsov, the Ukrainian filmmaker [who was arrested in Crimea in May 2014, accused of plotting terrorism, and sentenced to twenty years imprisonment in what Amnesty International has described as a show trial. Sentsov's plight is one subject of the show *Burning Doors*]. And within the film, while we were filming, he came up with the idea of giving a concert 'for the land', because he does lots of concerts for people, and this would be a concert 'for the stolen land', on the strip separating Ukraine from Russian-held Crimea, where there are military positions. So in July last year we organized that concert jointly with his band, and it was something truly incredible, that I will never forget.

JAEC   Was it in Kyiv that the concert took place?

NK   The concert was played in Crimea, on that border strip. And the idea was that there would be no people there, for safety and security, because information had been received that there were Russian snipers behind bushes, and landmine signs everywhere, so it was necessary for us to walk along special paths to avoid those. It was pretty tense, and so the concert ... his songs are all about love, all his life, and it's amazing how this conception of love could be applied to the war, how it could be perceived, and it was an incredible moment, when word got out, and many people got involved, and came from occupied Crimea to listen to the concert. I don't know how many of them were there, but first they crossed the border, and the moment they crossed into the Ukrainian side they would wave Ukrainian flags and put on wreaths of flowers, it was something extraordinary ...[2] And now we're editing it.

JAEC   So what's it going to be called?

NK   We're still trying to decide ... It started as 'Return Ticket for Oleg [Sentsov]', and now at the moment it's called 'Love Songs for Crimea', so we'll see how it ends up ...

JAEC   I'm also interested to know what's been happening to Kirill Serebrennikov [the cinema and theatre director who spent eighteen months under house arrest in Moscow in 2017–19, on dubious charges of embezzlement].

NK   I think it's very striking with Russia (and this would never happen in Belarus) that the Russian regime sent out clear signals in advance. It was the same with Mikhail Khodorkovsky [the businessman who spent ten years in prison from 2003 to 2013, on dubious fraud charges]. It was announced very openly: 'you have to leave the country, otherwise you will get arrested' ... And similarly, with Kirill Serebrennikov, it was very clearly said – but when you're inside those situations, you never think it will happen to you ... And I think it's much easier when these leaders have no specific ideology, neither Lukashenko, nor Putin: they're just people who are obsessed with power, and there is no humanity left in them.

Notes

1   It was the Bush administration which tagged him 'the last dictator in Europe'. See https://www.nytimes.com/2005/08/01/opinion/the-tyrant-of-belarus.html
2   A video of this event can be found at: https://vidos.top/v/1803344

Pavel Priazhko: the Text as an Instant Photograph (2012); Conversation with Pavel Priazhko (2011); Essay on Pavel Priazhko's Methods

Tania Arcimovich

> In her 2012 lecture on one of Belarus's most successful playwrights, Pavel Priazhko, Tania Arcimovich reflects on the fact that as someone who is so often staged in Russia, he might almost be regarded as a 'Russian' dramatist. In Tania's earlier, 2011 conversation with him she asks about his play *The Soldier*, which consists of just two short sentences of text. He comments on his reluctance to write anything autobiographical, and insists that he does not create characters: instead he eavesdrops on people and records their words. Priazhko is also reluctant to become a writer who describes life in Belarus to the outside world in terms which make it sound anomalous. In her more recent essay on Priazhko's methods, Tania notes that he writes documentary material but refuses to use a voice recorder, which he views as artificial: his texts belong to the here-and-now, rather than aspiring to the universal.

Extracts from lecture 'Pavel Priazhko: the Text as an Instant Photograph', Minsk, 2 June 2012

Pavel Priazhko is a Belarusian playwright who was born in Minsk in 1975. He started off as a law student, then abandoned that, and joined the Literature Department of the Institute for Culture. There again he didn't complete his studies. He began to write in the early 2000s, and his first play dates from 2004. But Priazhko himself dates the start of his creative career from his 2008 play *Panties* (*Trusy*), dismissing his early works. You can understand why, in one respect: these are plays where the author was still seeking not just a language but also a method for working with the theme of the everyday. What's more, his early plays are essentially very different: in them the author, one way or another, was working with his own experiences, and using facts from his own biography, for example in his *Sun of Arcadia* (*Solntse Arkadii*), and that is something which effectively disappears from his later plays.

[...]

In 2010 a production of his play *Life Has Gone Well* (*Zhizn' udalas'*), directed by Mikhail Ugarov and Marat Gatsalov at Teatr.doc and at the Centre for Playwriting and Directing in Moscow, won a special prize at Russia's Golden Mask festival. At the presentation Anatoly Smeliansky, Professor of the Arts and Rector of the Moscow Art Theatre Studio School, a man who in his time had uncovered for Russian readers the long-banned work of Mikhail Bulgakov, spoke for about ten minutes. He explained why Priazhko's controversial play, which had provoked heated arguments and discussions, was receiving an award. 'Modern Russian theatre is attempting to offer a cross-section of the life of the masses, which I, as a man who lives in the metropolis, and who goes out in the evenings to stroll around Patriarchs' Ponds [the opening setting for Bulgakov's novel *The Master and Margarita*], can observe to its full extent', said Smeliansky. 'I don't want to say that this is a problematic phenomenon or an alarming one. Chekhov would have described it as a process of diagnosis. And what's more, it's all being staged skilfully, with an extremely nuanced ear.'[1] [...] It is thus important to note that, yes, Priazhko has basically been staged and read by Russian directors, and it is probably true to say that in the future Russian theatre will have the right to call Priazhko a Russian dramatist, because it was precisely over there that his plays proved to be in demand, rather than in Belarusian theatres. [...]

Before he wrote *I Am Free* [*Ia svoboden*, a non-verbal 2012 composition consisting of thirteen captions and 535 photographs, each projected for seven seconds] there was another text of Priazhko's called *Three Days in Hell* (*Tri dnia v adu*). It's a piece written in continuous prose, evoking the trivial preoccupations of the inhabitants of Minsk over two or three days, though it's not fiction but specifically playwriting. And that is what is interesting about this text. In his outlook Priazhko is a globalist, and according to him he is not particularly interested in local settings and themes. However, in some respects it's obvious that he is working precisely in a Belarusian context, because he describes the people and situations that he observes here. But last year, after the economic crisis, he suddenly began to talk in one of our conversations about the political and the social in Belarus. And this was the text which then appeared, in which the Belarusian context is quite explicit.

Tania Arcimovich: Conversation with Pavel Priazhko (2011)

'I don't want to become the vehicle for communicating anomalies'.

Pavel Priazhko

PP I like commuter suburbs.

TA In Minsk do you often walk around the commuter suburbs?

PP Why, there's no lack of them here, is there?

TA Well, you could make a special visit to a commuter suburb, for example to Chizhovki [a suburb of high-rise buildings dating from the 1960s].

PP If I were an artist or a photographer, perhaps that's what I would do. But I don't make any particular effort to do anything specially.

TA This year the St Petersburg director Dmitry Volkostrelov has been preparing a production of your *Soldier* (*Soldat*, June 2011). How did that all turn out?

[The entire text of the play *Soldier* is as follows:

Soldier

A soldier came home on leave. When it was time to go back to the army, he didn't go back.]

PP The premiere has already taken place, and you can find a recording of the show on openspace.ru, together with Dima [Dmitry Volkostrelov]'s rehearsal diaries. I know the play is being included in the repertory of Teatr.doc in Moscow. It's going to be a joint project with the Petersburg Teatr Post. Dmitry Volkostrelov is the director for the production. In my opinion Teatr.doc and Teatr Post are the most interesting theatre spaces of all the ones I know. And I've become truly very close to that group of guys in St Petersburg.

TA In your preliminary conversation with Dima you told him that the text turned out as something of a surprise for you yourself, and that it seemed odd that it hadn't occurred to anybody previously to write a play like this. That is, you were consciously aware that this was some sort of new form?

PP You can't really speak of a new form as such here. It's just that I discovered something new for myself. But that doesn't mean that my next text is going to consist just of two sentences. In this particular case it is a concrete utterance precisely for this story, precisely for *Soldier*. But for me it isn't a question of seeking out a new form.

TA And why was such a laconic form required for this story?

PP I was preoccupied by the subject of how a soldier comes home on leave. I began to devise one sort of story, then another, then a third. And then I realized that I couldn't convey precisely what I wanted. Yes, I'm following the rules for constructing a plot, I introduce some characters, but in actual fact I'm occupying myself with nonsense, and I'm departing entirely from the utterance which was so important to me. And suddenly I understood that the form I needed was – two sentences: that was the only possible variant. And Dima decided to put it on. Thanks to him, the text did not get lost from sight. Because I did send the text to one other director, but he thought it was a joke. Whereas for me it was a serious piece of work. I'm glad that Dima saw that.

TA You and I once had a discussion about works by contemporary playwrights, and you said to me that you didn't find that texts in which the author speaks about him/herself were interesting.

PP Yes, because if I once wrote a first-person text, then I would not be able to do it again for a long time. I can't imagine what else I'd be able to share about myself. [He is referring to the text *The Coffee-Shop Owner* (*Khozyain kofeyni*, 2011) – note by TA. The text consists of a one-hour first-person monologue containing reflections on writing with references to Vyrpaev, Ugarov and Volkostrelov, the quest to find a 'normal person' rather than an 'anomaly' as a subject and the speaker's sense of his own 'infantilism' – JAEC.] If I were to set myself the task of only investigating myself, then I would write, for example, about how I brush my teeth or get dressed: that's how I would construct my investigation. But for the moment I don't see anything interesting about myself. In which case how could I be of any interest to others? In my opinion there are more interesting things happening all around. So if I am going to propose anything, then it will be about what's happening out there, externally.

TA How do you select your characters?

PP What characters? Characters are characters, and people are people. I write about people. I can't exactly answer the question, why them? I've only started to analyse my choices recently, because I suddenly realized that I could repeat myself, and I don't want to do that. These days my selection process is rather more strict.

TA Your texts are widely staged in theatres in Russia, such as Praktika and Teatr.doc in Moscow and Teatr Post in St Petersburg. These are all experimental, studio spaces. Is it possible for your texts to be heard in more traditional theatres?

PP There are a certain number of texts which I could offer for larger stages. But essentially I don't have any narratives for the wider world that could be shouted or spoken loudly. And it's for that reason probably that my texts sound better precisely in studio spaces. And as for carrying out a revolution by showing some hypermodern text in a mainstream context: well, that's never been my aim. That's what interests me least of all.

TA How important are audience reactions to you?

PP If I submit a text to be developed further, that's because I'm one hundred per cent confident about it. And if I'm not confident about a text, then I don't show it to anyone. And for that reason I'm not bothered by negative audience reactions: I have complete trust in my own taste.

TA But is it important to you that the meaning with which you have invested a text should be heard?

PP I don't especially make it my aim that the underlying ideas of my work should be clear and obvious. If someone does pick them up, that's fine. But if not, that's not a problem. And if they hear something different in it, that's fine too.

TA So it would seem that you are really writing for yourself?

PP   I wouldn't say that either. Rather, I am attempting to remain true to myself. That's why, for example, writing serials doesn't really work for me. When there are several parts to a serial, you have to work constantly on the sequence of events, which sometimes become rather absurd and unnatural, where events are forcibly embedded into the plot, and you have to write them up. And how are you going to write them up if it's unnatural? And that means that the dialogues become unnatural. The text turns into a sort of farce. Or perhaps not a farce, but something which in my opinion is not good.

TA   So what is good?

PP   I don't know, but I do know what is bad – and that's when there is some kind of inconsistency. For example, let's say there are certain things which are not characteristic of a certain individual. And suddenly he is asked to do them. And he knows it will go badly because these things are not characteristic of him. For example, lines of dialogue are added to a screenplay in order to move the plot on further. But I realize that people don't speak like that in real life ... Although on the other hand, and I've only just thought of this, there are fantasy films which are watched by scientists, and they know perfectly well that things can't really be like that. And then people say to them: 'Calm down, this is fantasy!' Maybe my objections to serials are equally unfounded ...

TA   So in other words it is important to you that what you write should be true to life?

PP   What's important to me is that it should be good enough. True to life – well, that's a subjective category in any case. I can simply sense what works for me, and what doesn't. And for that reason I don't like adaptations, when, for example, they take a text by an English author, and adapt it to the realities of our lives. Because there's a different view of life there, and different lines of dialogue in different societies. It's very important to think about that, because otherwise it turns out artificial.

TA   Would you be capable of writing a text based on historical material?

PP   No. I have thought about it, but it would become a documentary text. In which case why would I do it? For example, not long ago I read the diary of Miklukho-Maklay, *The Man from the Moon*. [Nikolai Miklukho-Maklay was a nineteenth-century Russian traveller and anthropologist, who was believed by the inhabitants of Papua New Guinea to have come from the moon – JAEC.] I sense that there are some possibilities there, there's a story to be told. But I could simply offer these materials to a director, because why would I copy out those diary entries, when someone else could make an entire show out of it? There would be no work of my own in it.

TA   Do you take an interest in what is going on around you?

PP   Yes, and above all I am looking out for people who interest me, and upon whom I will then eavesdrop, in order to note down how they speak. If I don't succeed in eavesdropping, then I will try to find people similar to them. But I'm not going to use my own speech or my own responses in order to describe their stories, and I'm not going to make use of those people in order to explore my own concerns. I try to be as accurate as possible, and then the story will rise to quite another level. I'm not going to make generalizations or reduce people to clichés, for example: this man is a layabout, and this one is a botanist, and now I'm going to make their paths cross, and so on.

TA   Do you specially seek out the protagonists of your plays?

PP   No. I try not to stir up the space around me too much. But once something has caught my attention, then I get down to work. That's my personal method, but each author works in the way which suits him and is comfortable for him.

TA   Do you edit your protagonists' words?

PP   No. Why would I? Then I would end up with some sort of 'ideal', closed construct. But it needs to be open, it needs to be open to interactions. If you manufacture some phrase which fully conveys a meaning, then in my opinion that is something closed. And that doesn't suit me. For me a line of dialogue has to be grubby, it has to interact with the surrounding world, it shouldn't convey meaning directly. If I need to depict a situation where a boy declares his love to a girl, then it's definitely not going to be a seashore, feet in the sand, a setting sun. If I write it like that, then that means I'll be taking the piss. I admit that such a young man may possibly exist, who declares his love exactly like that, but how sincere is it? Maybe he just wants to go to bed with the girl. Or maybe not. Perhaps they are very pure people. I don't know.

TA   So it turns out that you simply operate as a mediator between the real story and what goes down on paper? How do you yourself define your function?

PP   It's probably that I simply get satisfaction from something, perhaps so that someone else can obtain satisfaction. I don't know. There's a certain type of creative artist who says that something is an important theme for society, that you need to speak out about something directly. But that's not the path for me. I don't raise problems, I'm not concerned with themes which are important for society. I simply try to follow closely what is happening all around me.

Not long ago I had just come back from Poland and I was walking through Minsk – and suddenly I got the feeling that I had landed in the midst of some sort of art installation, as though I was walking along some clearly defined route: you must turn right here, and then left here. It felt as though there was an all-encompassing installation all around me. I suddenly got the impression that a certain idea was in existence which had been realized by someone or other in this space. It was a certain system of values which had seized the land, and which was creating a sense of how unnatural everything was that was happening. After that experience, for the first time I felt I wanted to leave the country.

TA   How would you define that system of values which felt so unnatural on the territory of Belarus?

PP A sense of an order that was imposed externally. I don't really want to draw parallels and make comparisons, but I get the impression that people may have experienced something similar in 1937, for example [at the height of Stalin's Terror in the USSR – JAEC]. Some sort of regulated system which has taken over everything around you. Previously when I used to come back to Minsk I would feel a sense of melancholy or depression. But on this occasion something different happened. You could of course write about it, but if I write about it once, and I'm constantly immersed in it, then I'll feel obliged to write only about that. Or else I'll have to write about some sort of made-up life. And that's why the sense was aroused in me that I needed to leave. But then there's the question of language. My profession is connected to my language, and if I were to go abroad, then I wouldn't know the language well enough to be able to write in it fluently.

TA What about moving to Russia?

PP Yes. But I like it in Minsk. Although I'm horrified by what I am observing nowadays. For example, there's a woman buying fifteen bottles of sunflower oil in a shop, and the woman on the till turns round and says to her: 'What on earth are you going to do with so much oil?' I can't understand this gulf in sympathy between people. This woman on the till, who almost certainly knows that the cost of oil is going up, has bought up a whole case of it for herself, but then reproaches the woman for doing the same. And a situation where people feel obliged to buy fifteen bottles also gets me down.

TA But that's something you can write about?

PP Yes, you can do it once. And then what?

TA Well, there could be various themes within that one situation.

PP But they would all come down to one and the same thing. The names might change, but it would all be the same thing, because it's all part of one closed system. And so it turns out that I'm limited in my choice of themes.

TA Do you watch TV?

PP No. The internet is enough for me. But I can't say that I follow the news particularly closely, I simply follow up certain links. And as a rule I don't need the media to mediate things for me. And that's why that sense of a certain order all around began to oppress me. It turns out that I can't see anything for myself, that I need to obtain information from certain places. When you have an open system, then everything that is taking place thousands of kilometres away is also happening here. Sitting here, you can tell the story of what is happening over there. But if you have a closed system, then what happens here won't be understood over there. A small, closed territory like this one will be regarded as something anomalous, and any signals that emanate from here will only convey the anomalies. But to become a constant communicator of anomalies, to trace the misery and greyness of life is also something I don't want to do. But I don't think there's any reason to get into a state about this. You have to accept that in a given spot on the planet that's precisely how things are. You accept that, or you don't, and if you don't, then you either try to change things or you leave. Each person has to choose for himself. You can't say that this is bad. And what serves as proof is that in these conditions hypermodern groups can still emerge, or new communities. It's rare, but it does happen. I'm thinking of the Belarusian [experimental pop] group LILAC. Of all the things that are happening in contemporary music at the moment, they're the most precious for me. They're amazing young people, and the female vocalist sings really well. I simply never expected that in our country, where there is bad – actually, in my opinion, terrible – rock music, and endless folk music, suddenly an absolutely modern group should appear. You can accuse them of being hipsterish, and attach various labels to them, but that doesn't change anything. They're cool. I'd like as many people as possible to find out about them. Wherever I am, I'm going to talk about them everywhere. I couldn't care less if people consider that to be PR. It's the first time I've had such strong reactions to Belarusian music. So there you are.

[Published on 16 November 2011, in the internet journal *Novaya Evropa*, and available at: http://n-europe.eu/tables/2011/11/16/dialogi_s_pavlom_pryazhko_byt_transferom_anomalii_mne_ne_khochetsya]

Essay on Pavel Priazhko's methods

The years from 2011 to 2013 became for Pavel Priazhko a period of active experiments in drama when, as the Russian critic Pavel Rudnev observes, he raised doubts about the limits of art in almost every new text of his. Over the course of just a few years Priazhko created iconic texts such as *The Closed Door* (*Zapertaia dver'*, 2010, a text in which the stage directions occupy more space than the dialogue –JAEC), *Three Days in Hell*, *The Soldier*, *The Coffee-Shop Owner*, *The Mournful Hockey-Player* (*Pechal'nyi khokkeist*, 2013, where a disillusioned ice-hockey player's life is conjured up in his former poems – JAEC), *I am Free* and so on. In these texts he more or less renounced dialogue, experimented with dramatic structure, made use of poetry as well as prose, and assembled texts by embedding new media in them such as images and hyperlinks. His explorations have done much to determine the course of contemporary playwriting in Russian, and have been seized upon by other [Belarusian] authors such as Maksim Dos'ko (*Radio Culture, London, LabRoom* and other texts) or Dmitry Bogoslavsky (*Points on the Axis of Time*).

However, beginning with the 2014 text *We Are Already Here* (*My uzhe zdes'*, set on the planet Mars – JAEC), Priazhko turned back towards the traditional format of dialogue. The speech of the characters is foregrounded, and capturing it in detail becomes the most important task for the author. This method of Priazhko's reminds one of micro-sociological approaches, when a conversation with an informant is noted and communicated with minimum interventions from the author. You would think that such a degree of authenticity would be possible only thanks to the use of a voice recorder, a method which is typical of verbatim techniques. But Priazhko himself has said that he doesn't use a voice recorder, as he feels that it becomes an intermediary between himself and the person he is listening to, and establishes an artificial barrier between them.² And speech is what interests Priazhko more than anything else. First of all a theme comes to him, and then he finds an environment and protagonists, and listens to them, trying to remember people's intonations and lexicon. He says that the text itself gets written quickly, virtually without stylistic editing or corrections. It is important to Priazhko that he should preserve the originality of the sound-world of the everyday. It is precisely by means of this detailed rendering of speech – the intonations, the phrasing and the lexicon of those who are speaking – that he succeeds in making a representation of a social context, and to move on from there towards broader narratives. These would include, for example, the theme of the stagnation of time in the post-Soviet era, and the sidelining of political realities by the everyday (*Three Days in Hell*, *The Mournful Hockey-Player*, *15 Swimming Pools* [15 *basseynov*, 2014], *The Black Box* [*Chernaia korobka*, 2016], set in a 1980s Soviet school – JAEC). Conflicts between generations in his texts move beyond a clash between the old and the new, and offer a diagnosis of the lengthy transitional condition of post-Soviet society, in which a battle has been taking place between fundamentally different value systems and orientations:

> I don't care where I live. Because as a rule everything is just the same wherever you are nowadays. Why should I defend McDonald's and seven hypermarkets, you can find them in other places, and I can go there too and use electricity and all the rest. And I don't think that's childish, it's childish to believe that you need to go and defend the motherland. The whole earth is our motherland.
>
> The Coffee-Shop Owner

> 'Dad? Dad, why won't you talk to me? . . . It's because I don't love the USSR, isn't it?'
>
> 15 Swimming Pools

But global themes such as these are spoken about in the texts as it were between the lines, as though they don't really interest the author. Priazhko attempts as far as possible to preserve a distance from any benchmarks of reality, or rather, he tries to understand the moment, to empathize with it rather than resist. And thanks to this detailed and non-judgemental recording, his texts become witnesses to the here and now, the documentation of which has become the author's principal task.

Notes

1 Anatoly Smeliansky, 'Muttersprache', available at http://news.students.ru/index.php?newsid=21134
2 Priazhko has told me that he has only once used a voice recorder, in the context of a drama workshop in New York: this was one of the conditions that had been imposed. But according to him the text which was created was not successful, and it has never seen the light of day.

18

The artistic space shared by Eastern Slavs, and the ways in which that is created

The Way People Love by the Belarusian dramatist Dmitry Bogoslavsky

Natalia Osis

> Natalia Osis considers a play by the Belarusian playwright and director Dmitry Bogoslavsky, who has staged Russian and Ukrainian plays in Minsk as well as plays in Belarusian. She argues that in *The Way People Love* Bogoslavsky contrives to depict the life of peasants and the folkloric traditions they have inherited in ways which are familiar and recognisable to other Eastern Slavs (i.e. from Russia and Ukraine). Natalia's analysis is shaped by the concept of 'artistic space', as articulated by the Russian semiotician Iurii Lotman. The geography of the 'artistic space' in this play is mythologised: time, distance and frontiers all become irrelevant in what is in fact a transnational, regional culture. Natalia compares Bogoslavsky's rural landscape to that created by Nikolai Gogol' in his Dikan'ka stories, written in the 1830s; and both texts combine the use of different languages for aesthetic and spiritual purposes. She also finds similarities between Bogoslavsky's handling of obscenities with that of the novelist and playwright Mikhail Bulgakov (1891-1940). Bogoslavsky's play culminates in a spiritual poem or song called 'Three Angels', which exists in both Russian and Belarusian variants.

The Way People Love (2011), by the Belarusian playwright and theatre director Dmitry Bogoslavsky, had considerable success in Russia: it reached the shortlist of the Eurasia competition based in the Urals, created a stir at the Liubimovka Festival of Young Drama (Moscow) and came top in the 'Competition of Competitions' internet voting at Russia's Golden Mask theatre awards and festival, and in the competition called 'Cast-List 2012'. Bogoslavsky does a great deal to support the development of contemporary theatre in Belarus, and was one of the initiators of The Studio for Alternative Drama (SAD) in Minsk in 2011. He draws the public's attention to contemporary issues in Belarus, and also stages contemporary Ukrainian plays (*Sasha Take out the Rubbish* by Natal'ia Vorozhbit, 2014) as well as Russian ones (Dmitry Danilov's *The Man from Podol'sk*, 2016).

Bogoslavsky's success, not only in Belarus but also in Russia, is determined among other things by the fact that in his work he constructs an artistic space depicting the countryside, and a picture of the everyday life of peasants, which is instantly perceived by all Slavs who speak or understand Russian as 'familiar territory'.

In this essay I will undertake an analysis of those instruments – primarily linguistic ones – which the author uses in order to draw an unbroken line between the oral, folk culture shared by all Eastern Slavs, and the modern-day countryside. In this village life the 'peasant' is just as inextricably associated with the notion of a 'Christian' as was the case in legendary times – and this is not just a question of language, but also of significance. The countryside depicted by Bogoslavsky in *The Way People Love* could just as easily be Russian as Belarusian – and in some respects it is both, for its inhabitants travel to Moscow as though it were the town just down the road, but also sing Belarusian folk songs.

The play's plot seems simple at first glance: in her desperate wish to live 'a decent life' the married woman Lius'ka murders her violent drunkard of a husband Kolia. She conceals the crime and marries a nice young man, Sergei the district policeman, who has loved her since their schooldays. But the spirit of the dead man will not leave her in peace. Her mother and new mother-in-law sincerely try to help their children, and Lius'ka and Sergei attempt to make a happy life for themselves. But neither of them is confident that life can and should be happy. Lius'ka is now having visions of her dead husband Kolia, and talks to him. Unlike the live Kolia, the ghost of Kolia doesn't drink, and Lius'ka can at last talk to him as she never could when he was alive. There is no room left in Lius'ka's life for the good and kind Sergei. In a fit of despair he almost kills Lius'ka, and then commits suicide. And now Lius'ka can talk day and night with both of her two dead husbands. At the wake the mother and the mother-in-law sing a song in Belarusian:

> Oh it is merry to live
> In our paradise,
> It is merry,
> but there's nobody to do that![1]

The framework for my study is provided by the term 'artistic space' as defined by Iurii Lotman:

> The plot of narrative literary texts usually unfolds within the confines of a specific continuum of setting. A naïve response by the reader strives to identify this with the way the consistent setting of the episodes corresponds to some sort of real (for example, geographical) space. However, the existence of a special artistic space, which can by no means be reduced to the simple reproduction of certain characteristics of a real landscape, soon becomes apparent.[2]

What, then, is the topography of the artistic space of the play *The Way People Love*? Within the internal geography of the play there is a road which is very nearby, very convenient and understandable, which leads to Moscow. This is of course a paradox, since in the real world Moscow is situated in a different country from Belarus, and in order to get there you need to cross frontiers, pass through customs and so on.

The geography of the artistic space of Bogoslavsky's play is constructed according to its own laws: distant Moscow appears to be close, whereas everything that lies around the village is far away and inconvenient. It turns out that the distance which it is hardest to overcome is the one which lies closest to hand. As you go further away from your own village the distances become shorter, and difficulties diminish (that is to say, it is very complicated to get from the village to the junction at Rechnoe, but travelling from Rechnoe to Moscow happens almost automatically). From this it is possible to conclude that the closer you get to this rather mythical – judging by the text of the play – Moscow, the more the world becomes noticeably simpler and better.

The artistic space in this Belarusian author's play acquires interesting characteristics: its political geography is suspended, and the characters live in a world without borders, but at the same time the two essential centres of attraction – Moscow and the home village – refract reality in different ways. Around the village everything is complicated and tangled, whereas Moscow somehow 'straightens' roads and 'speeds up' time. Moscow itself figures as the epicentre of structure and harmony in the mythological consciousness of the inhabitants of Bogoslavsky's village. For example, this is what Lius'ka says about her husband Kolia:

> **Lius'ka** He'd given up drinking. It was as though everything was sorting itself out, [...] and he was on his way to Moscow, to work on Chubas's building site. (p. 83)

The idea of 'sorting itself out' [*nalazhivalos'*] resonates etymologically in Russian with the idea of 'harmony' [*lad*], and defines in the broadest terms the process of transformation that was to have been achieved for Kolia in Moscow. Zalizniak and Shmelev define 'harmony' as a key concept in the Eastern Slav picture of the world. Vasilii Belov has devoted an entire book to the concept of 'harmony', in which he emphasizes that harmony is one of the most ancient of Eastern Slav concepts, representing the ideal of the simple and organic life of the village.[3] The inhabitants of Bogoslavsky's village have never been to Moscow, and so the way they picture it to themselves corresponds to their own fundamental assumptions about life. Let us offer a few examples.

Once you have moved to Moscow you can immediately resolve all the problems in your life thinks another character, Nastia, complaining about her own husband:

> **Nastia** He's a weakling, a wet rag. It's all lisping and grovelling! Yuk! If he'd wanted to, we could have moved to town ages ago. If he'd only asked to join Chubas, we'd have gone to Moscow. But he just can't do it, you understand? You just need to take one step in your life, but he can't do it. It's important to him never to ask anyone, or beg anyone. Do you know, his brother offered a hundred and fifty times: just move, you can get a job as a chauffeur driving some director around, but no, he says, he can't do it. His brother promised him an apartment to go with the job, but he just can't do it, he can't fucking do anything... (p. 89)

In Moscow they can do anything – including curing any illness, even her husband Van'ka's sterility:

> **Nastia**   They wanted me to have an operation, then they did some tests, then you had to wait, and then they said I was perfectly OK, it was Van'ka who couldn't... I said, we have to go to Moscow, but he's always afraid. [...] Maybe in Moscow they might have been able to do something. They might have cured him. There are plenty of clinics there, private ones and the rest. Maybe they'd have dealt with it all, but he... (p. 91)

In the artistic space of the play *The Way People Love* Moscow figures as a kind of 'magical' place in which there is 'structure' and 'harmony', where everything should be fine, and this heaven on earth is constructed according to the laws of the imagination of the inhabitants of Bogoslavsky's village.

One of the most famous of literary villages, which brought fame not only to its author, but also to the whole of Russian literature, was Nikolai Gogol's Dikan'ka. Although he is considered a classic Russian writer, Gogol' was brought up in Ukraine, near Poltava, and wrote his collection of stories *Evenings on a Farm near Dikan'ka* during the first years after he had moved to Russia, to St Petersburg. The stories offered a rich blend of primitive Ukrainian folklore and of the kind of mysticism that was fashionable in the early nineteenth century. The two volumes of the *Evenings on a Farm near Dikan'ka* (1831, 1832) not only promoted the young author to the first ranks of contemporary writers, but also demonstrated the depth of interest among Russian readers at the time in what was known, to use the imperial parlance of the day, as 'Little Russia'.

> Gogol' took Ukrainian folklore, added in some from Germany, and then got carried away... In the space of two years, sitting in St Petersburg and feeling homesick for the Poltava region, he wrote an entire corpus of national legends, in which are gathered together all the archetypes of Ukraine. [...] Although the *Evenings on a Farm near Dikan'ka* are written in Russian, they have preserved all the melodiousness of the Ukrainian tongue.

Broadly speaking, this is the most important book of Ukrainian literature, observed one of Russia's leading modern literary critics, Dmitry Bykov.[4]

In this first major work Gogol' figures not so much as a mystificator (a role he would subsequently become very fond of), but as a popularizer, or to use a modern term, a cultural mediator (German: *Kulturträger*). In his desire to popularize everyday Ukrainian village life and folklore, and to reveal all its charms to the citizens of the Russian capital, he was pursuing two goals. On the one hand he didn't want to impede people's grasp of information about Ukraine – and to that end he created an entirely Russian speech for his characters, just adorning them with colourful local turns of phrase, which were more folkloric than they were linguistically accurate. However, as though wishing to display his own absolute ease in understanding the Ukrainian language, he included fairly lengthy epigraphs in Ukrainian to each story, thereby showing off his beloved language in all its beauty and revealing its musicality. He also provided his readers with a short vocabulary list at the end of each volume, to explain the Ukrainian words they might not understand.

Bogoslavsky deploys a similar method. The inhabitants of his Belarusian village speak Russian, and the Belarusian language only appears at the moment when you move from the sphere of the everyday to the elevated sphere. And it is for that reason that the author translates the most important moment – the finale – from Russian into Belarusian. The ending of the play, written in Belarusian, instantly removes the narrative from the plane of normal life, which the author had been describing in such detail in order to achieve an especial degree of verisimilitude. This shifts our perception towards a metaphysical interpretation of the play. Without the use of the Belarusian language it would have been impossible to achieve such an instantaneous effect, such swiftness in shifting from one plane to another, from the grim reality of the everyday to vertiginous heights, to a sonorous distance.

The linguistic basis of the play is a deliberately impoverished use of the Russian language. The features of the protagonists' dialogues might appear at first glance to be rather undifferentiated, at times almost impersonal. But in order not to justify any reproaches to him for the poverty of his language, the author almost casually demonstrates a truly Pushkinian sensitivity in the way he handles words in his stage directions.[5]

It is very important to examine how the problem of expressive phrases gets resolved within the narrow linguistic limits which the author imposes upon himself. In most of the scenes Bogoslavsky avoids obscenity, even at the cost of some improbability, and obscene expressions appear only in scenes of the utmost harshness. In the other dialogues Bogoslavsky often deliberately smoothes over the expressive linguistic characteristics of his heroes, and coarse language, except in two scenes which will be discussed below, does not appear at all – something which is entirely untypical for contemporary plays in the 'New Drama' format.

The vocabulary of obscenity was from the very start of 'New Drama' one of the most controversial issues, but with time it became a characteristic marker not only of 'New Drama', but also subsequently just of modern playwriting – as an indicator of truthfulness, of maximum verisimilitude, or, in the phrase of one critic, as the 'most vivid and striking vocabulary, reflecting real life'.[6] 'If for some people obscenity is just a standard feature, for others it is almost like a magical incantation', writes the critic Il'mira Bolotian, noting at the same time that obscene vocabulary in one way or another is to be found in all the plays of 'New Drama', even if it fulfils a variety of functions.[7]

Why did Bogoslavsky remove obscenity from the main part of his text, leaving it in only in two key scenes? And what should happen to the text of a drama from which the obscenity has been removed?

One characteristic example is Mikhail Bulgakov's self-censorship in the play *The Days of the Turbins* (1926), based on his Civil War novel *The White Guard*. Since it was unthinkable to imagine obscene swearing on the stage of the Moscow Art Theatre in the period when *The Days of the Turbins* was staged, so the 'obscene words' and 'vulgar language of the streets' used by Lieutenant Myshlaevsky, as mentioned in the author's original novel, had to be transformed by Bulgakov into something else for the stage, and we cannot deny that he found effective ways of doing so. Bulgakov simply increased the expressive force of most of Myshlaevsky's speeches in the play, thereby compensating for the absence of what was a lengthy obscene monologue in his novel.

And what happens to the linguistic features of the characters from *The Way People Love*? In which scenes does Bogoslavsky include obscenity? The author injects obscene vocabulary for the first time near the beginning of the play, in the fourth scene:

Kolia   Lie down. Lie down, I said.

Lius'ka   No, no. Let me go.

Kolia   Lie down, you cunt. Stop wriggling. And now you're going to love me. Oh, you're really going to love me, oh, how you're going to respect me. I'll make you stop being stuck-up, you're going to behave as soft as silk.
  Now, then? Do you like that?

Lius'ka   Kolia, no! Kolen'ka, Kolen'ka, no, let me go. Kolia ... let me go ...
  No ... Kolen'ka, please, not in front of the kid, not in front of the kid, I'm begging you ... Kolia. No. No. No.
Kolia   Yes. Yes. Yes, cunt. Here I am. Here's my heart for you, here you are! (p. 62)

The second time is much later in the play (scene 16), when Sergei has a drunken fight in the snow with Van'ka:

Sergei   I'll ... you fucker ... I'll ... you fucker, you fucker (*hits him*). [...] *Van'ka looks at him fearfully.* (*Sergei staggers back under this gaze, and a few steps further on turns around and then falls face down in the snow.*) You fucker! You fucker! You fucker! (*He abruptly jumps up, rushes over towards Van'ka and embraces him.*) Forgive me, forgive me, you're like my own brother, forgive me, Vanechka. My dear brother, forgive me, I don't know what came over me, forgive me my friend, forgive, forgive me, Vanechka. Here. Here, you beat me, beat me, kill me, forgive me! I don't know what I was thinking, forgive me, Van'ka ... Ooh, fuck. What's going on in my head ... And this fucking snow ... (*Stands up, brushes himself down with a shudder, and leaves.*) (pp. 95–6)

The repetition is what makes this scene so dreadful. It creates an impression of monotony, and therefore of this being the everyday. And it is in the very ordinariness of such terrible things that the full horror lies. This diminished level of expressiveness also makes it possible to tackle yet another important theme, that of endurance, which during the course of the play begins to seem like endurance at the limits of the possible, and in the finale appears superhuman.

The finale, which takes place after a string of terrible events recounted with alarming normality, is marked by the transition into the Belarusian language: and this choice of language turns out to be extremely important. The characters' use of Russian hitherto could be described as 'stylized Russian'. It is a Russian which has been worn down and is almost characterless: the linguistic features of individual protagonists are almost stripped of any individuality, with the exception of those scenes which are connected with memories.

The absence of metaphors and of imagery in the protagonists' speeches during the main action is abundantly compensated for by the linguistic richness of the folkloric song at the end. All the threads lead towards this, and it is this song which has to 'go off with a bang' as they say in the theatre: the author stakes everything upon it, and he has not misjudged it.

The Russian spectator (like the reader) perceives the Belarusian language in the finale as a manifestation of a long-growing necessity of speaking out at last about the most important thing, about the thing which the protagonists have painstakingly avoided in their everyday conversations – about the human soul.

> Oy, and so my soul,
> Why have you missed out on paradise?
> Oy and in what way my soul,
> Were you guilty?
> You, out of miserliness,
> You, out of stupidity,
> You ruined your soul,
> You destroyed the crown.
> In the midst of paradise
> Stands a tree,
> Stands a tree,
> A cypress.
> So on that tree,
> There are heavenly little birds.
> Their little voices
> Are those of the seraphim
> Their little voices
> Are those of the seraphim.
> They sing songs
> Like cherubs.
> Oh it is merry to live
> In our paradise,
> It is merry,
> But there's nobody to do that! (p.110)

For the finale of his *The Way People Love* Bogoslavsky selected this spiritual song, recorded in the Gomel' region in south-eastern Belarus, called 'Three Angels', in the edition made by the well-known collector and performer of Belarusian folklore Ivan Kirchuk.[8] You can also find variants of this song in the form of a spiritual poem in ethnographic sources, whose wide geographical spread is striking: for example 'The Poem about the Sinful Soul' recorded at the beginning of the twentieth century in the Perm' region, in the distant Ural mountains.[9]

In modern song culture there are several variants of the song 'Three Angels', including 'You my dear...' and 'Heaven', available in the Russian language. All these variants are extremely popular, and are performed by folk groups such as the ensemble The Cossack Circle', and by well-known musicians such as Elena Kamburova. In its Belarusian variant the song 'Three Angels' is also performed by monastery choirs.

Just to dwell on this a little further: the modern Russian versions of the song 'Three Angels' are much closer in their words to the Belarusian version recorded by Kirchuk. Ivan Kirchuk says that he does not usually perform the opening of the folkloric song, but the differences are much more noticeable towards the end of the song.[10] If the earlier spiritual poem from the Perm' region ends with the words 'The angel of the night said: Down in our hell fire burns, and pitch bubbles, and thirsting worms crawl about. Amen',[11] then the Belarusian song from the Gomel' district culminates in a very striking conclusion to the effect that life in heaven is merry, only there's nobody to live there. This poetic premonition in the folk song can, in historical perspective, be applied to the catastrophe at Chernobyl', a tragedy of truly universal scale. And thus, through its continuing existence in the genre of a spiritual verse, 'Three Angels' acquires an additional epic force.

The author of the play has no doubt at all that Russian spectators will understand the Belarusian language. But the use of the two languages is only a technical aspect of the device. The purpose is far more complex and interesting: to create an opportunity to escape the everyday and rise above the humdrum. During the entire action of the play the protagonists speak and act as though they never raised their faces upwards, and the impact of their unexpected impulse towards something higher, towards heaven and towards the soul is all the more powerful for that. And this effect is achieved primarily by the author through linguistic means.

In this context the choice of a spiritual folk song turns out to be an ideal one. Firstly, because it is plausible, both historically and in this particular situation: Liliia Barankevic, one of the most authoritative researchers of Belarusian folklore, has noted that her observations in recent years allow her to speak about a new tendency that has become apparent, involving the performance of eschatological verses during funeral rites.[12] Thus it is possible to state that the author's choice of a song for Sergei's wake is not just a product of his creative intention, but also fits with a ritual which has already begun to establish itself in the lives of the common people.

Furthermore, the spiritual song is associated on the one hand with religion, and on the other with folklore. The shared historical heritage of the Russian, Belarusian and Ukrainian languages has meant that the song 'Three Angels' gets performed by Ukrainian folklore groups as well as Russian ones, as previously mentioned. It is very important to note that the religious musical groups, not only in Belarus, but also the Russian monastery choirs, perform the song precisely in Belarusian, notwithstanding the existence of a Russified version. For this departure from the usual Russian language of everyday life, and this transition into the sphere of one of the two other East Slav languages, creates a similar effect as would a switch into Old Church Slavonic, which to a similar extent as folklore coexisted over a long period of time contemporaneously in the lives of all three East Slav nations.[13] And so it turns out that this spiritual song (or spiritual poem) embodies at one and the same time a religious and a folkloric and mythological mindset which is common to all the Eastern Slavs.

The collecting of spiritual verses and songs has a long tradition in literature and scholarship. P. V. Kireevsky, for the first edition of his *Russian Folk Songs* in 1848, precisely selected the spiritual verses out of all of his enormous collection, which had been assembled from the notes taken by a number of people – among them the writers Pushkin and Gogol'.[14] The most thorough investigation of Belarusian folklore in pre-Revolutionary Russia was undertaken by Evdokim Romanov: between 1885 and 1912 he published nine *Belarusian Collections* with spiritual verses, together with proverbs, riddles, apocrypha, spells and so on, and a significant amount of material was also collected and published by Pavel Sheyn in 1902.[15] The collecting of Belarusian spiritual verses still continued into the 1920s, but then for a long period of time under Soviet rule, effectively from the 1930s to the 1970s, spiritual verses became a blank space in Belarusian ethnomusicology.[16] However, beginning in the 1970s, folklore expeditions under the direction of Professor L. F. Kostiukovets not only provided ethnographers and folklorists with new materials, but also served as the basis for the popularization of Belarusian folk songs outside the borders of Belarus.

The genre of the spiritual poem not only stimulates an aspiration towards the higher realm and towards the eternal, but also provides a sense of engagement with the culture and with history. Representatives of the mythological tendency in literary criticism of the nineteenth century tended to correlate the emergence of spiritual verses with ancient times, and were inclined to see pagan roots in them. To be more precise, they found in Russian everyday life of ancient times, and in the visions of the world associated with that, the foundations upon which was formed the 'generative model' (to use a term from Structuralism) of the spiritual verse. I. Iu. Nekrasov, for example, was convinced that spiritual verses were being sung even before the tenth-century conversion of Kievan Rus' to Christianity, and in the times of Prince Vladimir.[17]

In the finale of Bogoslavsky's play *The Way People Love*, when the song 'Three Angels' is heard, the heroine is sitting between her two husbands, with her head resting on the shoulder of one, and taking the hand of the other. They have died, but they have not left her. The pagan and Christian worlds in which the protagonists find themselves thanks to this song is a space in which everything is mixed up together, good and evil, heaven and hell, vice and virtue, the living and the dead.

The artistic space of the ordinary village gradually becomes a pagan spiritual space, where not only political but also temporal and religious boundaries have ceased to exist. Everything is mixed up here, but everything belongs. Moscow is an alien heaven, and none of the main protagonists ever gets there alive, any more than any of them attain heaven once they are dead.

For the protagonists of the play heaven is empty. In the middle of it there is a tree, and there are little birds on the tree singing cherubic songs in seraphic voices, but there is nobody to live in heaven. And why? Because they are sitting there dead, alongside those whom they loved, as we all are, with our terrible capacity for endurance and our love, which is given once and for all, and for an entire life. For that is the way people love.

In conclusion it is possible to argue that Dmitry Bogoslavsky unfolds the action of his play in an artistic space which corresponds to the age-old peasant world view of the Eastern Slavs, and by skilfully combining two languages together. The artistic space of *The Way People Love* possesses distinct characteristics, in the sense that time, distance and frontiers all become irrelevant.

Translated from the Russian by J. A. E. Curtis

Notes

1. Dmitry Bogoslavsky, *The Way People Love*, in *Luchshie p'esy 2011: Sbornik*, (Moscow: NF Vserossiyskiy dramaturgicheskiy konkurs "Deystvuyushchie litsa", Livebook/Gayatri, 2012), 110. Page references to this edition will be given in brackets after further quotations from the text.
2. Iurii Lotman, *O russkoi literature* (St Petersburg: Iskusstvo-SPB, 1997), 621.
3. Anna Zalizniak, Irina Levontina and Aleksei Shmelev, *Kliuchevye idei russkoi iazykovoi kartiny mira* (Moscow: Yazyki slavyanskoy kul'tury, 2005), 121; and Vasilii Belov, *Lad* (Moscow: Molodaya gvardiya, 1982).
4. Dmitry Bykov, *Na pustom meste: Stat'i, esse*, (St Petersburg: Limbus Press, 2016), 5.
5. Bogoslavsky follows in the tradition of Mikhail Bulgakov in keeping stage directions to a minimum, or in removing them altogether. This minimalization of the stage directions allows him to accord maximum weight to every 'authorial' remark. And the author uses this in order to create a soundscape of the village. The reader immediately gets a sense of a real village in this play, in which there is no din, but in which there are sounds, and each sound has its own importance: '*The doors creak. The boots shuffle. / The latch makes a clangour. The unoiled metal rings squeak. / The water pours from the hose. The dog barks.*' Modern-day theatre directors working on contemporary drama often find a way of ensuring that the spectators become aware of these stage directions in a play.
6. Larisa Vetelina, '"Novaia drama" XX–XXI vv.: problematika, tipologiia, estetika, istoriia voprosa', *Vestnik Omskogo Universiteta* 1 (2009): 108–14 (112).
7. Il'mira Bolotian, '"Novaia drama" mezhdu zhizn'iu i internetom', *Sovremennaia Dramaturgiia*, 1 (2008): 187.
8. Ivan Kirchuk is a professional ethnographer by training. He not only studies the folkloric heritage of Belarus, organizing research expeditions himself and arranging re-creations of ancient rituals, but he also performs all over the world with his folk group Troitsa, presents programmes on TV, holds master classes, writes books and teaches at a university in Minsk. See Ivan Kirchuk, *Avtobany i menestreli* (Mytishchi: OOO "Kovcheg", 2009; first published in Minsk, 2008).
9. Petr Bogoslovsky, *Materialy po narodnomu bytu, fol'kloru i literaturnoy starine*, vol. 1 (Perm': tip. raypotrebsoyuza, 1924).
10. In conversation Ivan Kirchuk explained that he just performs a fragment of the folk song: 'What I remember is that it is a fragment (the portion that I perform) of a spiritual poem recorded in the village of Varfolomeevka in the Gomel' region not far from Chernobyl', before the disaster there. I don't sing the beginning.'
11. *Golubinaia kniga: Russkie narodnye dukhovnye stikhi XI–XIX vv.*, L. F. Soloshchenko and Iu. S. Prokoshin (eds) (Moscow: Moskovskiy rabochiy, 1991), 229–30.

12 See Liliia Barankevic, *Printsipy klassifikatsii dukhovnykh stikhov* (2008), available online at: https://docplayer.ru/29052470-Principy-klassifikacii-duhovnyh-stihov.html
13 The decline of Old Russian took place at the same time as the decline of the single version of the Church Slavonic language used in the liturgy. It was on the basis of the Old Russian revision of the Church Slavonic language in the Great Lithuanian Principality that Ukraino-Belarusian was formed (which is now used in the Ukrainian Greek-Catholic church), and in the Great Muscovite Principality it was Old Muscovite (which is now used by Old Believers) recensions of Church Slavonic. See B. A. Uspensky, *Istoriia russkogo literaturnogo iazyka. XI–XVII vv.*, 3rd rev. edn (Moscow: Aspekt Press, 2002).
14 See P. V. Kireevsky, *Russkie narodnye pesni, sobrannye Petrom Kireevskim* (Moscow, 1848).
15 Evdokim Romanov, *Beloruskii sbornik v 9-ti tomakh* (Vitebsk, 1886–1912); P. V. Sheyn, *Materialy dlia izucheniia byta i iazyka russkago naseleniia Severo-Zapadnogo kraia: Sobrannye i privedennyia v poriadok P. V. Sheynom* (St Petersburg: Tipografiya Imperatorskoy Akademii Nauk, 1887–1902).
16 See M. Garetski, V. Dziarzhynski, and P. Karavay, *Vypisi z belaruskay litaratury* (Minsk, 1925); and M. Garetski and A. Iagorau, *Narodnyia pesni z melediyami* (Minsk, 1928).
17 I.Iu. Nekrasov, 'Zamechaniia po povodu russkogo narodnogo skazaniia o 12-i piatnitsakh: K voprosu o proiskhozhdenii dukhovnykh narodnykh stikhov', *Filologicheskie zapiski* 3 (1870): 1–26.

Conclusion

Summer of 2019

J. A. E. Curtis

Exactly ten years ago Birgit Beumers and Mark Lipovetsky predicted that 'New Drama' in Russia had run its course, and that cinema was the medium that would dominate the second decade of the twenty-first century:

> Many playwrights of New Drama have moved into film [...]. Maybe what has been outlined [...] for the 'theatrical period' will be developed in full through cinema – documentary, fiction or a hybrid form. New Drama has doubtless been one of the most promising phenomena in modern Russian culture, but then – many brilliant projects have ground to a halt, dissolving in self-repetitions or ending in the commercial cycle.[1]

As several accounts in this volume have demonstrated, this prediction with regard to Russia – but also in relation to Ukraine and Belarus – has proved to be somewhat premature, and the 'New Drama' movement has continued to fuel and energize innovation in playwriting across the entire region. But during the second decade of this century political and social developments in those three countries have also introduced new pressures and strains to the activities of leading Russian-language theatre-makers, and the decline of 'New Drama' may indeed by 2019 have become irreversible.

By way of a conclusion, I have invited the knowledgeable academic scholars and theatre-makers who have contributed to this volume to offer some further, updated reflections on the situation in these three countries, as they have seen it developing over the summer of 2019. I have shaped these contributions into an informal account, without necessarily identifying the source for every comment. This is a story which is still unfolding and being transformed.[2]

Russia

The aftermath of the deaths of Mikhail Ugarov and Elena Gremina in the spring of 2018 has proved to be an extremely challenging period for the independent theatre they founded, Teatr.doc. It is scarcely surprising that no one individual was prepared to take on all the strains of running the theatre in the fearless and exhausting way in which Gremina and Ugarov had been doing it. Instead, the management of the theatre has been devolved to a younger generation of directors and administrators, who are sharing the burdens among themselves and pursuing a variety of projects. Once again, however, Teatr.doc has also been forced to move premises, and it is now established in two separate locations, one on Sadovnicheskaia Embankment (named 'Doc on the Island'), and the other in a newer space just behind the Gogol' Centre on Kazakov Street. This is where Moscow's Liubimovka Festival took place in early September 2019. These several factors will perhaps prove to become, as one or two commentators have suggested, a force for fragmentation in the longer term. Some have suggested that the modes of documentary theatre established under Gremina and Ugarov had already begun to lose their freshness, and that new forms and languages of theatre are needed now, to articulate the realities of life in Russia during Putin's fourth term as president. Molly Flynn quotes the controversial opinion of the theatre critic Elena Koval'skaia, who has even suggested that 'it would be better to let Teatr.doc close and to create something new, than to try to preserve a project whose time has passed'.[3]

Meanwhile, harassment continues and seems to be intensifying. On the very day after Ugarov's death in early April 2018, a group of people bought ten tickets to a Teatr.doc play and announced their intention to disrupt the evening's performance. The theatre published the threats – and many of their supporters turned out to protect the actors. In the event, the threatened disruption never materialized, and those who had made the threats never showed up. During the summer of 2019 no fewer than three similar and separate acts of provocation were organized, in an attempt to prevent Teatr.doc staging its productions on a given evening. On 28 August a performance of *Vyyti iz shkafa* (*Coming Out of the Closet*), a play which has been running since 2016, about two young gay men discussing the difficulties of coming out, was disrupted by activists including members of the anti-liberal Russophile group SERB. One of them may have brought in fake documents to suggest he was over eighteen, when in fact he was a minor, so as to 'prove' that the theatre was exposing children to 'propaganda of non-traditional relationships', in contravention of the law. Objections were shouted about the theatre's use of obscenities, and about its critical stance towards President Putin. The production's director, Anastasiia Patlay, was obliged to accompany the police back to the station to respond to the protestors' complaints, but in the end it was one of the protestors who was eventually charged with 'petty hooliganism'. On 20 September a production of *Voyna blizko* (*War is Close*), originally staged by Gremina, was disrupted by SERB activists. The play, which includes a diary written by a civilian during the fighting in Eastern Ukraine, followed by a section written by Mark Ravenhill about media manipulation of the truth, has a third section about the Ukrainian film director Oleg Sentsov, who was detained by the Russians after the 2014 annexation of the Crimea, and who had been released in a prisoner exchange just recently. It was this third section which was disrupted, with activists chucking some foul-smelling substance into the small auditorium, which had to be evacuated and cleaned before the performance could continue. And then on 28 September Teatr.doc hosted a show by Ekaterina Nenasheva with GRUZ 300 called *Rave No. 228*, 'an immersive project about drug abuse and the falsification of cases under article 228' (of the Russian legal code). This performance was disrupted by police officers, who had to be persuaded in lengthy discussions that the actors were not in fact engaged in drug dealing.

Commentators disagree about whether Teatr.doc has moved entirely away from its early 'zero position' towards becoming more and more politically engaged, or whether it is more accurate to describe it as being committed to human rights activism rather than political theatre as such. On the one hand, there has been a new focus on re-examining the traumas of the Soviet era (Communist rule, the Second World War, Stalin's Terror and the Gulag) in the context of modern-day repressions and the promotion of 'official' versions of history. But a couple of more recent productions seem to be less overtly related to politics. One of these, *Budushchee.doc* (*Future.Doc*), written by Ugarov's son Ivan, is made up of verbatim interviews with young people all over Russia. Adolescents whose age corresponds roughly to that of Teatr.doc itself are asked how they see prospects for the future. Another recent project was a one-off 'act of solidarity' initiated by Zarema Zaudinova and others called *Tri sestry* (*The Three Sisters*), to express support for the Khachaturian sisters – three young women who killed their father after years of rape and abuse, and were now facing prison sentences of eight to twenty years for murder. Many related protests highlighted the leniency of attitudes in Russia towards domestic violence and abuse. Whether it is explicitly political or not, human rights activism based on documentary techniques has become and more and more central to Teatr.doc's work. The authorities – and right-wing pressure groups – clearly care little for such distinctions in any case, and at present the right to freedom of expression within the performing spaces of Teatr.doc is being challenged quite blatantly and aggressively.

During 2019 the release from house arrest of the film and theatre director Kirill Serebrennikov, like the release from prison as part of an international prisoner exchange of the Ukrainian film director Oleg Sentsov, might have seemed like signs of a more tolerant attitude on the part of the authorities towards those in the cultural sphere who stood up against the power of the state. Expert evaluation of the embezzlement charge against Serebrennikov and others concluded in mid-August that no money had in fact been stolen. It should be remembered, however, that Serebrennikov was still only released on bail, and to this day is forbidden to leave the country – even though he has residence rights in Germany. The summer of 2019 was characterized by widespread and frequent street protests in Moscow and elsewhere about local elections scheduled for early September, for which opposition candidates had been to a large extent decreed ineligible. Many arrests took place, but one which attracted particular attention in theatre circles was that of a young actor, Pavel Ustinov, who was given a prison sentence of three-and-a-half years for supposed violent behaviour during a demonstration on 3 August. The court refused to admit as evidence a video which clearly showed that Ustinov was not even taking part in the demonstration. Hundreds of journalists and cultural figures took part in carefully choreographed protests, and by the end of September the court reviewed the case and gave him a one-year suspended sentence instead.

In the legal sphere, the new law which 'forbids criticism "in indecent form" of symbols of power and of state bodies' came into force on 29 March 2019. There have already been several dozen cases of its implementation since then, with many fines (ranging from 30 to 100 thousand roubles) handed out, and materials from social media and the wider internet being forcibly taken down on the grounds that they 'disrespect the authorities'. Although the law primarily affects internet users and the public realm, it nonetheless feeds into the problem of self-censorship and uncertainty over what can and cannot be said on stage. In a not unrelated case, Dmitry Smolev, a leading actor at Moscow's Sovremennik theatre (who had played D'Artagnan in their show *Dumas*, and has appeared in Chekhov's *The Cherry Orchard*), was sentenced to eight days of detention for a twelve-second video in which he comically depicted a drunken traffic cop: the charges included the illegal wearing of an official uniform, plus petty hooliganism.

One of the many legacies of Teatr.doc and of 'New Drama' may prove to have been the nurturing of a new, younger audience for theatre, one whose members have become impatient with the classically contoured or more commercial repertoires of mainstream theatres. A number of our contributors have commented on the ways in which certain theatres in Moscow (the Gogol' Centre, Praktika, the Theatre of Nations and even more traditional venues such as the Pushkin Theatre or the Moscow Art Theatre) have started to adopt a more adventurous and innovative aesthetic, often exploiting multi-media technological resources. They have also promoted more liberal messages in relation to social issues, but without engaging in explicitly confrontational political programming directed against the existing regime. An artist like Ivan Vyrypaev has to some extent become institutionalized, and performances of his works are to be seen at a wide range of theatres. Teatr.doc, which once stood almost alone on Moscow's theatre scene, is now increasingly competing with rival venues.

'New Drama' has not only had a substantial and enduring impact on the capital's theatre scene, but also in other places such as St Petersburg, Ekaterinburg (in the Urals) and regional theatre more generally. However, according to Zaudinova:

> 'New Drama' died with Ugarov and Gremina. We live in a new reality and a different Russia to the one that existed during the period of 'New Drama'. [...] They stage contemporary writers even less now than they did before. [...] During the flourishing of 'New Drama', the country was freer, or at least it seemed freer, there was more money from oil, prosperity. That all changed after 2012.

Alexander Trustrum Thomas concludes that progressive, independent theatre remains starved of resources, unable to foster the kinds of cultural growth for which there is evidently considerable potential. If 'New Drama' was once a broad movement transcending national borders and encompassing the post-Soviet space in the spirit of the new, it is now a localized phenomenon: war, new borders – both physical and linguistic – and an absence of leadership have created a fractured cultural landscape. That said, the deteriorating conditions do continue to generate new work that responds in bold and challenging ways. The swelling protest movements and the rallying of the independent theatre scene to activist causes, as witnessed at the past two sessions of the annual Liubimovka festival, perhaps suggest that the apolitical disengagement of previous generations is giving way to a new wave of committed art in the remaining spaces of free thought and expression.

Ukraine

The essays and interviews offered earlier in this volume trace the many ways in which Ukrainian 'New Drama' has broken away from the close collaboration with Russian 'New Drama' which characterized the first fifteen years of this century. Nevertheless, in Ukraine as in Russia, perhaps one of the greatest benefits has been a renewed sense of vocation among playwrights: right up to the present day 'New Drama' has helped to legitimate their sense of doing something worthwhile and meaningful.

Molly Flynn reports, however, that the Theatre of Displaced People is no longer active, or at least not in the way in which it functioned previously. In the summer of 2017 Georg Genoux and Natasha Vorozhbyt handed over artistic directorship of the company to several of its members. Since that time the name has appeared as a producing organization for a playwriting festival at PostPlay and a few other events, but it no longer functions as a unified group in the way that it did in the early years. This is partly because Genoux and Vorozhbyt have moved on to other projects. Genoux has relocated to Germany, and Vorozhbyt has gone on to write several high-profile projects including a film scenario about the battle for Donetsk airport, *Kiborgi* (*Cyborgs*) (2017), and another called *Dikoe pole* (*Wild Fields*) (2018), based on a novel by Serhiy Zhadan. At the moment she is making her directorial debut with a film version of her play about the human costs of conflict, *Plokhie dorogi* (*Bad Roads*), with funding from the Ukrainian Cultural Foundation. Given that the fighting in Ukraine has been going on for five years now, with no end in sight, it is perhaps not surprising that it becomes impossible to sustain an explicit response to the war in the form of a project like the Theatre of Displaced People. There is no doubt that Vorozhbyt has had to confront the sheer sense of burn-out that working in such circumstances inflicts on someone with a creative vocation.

Certain playwrights continue to feel stifled by prevailing attitudes of social conservatism. In Ukraine, for example, there is no law against 'the propaganda of non-traditional values' such as there is in Russia. The Ukrainian Orthodox Church declared its independence from the Russian Orthodox Church in January 2019, but this is by no means a guarantee that more liberal social attitudes will hold sway there than in Russia, or that blasphemy and obscenity might be tolerated on stage. In the absence of any explicit bans, Maksym Kurochkin observes that there is little enthusiasm among audiences, for example, for drama which raises gender issues or treats themes of homosexuality, and that many Ukrainian theatres would still be reluctant to stage plays of this kind.

Even in the absence of a wider international sphere of contacts, there is nevertheless great energy among theatre-makers, and many works still emerge of considerable artistic originality. One difficulty for Ukrainian playwrights is indeed the problem of tearing their gaze away from the intense crisis in their own country in order to look towards broader horizons. To give an obvious example, global issues such as climate change, degrowth economics or green capitalism have yet to make a significant appearance in Ukrainian playwriting; gender issues have begun to be addressed in recent years, but in the absence of flourishing cultural links with other countries, there is still a risk (as indeed there is with Russia), that global topical themes emerge there somewhat later in time than they may do in some Western countries.

The postcolonial society that is Ukraine has rejected in many respects the cultural domination of Russia, and of the Russian language. The playwright Maksym Kurochkin has resolved only to write in Ukrainian in the future, and expects Ukrainian-language drama to blossom in the future. The annual festival of Week of Contemporary Plays project has recently been renewed, after some anxious moments, and for the time being will continue to accept submissions of plays written either in Ukrainian or in Russian. The legacy of the transnational project of Russian-language 'New Drama' still survives in Ukraine, in other words, but its future is somewhat uncertain. In the meantime Kurochkin also observes that women dramatists are acquiring a much higher profile in Ukraine than previously. But he notes that the absence of arts organizations (whether in the form of state structures or private foundations) means that it is very difficult for many young playwrights to progress beyond the staging of some early plays. There is little financial or career security, nor is Ukrainian contemporary drama underpinned by any kind of profound theoretical modelling or training. Others feel more confident, on the other hand, that new 'voices' will emerge in time. Ukraine is in such an existential, self-reflexive mode at the moment that good writing is likely to emerge, which will surely question and imagine an entirely different future.

Belarus

Tania Arcimovich comments that 'New Drama' has made considerable advances in Belarus in recent years. This form of playwriting has challenged widespread assumptions in Belarus that theatre has little to contribute in the socio-political sphere. Belarusian 'New Drama' addresses many topical problems of societies in the post-Soviet space, such as everyday violence, sexism, discrimination and nationalism. This in turn has engendered the emergence of new audiences, who see this kind of drama as means of engaging with social debates.

This shift in audience perceptions has been brought about by the activities of the Centre for Playwriting in Belarus and its peripatetic Laboratory for Contemporary Playwriting. These have staged performances in state theatres, but also in alternative spaces such as the OK16 cultural hub in Minsk. There have now been four rounds of the Festival and competition for contemporary drama called WriteBox (an independent initiative), which supports Belarusian playwrights, including those who write in the Belarusian language (as opposed to Russian). One significant playwright who has emerged through this festival is Ekaterina Chekatovskaya with her plays *Mastectomy* (2018) and *The Last Breakfast* (2019), both written in Belarusian. However, given the ongoing absence of any state schemes to support creative artists like her, Chekatovskaya still finds herself obliged to translate her plays into Russian and then submit them to Russian theatre festivals: *The Last Breakfast* was shortlisted for the 2019 Liubimovka Festival, and two other plays by Belarusian authors made it into the final programme – Mariya Bel'kovich's *Blagopoluchie* (*Well-being*) and *Vse normal'no* (*Everything's Fine*) by Vladislava Khmel', alongside Pavel Priazhko's new play *Komitet Grustiashchego Bozhestva* (*The Committee of the Mournful Deity*).

In recent years more and more women playwrights have appeared in Belarus, as well as texts with feminist themes, such as those by Yaro and by Viktoriya Biran. This is becoming increasingly widespread, although not all women writers define themselves as feminists. These writers have also begun to raise ethical questions around issues of playwriting (as with the example of Chekatovskaya's writing about the clinical experience of mastectomy, drawn from real experiences).

Despite the future looking brighter, in the sense that we can be more confident that 'New Drama' and contemporary playwriting in Belarus are going to develop in new directions, as well as being created in various linguistic registers, these positive shifts are, as before, all associated with the efforts of activists from the world of alternative theatre. Such plays rarely figure in state theatres, and if they do appear there, they undergo a process of 'editing' – especially in order to remove all obscenities. This happened, for example, with Priazhko's play *Harvest* when it was staged in the spring of 2019 by the Yanka Kupala National Academic Theatre in Minsk. And of course the effect of this 'editing' was significantly to distort the unique, original sound-world of Priazhko's text. A change in attitude in these theatres will only come about when cultural policy in the country as a whole is altered. And despite the numerous initiatives by cultural activists, it is difficult to know when this will be achieved.

The date of 24 September 2019 marked a new development in the Belarus Free Theatre's history of confrontational relations with the Belarusian authorities. One of their shows, under the title *Dom No. 5 (Building No. 5)*, was for the first time performed in an officially approved state venue in Belarus. Up until now all their shows and activist events have taken place in independent venues, and without the permission of the authorities. *Building No. 5* is based on a journalistic investigation of people with mental disabilities, weaving their experiences into a wide-ranging narrative and highlighting the ways in which their lives are restricted by social norms. The production displays pity and concern for its protagonists, but also showcases their exceptional qualities; the audience is confronted with the common human aspirations of people with a wide range of disabilities, and comes to understand the ways in which they are made to feel isolated and cut off from everyday life. The directors of the show were Nicolai Khalezin and Natal'ia Koliada.

If 1 October 2019 marks the cut-off point for our research investigations for this volume, then that date was marked by two revealing – and very contrasting – events in Belarusian culture. *The Moscow Times* on that day reported recent talks between the governments of Russia and Belarus to deepen their cooperation, talks which have fuelled anxieties about a possible de facto annexation of Belarus by its powerful neighbour. Russian proposals to go beyond agreements over economic, taxation and energy policies were met with wariness by the Belarusian government, and subsequently provoked public protests.[4] All this served to underline the closely integrated political and economic systems of the two countries, a form of integration which has extended to the realm of 'New Drama' as well, and still continues to this day.

On 1 October it was also announced that the Belarusian author Svetlana Aleksievich, who was awarded the Nobel Prize for Literature in 2015, was to be presented in London with the 2019 Anna Politkovskaya Award. This award was set up in honour of the campaigning Russian journalist Anna Politkovskaya (1958–2006), known especially for her fearless reporting of the brutal treatment of civilians during Russia's war in Chechnya, despite numerous acts of intimidation and violence against her. She was murdered in Moscow on 7 October 2006. Despite a police investigation into her murder, those who ordered it were never brought to justice. Aleksievich had met Politkovskaya in 2005, and shares with her a passionate concern about the traumatic impact of war on civilian populations. One of Aleksievich's books is a compilation based on verbatim interviews with people who had been traumatized as children by their experiences in the Second World War, and it was published in English in 2019 under the title *Last Witnesses: Unchildlike Stories*. Her work offers a counter-narrative to the official, triumphalist versions of the conflict promoted by the Soviet state, and by Putin's Russia today.

One of the many legacies of 'New Drama', and of the human rights activism associated with it, has been this prominence of women's voices speaking out across Russia, Ukraine and Belarus about issues of transnational concern. It would appear that the time has finally come now to move on from 'New Drama' in Russia; but in Ukraine and Belarus the impact of 'New Drama' is still shaping and inspiring playwrights of the new generation. The third decade of the twenty-first century will perhaps see the transnationalism of 'New Drama' left behind for good, while exciting new trends emerge in all three countries as they determine their own, more distinct theatrical destinies in the post-Soviet space.

Notes

1 Birgit Beumers and Mark Lipovetsky, *Performing Violence: Literary and Theatrical Experiments of New Russian Drama* (Bristol: Intellect, 2009), 304–5.
2 I am particularly grateful to Tania Arcimovich, Marie-Christine Autant-Mathieu, Noah Birksted-Breen, Molly Thomasy Blasing, Molly Flynn, Maksym Kurochkin, Valeriia Mutc, Natalia Osis, Alexander Trustrum Thomas and Zarema Zaudinova for contributing their thoughts to this concluding essay.
3 Molly Flynn, *Witness Onstage: Documentary Theatre in Twenty-First-Century Russia* (Manchester: Manchester University Press, 2019), p. 161.
4 https://www.themoscowtimes.com/2019/10/01/belarus-rejects-russias-unacceptable-terms-of-integration-a67540

Recommended reading

Reading suggestions relevant to each contribution are to be found in the endnotes of each essay or interview. Significant anthologies in English are mentioned below, but many other plays of Russian-language 'New Drama' have also been translated into English, and may be found in individual, small publications. Recommended here are texts (in English, Russian and French) of more general interest.

Autant-Mathieu, Marie-Christine (ed.). *Les Nouvelles Ecritures russes*. Pézenas: Domens, 2010.
Belarus Free Theatre: *New Plays from Central Europe (the VII International Contest of Contemporary Drama)*. London: Oberon Books, 2014.
Belarus Free Theatre: *Staging a Revolution (New Plays from Eastern Europe: the VIII International Contest of Contemporary Drama)*. London : Oberon Books, 2016.
Beumers, Birgit and Lipovetsky, Mark. *Performing Violence. Literary and Theatrical Experiments of New Russian Drama*. Bristol and Chicago: Intellect, 2009.
Davydova, Marina. *Kul'tura Zero. Ocherki russkoy zhizni i evropeyskoy stseny*. Moscow : NLO, 2018.
Flynn, Molly. *Witness Onstage: Documentary Theatre in Twenty-First-Century Russia*. Manchester: Manchester University Press, 2019.
Freedman, John (ed.). *Real and Phantom Pains: An Anthology of New Russian Drama*. Washington, DC: New Academia Publishing, 2014.
Gremina, Elena and Ugarov, Mikhail. *P'esy i teksty* (2 vols). Moscow: NLO, 2019.
Hanukai, Maksim and Weygandt, Susanna (eds). *New Russian Drama: An Anthology*. New York: Columbia University Press, 2019.
Kempf, Lucie and Moguilevskaia, Tania (eds). *Le Théâtre neo-documentaire: résurgence ou réinvention?* Nancy: PUN, 2013.
Rudnev, Pavel. *Drama pamyati. Ocherki istorii rossiyskoy dramaturgii 1950–2010e*. Moscow: NLO 2018.
Teatr. Zhurnal o teatre, no. 34 (2018), special edition: *Mikhail Ugarov: teoriya, praktika, politika, pedagogika*.
Vilisov, Viktor. *Nas vsekh toshnit: Kak teatr stal sovremennym, a my etogo ne zametili*. Moscow: ACT, 2018.

Index

Agureeva, Polina 101, 102, 108, 110, 111, 113, 114
Aleksandrovsky, Semen 34
Aleksievich/Alexievich, Svetlana 16, 265–6
  Last Witnesses: Unchildlike Stories 266
Alyokhina, Maria 5, 16–17, 47, 226
Anna Iablonskaia: The Return, memorial project 178
Apchel, Olena 142–4, 145, 146–7, 153
  Horizon 200 (with Oksana Danchuk) 142–3
Arbuzov, Aleksei 23
Arcimovich, Tania 14, 76, 264
Ar'e/Ar'ye, Pavel/Pavlo 12, 127, 129, 133, 144, 149, 160
Armianovsky, Piotr 151–2, 154
Azarov, Denis 202

Babchenko, Arkady 42
Barboy, Iury 30–1
Barlig, Oles' 148
Bartoshevich, Aleksei 30
Batalov, Talgat 97
Baudrillard, Jean 33
Beautiful Flowers Theatre (Kharkiv) 147
Beckett, Samuel 33, 101, 225
  Acts Without Words 33
  Krapp's Last Tape 101
  Waiting for Godot 225
Belarus Free Theatre (BFT) 7, 15, 16, 17, 41, 42–3, 44, 45, 46, 47, 50, 75, 77, 223–36, 265
  Being Harold Pinter 47
  Building No. 5 265
  Burning Doors 16, 46, 47, 48, 224, 228, 232, 235
  Counting Sheep 224, 231, 232
  Discovering Love 44
  Generation Jeans 43, 44, 45

Love Songs for Crimea (Return Ticket for Oleg), film 235–6
Master Had a Talking Sparrow, The 231–2
Minsk 2011: A Reply to Kathy Acker 227
Time of Women, The 46, 47
Trash Cuisine 46, 47, 226
Belenitskaia, Nina 84
Berkovich, Evgeny (Zhenia) 84
Berlusconi, Silvio 26
Beumers, Birgit and Mark Lipovetsky 4, 106, 110, 111, 181, 214, 259
Bialkovich/Bel'kovich, Maryya/Mariya 219, 264
  Well-being 264
Bilyts, Ihor/Igor 144, 147
Bilyts Art Centre (Kyiv) 202–4
Bilzho, Andrei 9
Biran, Viktoriya 265
Birksted-Breen, Noah 10, 15, 141–2,
Blasing, Molly Thomasy 14
Blok, Natal'ia 72, 74–5, 144, 147, 149, 151–2, 154, 160
  All This Fucking Mess Upsets Me 72, 74–5
  Bomb 152
  Woman! Sit Down! 147
Blue Blouse, theatre movement 25
Bogdanova, Polina 31
Bogomolov, Konstantin 6, 23, 30, 32, 33, 35
  An Ideal Husband 6, 32
  Musketeers: A Saga 32
Bogoslavsky Dmitry, 76, 77, 78, 214, 228, 244, 247–57
  Points Along/On the Axis of Time 78, 244
  Way People Love, The 247–57
Boiakov, Eduard 26
Bolotian, Il'mira 214, 251

Bol'shoi Drama Theatre (St Petersburg) 85
Bol'shoi Theatre (Moscow) 8, 60
   Nureyev 8, 60
Bondarchuk, Fedor 187
Bondarenko, Andriy 148
   Interview with a Friend 148
BoomBox, band (Ukraine) 228, 235
Borodina, Polina 6
   The Bolotnaya Case 6
Boyd, Sir Michael 11, 195
Brecht, Bertolt 44, 102, 132
British Council 2, 25, 82, 83
Brodskaya, Nadya 225
Brook, Peter 103
Bu-Ba-Bu, poetry collective 122–3
Bulgakov, Mikhail 48, 238, 247, 251–2
   Days of the Turbins, The 251–2
   Master and Margarita, The 48, 238
   White Guard, The 251–2
Butusov, Yury 30
Bykov, Dmitry 16, 250

Cage, John 33
   Lecture on Nothing 33
Carroll, Lewis 97
   Alice in Wonderland 97
Centre for Belarusian Dramaturgy (Minsk) 220
Centre for Playwriting and Directing (Belarus) 73, 264
Centre for Playwriting and Directing (TsDR, Moscow) 24, 123, 202–4, 238
Chekatouskaya/Chekatovskaya, Kacia/Ekaterina 219, 264–5
   Last Breakfast, The 264
   Mastectomy 264–5
Chekhov, Anton 24, 27, 32, 114, 234, 238, 262
   Cherry Orchard, The 262
   Seagull, The 114
Chenskii, Vitalii 122, 130, 147
   Vitalik – A Show About a Man 122, 130–1
Chykanas, Lekha/Liokha 15, 219
Clark, Katerina 10
'Class Act', project 69, 73, 81–93

'Class Act – East/West', project 81, 87–9, 148, 163, 167
Clover, Jack 10

Dadin, Il'dar 50
DAKh Contemporary Art Centre (Kyiv) 193
Danan, Joseph 28
Danilov, Dmitry 247
   The Man from Podol'sk 247
Davydova, Marina 55
Denisova, Aleksandra (Sasha) 95–7
   Alice and the Government 95, 97
   Country Villages.net 97
   Light My Fire 95, 97
   Mayakovsky Fetches Sugar 97
   Plus-Minus Twenty 97
Dépardieu, Gérard 13
Derrida, Jacques 108, 111, 113, 116–17
   'SignatureEventContext' 111
   Specters of Marx 113
Dikiy (Wild) Theatre, (Kyiv) 129, 130–1, 132, 134, 147, 149, 202–4
   Vitalik – A Show About a Man 122, 130–1
Dobrenko, Evgeny and Galin Tihanov, 9
   A History of Russian Literary Theory and Criticism 9
Dodgson, Elyse 2, 11, 14
Dodin, Lev 33
Dos'ko, Maksim 214, 244
   LabRoom 244
   London 244
   Radio Culture 244
Dostoevsky, Fedor 58, 234
Dozhd' (TV channel) 5
Dragunskaia, Kseniia 27
Drama.UA (International Festival of Contemporary Playwriting, Lviv) 125, 129, 130, 134, 144, 145, 148, 149
Dugdale, Sasha 2, 11, 125, 181
Durnenkov, Mikhail 15, 69–80, 83
   Brothers, The 79
Durnenkov, Viacheslav 69, 83, 84, 85
Dzhikaeva, Galina 132, 142, 144, 145, 146, 147–8, 158

Ellis, Jane 82
Ermolova Theatre (Moscow) 178
'Eurasia', drama contest 176, 214, 247

Faer, Varvara (Galina Sin'kina) 26, 60
  Bath-house Attendant, The 60,
  BerlusPutin 26
Felman, Shoshana 108, 112
  Scandal of the Speaking Body, The 112,
Fifth Theatre (Omsk) 178
Fischer-Lichte, Erika 29, 31, 34
  The Transformative Power of
    Performance: A New Aesthetics 29
Fisher, Mark 57–9, 62
Flynn, Molly 10, 13, 14, 260, 263
Fo, Dario 26,
  Two-headed Anomaly 26
Fortinbras Theatre Laboratory (Minsk)
    225, 229, 232, 233
Franko National Theatre (Kyiv) 127, 228
Freedman, John 3, 7, 178
Frolova, Tat'iana 41–2, 44, 45, 46, 49–50
FSB 6, 9, 14

Galin, Aleksandr 23
Gapova, Elena 217, 220
Gatsalov, Marat 30, 238
Genina, Anna 82
Genoux, Georg 13, 145, 163–4, 168–9,
    170, 263
GITIS, (Russian Institute for Theatrical
    Arts) 30, 168
Globe Theatre (London) 231
Gogol', Nikolai 28, 193–6, 198–9, 201, 202,
    204, 247, 250, 255
  Evenings on a Farm near Dikan'ka
    247, 250
  Mirgorod 194
  Viy 28, 193–4
Gogol' Centre (Moscow) 8, 69, 91, 187,
    260, 262
Goldberg, RoseLee 29
  Performance Art: From Futurism to the
    Present 29
Golden Mask, festival 97, 194, 238, 247
Golenko, Maksim 202
Gorbachev, Mikhail, President 23, 42
Gor'ky Literary Institute (Moscow)
    123, 168
Gremina, Elena 2, 4, 6, 10, 11, 12, 14, 23, 24,
    26, 41, 42, 43, 44, 45, 48, 50, 57, 75,
    146–7, 151, 170, 179–80, 186,
    259–60, 262

Grishko, Valery, 6
Grishkovets, Evgenii 27, 101, 105
  How I Ate a Dog 105
Grotowski, Jerzy 103
Gumennaia, Yana 131, 144, 147–8, 158
Gumennyi, Den 72, 122, 131, 144, 146,
    147–8, 149, 158
  Militiaman, The (with Yana
    Gumennaia) 122, 131

Havel, Václav 15, 43
Hayes, Daisy 151–2, 154

Iablonskaia, Anna 14, 124, 175–92
  Kyiv-Moscow 176–8
  Pagans, The (The Terrorists) 14, 175–92
Ianukovich, Viktor, President (*see*
    Yanukovych)
Ibsen, Henrik 27, 95, 103
Ignatov, Ilya 114
  Theatre and Spectators 114
International Contest of Contemporary
    Drama (ICCD) 17–18, 75, 229–30
Iudnikov, Aleksei 97, 146
  Carrier 146
Iukhananov, Boris 30
Iushchenko, Viktor, President 124, 125
Iushkova, Anastasia 91
Ivanov, Andrei 70, 76, 78
  From the College 78

Jirkov, Stas 127
Joseph Beuys Theatre (Moscow) 168

Kane, Sarah 25
Karachinskii, Aleksei 164, 169
Kavaliou, Siarhiej 215
Kazantsev, Aleksei 23
KGB (*see also* FSB) 6, 9, 10, 14
Khalezin, Nicolai/Nikolai (*see also* Belarus
    Free Theatre) 14, 15, 16, 17–18, 41,
    42–3, 44, 46, 48–9, 50, 214, 223–36,
    265
Khlyvnyuk, Andriy 228, 235–6
Khmel', Vladislava 264
  Everything's Fine 264
Khodorkovsky, Mikhail 4, 5, 46, 236
Khromeychuk. Olesya 166
Kitsenko, Tat'iana, 12, 142

Klavdiev, Yuriy 83, 84
KnAM Theatre (Komsomol'sk-on-Amur) 41–2, 43, 44, 45, 46, 48, 49–50
   A Dry and Waterless Place 42
   I Exist 49–50
   I Haven't Yet Started to Live 46, 49, 50
   My Mum 44
   Personal War, A 42, 44, 45
Koliada, Natal'ia/Natalia (*see also* Belarus Free Theatre) 14, 15, 17, 42–3, 46, 223–36, 265
   Dreams 15
Koliada, Nikolai 27
Kopylova, Tatiana 27
Kosodiy, Anastasia 129, 130, 133, 142–4, 146, 148–9, 151–2, 154, 160
   Greatest Pain on Earth, The 148
   Ministry of Education and Science of Ukraine, The 148
   Paradoxical Papa 148
   Song 149, 152
   Timetraveller's Guide to Donbas 142–4, 145
Kostiuchenko, Elena 146
   New Antigone 146
Koval'skaia, Elena 103, 260
Kozhevnikov, Konstantin 26
Krasovsky, Anatoly and Irina 44
Krivochurov, Dmitry 28
Kroupnik, Maria 69–80, 163
Kseshinskaya, Matil'da 7
Kukulin, Ilya and Mark Lipovetsky 9
Kureychik/Kureychyk/Kureichik, Andrey/Andrei 15, 16, 17, 214
Kurochkin, Maksym 11, 13, 27, 123, 124, 128, 132–3, 134, 141, 142, 146, 147, 149, 151–61, 228, 263, 264
   Kitchen, The 11, 123, 132–3
   Monastery, The 152
Kviatkovsky, Iury 28,

Left Front of Art (LEF) 25
Lehmann, Hans Thies 29–31
   Postdramatic Theatre 29–31
Lenin, Vladimir 7, 8, 25, 156
Lesia Ukrainka Academic Theatre (Lviv) 142–4
Levanov, Vadim 83
Levick, Jemima 82

LILAC, band (Belarus) 244
Lipovetsky, Mark (*see also* Beumers, Birgit, and Kukulin Ilya)
Lisovsky, Vsevolod 26, 28
Lomasko, Viktoria 186
Lotman, Iurii 247, 248
Liubimovka, festival 2, 3, 11, 14, 15, 25, 69–80, 124, 148, 193–4, 214, 230, 247, 260, 262, 264
Lukashenko, Alexander, President 14, 15, 16, 17, 41–2, 43, 44, 45, 46, 48, 77, 216, 217, 218–19, 225, 236

Maciupa, Olga 144, 148, 149, 160
Magnitsky Sergei 4, 45
Mai, Andrei/Andriy (*see also* Vorozhbit) 12, 124, 127–8, 133, 145
Maiakovskii Theatre (Moscow) 95
Makeychik, Aleksei 15
Malikov, Ruslan 27
Malinina, Kira 89
Markovsky, Evgeny 160
'May Readings', festival (Togliatti) 214
Maxwell, Douglas 82, 86, 89
McCartney, Nicola 72–3, 82, 87, 89, 90
McDonagh, Martin 60
   Pillowman, The 60
Medinsky, Vladimir 5, 6, 7, 8, 35, 54, 56, 187–8
Medvedev, Dmitry/Dmitrii 3, 45, 54, 78
Meierkhol'd, Vsevolod 8, 33
Meierkhol'd Centre (Moscow) 28, 34, 72, 83, 97
   Murmansk 28
   Shoot/Get Treasure/Repeat 34
Mezdrich, Boris 54
MIEFF (Moscow International Experimental Film Festival) 34
Mikhailov, Oleg, 76
Mikhal'kov, Nikita 187
Miklukho-Maklay, Nikolai 241
   The Man from the Moon 241
Ministry of Counter-Culture (online news service) 15, 232, 233, 234
Moguchiy, Andrey 30
Molière, J-B. Poquelin de 103, 112
   Don Juan 112
Moscow Art Theatre 6, 24, 32, 114, 179, 238, 251, 262

Moscow Times, The 3, 265
Mossoviet Theatre (Moscow) 123
Mukhina, Ol'ga (Olha Puzhakovska) 27, 144

Nabokov, Vladimir 195
Naval'ny, Aleksei 9
Nekliaev, Vladimir 17, 48
Nenasheva, Ekaterina 260-1
New Drama Festival 24, 25, 214
Nicholas II, Tsar 7
Novosibirsk Opera House 6
    Tannhäuser 6
Nureyev, Rudol'f, 8, 60

O'Hare, Jeanie 11
OK 16, cultural hub (Minsk) 264
Oskolkova Tat'iana 82
Ostrovsky, Aleksandr 24, 103

Pankov, Vladimir 24
    Red Thread 24
Patlay Anastasiia, 260
Patriarch Kirill 5
Pavis, Patrice 35
Pavlensky, Piotr 47
Pelevin, Viktor 32
Peskov, Dmitry 7
Petrova, Viktoria 130, 148
Petrushevskaia, Liudmila 23
Pogodina-Kuzmina, Ol'ga 42
Politkovskaya, Anna 265-6
Pomerantsev, Vladimir 25
    'On Sincerity in Literature' 25
Poroshenko, Petro, President 1, 126
Post-Play/PostPlay (Kyiv) 72, 129, 130, 131-2, 134, 142, 143, 145-8, 149, 152, 158, 263
    Girls-Girls 148
    Grass Breaks through the Soil 148
Praktika Theatre (*see* Teatr Praktika)
Pratt, Mary Louise 194-5, 202
Presniakovs, Oleg and Vladimir 24, 27
    Playing the Victim 24
    Terrorism 24
Priazhko, Pavel 15, 23, 33-5, 75-6, 104-5, 214, 215, 218, 220, 228, 237-45, 264
    Black Box, The 245

Closed Door, The 244
Coffee-Shop Owner, The 240, 244, 245
Committee of the Mournful Deity, The 264
Field, The 34
15 Swimming Pools 245
Harvest, The 265
I Am Free 238, 244
Life Has Gone Well 105, 238
Mournful Hockey-Player, The 244, 245
Panties 237
Soldier, The 237, 239, 244
Sun of Arcadia 237
Three Days in Hell (Collective Farm Workers) 220, 238, 244, 245
*We Are Already Here_*244
Prilepin, Zakhar 60
Prokhorova, Irina 8
Proskurnia, Sergei 178
Prusak, Volha 219
    Sikulakubuzuka 219
Punchdrunk, theatre company 28
Pushkin, Aleksandr 28, 251, 255
Pushkin Theatre (Moscow) 262
Pussy Riot 4, 5, 6, 7, 16, 24, 47, 48, 49, 50, 95, 226
Putin, Vladimir, President 2, 3, 4, 5, 6, 7, 8, 9, 10, 12, 14, 16, 18, 32, 42, 44, 45, 46, 53, 54, 55, 57, 58, 59, 60, 61-2, 80, 126, 225, 236, 260, 266

Ramanava, Volha 219
    Do You Want Me to Blow Up Kempinski? 219
Ravenhill, Mark 25, 26, 34, 48, 146, 260
Raykin, Arkady 7
Raykin, Konstantin 7
Romanov, Anton 147-8
Roshchin, Mikhail 23
Royal Court Theatre (London) 2, 14, 15, 24, 25, 42, 75, 123, 159, 161, 215, 230
Royal Shakespeare Company (Stratford-upon-Avon) 11, 14, 125, 195
Rozov, Viktor 25
Rubinshteyn, Lev 25

Rudnev, Pavel 17, 178, 214, 218, 244
Russian Drama Theatre (Ulan-Ude) 85
Russian Drama Theatre of Lithuania (Vilnius) 178
Ryzhakov, Viktor 108

Sardarian, Alik 165
   Product 165
Satirikon Theatre 7
Sauchanka, Andrei 217–18
   Bilingua, or Chicken with Heart 217–18
Savchenko, Oksana 12
Savukh, Aleksandr 214
Sentsov, Oleg/Oleh 7, 16, 47, 48, 146, 235, 260
Serebrennikov, Kirill 8, 24, 35, 53, 54, 60–1, 69, 79–80, 187, 214, 215, 236, 261
   Midsummer Night's Dream, A 8
   Nureyev, 8, 60
   Pillowman, The 60
   Punks 60
Seventh Studio 8, 54
Shakespeare, William 30, 32, 82, 84, 101, 102, 103, 108, 113
   Hamlet 100–1, 108
   King Lear 231
   Romeo and Juliet 32
Shakhnazarov, Karen 187
Shatrov, Mikhail 25
Shcherban, Vladimir 15, 43, 223, 227
Shevchenko, Vladimir 6
Shevkunov, Bishop Tikhon 8
Shvydko, Viktoria 130, 144
Sigarev, Vasily 24
   Plasticine 24
Siniavsky, Andrei 10
   'What is Socialist Realism?' 10
Skillen, Daphne 58, 61
Skorokhod, Natal'ia 30
Skripal, Sergei and Yulia, 6
Slavkin, Viktor 23
Smeliansky, Anatoly 238
Smolev, Dmitry, 262
Snyder, Timothy 16
Socialist Realism 10, 18, 23, 55, 56–7, 61
Sorokin, Vladimir 25, 32
SounDrama, group 28

Sovremennik Theatre (Moscow) 83, 262
   Dumas 262
Sputnik Theatre (*see also* Noah Birksted-Breen) 15
Stalin, Iosif 3, 5, 8, 11, 25, 50, 56, 57, 58, 60, 61–2, 80, 148, 152, 156, 261
Stanislavsky, Konstantin 32, 100, 101, 103, 114
Steshik, Konstantin 15, 76, 77, 214, 228
Stoppard, Sir Tom 15, 43, 229
Strindberg, August 27
Studio for Alternative Drama (SAD), (Minsk) 247
Sugakova, Svetlana 225, 233
Surkova, Valeria 178, 180, 187

Takidang, Andrus 219
Tarantino, Quentin 32, 105
Teatr Dakh (Ukraine) 123, 129
Teatr.doc (Moscow) 2, 3, 4, 6, 7, 10, 11, 14, 16, 23, 24, 25–6, 27–8, 35, 41–2, 44, 45, 46, 47–8, 49, 50, 69, 70, 77, 84, 95, 97, 109, 145–7, 151, 157, 158–9, 165, 168, 170, 178, 179–81, 186–7, 238, 239, 240, 259–62
   150 Reasons for Not Defending the Motherland 48
   Battle of the Moldavians for a Cardboard Box, The 44
   Bolotnaya Case, The 6, 26, 46, 47, 48, 186
   Co-defendants, The (The Bolotnaya Case 2) 26
   Coming Out of the Closet 47, 260
   Crimes of Passion 42
   Doc.tor 28
   Future.doc 261
   Great Guzzle, The 42
   History of the Russian State, The 28
   I Am a Thing! 28
   Keeping Silent on a Given Theme 28
   Lear the Parasite (Uncensored Songs) 28
   Monsters 28
   Obscure Influences 28
   One/An Hour and Eighteen Minutes 4, 26, 45
   Rave No. 228 260–1
   September.doc 26, 42, 44, 45

Silence of the Classics, The 28
Three Sisters, The 261
Tibetan Book of the Dead, The 28
To Forgive Betrayal 28
Two in our House/Two People in Your Home/Two in Your Home 26, 48, 146,
War is Close 26, 47, 48, 146, 260
When We Came to Power 26
Teatr Lesi (*see* Lesia Ukrainka Academic Theatre)
Teatr Post (St Petersburg) 33–5, 240
   I am Free 33
   Love Story 34
Teatr Praktika (Moscow) 26, 104, 105, 108, 109, 240, 262
'Theatre in Two Weeks: Silence Isn't Golden', theatre project 151–4, 157
Theatre of Contemporary Dialogue (Poltava) 130
Theatre of Displaced People (Ukraine) 13, 129, 143, 151, 163–73, 263
   Children and Soldiers 166–7
   My Mikolaivka 163–4, 168–9
   What My Mum and Dad Should Never Know 169–71
   Where is East? 169
Theatre of the Nations (Teatr Natsiy, Moscow) 69, 262
Théâtre Vidy-Lausanne (Switzerland) 193
Thomas, Alexander 9, 262
Tkachou, Cimafiej 220
Tolokonnikova, Nadezhda 5, 49, 50
Totem Centre Theatre Lab (Kherson) 130
Transformator.doc 26
Traverse Theatre (Edinburgh) 81, 82, 86, 90, 167
Troitskii/Troitsky, Vladislav 122, 123, 193–4
TsDR, *see* Centre for Playwriting and Directing (Moscow)
Trump, Donald, President 1, 225
Tsvetaeva, Marina 28, 148

Uchitel', Aleksei 7
   Matil'da 7, 146

Ugarov, Ivan, 261
Ugarov, Mikhail 2, 4, 6, 10, 12, 14, 23, 24, 26, 42, 43, 44, 45, 59, 75, 105, 146–7, 151, 238, 240, 259–60, 262
Ukrainian Theatre (Odessa) 178
Ulitskaia, Liudmila 16
Ustinov, Pavel 261

Vartanov, Aleksandr 27
Volkostrelov, Dmitry/Dmitrii 23, 30, 33–5, 239, 240
   Lecture on Something 33
   Monument to the Third International, The 34
   Shoot/Get Treasure/Repeat 34
Volodin, Aleksandr 25
Vorozhbit/Vorozhbyt, Natal'ia 11, 12, 13, 14, 72, 73, 75, 81, 87–8, 90, 122, 123, 124, 125, 127–9, 133–4, 144–5, 149, 151, 159, 160–1, 163–4, 167, 168–9, 193–210, 228, 247, 263
   Bad Roads, play and film 14, 144–5, 263
   Cyborgs, film 263
   Gal'ka-Mota'lka/Galka-Motalko 11, 123, 195
   Grain Store/ Grainstore, The 11, 125, 129, 195, 199, 201
   I Join Them 124
   Lives of the Common People, 123
   Maidan: Voices from the Uprising/Maidan Diaries (with Andrei Mai) 12, 122, 127–9
   Sasha Take out the Rubbish 247
   Viy: A Docudrama/Viy 2.0 193–210
   Wild Fields, film 263
Vyrypaev, Ivan 8–9, 26, 27, 33, 78, 97, 99–106, 107–18, 179, 181, 188–9, 240, 262
   Delhi Dance 100, 101–2
   Dream Works 101
   Drunks/Drunkards, The 101, 179
   Genesis-2 111
   Illusions 99, 100, 101, 103–4, 105
   Iran Conference, The 109
   July 99, 101, 102, 103, 104, 105, 107–18
   Oxygen 99, 104, 109, 111

Salvation (film) 109, 188–9
Solar Line 188–9

Wagner, Richard 6, 60
   Tannhäuser 6, 54, 60–1
Wanner, Catherine 199, 201
Weber, Samuel 108–9, 113
   Theatricality as Medium 113–14
'Week of Contemporary Drama/Week of Contemporary Plays/ Week of Relevant Plays', festival, (Kyiv) 11, 12, 73, 75, 124–5, 128–9, 134, 145, 149, 161, 230, 264
Weiwei, Ai 226, 229
Wild Theatre (*see* Dikiy Teatr)
Wilde, Oscar, 6, 32
   An Ideal Husband 6, 32
'WriteBox', festival (Belarus) 264
'Writing in the Cross-hairs', festival 142–3,

Yakovlev, Alexander 6
Yanka Kupala National Academic Theatre (Minsk) 265
Yanukovych, Viktor, President 12, 126, 166, 195, 225
Yaro 265
Young Vic Theatre (London) 15, 231
Youth Theatre (Kyiv) 123

Zabuzhko, Oksana 122, 123, 133
Zakhozhenko, Dmitrii 151–2
Zaudinova, Zarema 26, 158, 261, 262
Zelensky, Volodymyr 2, 13, 14, 161
Zelinskaia/Zelinskaya, Maria 84, 85
Zhadan, Serhiy 263
Zheleztsov, Aleksandr
Zviagintsev, Andrei 5, 6, 79, 187
   Leviathan, 5, 6, 79
   Loveless 187

www.ingramcontent.com/pod-product-compliance
Lightning Source LLC
Chambersburg PA
CBHW072127290426
44111CB00012B/1812